Women in Print

Print Culture History in Modern America

Women in Print

Essays on the Print Culture of American Women from the Nineteenth and Twentieth Centuries

Edited by
James P. Danky
and
Wayne A. Wiegand

Foreword by
Elizabeth Long

THE UNIVERSITY OF WISCONSIN PRESS

The University of Wisconsin Press
1930 Monroe Street
Madison, Wisconsin 53711
www.wisc.edu/wisconsinpress/

3 Henrietta Street
London WC2E 8LU, England

Published online by
University of Wisconsin–Madison Libraries
Office of Scholarly Communication and Publishing
http://parallelpress.library.wisc.edu/books/print-culture/women-in-print.shtml

In collaboration with
Center for the History of Print Culture in Modern America
A joint project of the Wisconsin Historical Society and the University of Wisconsin–Madison
http://slisweb.lis.wisc.edu/~printcul/

5 4 3 2 1

Printed in the United States of America

Library of Congress Cataloging-in-Publication Data

Women in print : essays on the print culture of American women from the nineteenth and twentieth centuries / edited by James P. Danky and Wayne A. Wiegand ; foreword by Elizabeth Long.
p. cm. — (Print culture history in modern America)
Includes bibliographical references and index.
ISBN-13: 978-0-299-21784-6 (pbk. : alk. paper)
ISBN-10: 0-299-21784-1 (pbk. : alk. paper)
1. Women in the book industries and trade—United States—History—19th century. 2. Women in the book industries and trade—United States—History—20th century. 3. Women—Books and reading—United States—History—19th century. 4. Women—Books and reading—United States—History—20th century. 5. Women editors—United States—History. 6. Women publishers—United States—History. 7. Libraries and women—United States—History. 8. Women authors, American. I. Danky, James Philip, 1947– II. Wiegand, Wayne A., 1946– III. Series.
Z473.W68 2006
381'.45002'0820973—dc22 2005021512

For Gerda Lerner, whose pioneering in women's history changed our campus along with the rest of the historical landscape.

Contents

Preface and Acknowledgements

On the afternoon of September 11, 2001, Wayne Wiegand and James Danky, co-directors of the Center for the History of Print Culture in Modern America, a joint program of the University of Wisconsin–Madison and the Wisconsin Historical Society, arrived at an obvious but not surprising decision. Namely, that the conference, "Women in Print," scheduled for September 14–15, 2001, and which had been planned for over two years, would need to be cancelled. In the days of sadness and anger following the tragedies of 9/11, the center determined that the conference could not be rescheduled, a great disappointment to those on the Madison campus as well as to the many scholars across North America who had made proposals and were preparing to come to Madison. We know that the conference would have been a great success, both in terms of intellectual content and local arrangements, because of the work of Jane Pearlmutter, assistant director of the School of Library and Information Studies, who has aided the Center so many times in the past.

However, we determined that we would proceed with our intention to produce a volume of the best papers, and we invited participants in the lost conference to submit finished drafts appropriate for publication. After careful review, the papers in this volume were selected. In this process Rima Apple, William J. Reese, Phyllis Holman Weisbard, and all members of the center's advisory board aided the editors. The committee's work was greatly facilitated by Fran Scharko Steele and Sarah Dauscher of the Wisconsin Historical Society's Library. The center's "home" is in the School of Library and Information Studies where it has benefited greatly from the support and advice of its director, Louise Robbins.

The center celebrated its tenth anniversary in October 2002 and it continues to help determine the historical sociology of print in modern America (ca. 1876 to the present) in all its culturally diverse manifestations. (See the center's WebPages for more details, including our mission statement http://slisweb.lis.wisc.edu/~printcul/.) In designing our colloquia, annual meeting, and biennial conferences we rely on the wisdom and energy of our advisory board members who include, in addition to those cited above: James L. Baughman, Paul Boyer, Sargent Bush (Chair), Kenneth Frazier, Peter Gottlieb, Robert Kingdom, Ginny Moore Kruse, Mary N. Layoun, Anne Lundin, Nellie McKay, Tony Michels, Richard Ralston, Stephen Vaughn, and David Woodward.

This volume, the fourth to be published by the University of Wisconsin Press as part of the series Print Culture History in Modern America, has benefited from the encouragement and support of press director Robert Mandel, and associate director Steve Salemson has been essential to the enterprise. *Women in Print* is the inaugural title to be published both online and as print on demand. The cooperative venture between the Press and the University of Wisconsin–Madison Library is an important development in scholarly communications. The Press has been an enthusiastic supporter of this initiative, especially Terry Emmrich, Scott Lenz, Adam Mehring, and Mary Sutherland. For the General Library System, the volume has benefited from the work of Eric Larson, Tom Murray, Lee Konrad, and Wayne Hayes.

The Volume

This book divides into four parts. The first consists of Barbara Sicherman's essay "Connecting Lives: Women and Reading, Then and Now," which was to have been the conference keynote. Sicherman locates women and reading in a much broader context of print culture history. By scanning the contemporary cultural landscape, she finds evidence of a "reading revival" at the beginning of the twenty-first century and sees women positioned at its center. In a theoretically grounded, well-crafted historiographical journey, she traces the kind of relationship between women and reading of which Oprah's Book Club is only the latest (albeit the best-known) manifestation since its mid-nineteenth-century origins.

Sicherman's introductory piece is followed by ten essays that conveniently divide into three sections. In the section titled "Print for a Purpose: Women as Editors and Publishers," Kristin Bloomberg seeks to rescue Clara Bewick Colby, editor of the *Women's Tribune* (Beatrice, Nebraska) from 1883 to 1909, from a women's history that has overlooked a generation of feminist activism between Seneca Falls (1848) and passage of the Nineteenth Amendment (1920). As editor, Colby used the *Tribune*'s columns as an agent to link the women's culture she inherited to a feminist activism she hoped would lead to true equality for women. June Howard resurrects the career of Elizabeth Jordan, editor of *Harper's Bazar* from 1900 to 1913 and editor of two composite novels, *The Whole Family* (1908) and *The Sturdy Oak* (1917). As editor, Jordan crossed and combined public and private worlds and commercial and cultural space in attempts to open up room for women in professional worlds. Terri Castaneda highlights the career of *Smoke Signal* editor Marie Mason Potts. *Smoke Signal* was a periodical representing the interests of the Federated Indians of California that was published between 1948 to 1978. As editor, Potts helped shape California Native Americans' political solidarity and cultural identity, and gave voice and cultural pride to marginalized people seeking land claims legislation. At the same time, Potts modeled behavior for several female American Indian editors who followed her. Toni Samek shows how San Francisco Public Library employee Celeste West founded the Booklegger Press in 1972 to articulate through *Booklegger Magazine* an alternative library philosophy. In its pages West challenged the professional ideology that libraries could provide "neutral" service and collections embracing "all points of view." In addition to *Booklegger*, the press also published *Revolting Librarians* (1972), a collection of forty essays on many topics, all demonstrating bias that exists throughout the library profession. *Revolting Librarians*, many have argued, marked the beginnings of critical analysis in library literature.

Three essays fit comfortably into the second section, entitled "Women in a World of Books." Michelle Cloonan analyzes the career of California bookseller Alice Millard, an aggressive arbiter of highbrow taste in a middlebrow book world. In the 1920s, Millard was the only woman in America running an antiquarian bookstore, and she did so on a shoestring budget by creating what she called "undeniable opportunities for those who wanted to possess fine things." Cloonan argues that the gospel of good taste she preached and practiced in the early twentieth century has endured in the rare book world. Jane Aikin looks at a number of highly educated women who assumed positions as bibliographers and subject-heading specialists at the Library of Congress at the beginning of the twentieth century, when the LC shifted its focus toward becoming a national library. In such positions these women became silent arbiters between publications and consumers by crafting rules and practices that have influenced librarianship and the world of books ever since. Although names like Harriet Wheeler Pierson, Malina Gilkey, Elizabeth Howard West, and Margaret D. McGuffey have long since faded into the pages of Library of Congress history, Aikin makes a convincing case for their pioneering work. Christine Pawley describes a mid-century Wisconsin Free Library Commission–sponsored project that funded a bookmobile library service to the rural parts of Door and Kewaunee counties in Wisconsin's Door Peninsula. With the project WFLC sponsors hoped to demonstrate to local citizens that libraries constituted "an important and informational asset." At the same time, they hoped to balance the gender profile of users away from primarily women and children, and to attract more men. During the project, circulation figures did rise by 160 percent, and although a majority were children, 95 percent of adult users were farm women and female teachers in rural schools, whose lives were transformed in many ways and who interacted directly with the female professionals providing the service. All used the project to challenge gendered domains and role definitions.

While women in previous sections focused on particular sites (periodical and book publishing and library institutions) as opportunities to effect change in the world of print, women profiled in the third and final section ("A Centrifugal Force: Gendered Agency Through Print") worked as authors and used print to effect change in women's lives. For forty years following the Civil War, Lois Waisbrooker published books and periodicals on female sexuality and women's rights. When she was arrested in 1894 for violating the Comstock Act of 1873, she declared, "If prison will advance the work, I am ready." Joanne Passet points out that her contributions constituted a site around which rallied a geographically dispersed community of female readers who were marginalized by the dominant patriarchy. Sarah Robbins analyzes several late-nineteenth-century religious foreign mission periodicals for gendered agency, and discovers that those women who wrote for and read from the pages of these periodicals used a set of shared social beliefs and activities to fashion a community for themselves. For example, for half a century a Presbyterian monthly titled *Woman's Work for Woman* offered space in its pages for "home letters" and other columns in which authors shared stories. These periodicals, Robbins shows, played a productive role in the everyday lives of their readers. In hundreds of variously titled articles in the "women's section" of *La Follette's Magazine* over a twenty-year period beginning in 1909, Belle Case La Follette sought to influence public opinion in her highly personalized column. She called upon her fellow women (who until 1920 lacked the franchise) to champion the cause of African Americans, another oppressed group. Her persistence reflected a deep and broad-based commitment to civil rights, since she refused to back away from criticizing the racism of some of her white sisters. What upset her most, however, were efforts of Woodrow Wilson's administration to racially segregate federal agencies. Nancy Unger concludes that the Wilson administration failed in its attempt to segregate federal civil service in large part because Belle Case La Follette used the printed word to challenge its segregationist activities.

Foreword

ELIZABETH LONG

At a time of concern about whether feminist scholarship has become overdisciplined within the academy and irrelevant to some of the broad questions that animated an earlier generation's contributions, this strong, vital collection of essays is inspirational. Drawing on scholarship in history, literature, religion, and sociology, this volume is animated by interdisciplinary traditions in the study of print culture as well as in feminism, giving the book a breadth and unity rare among edited collections.

Many of the essays document individual woman's involvement with print culture, such as Clara Colby's editorship of *The Women's Tribune* during the generation between Seneca Falls and the attainment of woman suffrage, or the pioneering work of Alice Millard, who spread the gospel of taste and beauty through antiquarian bookselling. Others focus on groups (women missionaries and their writings, and the first cohort of professional women cataloguers and bibliographers at the Library of Congress), or on programs (the rural library and bookmobile program in Wisconsin's Door and Kewaunee counties). All, however, are case studies. Paradoxically, this particularistic focus enables them, as a collection, to bring valuable theoretical and empirical nuance to some of the overarching themes the book addresses. The introduction discusses two of these themes, leaving to other readers the pleasant task of mining the volume for different lines of inquiry.

Domesticity, as lived experience and ideology, figures centrally in many of the chapters, perhaps in part because many of the essays deal with the period between the mid-nineteenth and mid-twentieth centuries. The essays highlight complex relationships between domesticity, whether as lived experience or ideology, and the public sphere, with print culture serving as a vital and complex intermediary connecting the two domains.

Ironically, women's domestic role and the moral authority that sprang from it often enabled their emergence into the world beyond the family. Domesticity could be experienced as a constraint, even a prison, as was the case for freethinker and Spiritualist writer Lois Waisbrooker, who became pregnant at age seventeen and was forced into a loveless marriage, and then, upon her husband's death, worked as a live-in maid. Yet her experience of the sexual double standard also served as the motive for her entrance into print as an impassioned defender of sexual freedom and a critic of women's enslavement in marriage. And perhaps even more ironically, the woman she worked for as a domestic was responsible for Waisbrooker acquiring the education she needed to make the leap into the world of letters.

Even in less extreme cases, these essays show how important domesticity was in shaping women's career paths and reading choices. For example, Marie Mason Potts, editor of the path breaking Native American newspaper *Smoke Signal*, began her career of print activism only at age fifty-three, after her children had become adults. Similarly, the first generation of women librarians at the Library of Congress often left that institution after only a few years' experience, either to relocate near their families or to form families of their own. This gave the Library of Congress an important role as a training institution. In turn, this helped disseminate innovative cataloguing and bibliographic practices, including those that kept women writers visible. For example, women bibliographers at the Library of Congress appear to have been responsible for the practice of tracking women authors under all their single and married names, while a largely female cataloguing department made sure to include women's associations, accomplishments, and activities under other headings than the subject "woman."

Other essays follow the varied inflections of domesticity in the lives of women readers and writers. The chapter on the rural library experiment in Wisconsin, for example, details the largely domestic concerns expressed by usage records of women patrons in the 1950s. It also makes the point that the novels, craft, and cookbooks these farming women sought out initiated them into a new kind of social interaction with librarians, a broadening of horizons that then galvanized these homemakers into public action to establish a branch library in southern Door County. The women missionaries of the late nineteenth century who used print to stitch together their efforts in foreign missions with groups of women supporters at home had ventured far from the family circle. Yet their work abroad was gendered "domestic." They served almost exclusively as caregivers and educators for women and children. This selfsame traditionalism enabled their letters and newsletters home to spark identification and garner material support for an endeavor that gradually ushered in a new set of professional roles for women mission workers.

Domesticity, then, appears in some essays as a boundary or constraint, but in others figures importantly as a resource. On a relatively homely level, several essays detail the ways that men served as mentors and brokers of extradomestic opportunities for their women kinfolk. For instance, Belle Case La Follette was not only the respected advisor and companion of her husband, Wisconsin's progressive "Fighting Bob" LaFollette, she also found an important political platform for her own views in *La Follette's Magazine* (now *The Progressive*). Other husbands, though less influential, were equally supportive. Alice Millard, for example, learned the trade of selling rare and beautiful books from George Madison Millard, whom she first met at his antiquarian bookstore in Chicago and later married. And although Clara Colby's *Women's Tribune* was staffed and owned entirely by women, she first worked as a journalist for her husband at the *Beatrice Express*. Elizabeth Jordan, editor of *Harper's Bazar* and initiator of two round-robin novels, found her vocation not through a husband but a father. Early in life, she wanted to become a nun, while her mother urged her to become a pianist. As a compromise—and because of her love of literature—her father suggested journalism and secured her first position on *Peck's Sun* in Milwaukee.

If domesticity could serve some women as a material resource, it figured even more importantly as a ground for claims to expertise and the rubric under which women—through print—could achieve voice, find an audience, and ultimately change their lives and the broader social fabric. The reason this worked so well for many of the women showcased here had to do not only with women's experience in a gendered division of labor but also with the power of domesticity as an ideology. At the level of ideas and affect, domesticity legitimized women's everyday practices, gave them authority, and kindled intimate identification between women writers and editors and the women who read their work. The women mission workers mentioned above provide one obvious example of this process. But journalists as differently situated as Clara Colby, Elizabeth Jordan, and Belle Case La Follette used women's departments or women's pages both to affirm the worth of women and their work at home, and to push for the expansion of women's sphere. This initiative was differently inflected depending on the nature of their audiences. When Elizabeth Jordan imagined and constructed in print her vision of a women readership for *Harper's Bazar* whose minds would be as cultivated as their fashion sense, she was clearly addressing a more privileged group of readers than did Clara Colby, who kept subscribers on the list of the *Women's Tribune* even if they couldn't pay. But Colby's paper also provided her mainly rural women readers with an expansive view of women's culture. The paper featured departments on Industry, Political and Social Science, Law, and Hygiene and Medical Progress, as well as Notes about Women, which publicized the accomplishments of women's inventors, suffragists, and other "new women." In much the same way the Home and Education department in *La Follette's Magazine* became a platform for Belle Case La Follette's progressive views on world peace, feminism, public service, and race relations. Letters from readers show the importance of print culture for satisfying women's hunger for substantive intellectual and political fare, and also for giving them a sense of companionship and common purpose with other like-minded women.

The places and times where domesticity as practice and ideology does not figure so centrally in the relationship between women and print are also instructive. Consider, for example, Marie Mason Potts and *Smoke Signal*. She addressed an audience of Native Americans just a generation removed from a life that did not separate a "public" from a "domestic" sphere, and she targeted male as well as female readers. Her notes on traditions, crafts, and rituals helped revitalize a holistic cultural identity that could resist the depredations of a more fragmented white

America. Consider also Celeste West and her radical library journal *Booklegger Magazine*. One could claim that she drew on women's experience for her critique of the mainstream bias in the supposedly neutral role of librarians as cultural conservators, but she did not do so in the name of domesticity. Rather, she wanted to save the printed ephemera of the radical social movements of the 1960s and 1970s. Similarly, her defense of librarians' rights to free speech as citizens and workers can be parsed as a critique of a feminine ideology of silent service, though West appears to have been more invested in a gender-neutral application of the First Amendment.

Counterposing these significantly different ways women have related to domesticity in print leads to important questions about what has been lost as well as gained by different groups of women as the sphere and ideology of domesticity have faded. It also raises the issue of what role women—whether as women, or more specifically, as readers, writers, editors, and publishers—can play in confronting the almost unmitigated expansion of marketplace institutions, priorities, and values that mark this new century.

The question of differences among the women described in this volume leads quite naturally into a consideration of how factors aside from gender shaped their lives and interventions in print culture. The question of intersectionality usually leads to an analysis of race and social class alongside gender as important dimensions of social differentiation. Once again, these essays productively complicate an important theoretical discussion. First, they show the necessity of taking into account other factors than the triad of race/class/gender in understanding women's actions and the social world. For example, Celeste West's later career as a publisher of lesbian literature as well as Lois Waisbrooker's critique of heterosexual marriage show the necessity of taking into account sexuality as well as gender. Religion's importance for many women is sharply limned in Robbins' discussion of missionary workers. Similarly, Clara Colby's orientation to an audience of tallgrass prairie women and Belle Case La Follette's close ties to midwestern progressivism demonstrate the importance of region. Their work, and that of the rural librarians in Wisconsin, also shows how crucial the rural/urban dichotomy was for structuring women's writing, reading, and activism. Clearly, the social factors constituting "intersectionality" must be broadly conceived in order better to understand both social inequality and its contestation.

Second, the biographical focus of many chapters also shows the subtle and unexpected ways these social factors surface in individual women's lives, shaping their patterns of connection and alliance, whether in print or beyond. For example, Clara Colby's adoption of a Lakota daughter seems connected to the *Women's Tribune's* supportive stance toward Native Americans, African Americans, and women—such as those in Cuba, Hawaii, and the Philippines—who were oppressed by American imperialism. Sometimes the reasons for such connections are unclear. What were the sources, for instance of Belle Case La Follette's outspoken campaigns for racial integration? How did Lois Waisbrooker's own childhood as the daughter of an impoverished farm laborer influence her later closeness to the largely urban anarchist press? In beginning to map the intricacies of individual women's social and discursive positioning, these essays point to important new areas of research.

Third, these essays show the creation and mobilization of "sisterhood" as a deliberate strategy undertaken by politically aware editors, publishers, and librarians. Taken together, they make a powerful case for the necessity of understanding the role of print in enabling women's identification with other women and with other social groups quite different than themselves. This is an important contribution, as both a guide and a provocation to further scholarship engaging the intersection of feminism and print culture.

One of the pleasures of reading this volume is the way individual chapters and the book as a whole move between bringing the cultural work of relatively unknown women to light and reflecting on what their interventions mean for conceptualizing more abstract questions about voice, identity, and social change. The fruitfulness of this oscillation calls into question the "stage" theory of feminist scholarship. In the same volume, what has been regarded as "the first stage"—making invisible women visible—stands side by side with what some scholars regard as the most fully developed stage, that of analyzing the gendered nature of careers, ideologies, and institutions. This is disheartening, on the one hand, because it shows how easily women's contributions to print culture fade from view—one effect of their social and ideological marginalization. On the other hand, it also shows how productive the scholarship in volumes such as this—itself an intervention in print culture—can be.

Finally, and perhaps most importantly, these essays provide an extremely valuable point of purchase on the relationship between structural constraint and human agency. For example, Terri Castaneda's essay on Marie Mason Potts, editor of the California Native American publication *Smoke Signal*, shows how Potts's life was shaped by the destruction of traditional Indian lifeways (including her mother's rape and abandonment by a white man). It also shows the brutality of the deracination that occurred when native children were shipped off to white-run boarding schools during the assimilationist period. Yet the same essay demonstrates that Potts was able to use the literary and printing skills she acquired in boarding school to publish a newspaper that built solidarity among California's Native Americans and ushered in innovative campaigns for civil rights. Reading and reflecting on lives such as hers not only makes fine scholarship; it also forges the kinds of inspirational connections that Barbara Sicherman's introductory essay so eloquently describes.

Women in Print

Connecting Lives

Women and Reading, Then and Now

BARBARA SICHERMAN

Despite the dire prophecies of cultural pessimists who forecast the imminent overthrow of books and reading by electronic and other media, these reminders of the age of Gutenberg are surviving, even thriving.[1] So much so that, to adapt Mark Twain's familiar adage, reports of the demise of reading are greatly exaggerated. Beginning in Seattle in 1998, recent efforts to have entire cities read the same book (Harper Lee's *To Kill a Mockingbird* in Chicago, Edwige Danticat's *Breath, Eyes, Memory* in Hartford, both available in languages other than English) are among the signs that we may be in the midst of a reading revival. If so, women are at the center of it. Women are increasingly visible as writers as well as readers: there are significantly more female than male authors under forty, a trend that prompted one journalist to conclude that literature is "a woman's world now."[2]

Certainly women are the mainstay of the book clubs that are so conspicuous a feature on the contemporary cultural landscape. Although some are mixed-sex and all-male, reading groups appeal mainly to women, just as they did in the nineteenth century. A few have had a continuous existence since then, survivors of a social movement that originated as women's study clubs; most are of relatively recent origin. The current movement has roots in the 1980s and took off in earnest in the nineties, when just about everyone seemed to be joining one. Some have distinctive identities, such as women-of-color and mother-daughter groups; others are organized more haphazardly. A longtime professional group leader estimated in 1999 that there were some 500,000 groups, double the number in 1994, with an estimated membership of between five and ten million. The large margin of error represented by the unknown millions suggests the difficulty of keeping track of a grass-roots phenomenon that typically begins when a handful of people decide to read books and talk about them together. Whatever the accuracy of the statistics, reading groups are here in force. And they are good business: asked whether reading groups sell books, one bookstore owner exclaimed: "Oh yes! Oh yes!" The book industry assists in a number of ways: special advisers at independent book stores (Denver's Tattered Cover offers advice to some three hundred groups a year) as well as bulletin board lists of those wanting to join; newsletters; groups that operate out of the large book chains; and reading-group guides produced by publishers to foster discussion, a practice begun in 1993. Several guides to reading groups that include how-to advice, reading lists, and testimonials date from the same period.[3]

What accounts for the popularity of an activity that has been hailed as obsolete and lacks the kind of tangible purpose associated with so many contemporary self-directed endeavors? To restate the question posed by a team of social scientists in 1940, "What is Reading Good For?": what do women find in reading that makes it so compelling for them? There is no single or simple answer.[4]

Reading-group aficionadas answer the question by talking about self-discovery and intimacy, "verification" and self-esteem, connection and community. Some join, they say, "because they want 'to do something for me,'" some because they "want to have someone besides an uninterested husband, roommate, or baby to share their book-related thoughts with." Others talk about the expanded horizons that follow serious encounters with books, especially books they would not read on their own. But when members speak of groups as "life support" and "safe places," it is clear that groups are "more than talking about books." Whatever the initial motivation, a women's book group is also about female bonding. It is the personal dimension of the interchanges—the emotional satisfaction that comes from shared moments of intimacy over book talk—that is often most compelling. As one book club leader put it: "The books and the groups serve as a starting point for connection. Women want to explore issues in depth and search for meaning. Books and the structure of book groups allow that." Book clubs blend the intellectual, the personal, and the social—a powerful combination for women.[5]

In an article titled "Reading Groups: Where Are All the Men?," a freelance male writer who belongs to a book group observed that men rarely join them for the same reason they do not read Amy Tan or go to see the latest version of *Little Women* or cry at Beth's death if they do: because doing so would "violate the 'Guy Code.'" Men view book clubs as "one more form of 'women's work' to be avoided at all costs"; many prefer more "'objective,' impersonal groups" to those that minimize formal structure and place a premium on everyone's participation. (Shades of 1970s consciousness raising!) Then, too, many groups concentrate on books by women authors and, he might have added, on fiction, a category more appealing to women than to men.[6]

It is a wonderful irony that the greatest boost to reading in the recent past has come from the most unlikely source: television. I refer of course to Oprah's Book Club, launched in September 1996 "to get the country reading." During its six years on air, the venture was a runaway success, at least as far as women were concerned: Oprah readers, like Oprah viewers, are predominantly female. In the process the program's host became the nation's most important gatekeeper for fiction—an unlikely position for an African American woman of humble origin. Some thirteen million viewers reportedly watched the monthly book club segment of *The Oprah Winfrey Show*, and it is claimed that at least half a million had read or at least dipped into the featured book by air time. Sales of books that made the cut increased by an estimated minimum of 500,000 to 750,000 copies and in some cases by more than a million. All of them became best sellers. The designation "Queen Midas of the Midlist" is no idle manner of speaking. Oprah's Book Club did more for Toni Morrison's sales than the Nobel Prize in Literature, although not even Oprah could make a box-office success of *Beloved*: there she was operating beyond the reach of her brand name.[7]

Unlike reading groups, which appeal mainly to women who are self-described "great readers," Oprah's Book Club drew women who claimed they had not read a book in years. Some professed that the Club changed their lives, as Winfrey claimed reading had changed hers.

Like many group members, she highlighted the personal impact of reading: "'The reason I love books is because they teach us something about ourselves.'" In the program on *Stolen Lives: Twenty Years in a Desert Jail* by Malika Oufkir, an upper-class Moroccan woman imprisoned with her mother and siblings after the failure of her father's attempted coup, Oprah underscored the point: "We all look for the parts of ourselves that are in your story." This understanding of what reading does linked Oprah's Book Club to the self-help movement that constitutes such an important feature of the program and of contemporary American life. Since her show became "motivational" rather than "confrontational" in 1994, its primary message has been self-empowerment: each of us is responsible for our own life, take charge of it. Book selections advanced this project. An "Oprah-type novel" has been described as a "'moving, painful human story,'" usually written by a woman. Treating such subjects as dysfunctional families, abusive relationships, and mental illness, many feature heroines who come through harrowing experiences with new self-awareness and determination. Oprah's Book Club readers connected with such heroines, their trials and triumphs. Thanks to modern technology, they also connected with one other—on line in a number of virtual reading communities.[8]

In view of its high visibility, it is hardly surprising that Winfrey's surprise announcement in April 2002 that "'this is the end of the book club as we know it'" caused such a stir in the media. Few gave much credence to her explanation that "'It has become harder and harder to find books on a monthly basis that I feel absolutely compelled to share.'" Speculation centered on her possible boredom with the cycle; her sense that it was time to move on to keep the show fresh; and the diminishing impact of her endorsement: the sale of half a million extra copies is hardly insignificant, particularly to publishers and authors, but sales figures attributed to Oprah's Book Club had declined from the early years.[9]

It is possible, too, that the contretemps with Jonathan Franzen played a part in Winfrey's decision to move on. When his highly regarded novel, *The Corrections*, became an Oprah's Book Club pick the previous fall, Franzen publicly aired his angst about the company he was in, challenging both Winfrey's taste and her cultural authority. (Later he did apologize for hurting her feelings.) Winfrey responded by withdrawing her invitation to appear on the show, but not her endorsement (estimated to be worth a cool $1.5 million to the author). Franzen voiced discomfort on several grounds. He disliked the Oprah's Book Club logo on the cover, an emblem of "corporate ownership" that violated his sense that the book was his individual creation. He thought of himself as "solidly in the high-art literary tradition," presumably unlike the majority of authors and books endorsed by Oprah (she had made some good selections, he observed, but "She's picked enough schmaltzy, one-dimensional ones that I cringe, myself, even though I think she's really smart and she's really fighting the good fight"). He feared that men would be put off by the endorsement because Oprah's choices were seen as appealing mainly to women (he did not need to mention that most of the authors were female). And he believed that book clubs somehow undermined the seriousness with which literature should be considered.[10]

Gender considerations were clearly at play in Franzen's eagerness to distance himself from the queen of daytime television (a medium he deplored in any event) and from her viewers—and not just in his fear of losing male readers. Although Franzen later repudiated his distinction between cultural levels as a "mistake," his invocation of the literary class system was at the heart of the controversy, one with a long history. Critics who identify with high culture have frequently disparaged women writers and their output as sentimental and therefore less than serious; they have also ridiculed women's literary clubs as shallow and/or pretentious.[11]

Whether or not this well-publicized incident contributed to Winfrey's decision to curtail her book club, other television programs stepped in to fill the vacuum by starting book clubs of their own, among them *Today*, which announced its plans just seventy-two hours after Oprah's retreat, and *Live with Regis and Kelly* and *Good Morning America*. Clearly the connection between television and reading is far from over, although none of these programs has attained anywhere near Winfrey's cachet—or sales power.[12]

Turning from the contemporary scene, I would like to reflect on some patterns of women's reading by focusing on the beginning of the era covered by this volume: on continuities, changes, above all connections. Just as connections are central to the current reading-club phenomenon, they are critical for understanding the role of reading in women's lives in the past: connections to self, to others, and even to some larger community, visible or virtual. Far from making nothing happen, as has been said of poetry, reading has been a connecting factor for women past and present, mediating between dreams and lived experiences, between private and public. The appeal of literal as well as virtual reading communities has been strong in both eras. But the reading culture of the Gilded Age drew women outward as well as inward, encouraging not just personal development but public engagement. And in this I see a critical difference.[13]

The association of women and reading—the reading of fiction in particular—is far from new: recall the early laments that novel reading would promote female sensuality, addiction, and dereliction of duty and the entranced female readers depicted in paintings by Jean-Honoré Fragonard (*La Liseuse*) and Winslow Homer (*The New Novel*). By the late nineteenth century, reading was gendered female, as were cultural pursuits more generally—by then in largely positive ways. In the context of men's pursuit of business and the conquest of a continent, the gendered thinking that ascribed to women inherent nurturing traits also assigned to them the province of culture, at least those aspects that radiated out from the home or were locally based. Contemporary understanding of this division was symbolically displayed at the landmark 1893 World's Columbian Exposition, where art and imagination were represented as female, science as male. School texts, magazines, and paintings too depicted women, especially young women, as the paramount readers. Some of these images (such as those of girls giggling over books in idle moments) were equivocal. But an older image of women as frivolous readers diminished as the century progressed. It is difficult to imagine anyone in 1880 writing the female counterpart of an article on "How to Make Dull Boys Read": too much rather than too little reading was the besetting female vice.[14]

As the bourgeois family evolved and the years of childhood lengthened, women took the lead in providing their offspring with the requisite cultural capital for life in a society increasingly differentiated by class. As the principal means of entertainment, literary activities permeated daily life to a degree unimaginable in the age of television. Reading aloud, playing word games, and writing occasional poetry for family celebrations were enjoyed across the generations. For the younger set, there were also parlor theatricals, home newspapers, and recitations of set pieces. Although men and women of the comfortable classes grew up with books together, young women developed an especially complex and elaborated relation to reading. Many became adept in its ways, often more so than their brothers. Because literature was in some respects women's province, it was an arena in which girls were permitted, indeed expected, to excel. Because domestic literary culture was both participatory and collaborative, contemporary structures of reading intertwined with women's lives in synergistic ways. At once study and play, a source of knowledge and pleasure, public performance and private dreaming, reading opened up space unlike any other. As an esteemed cultural practice, a wellspring of aspiration, and a frequently intense social ritual performed with members of their own sex, reading assumed a central place in young women's lives in ways that were less true for men. In this instance, female socialization and opportunity went hand in hand.[15]

At a time when women lacked direct political power and when opportunities for female self-support were just emerging, literature in many ways offered women a significant, perhaps even their best, opening onto a larger world. This was more than a matter of honing skills necessary for employment in the professional and service sectors, necessary though these were. Women's literary proficiency gave them a valuable and valued space (both literal and psychological) from which to move out of the parlor and into more public sites. For adult women, reading clubs began as literally intermediate places in this regard, they were "semi-public" as Elizabeth Long aptly suggests.[16] At an individual level, reading extended, as it still does, what Hans Robert Jauss calls the "horizon of expectations," anticipating "unrealized possibilities" and opening up "new wishes, demands, and goals, and thereby . . . avenues for future experience." In particular, the "personal experience and free creative imagination" that Mikhail Bakhtin finds at the core of the novel permitted a reader to experiment with subjectivity and thus to "change the nature of his [or her] own image." Breaking down the separation between private and public in this way, the late-nineteenth-century culture of reading not only enabled women to extend their experiences but also provided the basis for a new kind of female identity. This was particularly the case during adolescence, a time of intense longing, when imagination plays a crucial role in the formation of identity.[17]

Take the case of M. Carey Thomas, later president of Bryn Mawr College, who read voraciously and widely from an early age. Born in 1857, she grew up in upper-middle-class white privilege, tempered somewhat by the family's Quaker heritage. Though unusual in her precocity and determination, in early adolescence she engaged in literary pursuits common among her peers: between the ages of thirteen and fifteen she kept a journal, a commonplace book, lists of favorite poems and of books she had read or wanted to read. She wrote poems and short stories and sent one of each to *Harper's* (neither was accepted). Reading was at once an occasion for fantasy and wish fulfillment; a source of emotional connection not only to characters and authors but also to the larger world in which Thomas longed to make a mark; a stimulus to friendship and an accompaniment of romance, mainly with women; a means of escape in times of stress; and a catalyst for what she called "the thought life." Reading was as necessary to Thomas as breathing: "It is the purest happiness—the one thing wh[ich] no man taketh from you."[18]

For Thomas's generation, books were a source of private dreaming, social exchange, and collective purpose. For girls raised in a culture that encouraged and restrained them in curiously mixed ways, reading created space for imaginative play, offering not only role models but entry into a larger life. When Thomas started a journal at age thirteen, she did so in the persona of Jo March. A tomboy and a bookworm like Thomas, the heroine of *Little Women* appealed because, as "Jo (not Joe)" she demonstrated that women could be writers and in other ways aspire. When Thomas later embarked on graduate study in Germany, her closest childhood friend, Bessie King, who had joined her in adolescent role-playing centering on *Little Women*, reflected: "Somehow today I went back to those early days when our horizon was so limited yet so full of light & our path lay as plain before us. It all came of reading over Miss Alcott's books now the quintescence [*sic*] of Philistinism then a Bible. . . . Doesn't thee remember when to turn out a 'Jo' was the height of ambition. . . ."[19]

Crossing both gender and genre boundaries, Thomas read herself into a host of texts, ancient and modern, fiction and nonfiction. At fourteen she hoped to show "that the woman who has fought all the battles of olden time over again whilest reading the spirited pages of Homer Vergil Heroditus . . . been carried away by Carlyle & 'mildly enchanted by Emerson' . . . is not any less like what God really intended a woman to be than the trifling ballroom butterfly than the ignorant wax doll baby which *they* admire." The passage reveals the possibilities for female heroism Thomas found in classic texts and demonstrates as well the reciprocal relation between her reading and her ambition, concluding: "[M]y greatest hope & ambition is to be an author an essayist an historian to write hearty earnest true books that may do their part towards elevating the human race." Diary entries such as these suggest the fluid and imaginative possibilities of reading that went beyond conventional role models.[20]

To a remarkable degree, Thomas "[wrote] her own life in advance of living it," in Carolyn Heilbrun's telling phrase.[21] One of the most explicit foretellings was a fantasy of literary achievement at age fifteen that she spun out with Bessie King. The focal point was "a library with all the splendid books with a bright wood fire always burning[,] dark crimson curtains & furniture, great big easy chairs where we could sit lost in books for days together." Far from being idle dreamers, the companions were authors and laboratory scientists of whom people would say: "'Their example arouses me, their books enoble [*sic*] me, their deeds inspire me & behold they are women.'"[22] This fantasy, with its masculine accoutrements and female companion (they gave themselves gender-neutral names), prefigured not only the decor of Bryn Mawr College but also the high standards for female intellect for which the college was renowned under Thomas's leadership.

The life she wrote included an ambitious career for herself as well as a script for the advancement of her sex. Her goal in later years remained essentially unchanged: to vindicate and advance women's intellectual equality. While preparing herself for public life through difficult years of study, culminating in a PhD summa cum laude from the University of Zurich, she received emotional and intellectual support from a like-minded feminist reading circle. Daughters of Baltimore's elite, members of the "Friday Night" shared literary passions (among them writers like William Godwin and Algernon Charles Swinburne who transgressed bourgeois political and aesthetic standards), submitted their literary productions to the group (including an essay on Bolognese women intellectuals of earlier centuries), and tried their hand at joint composition (a novel and essays). Forging a collective feminist identity, they schemed as well as dreamed together. Their most impressive achievement in later years was securing the admission of women to the Johns Hopkins University Medical School.

Of course, Thomas's class and racial subject position, her family's support, and her ties to friends from well-connected families, enabled her to give practical shape to her dreams and schemes. (Class and especially racial privilege also help to account for her racist and anti-Semitic views as an adult.) But many elements of the reading culture maintained by Thomas were widely dispersed in the Gilded Age, among middle-class women of African American as well as European descent. Though reading practices and ideologies varied according to social location and temperament, for the less privileged, too, reading was often a vehicle for articulating individual aspirations and intensifying desires. Women's reading groups, both formal and informal, looked outward as well as inward; they had connections to a larger community, public as well as private commitments.[23]

Where the public aspect of white women's reading developed over time, for African American women the connections between literature and politics—what Elizabeth McHenry calls "public literacy"—prevailed from the start.[24] For Ida B. Wells reading was centrally, though not exclusively, tied to race: "My earliest recollections are of reading the newspaper to my father and an admiring group of his friends. He was interested in politics and I heard the words Ku Klux Klan before I knew what they meant."[25] Born in the waning days of slavery, Wells belonged to the cohort that could not take basic literacy for granted. She was fortunate to grow up in Holly Springs, Mississippi, site of one of the missionary schools founded to instruct the newly freed, and to have parents who urged her on.

Reading was central to Wells, as avocation and vocation. Like Thomas, she called herself a "voracious reader" who read for pleasure, for self-improvement, for sociability, and as a way of forgetting her troubles. In her autobiography she cited literature as her primary source of values: "I had formed my ideals on the best of Dickens's stories, Louisa May Alcott's, Mrs. A. D. T. Whitney's, and Charlotte Brontë's books, and Oliver Optic's stories for boys. I had read the Bible and Shakespeare through, but I had never read a Negro book or anything about Negroes." Except for the last point, this statement might have come from a middle-class white woman of her generation. In fact, Wells combined both European and African American traditions of reading, writing, and speaking.[26]

While establishing herself as a teacher in Memphis in the mid-1880s, Wells engaged in a variety of self-improving activities, oral and written, public and private. These included elocution lessons from a fellow teacher and membership in the Chautauqua Literary and Scientific Circle, a national home-study program that operated through local reading groups (four-fifths of the members were women). Most important, she joined a lyceum with other African American men and women, many of them teachers, who were trying to establish themselves professionally and to survive with dignity in a deteriorating racial climate. The lyceum featured "recitations, essays, and debates interspersed with music," and it may have been there that Wells recited Lady Macbeth's letter-reading and sleepwalking scenes in her nightdress. Mixing high culture with racial politics and opportunities for vocational advancement, the lyceum was, Wells claimed, "a breath of life to me." She was elected editor of the *Evening Star*, "a spicy journal prepared and read by the editor" at the close of each lyceum meeting that included "news items, literary notes, criticisms of previous offerings on the program, a 'They Say' column of pleasant personalities—and always some choice poetry." When a Baptist minister in the audience invited her to write for a local religious weekly, her career as a journalist was launched. By the time she burst on the national scene in 1892 with her uncompromising stand against lynching following the murder of three African American men, she already had a large reputation in the African American press and was part-owner of her own newspaper.[27]

Wells's literary interests were much in evidence at this time, as they were throughout her life. During the Memphis period, she played with the idea of writing a novel, "in partnership" with a young male journalist who encouraged her to make the book "classical, representative and standard." We don't know what he meant by these terms or how she understood them. But we do know that Wells kept notes on incidents of racial offense. One involved a black girl sentenced to a workhouse for resisting a white girl's efforts to push her off a narrow path, an incident Wells wanted to remember when she wrote her novel—perhaps the "Negro book" she had never had an opportunity to read. She never got around to writing it—she lived her own adventure instead—but her interest anticipated that of other African Americans eager to create a "race literature" in the 1890s.[28]

Spelling out the relationship between fiction and social change, Mary Church Terrell, first president of the National Association of Colored Women (NACW), observed: "It has been a bitter disappointment to me that I did not succeed as a story writer. I have thought for years that the Race Problem could be solved more swiftly and more surely through the instrumentality of the short story or novel than in any other way." If this faith seems naive to us, Terrell had in mind the astounding impact of *Uncle Tom's Cabin* and longed to write a work of comparable power. Instead, she wrote an article about Stowe, who remained an important writer in this African American reading community long after her reputation among white critics had declined.[29]

For African American women, the connection between literature and politics, especially racial politics, was strong.[30] Unlike white women's clubs, which began as purely cultural, African American women's groups were political from the start. Not only were they among Wells's chief supporters, but some of them first organized around her antilynching crusade. At the height of the campaign, Wells herself took time to lecture on "The Afro-American in Literature" to the Concord Literary Circle of Brooklyn and also reported on an exhibition of African American artists shown at the home of a member of the Women's Loyal Union of New York and Brooklyn.[31] Leaders of the union helped to organize a testimonial for Wells in Lyric Hall in New York City to raise funds for her cause.[32] A few years later, the group's co-founder, Victoria Earle Matthews, a writer, journalist, and reformer, organized a collection of "Race Literature" at the White Rose Mission, a nondenominational settlement she founded to assist black girls and women migrating from the South to New York City.[33]

Unlike all-male or mixed-gender African American literary societies, like the Bethel Literary and Historical Association of Washington, D.C., few of the women's clubs affiliated with the NACW devoted themselves exclusively to literature or intellectual pursuits. Like the Women's Loyal Union, many combined cultural work with socially useful projects, among them the Sojourner Truth Club of Montgomery, Alabama, which divided its time between literary and social service evenings and also established a Free Reading-Room and Library following the exclusion of African Americans from the local Carnegie library.[34] Such a project was by nature political.

Although faith in the civic uses of literature had a special urgency for African Americans, it was by no means unique to them. No one articulated the social and political dimensions of reading, and the responsibilities that accompanied privileged literacy, more articulately than Jane Addams. Indeed, the founder of Hull-House, America's most influential social settlement, provides a fascinating contrast to her fellow Chicagoan, Oprah Winfrey. (Nor is the juxtaposition as implausible as might appear. In addition to being the city's most famous women of their respective eras, Winfrey in 1994 announced that her proposed $3 million program to improve public housing would be administered by the Hull-House Association, a social service organization in downtown

Chicago.)[35] For both women, reading was an important vehicle for personal development. Both made available their reading proficiency and preferences to others less favored, Oprah through her Book Club, Addams through reading parties and classes at Hull-House. In Winfrey's account: "'Books opened windows to the world for me. If I can help open them for someone else, I'm happy.'"[36] Addams, though an impassioned critic of the elitism of the culture of reading in which she grew up, believed so strongly in the value of literature that she often quoted the Italian revolutionary patriot and nationalist, Giuseppi Mazzini, that education was a "'Holy Communion with generations of dead and living.'" Affirming that every person had a right to this communion, Addams and Hull-House co-founder Ellen Gates Starr launched a variety of clubs and classes at the settlement—all resolutely high culture—beginning with a reading of *Romola*, George Eliot's difficult historical novel set in Renaissance Italy.[37]

Drawing on Leo Tolstoy's view of art as infection, Addams stressed its emotional as distinct from intellectual power: "[A]rt makes us understand and feel what might be incomprehensible and inexpressible in the form of an argument."[38] Through its capacity to stir the imagination, literature satisfied some of the deepest human longings—for emotional connection with one's fellows and truer understanding of them. By permitting readers "to know all sorts of men, in an indefinite way," novels enabled individuals to "find in ourselves a new affinity for all men." Such imaginative engagement was, she believed, a first step toward an aroused public conscience and therefore a pathway to finding remedies for social ills: "We have learned as common knowledge that much of the insensibility and hardness of the world is due to the lack of imagination which prevents a realization of the experiences of other people."[39] Addams even anticipated that readers for whom immigrants or the unemployed had been individualized in this way would never again cast ugly words or thoughts in their direction.[40] Though her views on these subjects may seem naive or utopian, they reveal her affinity with other progressives of her generation who believed that for people of good will, becoming aware of something was a virtual guarantee for acting on it.[41]

Despite their common faith in reading, Winfrey's and Addams's views on its goals are strikingly different. As we have seen, Winfrey's originate in a self-help perspective, while Addams's more fully elaborated ideas derive both from an analysis of class and from her expectation of service from those who lived in comfort. There is a self-help vein in Addams, for she believed that literature provided a form of emotional education necessary for men and especially women of the comfortable classes if they were to move outside their class cocoons. But in Addams's view, "The question is after you have learned reading and writing, to what use do you intend to put them, not how well have you learned them, but what stimulus are you given by learning them? The old foolish notion that they are the property of a special class, must be destroyed. . . . [T]he real question is not what we read, but what social use do we make of the mental and physical life we have thus acquired."[42] Reading and education broadly considered became for her a potential vehicle for diminishing the gap between rich and poor. Addams would certainly have approved of "literacy volunteers" as a starting point, but she would have gone beyond the acts of individual compassion involved in transmitting basic skills to advocating programs that promoted social justice as well as personal well-being.

Like Winfrey, then, Addams began with reading's emotional power, but she went on to articulate its transformative cultural and political force. In her articulation, reading certain kinds of literature was a kind of experience that had profound social consequences. Considering both Addams and Winfrey as cultural leaders of their times, their differences tell us a great deal about changes in American life, then and now.

One of the most striking of these is the changed professional and political situation of American women. Today, when roughly half of law and medical students are female, girls grow up with expectations about their lives that those of us raised during the first half of the twentieth century—let alone the nineteenth—did not. At the same time, new opportunities brought about in part by two women's movements result in less leisure for the middle class. If, 125 years ago, voluntary organizations like the literary clubs provided a launching pad for public activities of various sorts, today's clubs seem more like places of refuge. Then, when women were assumed to be limited to private life, they fashioned an ostensibly private activity (reading) into a public instrument. Of course, feminist theorists and historians have demonstrated that the supposed gap between public and private masked more complex realities. And Elizabeth Long has shown us that all reading is socially based.[43] But women used what was most readily available to them, what began at home—literary endeavors—to carve out first semipublic and then overtly public space.

Today, reading seems to have lost most of its political edge. Reading clubs offer time out from busy professional and personal lives—to use a concept developed by Janice Radway—whether these lives are lived mainly at home, or in the paid work force, or both.[44] They also offer occasions for female bonding otherwise often less available today, when gender-segregated activities are fewer than they once were.

What are the possibilities of reading groups becoming more politically engaged? I'm not holding my breath. The words of a professional book group leader give one pause: "'My groups are an exploratory avenue for people who would be uncomfortable with the label 'feminist,' . . . These people would never be interested in being activists, but they see themselves reflected in feminist books and find themselves cheering for feminist characters. . . . Groups are essentially a safe place. Members can express their views there without fear of reprisals. They can avoid labels they find uncomfortable while they explore new ideas.'"[45] This language is disconcertingly reminiscent of the predicament of those early study club members in the 1870s and 1880s who had to justify every move outside their homes. Perhaps things have changed less than we think.

Perhaps, on the other hand, each generation must find new ways to promote female agency in the face of continued impediments. In that sense, reading groups may be as good as it gets, as near as we get, at this historical moment. Perhaps they will help to fan the spark of change, whenever that may come.

Notes

I want to thank Joan Hedrick for her thoughtful comments on an earlier version of this essay; Elizabeth Long for allowing me to read two chapters of her then unpublished book, *Book Clubs: Women and the Uses of Reading in Everyday Life*; Scott D. Taylor for generously sharing his thoughts and information on Oprah's Book Club; and Mary Curry for interlibrary loan assistance.

1. For an influential statement of this position, see Sven Birkerts, *The Gutenberg Elegies: The Fate of Reading in an Electronic Age* (New York: Ballantine Books, 1994).

2. Jonathan Yardley, "The real readers of literature do not fit the stereotype of tweedy male," *The Times (Trenton)*, Sept. 3, 1989. On the one book movement, see Stephen Kinzer, "Quiet, Please; Chicago is Reading. The

Same Book at the Same Time," *New York Times* (Aug. 28, 2001): E1, and Alan Bisbort, "Everyone on the Same Page," *New York Times* (March 31, 2002). It is unclear just how successful these programs, usually initiated by libraries, have been. One writer suggested that in Chicago and New York "whole populations shrugged." Richard Lacayo, "Oprah Turns the Page," *Time*, 159 (April 15, 2002): 63.

3. D. T. Max, "The Oprah Effect," *New York Times Magazine* (Dec. 26,1999): 36; quotation from Robert Dahlin, "This '90s Group Activity Is All the Rage," *Publishers Weekly*, 243 (Nov. 18, 1996): 43. For a scholarly analysis of the contemporary reading club phenomenon, see Elizabeth Long, "*Book Clubs: Women and the Uses of Reading in Everyday Life*" (University of Chicago Press, 2003).

Three guides to reading groups appeared in the mid-nineties: Ellen Slezak, *The Book Group Book: A Thoughtful Guide to Forming and Enjoying a Stimulating Book Discussion Group* (Chicago: Chicago Review Press, 1993); Rachel W. Jacobsohn, *The Reading Group Handbook: Everything You Need to Know, From Choosing Members to Leading Discussions* (New York: Hyperion, 1994); and David Laskin and Holly Hughes, *The Reading Group Book: The Complete Guide to Starting and Sustaining a Reading Group, with Annotated Lists of 250 Titles for Provocative Discussion* (New York: Plume Books, 1995). Books with a more specialized focus are: Pat Neblett, *Circles of Sisterhood: A Book Discussion Group Guide for Women of Color* (New York: Harlem River Press, 1997) and Shireen Dodson, with Teresa Barker, *The Mother-Daughter Book Club: How Ten Busy Mothers and Daughters Came Together to Talk, Laugh and Learn Through Their Love of Reading* (New York: Harper Perennial, 1997).

4. Douglas Waples, Bernard Berelson, and Franklyn R. Bradshaw, *What Reading Does to People: A Summary of Evidence on the Social Effects of Reading and a Statement of Problems for Research* (Chicago: University of Chicago Press, 1940).

5. Quotations from Robin M. Neidorf, "Feminist Book Groups: The New C. R.?" *Ms.*, 5 (January/February 1995): 64–67 (an excellent overview of the psychological and social impact of groups); Neblett, *Circles of Sisterhood*, pp. 18–19; and Carol Huber, "Once Begun, We Are Mighty," p. 5, and Ellie Becker, "Talking as Quilting," p. 95, both in *The Book Club Group*, ed. Ellen Slezak. See also Dorian Burden, "Reading Groups: A Working Woman's Retreat," *Executive Female*, 17 (July/August 1994): 76–77.

6. Bob Lamm, "Reading Groups: Where Are All the Men?" *Publishers Weekly*, 243 (Nov. 18, 1996): 48.

7. On Oprah's Book Club, see Gayle Feldman, "Bookend: Making Book on Oprah," *New York Times Book Review* (Feb. 2, 1997): 31; Max, "The Oprah Effect," 36–41; Martha Bayles, "Bookend: Imus, Oprah and the Literary Elite," *New York Times Book Review*, (Aug. 29, 1999): 35; Deborah Tannen, "Oprah Winfrey," *Time*, 151 (June 8, 1998): 197–98 (Special Issue on "Artists and Entertainers of the 20th Century").

8. Max, "The Oprah Effect," p. 37; Lynette Clemetson, "Women of the New Century: Oprah at a Crossroads," *Newsweek*, 137 (Jan. 8, 2001): 38–46 (cover story); "Touched by an Oprah," *People Weekly* 52 (Dec. 20, 1999): [113]. Malika Oufkir's *Stolen Lives* was featured on June 20, 2001. Exchanges about Oprah's Book Club selections may be found on the show's website, Oprah.com. For a critique of the recovery movement that includes Winfrey, see Wendy Kaminer, *I'm Dysfunctional, You're Dysfunctional: The Recovery Movement and Other Self-Help Fashions* (Reading, Mass.: Addison-Wesley, 1992), esp. pp. 33–43. Trysh Travis discusses the literary context of the recovery movement in "Heathcliff and Cathy, the Dysfunctional Couple," *The Chronicle of Higher Education* (May 11, 2001): B13–14.

9. David D. Kirkpatrick, "Oprah Will Curtail 'Book Club' Picks, And Authors Weep," *New York Times* (April 6, 2002); Lacayo, "Oprah Turns the Page," p. 63; "Winfrey Provokes Range of Reaction and Speculation," *Publishers Weekly*, 249 (April 15, 2002): 20; and "Oprah's Book Club, The Final Chapter," *The Economist* 363 (April 13, 2002): 80. A perceptive account that credits Winfrey's desire to be free of the constant pressure of finding contemporary books she "really passionately love[s]," is Kathy Rooney, "Oprah Learns Her Lesson," *The Nation*, 274 (May 20, 2002): 56–60. Although the announcement stated that Oprah's Book Club would be curtailed, most perceived it as the Club's death knell.

10. David D. Kirkpatrick, "Winfrey Rescinds Offer to Author for Guest Appearance," *New York Times*, Oct. 24, 2001; David D. Kirkpatrick, "'Oprah' Gaffe By Franzen Draws Ire and Sales," *New York Times* (Oct. 29, 2001); Margo Jefferson, "There Goes the Neighborhood," *New York Times Book Review* (Nov. 25, 2001): 35. Press commentary on the affair has been extensive; a sampling of magazine articles may be found at: http://relayweb.hwwilsonweb.com/cgi-bin/ . . . Thomas R. Edwards, "Oprah's Choice," *Raritan*, 21 (Spring 2002): 75–86, combines discerning commentary with a review of the book. *The Corrections* went on to win a National Book Award.

11. It is perhaps significant in this context that the title of Franzen's recent collection of literary essays is *How to Be Alone: Essays* (New York: Farrar, Straus and Giroux, 2002); the final essay, "Meet Me in St. Louis," centers on his discomfort at being filmed for the program.

The disdain of high-culture purists for commercialism and popular status, and its relation to both gender and race, is ably captured by John Young, "Toni Morrison, Oprah Winfrey, and Postmodern Popular Audiences," *African American Review* 35 (Summer 2001): esp. 186–87. The impact of gender on debates on literature is analyzed in several contexts by Joan D. Hedrick, *Harriet Beecher Stowe: A Life* (New York: Oxford University Press, 1994); Nancy Glazener, *Reading for Realism: The History of a U.S. Literary Institution, 1850–1910* (Durham: Duke University Press, 1997); and Janice A. Radway, *A Feeling for*

Books: The Book-of-the-Month Club, Literary Taste, and Middle-Class Desire (Chapel Hill: University of North Carolina Press, 1997).

12. See Kate Santich, "In Wake of Oprah Book Club, Others Spring Up and Spike Sales," *Hartford Courant* (June 22, 2002); Bill Goldstein, "TV Book Clubs Try to Fill Oprah's Shoes," *New York Times* (Dec. 16, 2002): C17. Selections for "Today" and "Good Morning America" are made by writers rather than by the programs' hosts. Choices for "Reading with Ripa," the club hosted by Kelly Ripa, are resolutely anti-Oprah. The goals are to "be fun, frivolous, fast and fiction," with selections tending toward romances and mysteries.

Also attempting to fill the gap left by the demise of Oprah's Book Club, which featured many books by African Americans, *Essence*, the premier monthly magazine for black women, announced its plans to establish a book club centered on the African American experience. Martin Arnold, "Black Magazine Tries Book Club," *New York Times* (Sept. 12, 2002): E3. Unlike some of the television clubs, where experts make the choices, final selections were to be made by readers.

In fact, Winfrey herself recently announced plans to bring back her book club, although in a different form. This time she wished to celebrate writers she admired from the past, such as Shakespeare, Faulkner, and Hemingway. The lineup suggests that Franzen may indeed have had an impact. See "Oprah Bringing Book Club Back," *Hartford Courant*, Feb. 28, 2003: D10.

13. This article is informed by my ongoing research on women's reading in the late nineteenth century. Published pieces include: "Sense and Sensibility: A Case Study of Women's Reading in Late-Victorian America," *Reading in America: Literature and Social History*, ed. Cathy N. Davidson (Baltimore: Johns Hopkins University Press, 1989), 201–25; "Reading and Ambition: M. Carey Thomas and Female Heroism," *American Quarterly* 45 (March 1993): 73–103; "Reading *Little Women*: The Many Lives of a Text," *U.S. History as Women's History: New Feminist Essays*, ed. Linda K. Kerber, Alice Kessler-Harris, and Kathryn Kish Sklar (Chapel Hill: University of North Carolina Press, 1995), pp. 245–66, 414–24; and "Reading and Middle-Class Identity in Victorian America: Cultural Consumption, Conspicuous and Otherwise," *Reading Acts: U.S. Readers' Interactions with Literature, 1800–1950*, ed. Barbara Ryan and Amy M. Thomas (Knoxville: University of Tennessee Press, 2002), pp. 137–60.

14. Joseph Cook, "How to Make Dull Boys Read," *Hints for Home Reading: A Series of Papers on Books and Their Use*, ed. Lyman Abbott (New York: G. P. Putnam's Sons, 1880), pp. 70–77.

On representations (pictorial and verbal) of women readers in Great Britain, see Kate Flint, *The Woman Reader, 1837–1947* (New York: Oxford University Press, 1993); for illustrations of women's pleasure in group reading in *Godey's Lady's Book*, see Patricia Okker, *Our Sister Editors: Sarah J. Hale and the*

Tradition of Nineteenth-Century American Women Editors (Athens: University of Georgia Press, 1995).

On women as the chief readers of fiction in recent years, see Nicholas Zill and Marianne Winglee, "Literature Reading in the United States: Data from National Surveys and Their Policy Implications," *Book Research Quarterly*, 5 (1989): 24–58, a summary of a longer survey.

15. I treat nineteenth-century reading culture in greater detail in "Reading and Middle-Class Identity in Victorian America" and in "Growing Up With Books in the Gilded Age: The Gendering of Reading," chapter 3 of my forthcoming book, *Reading Lives: Women and Literary Culture, 1860–1920.*

16. Long, *Book Clubs*, chapter 2.

17. Hans Robert Jauss, "Literary History as a Challenge to Literary Theory," *New Directions in Literary History*, ed. Ralph Cohen (Baltimore: Johns Hopkins University Press, 1974), 37 and *passim*; M. M. Bakhtin, *The Dialogic Imagination: Four Essays*, ed. Michael Holquist, translated by Caryl Emerson and Michael Holquist (Austin: University of Texas Press, 1981), 39, 38; see also 31–40 and 247. See also Erik H. Erikson, *Identity: Youth and Crisis* (New York: W. W. Norton, 1968) 53, 87, and *passim.*

18. M. Carey Thomas Journal, Aug. 23rd [1878], *The Papers of M. Carey Thomas in the Bryn Mawr College Archives*, ed. Lucy Fisher West (Woodbridge, Conn., 1982), reel 1; microfilm edition, hereafter MCTP). A fuller analysis of Thomas's reading may be found in Sicherman, "Reading And Ambition." For an interpretation that emphasizes the importance of Thomas's reading in fostering an alternative sexual identity, see Helen Lefkowitz Horowitz, "'Nous Autres': Reading, Passion, and the Creation of M. Carey Thomas," *Journal of American History* 79 (June 1992): 68–95. See also Horowitz's full-length biography, *The Power and Passion of M. Carey Thomas* (New York: Alfred A. Knopf, 1994).

19. MCT Journal, June 20, 1870, MCTP, reel 1; Elizabeth King Ellicott to MCT, Nov. 23 [1879], reel 39.

20. MCT Journal, Nov. 10, Feb. 26 [1871], MCTP, reel 1.

21. Carolyn G. Heilbrun, *Writing a Woman's Life* (New York: W. W. Norton, 1988), p. 11.

22. MCT Journal, March 14, 1872, MCTP, reel 1.

23. The literature on white women's study clubs is extensive. Among the most useful studies are Theodora Penny Martin, *The Sound of Our Own Voices: Women's Study Clubs, 1860–1910* (Boston: Beacon Press, 1987) and Anne Ruggles Gere, *Intimate Practices: Literacy and Cultural Work in U.S. Women's Clubs, 1880–1920* (Urbana and Chicago: University of Illinois Press, 1997), which offers comparative class, racial, and ethnic data, as does Anne Ruggles Gere and Sarah R. Robbins, "Gendered Literacy in Black and White: Turn-of-the-Century African-American and European-American Club Women's Printed Texts," *Signs*,

21 (Spring 1996): 643–78. See also Elizabeth Long, *Book Clubs*, chapter 2, and Christine Pawley, "'Not Wholly Self Culture': The Shakespearean Women's Club, Osage, Iowa, 1892–1920," *The Annals of Iowa* 56 (Winter/Spring 1997): 12–45, as well as Pawley's study of reading in a midwestern community, *Reading on the Middle Border: The Culture of Print in Late-Nineteenth-Century Osage, Iowa* (Amherst: University of Massachusetts Press, 2001).

24. See Elizabeth McHenry, *Forgotten Readers: Recovering the Lost History of African American Literary Societies* (Durham: Duke University Press, 2002), esp. p. 241, and her earlier articles, "'Dreaded Eloquence': The Origins and Rise of African American Literary Societies and Libraries," *Harvard Library Bulletin*, NS, 6 (Spring 1995): 32–56 and "Forgotten Readers: African-American Literary Societies and the American Scene," *Print Culture in a Diverse America*, ed. James P. Danky and Wayne A. Wiegand (Urbana and Chicago: University of Illinois Press, 1998): 149–72. See also Anne Meis Knupfer, *Toward a Tenderer Humanity and a Nobler Womanhood: African American Women's Clubs in Turn-of-the-Century Chicago* (New York: New York University Press, 1996), esp. 108–22.

25. *Crusade for Justice: The Autobiography of Ida B. Wells*, ed. Alfreda M. Duster (Chicago: University of Chicago Press, 1970), p. 9.

26. *Crusade for Justice*, pp. 21–22.

27. Wells discusses her lyceum activities in *Crusade for Justice*, pp. 22–24; a contemporary account of this and Wells's other literary and self-help activities may be followed in *The Memphis Diary of Ida B. Wells*, ed. Miriam DeCosta-Willis (Boston: Beacon Press, 1995). Wells's career may be followed in two recent studies: Linda O. McMurry, *To Keep the Waters Troubled: The Life of Ida B. Wells* (New York: Oxford University Press, 1998) and Patricia A. Schechter, *Ida B. Wells-Barnett and American Reform, 1880–1930* (Chapel Hill: University of North Carolina Press, 2001).

28. *Memphis Diary*, pp. 53, 35–36, 46, 101, and passim. Wells wrote a classic temperance tale, "Two Christmas Days: A Holiday Story," published in the *AME Zion Church Quarterly* in 1894; it is reprinted in Mildred I. Thompson, *Ida B. Wells-Barnett: An Exploratory Study of an American Black Woman, 1893–1930* (Brooklyn: Carlson Publishing Inc., 1990), pp. 225–34. On race literature, see Victoria Earle Matthews, "The Value of Race Literature," *Massachusetts Review* 27 (Summer 1986): 169–91; this is a reprint of a talk originally delivered in 1895. See also McHenry, *Forgotten Readers*, pp. 191–97.

29. Terrell, *A Colored Woman in a White World* (Washington, D.C.: Ransdell Inc. Publishers, 1940), p. 234. On the Stowe connection, see Dorothy Sterling, *Black Foremothers: Three Lives*, 2d. ed. (New York: The Feminist Press, 1988), p. 136; Terrell, *A Colored Woman*, p. 233; and Mary Church Terrell, "Harriet Beecher Stowe," Mary Church Terrell Papers, Moorland-Spingarn Research Center, Howard University, Washington, D.C. Terrell tried her hand at fiction, but had trouble getting it published.

30. McHenry makes this point in *Forgotten Readers*, chapter 4, an excellent analysis of the literary activities of African American women's clubs in the late nineteenth century.

31. Notice of Ida B. Wells lecture, *Washington Bee*, XI (Oct. 22, 1892): 3.

32. Wells dedicated her first anti-lynching pamphlet, "To the Afro-American women of New York and Brooklyn . . . [who] made possible its publication." *Southern Horrors. Lynch Law in All Its Phases* (1892; rpt in *Southern Horrors and Other Writings: The Anti-Lynching Campaign of Ida B. Wells, 1892–1900*, ed. Jacqueline Jones Royster (Boston: Bedford Books, 1997), p. 50.

33. "White Rose Mission Settlement," brochure reprinted from the *New York Evening Post*, White Rose Folder, Schomburg Center for Research in Black Culture, New York Public Library (courtesy of Gabrielle Foreman). The race literature collection at the Mission included "books written for and about the Negro in America."

34. W. E. Burghardt Du Bois, ed., *Efforts for Social Betterment among Negro Americans*, The Atlanta University Publications, No. 14 (Atlanta: Atlanta University Press, 1909), pp. 117–18. The volume contains considerable information about African American women's organizations. See also Dorothy Salem, *To Better Our World: Black Women in Organized Reform, 1890–1920* (Brooklyn: Carlson, 1990); *A History of the Club Movement among the Colored Women of the United States of America* . . . (Washington, D.C.: National Association of Colored Women's Clubs, Inc. 1902 [rpt 1978]); and Knupfer, *Toward a Tenderer Humanity*, pp. 108–22. *The Woman's Era* and *National Association Notes*, successive publications of the National Association of Colored Women, included summaries of club activities.

35. A year earlier, Winfrey donated proceeds from the auction of her dresses to the Association. Shannon Jackson, *Lines of Activity: Performance, Historiography, Hull-House Domesticity* (Ann Arbor: University of Michigan Press, 2001), pp. 38–39.

36. Quoted in "Touched by an Oprah," p. [113].

37. See, for example, Addams, "The Subjective Necessity for Social Settlements," *Philanthropy and Social Progress* (New York: Thomas Y. Crowell, 1893), p. 10. Addams's views are analyzed in greater depth in my *Reading Lives*.

38. Addams, "A Function of the Social Settlement," *Annals of the American Academy of Political and Social Science* 13 (May 1899): [326]. Tolstoy's *What Is Art?* appeared in an English translation in 1898. Addams visited Tolstoy at Yasnaya Polyana in 1896 and subsequently read him avidly. Though deeply influenced by his views, she did not accept his controversial aesthetic or other theories uncritically (he dismissed Shakespeare and other celebrated writers and artists because they did not reach the masses). See Addams, "Tolstoy's Theory of Life," *Chautauqua Assembly Herald*, 27 (July 14, 1902): 2–3 and *Twenty Years at Hull-House* (1910; rpt. New York: Signet, 1960), pp. 186–199.

39. Addams, *Democracy and Social Ethics* (1902; rpt. Cambridge, Mass.: Harvard University Press, 1964), pp. 8–9. Addams's choice of language here echoes the title of Walter Besant's *All Sorts and Conditions of Men*, one of several books proposing cultural remedies to social problems that electrified American as well as British readers in the late 1880s.

40. "The Newer Ideals of Peace," *Chautauqua Assembly Herald* 27 (July 8, 1902): 5.

41. The role of the literary imagination in promoting empathy and social justice has recently been highlighted by Martha C. Nussbaum. In *Poetic Justice*, Nussbaum looks back to an earlier era—the time of James and Dewey, which was also the time of Addams—when novels had an acknowledged contribution to make to moral discussion, to public life. Though lacking a gendered analysis, Nussbaum argues for the importance of the literary imagination (with its emotional impact) in fostering empathy and compassion for individuals and groups who would otherwise be seen as alien and lacking in individuality. *Poetic Justice: The Literary Imagination and Public Life* (Boston: Beacon Press, 1995), esp. xiii–xix and 1–12.

42. Addams, "Democracy and Education," *Chautauqua Assembly Herald*, 25 (Aug. 9, 1900): 2. See Charlene Haddock Seigfried, *Pragmatism and Feminism: Reweaving the Social Fabric* (Chicago: University of Chicago Press, 1996) for an analysis of the connections between Addams's views (and their implementation at Hull House) and the pragmatism of John Dewey, esp. pp. 73–79, 227–33.

43. Elizabeth Long, "Textual Interpretation as Collective Action," in *The Ethnography of Reading*, ed. Jonathan Boyarin (Berkeley and Los Angeles: University of California Press, 1992), pp. 180–211.

44. See Janice A. Radway, *Reading the Romance: Women, Patriarchy, and Popular Literature* (Chapel Hill: University of North Carolina Press, 1984).

45. Quoted in Neidorf, "Feminist Book Groups," p. 66–67.

Part 1

Print for a Purpose

Women as Editors and Publishers

Cultural Critique and Consciousness Raising

Clara Bewick Colby's Woman's Tribune *and Late-Nineteenth-Century Radical Feminism*

KRISTIN MAPEL BLOOMBERG

For Clara Bewick Colby (1846–1916), editor and publisher of the suffrage journal the *Woman's Tribune* from 1883 to 1909, radical feminism was an ideology foundational to her editorial vision. But who *was* this influential suffrage presswoman, and what was the *Woman's Tribune*? While Colby was not on the earliest "front lines" of the suffrage movement when the landmark "Declaration of Sentiments" was read at Seneca Falls in 1848, she was a member of that generation of women who were to become the foot soldiers of late-nineteenth- and early-twentieth-century feminist activism. These were the women who did the vast majority of the work for woman suffrage; yet they were neither its initial revolutionaries, nor were they present to stand in the winner's circle when the Nineteenth Amendment was ultimately passed in 1920.

Because she was part of this "sandwich" generation, Clara Bewick Colby and an account of her influential periodical were lost in the shuffle of politics and time; as a result, they need to be returned to the historical dialogue regarding woman-edited periodicals. This essay is intended as a contribution to that dialogue, especially in light of the fact that Colby's editorial emphasis, which favored what E. Claire

Jerry terms "the broader arena of women's rights" over a narrow push toward legislative reform, caused Colby and her paper to be seen as "fringe, radical, even as detrimental to the cause."[1] A wholesale review of Colby's history as a suffrage editor and publisher would require another forum, but it is possible to focus here on the editorial strategies Colby established in earlier editions of the *Tribune*. Through an analysis of Colby's editorial philosophy, readers today can understand how her concept of radical feminist activism was built upon notions of a late-nineteenth-century domesticity that was shaped by the peculiarities of her geographic location—on the Nebraska frontier. Through this process, we may discern how Clara Bewick Colby worked to create a political periodical that eschewed didactic notions of women's rights and instead focused on a many-layered awareness of the daily realities of her readers, and how those realities intersected with radical politics.

Radical feminism, which is often assumed to have been the creation of feminists of the 1970s, was in fact rooted in the feminist movement of the 1870s. Like their sisters one hundred years in the future, late-nineteenth-century radical feminists like Clara Bewick Colby believed there existed a system of men's oppression of women that reached beyond simple gender discrimination, and that this social oppression was legitimized within the law, medicine, religion, family, and other social institutions. Moreover, this late-nineteenth-century awareness of how women were oppressed was coupled with the belief that women were, in some ways, culturally superior to men. This was a worldview not altogether incompatible with shifting conceptions of late-nineteenth-century domesticity found in the cultural traces of Republican Motherhood, which stressed education for women so that they could, in turn, educate their sons to become model citizens; and True Womanhood, which stressed traditionally feminine values as the only appropriate social roles for women. This "domestic ideology," argues historian Robert L. Griswold

> was central to the world view of Anglo women in the West. . . . The cultural values of domestic ideology had a powerful appeal to female settlers: they gave meaning to women's domestic work, made the blurring of sex roles culturally intelligible, helped confirm women's self-worth, offered a sense of stability in an inherently unstable world, and fostered bonds of friendship with other women. Domestic ideology, furthermore, legitimated women's efforts to "civilize" the West.[2]

Griswold rejects proscriptive notions of late-nineteenth-century domesticity for a more fluid notion of domesticity as a cultural ideology that in the American West functioned as "a tie to the past, a way one connected new surroundings to older roots," to provide a comfortable cultural framework used by western women to interpret "the uncertainties and upheavals characteristic of life in a new land."[3]

Domesticity in the nineteenth century was a cultural ideology in the process of transformation, and, Martha M. Solomon argues, "this shared identity, which was so carefully inculcated in women of the age, in some ways provided the basis for its own rejection."[4] As an editor aware of the cultural location of her readers, Colby made a conscious political choice to target female readers who were already unified by a shared social sense of both domesticity and a vocation. Thus, through the *Woman's Tribune*, she could engage for movement toward social change a population of women who had already rejected narrow definitions of domestic women's roles. Western women's shared experience of domestic ideology, then, could be tapped as a force for creating new social institutions. As Nancy F. Cott observes, "because it [the ideology of domesticity] included 'all' women, and was endowed with social and political meaning, the domestic vocation gained enormous persuasive strength. It gave many women a sense of satisfaction as well as solidarity with their sex."[5]

This sense of satisfaction was embraced especially by frontier women who saw themselves as progressive "civilizers" of a new society. But keeping the changing notions of domesticity in mind, Griswold explains that "their quest was not to establish a lofty, other-worldly abstraction called *civilization* but to create the institutions—the schools, churches, charity associations, reforms—that would check male-inspired disorder, assist the victims and losers of the male dominated society, and secure a social order within which domestic virtues and family life could flourish."[6] By focusing on domesticity as a seemingly natural way to women's power, radical feminist editors like Clara Bewick Colby built on an existing cultural ideal to cleverly manipulate the means of these social ideologies to justify the ends of increased empowerment for the literate Anglo women who would read and subscribe to her periodical. In this way, she could both affirm and radicalize women's lived experiences to transform True Women and Republican Mothers into New Women looking forward to a new century where they would discover together their "shared and special destiny" as American women.[7]

By elevating traditional female qualities and simultaneously locating them within a political movement—in this case suffrage—radical feminist editors like Colby sought to empower half the population in order to transform the world. Judith Lorber explains the social ideals foundational to the radical feminist philosophy:

> Radical feminism is not only critical of men's violence and sexuality, it turns male-dominated culture on its head. It takes all the characteristics that are valued by men in Western societies—objectivity, distance, control, coolness, aggressiveness, and competitiveness—and blames them for wars, poverty, rape, battering, child abuse, and incest. It praises what women do—feed and nurture, cooperate and reciprocate, and attend to bodies, minds, and psyches. The important values, radical feminism argues, are intimacy, persuasion, warmth, caring, and sharing—the characteristics that women develop in their hands-on, everyday experiences with their own and their children's bodies and with the work of daily living.[8]

Importantly, Lorber continues, "Radical feminism's view is that the presence of significant numbers of women can alter values and behavior because their ideas, their outlook, and their experiences are different from those of most men, almost to the point of giving women a different culture."[9] The *Woman's Tribune*, then, reflected late-nineteenth-century radical feminist culture in the sense that Clara Bewick Colby created a periodical that celebrated all the achievements of women—both mundane and extraordinary. What is more, Colby's reflection of intimate women's culture in the pages of the *Tribune* functioned as a connecting link to which she could couple her radical political program and, ultimately, persuade her readers of the need for women's true equality.

By establishing connecting links among women's culture and feminist activism, the *Woman's Tribune* reflected a fundamental kind of radical feminism—in the notion of "radical" as "of the root or source." This was a radical feminism that had its roots in domestic women's culture, one that touched on the daily realities of her women readers. Through this editorial practice, Colby marked a shared solidarity among a readership of women with diverse life experiences not unlike her own family's middle-class frontier life. Like those of its editor, the daily lives of the *Tribune*'s readers were still framed by cultural notions of domesticity; as a result, Colby realized it was important to emphasize a broad-based political movement that kept its roots in an accepted set of ideas about women's roles and women's place in the world.

As with many other late-nineteenth-century progressives, Colby believed with her readers that she was among those women who saw domesticity as a fluid social ideology that could be used as a cultural framework to "connect new surroundings to older roots."[10] Like many of her readers, Colby was raised on a midwestern homestead in the 1850s, and as a young adult moved farther west to the Nebraska frontier in the 1870s, to help build a better American society. Because of her deeply held progressive ideals, Colby's editorial vision for the *Woman's Tribune* was both educational and political. Her focus was to teach her readers to see themselves outside of traditional, male-identified social models, while simultaneously affirming their current social roles and responsibilities as guardians of the family and shapers of a new society. By drawing on these shared ideas about women's place in the world, she could work to bind together nonrelated women through an ideology Griswold calls "a shared belief about women's duties, responsibilities, and prerogatives."[11]

The *Woman's Tribune* entered the world of women in print in a timely fashion, for the world was ready to receive a woman-focused political periodical. Patricia Okker writes that earlier in the nineteenth century, increased readership for American periodicals provided opportunities for women editors to gain experience and establish credibility in the field. She identifies six women editors of American periodicals in 1828: "a 'Lady of Providence' at the *Toilet; or, Ladies Cabinet of Literature*, Sarah J. Hale at the *Ladies' Magazine* [later of *Godey's Ladies' Book*], Katherine Ware at the *Bower of Taste*, Eliza L. Follen at the *Christian Teacher's Manual*, Julia L. Dumont at the *Chrystal and Ladies' Magazine*, and Frances Wright at the *New Harmony Gazette*."[12] These early-nineteenth-century women editors oversaw nonpolitical periodicals aimed at an audience of women and children; but, more importantly, they opened the door for later nineteenth-century political newspaperwomen like Clara Bewick Colby.

After early-nineteenth-century women gained a foothold as respected editors and publishers, it is possible to view the evolution of the woman-edited and woman-published women's rights periodical into three stages.[13] The first can be seen as a kind of "moral uplift" political periodical that grew out of the temperance movement and other reform movements of the day. These early politically oriented periodicals included Amelia Jenks Bloomer's the *Lily* (Seneca Falls, NY, 1849–56) and the short-lived *Una* published by Paulina Kellogg Wright Davis (Providence, RI, 1853–55). Other politically minded woman-published papers emerged at this time, turning the focus more to women's rights, including Anne Royall's *Huntress* (Washington, D.C., 1836–54) and Jane Grey Swisshelm's *Pittsburgh Saturday Visiter* (1847–51). Elizabeth Cady Stanton, Susan B. Anthony, and Matilda Joslyn Gage's *History of Woman Suffrage* notes that political periodicals such as *The Lowell Offering*, "edited by the 'mill girls' of that manufacturing town, was established in 1840, and exercised a wide influence. It lived till 1849. Its articles were entirely written by the girl operatives, [. . . . while] Harriet F. Curtis, author of two popular novels, and Harriet Farley, both 'mill girls,' had entire editorial charge during the latter part of its existence."[14]

The second stage of woman-published and woman-edited women's rights periodicals began after the Civil War, when Elizabeth Cady Stanton and Susan B. Anthony collaborated with George Francis Train, a proslavery Southerner, to publish the *Revolution* (1868–71). The authors of the *History of Woman Suffrage* assert the *Revolution*'s important place in this new stage of women's political journalism, declaring, "From the advent of *The Revolution* can be dated a new era in the woman suffrage movement. Its brilliant, aggressive columns attracted the comments of the press, and drew the attention of the country to the reform so ably advocated. Many other papers devoted to the discussion of woman's enfranchisement also arose."[15] Importantly, the *Revolution*'s new exclusive focus on national suffrage events established what Lynne Masel-Waters describes as beginning "a century-long tradition of women's political journalism."[16] However, the leftist posture of Stanton and Anthony's *Revolution* and their alliance with an avowed supporter of slavery solidified the split between Stanton and Anthony and others who came to the suffrage movement through abolitionist activism. As a result, in 1870 Lucy Stone and her husband Henry B. Blackwell established the American Woman Suffrage Association, and their own competing suffrage paper, the *Woman's Journal* (Boston, 1870–90).

While Stanton and Anthony's *Revolution* ceased publication a mere three years after it began publication (in part because Train left the country and withdrew his financial backing of the paper),[17] the success of Stone and Blackwell's *Woman's Journal* set the stage for establishing a robust print culture devoted to the cause of women's rights. E. Claire Jerry reports that by 1873 there existed four periodicals focused exclusively on suffrage: the *New Northwest* (Portland, Oregon), the *Pioneer* (San Francisco), *Woodhull & Claflin's Weekly* (New York City), and the *Woman's Journal* (Boston). By 1884, nine suffrage papers were published regularly, including *Fortschritt* (New York City), *Our Herald* (Lafayette, IN), the *Queen Bee* (Denver), the *New Northwest* (Portland, OR), the *Woman's Exponent* (Salt Lake City), the *Woman's Herald of Industry* (San Francisco), the *Woman's Journal* (Boston), the *Woman's Own* (Indianapolis), and, not least, Clara Bewick Colby's *Woman's Tribune* (Beatrice, NE).[18]

Like her sister editors, Clara Bewick Colby was aware of the need for woman-centered journalism, noting in the January 1, 1884, issue of the *Tribune* that "men for the most part manage the tone of the press."[19] Defining her own niche as a front-runner in this new assemblage of women's political periodicals, Colby and the *Woman's Tribune* strove to create a journalistic cultural critique that would not only report news of important happenings, but also provide backgrounds and contexts for her readers that were different from both the traditional male-dominated press and other woman-run periodicals. In this task, she would blend together the documentation of women's culture, radical feminist activism and education, and a purposeful sense of recording the history of the women's movement.

Clara Bewick Colby's early experience as a woman journalist in the man's world of newspaper publishing uniquely situated her to produce a successful feminist paper. Not unusually for a woman of her time, Colby began her professional career in journalism working for men—among them her husband at the *Beatrice Express* (Beatrice, NE, 1871–78) and Erasmus M. Correll at the *Western Woman's Journal* (Lincoln, NE, 1881–82), where she was able to practice her craft within the limited boundaries set by men who were sympathetic to the notion of equal rights for women.[20] But in the pages of the *Woman's Tribune*, Colby was free to create a newspaper that was wholly conceived, funded, and undertaken in all aspects by women. With Colby as editor, the *Woman's Tribune* was established in 1883 by the Nebraska Woman Suffrage Association when "it was decided that the suffragists of the State must have a paper."[21] Soon thereafter, Colby took over independent operation of the paper. Indeed, the editors of the influential *History of Woman Suffrage* wrote that Colby was a clear choice for permanent editor since the *Tribune* was "a paper whose columns show that Mrs. Colby has the true editorial instinct."[22]

The birth of the *Woman's Tribune* was in many respects unique. Unlike many other late-nineteenth-century women's papers, which were edited by women but funded and published by men, or edited by women who inherited their tasks from fathers or husbands, for its entire twenty-six-year run the *Tribune* relied on neither economic nor intellectual support from men. The *Tribune* was for Colby a labor of love, not a vehicle for building wealth. As she explained in January 3, 1898, "In these fourteen years scores of woman's papers have flourished for a time and then succumbed to the financial pressure. In cases where men have been associated with the enterprise, it has started out with a bigger flag but has made the shorter journey. Few men, perhaps, could be found so devoted to woman's cause that they would be willing to give time and talent to an undertaking doomed from the start never to be a paying investment."[23] Because of its woman-centered focus and woman-organized history, the *Tribune* was in an unrivaled position to serve as the voice of the more radical ideals of the feminist movement. And Jerry notes the impact of this position, compared to its suffrage peers, caused the *Woman's Tribune* to be "freer to explore a variety of issues related to woman's rights from a broader spectrum of women's viewpoints."[24] In this sense, the *Woman's Tribune* was a newspaper created for women, about women, edited and written by women, and guided exclusively by the radical feminist editorial vision of one woman: Clara Bewick Colby.

As a feminist editor devoted to the cause of radicalizing everyday women to participate in the movement for women's rights, Colby was among a group of women editors who, Solomon explains, "recognized the vital importance of . . . the periodical edited and published by sympathizers. Through this channel, the movement could reach, educate, and inspire scores of women who could not be tapped by other means."[25] But to do this, Solomon explains, those who published suffrage periodicals "faced the difficult task of raising the consciousness of other women."[26] She breaks this task into three stages:

> First, offering a persuasive analysis of the barriers women faced in common; second, convincing women of their own ability to effect social change; and finally, molding them into an organized, committed group. In essence, each woman had to become convinced that she shared many of the same problems and faced many of the same barriers as other women. She had to come to perceive herself as part of an extensive, oppressed group and to be persuaded of her right and ability

> to seek remedies. These tasks had to be accomplished while offering her an alternative role model to the prevailing, restrictive social stereotypes. The "true woman" ideal had to be transformed into that of a "new woman." To be acceptable to many women acculturated into fixed social roles, the "new woman" had to evince allegiance to traditional values as she embraced new roles and responsibilities.[27]

Solomon's analysis of the role of suffrage editors can be applied to the editorial strategies used by Clara Bewick Colby, who framed the triumphs of real women not only as individual successes but also as examples of political successes that could be shared by her readers. Using this strategy, she moved purposefully from recognizing the limitations of traditional notions of domesticity to celebrating alternative roles embraced by new women—roles that were already practiced by many frontier women. By affirming and extending these examples, Colby showed her readers how they could not only view themselves as true women who have the cultural and spiritual authority to act for women's rights, but also, as Colby explained, "overcome their age-long habit of seeing themselves only in their relations to mankind, forgetting that whatever develops them as human beings fits them to fill all relations more perfectly."[28] She declared: "This educational effort in both directions is Feminism."[29] Thus the *Woman's Tribune* became a woman-centered social, educational, and political tool used to develop a broad-based readership of diverse women who would become active agents in the campaign for women's rights.

When Clara Bewick Colby moved with her husband Leonard to Washington, D.C., in 1889,[30] she continued to publish the *Woman's Tribune* and to focus primarily on a readership comprised of women who formed the roots of the woman suffrage movement . Like Colby's readers on the Plains, these were women who did not normally see themselves as radical activists—they were housewives and mothers, farm women, and shopkeepers. Keeping these readers always in mind, Colby crafted her paper so that they could learn to see themselves as a unified group motivated for the cause of women's equality, and not merely as individual women learning and striving alone. In every aspect of her paper, Colby spoke directly to the root source of feminist movement—the women who would ultimately be the standard-bearers, soldiers, and beneficiaries of the fight for freedom.

This strategy was not without merit. Linda Steiner argues that women's rights periodicals were a necessity, "given that 'new women' then had relatively few opportunities to meet in person, to see what these new women actually looked like. . . . These publications dramatized what it was like to be a woman's rights activist and reassured readers they were not alone in taking on this identity. As such, their lives took on significance and purpose."[31] But this identity reconstruction had to be done with care. Steiner notes: "Stimulating an awareness of shared difficulties and past oppression may even discourage audience members unless they develop an alternative images of themselves as agents of change. Woman's rights editors and their readers, then, together constructed the new women they would become."[32]

It is because of this editorial focus, Jerry explains, that "the *Tribune* was in a slightly better position to represent the very women who were not involved in mainstream movement activity."[33] By placing woman suffrage among the broader social aspects of empowering women and celebrating their lives, the *Tribune* located the source of feminist activism in the daily realities of its female readers. Furthermore, by targeting women as a class based solely on their sex, Colby was able to rally her readership by speaking to their shared experiences as women living in a man's world. Ultimately, her target audience was ambitious—half the nation's population.[34]

Carefully constructing an editorial vision that drew its power from the experiences of her women readers, Colby's goal in the early editions of her paper was to build a feeling of shared solidarity among a grassroots community of women. The practical application of this lofty ideal meant literally reaching out to women isolated on the tallgrass prairie. In a column entitled "To the N.W.S.A." (the Nebraska Woman Suffrage Association) published in the second issue of the *Woman's Tribune* on November 1, 1883, Colby spoke explicitly of her vision to create a newspaper that could bind together all women—including rural and working-class women who were too often left out of national political discussions:

> It has been decided to have from the start a circulation of 10,000, for this, apportioned among the counties according to population, seems to be the smallest number by which the influence of this educational measure may be felt all over the state, and in any degree by the population outside of the cities and towns. The great drawback to

> successful work in reforms has been almost exclusively confined to the cities, where are congregated the classes that are inevitably antagonistic, but those with whom favorable impressions are most likely to be transient. With our proposed method of distribution we shall especially strive to reach dwellers in the country. . . . In case you cannot pay the money at present but would like to receive the paper, just drop a card to the TRIBUNE to that effect. . . . We shall all feel more like working for it knowing that it is going into so many homes and will be a connecting link between so many hearts.[35]

Part of Colby's radical feminist vision for the *Tribune* was for it to engage in a form of intimate woman-to-woman communication so desperately needed by women on the prairies and plains of the American West. Speaking explicitly to a readership that included isolated rural women, Colby's vision of the *Woman's Tribune* as the "connecting link between so many hearts" resonates with the feminine language of late-nineteenth-century women, for whom weekly correspondence was the blood of life. Moreover, by making the claim that city-dwellers often provide the most difficult obstacles for successful reform work, she anoints those who live in the country—the majority of the nation's population at that time—as the group most likely to reflect America's progressive values. If her political goal was to change the mind of a nation, this was the group of readers to secure.

Targeting this readership was a shrewd editorial act on Colby's part. In 1883, Nebraska was entering upon a decade that would see its total population double, with most of its population residing in rural areas.[36] Furthermore, by locating the root source of power for the feminist movement in a solid base of rural women, the *Tribune* nurtured family-style connections along a network of a growing female population that was separated from long-standing women's family networks in the East. Like letters exchanged among friends, the issues of the *Woman's Tribune* reflected and addressed the particular concerns of its readers in all matters political, educational, and social. As Colby wrote to her readers in 1884, "This is your paper."[37]

Clara Bewick Colby's editorial plan to earn the readership of ordinary women in the West dovetailed with what historian Glenda Riley describes as an important "survival technique" practiced by women in the West; notably, the "ability to bond with other women."[38] The lack of well-established women's communities on the new frontier caused many women émigrés to feel isolated and lacking in the resources for social and intellectual enrichment. While the expanding frontier was a site of liberation and freedom for many women, it was also a place of extreme isolation for others who were torn from close-knit kinship networks in the name of westward expansion and Progress. As Everett Dick, an early-twentieth-century historian of the Great Plains dramatically paints it, a woman's life on the frontier could be a depressing place. Only when a woman "got her first view of a dugout and realized that such a hole in the ground was to be her home [did] she sense the utter loneliness and drab realities of her future life. Many women were reduced to tears when they first caught sight of their future dwelling."[39] Dick observes that for some women, "There was nothing to do or see and nowhere to go. The conversation each day was a repetition of that of the day before and was primarily concerning the terrible place where they had to live."[40]

Whether it was a result of this isolation, or of their allegiance to domestic culture, Riley explains, "Most women seemed to regard the need for female companionship as a given fact of life."[41] Colby understood that this was not always physically possible for frontier women; therefore she formatted her paper to help her readers cope with the challenges of their new lives through the female companionship provided by the *Woman's Tribune*. Her paper filled an important intellectual and social need for a population of women cut off from the vital women's communities they had left behind, and it became a tool with which plainswomen could deal positively with the often harsh conditions of frontier life. Along with other activities, interacting with the *Tribune* tapped into a frontier women's culture described by Riley as coming from "their ability to create a rich social life from limited resources, the tremendous reward they derived from their roles as cultural conservators, and their willingness and ability to bond to each other."[42]

Unlike other suffrage periodicals that were tailored for a more urban and urbane readership, Clara Bewick Colby's self-identified position as a western "free lance" editor and publisher allowed her to speak "to and for an audience not specifically addressed" by more urban and conservative suffrage papers such as Lucy Stone's and Henry Blackwell's *Woman's Journal*.[43] As Steiner explains, Colby

> had staked her own identity and status to a cause, which itself could in part be defined in terms of its ability to provide women outside the inner

> circle of suffrage leaders with a sense of significance, importance. New women of the late nineteenth and early twentieth century demanded suffrage not because they had realistic hopes of using the ballot box to end their own political oppression or to enact other reforms. Rather, they needed to proclaim the legitimacy of their emerging style of life. So Bewick Colby drew upon common strategies for bolstering the image of suffragists—in their own eyes as well as in others'—by educating them on political issues and by glorifying their participating in a historic nationwide cause.[14]

The political goal of bolstering the image of suffragists was furthered by Colby's editorial goal of building community among women through the *Woman's Tribune.* Indeed this endeavor was so important that she often disregarded the cost. Four years into the *Tribune*'s run, she explained: "Unless so requested, [the *Woman's Tribune*] is not discontinued when subscription expires, except [when a] subscription was given by another party. . . . No person need stop the paper because unable to pay. Time will be given; or if circumstances make it necessary, the account will be marked paid."[15] Women who could not afford an individual subscription to the Tribune were encouraged to form a subscription club, with each member contributing a portion of the cost. Riley notes that this was a common practice among women on the prairie: "When the journal arrived, members shared it, then passed it on to friends, neighbors, and relatives, who also read the articles and stories."[16] To this end, Colby kept the paper at only one dollar per year throughout its entire twenty-six-year run in order to keep it accessible to the widest readership. Such was her passion, and her generosity, that sometimes Colby herself would ride out to deliver samples of the paper free of charge to women who were unable to leave the homestead.[17]

The *Tribune*'s original readership was comprised of rural western women who did not have the urban conveniences of public lectures, weekly papers, monthly magazines, or a ready-made community of like-minded sisters with whom to share their views. As a result, Colby structured the *Tribune* to meet the needs of women hungry for both social and intellectual stimulation. Carefully considering the position of her rural readers, for whom "current" news was often stale by weeks or even months, Colby contextualized the content of the *Tribune* so that isolated rural women would have access to the full context of the ideas and activities of the women's movement. For example, Jerry explains that, "Although suffrage news was reported in detail, the mere reporting of suffrage work was not enough. Movement efforts had to be recounted in ways especially meaningful for isolated women; this included covering activities ignored by the general circulation press or reported incompletely."[48] These included printing nuts-and-bolts items from suffrage meetings such as the full texts of speeches and resolutions, notice of elected officers and standing committees, reprinted excerpts from speeches made for and against pending legislation, or correspondence from major pro- and anti-suffrage figures.

Colby explained the transformational role of her suffrage paper in the November 1886 edition of the *Tribune*:

> Knowledge of the change of sentiment produced in readers of the paper who were before not favorable to its objects leads the editor to believe that the wide dissemination of a suffrage paper advances the cause far more than the same money spent in securing lectures, although this should also not be neglected. But while the lecture amuses and interests for an hour or two, often the many cares and interests of our complex life sweep away the impression immediately, while the paper read in quiet moments gradually makes conviction, and the reader instead of being transitorily influenced by the opinion of another, builds up opinions of his [*sic*] own from the logic of events, a faith that cannot be shaken.[49]

As an editor, Colby believed that suffrage periodicals were of greater importance than conventions and speeches in that they allowed readers to "digest" the material on their own terms. She returned to this philosophy time and again, keeping this mission of the *Tribune* always foremost in her readers' minds. Sometimes, she would enter into a dialogue with her readers by reprinting correspondence that reinforced these ideals. For example, Colby printed this letter from "Mrs. A. G. B." in June of 1891:

> Your thoughtful kindness in placing my name on the complimentary list when I could not continue my subscription is most gratefully appreciated. We feel that we could not do without the Tribune. It is invaluable as an educator on the subject of Equal Suffrage, and the ultimate extension of woman's sphere. While I am precluded by circumstances from taking any public part in the grand work to which your noble life is devoted, yet I am doing what I can to train our five daughters and

> three sons in the fundamental principles of liberty and equality. The Woman's Tribune is a great help to me and I enclose $1.00 postal note, so that you may be able to send my free number to some other poor mother who is hungering for mental food, or straining weary eyes to catch a ray of hope upon a darkened path.[50]

In addition to reprinting letters from her readers, Colby saved especially meaningful correspondence—for example, this letter of May 12, 1897, by Mrs. Delia Dunton of Lebanon, Kansas, which nicely captures the feelings of many of the *Tribune*'s loyal readers (Mrs. Dunton's spelling and grammar have been left unchanged):

> Dear Editor. Once more I will send a years subscription to your most valuable paper. Nine years ago I thought of discontinuing it, but there seemed to be a something about it that I could not do without. In my own mind I termed it an aroma that effected other, for finer muses, than the olfactorys, something that if one had an afinity for, could be inbibed regardless of distance.
>
> It seemed as iff the verry forms on which it was printed was effected by a great tender mind, strong enough so the little sheet could carry that strange inexpressable message to the verry ends of the earth; and could do much good, if received by those who could appreciate it, and each year since I have marked its rapid growth in many different lines. It seems to choose from, and advocate the best and noblest, from whatever subject it investigates. [. . .]
>
> Success to The Tribune. I very much regret that those who are in condition to make it possible, do not give more towards the Best Friend. It is due to the great noble souls who for fifty years have championed *our cause*. [. . .]
>
> One dollar to pay for a Perfection
> [. . .]
> Mrs. Delia Dunton,
> Lebanon, Kansas
> Smith Co.[51]

Clearly, readers responded emotionally to Colby's foundational editorial approach of creating "the connecting link between so many hearts."[52]

As the *Tribune*'s readers noted, suffrage news was but one component of its vision of the whole, free, woman. To this end, the *Tribune*'s editor also included articles of interest that would help to expand traditional notions of women's culture and provide its readers with a broader intellectual and social horizon. In this way, the *Tribune* would provide the flame with which to light the lamp of liberty. Because Colby believed that women's political rights were fashioned as an integral part of the whole, thinking woman, she viewed her readers as well-informed, thoughtful authorities on all aspects of women's culture—including politics and public affairs—and tempered her suffrage reportage with general news of interest to a specific audience of independent women.

As an editor, Clara Bewick Colby set herself a complicated, many-layered task. She sought to create a newspaper that would function simultaneously as a forum for radical suffrage; as a historical record for the cause; and as an intellectual, educational, and social journal devoted to issues germane to the "thinking woman." As early as January 1, 1884, Colby stated her goal of structuring the *Tribune* "in such a way as to make it most helpful to the women of the State in all their varied interests."[53] She wrote:

> The main features of current history and national politics will be given in as brief space as possible, that busy men as well as women may learn to look here for a mention of such things about which no intelligent person should be ignorant. It will be the endeavor of the Woman's Tribune to give, not so much argument and theory, but facts and information, as a help to people to do their own thinking and draw their own conclusions.[54]

Note here how Colby does not impose a polemical agenda on her readers, but instead presents the content of her paper in a way that allows women to think and speak for themselves from their own experiences as women. By treating her readers with dignity and respect, and leaving strident suffrage discussions to other venues, Colby created a "reform and educational paper" that promised to "faithfully represent not only the woman suffrage work, but women's work in every field. It aims to be a good family and literary paper, such that people will want, even if they do not agree with its positions."[55]

In this manner she was able to create a reform paper that would expand the world of her women readers. As she wrote in the January 3, 1898, edition of the *Tribune*:

> Perhaps because the suffrage matter in the Tribune is taken for granted, it is those features of the paper which do not directly pertain to suffrage that have brought in the most words of approval. . . . The Tribune

> therefore feels that it is taking the course most acceptable to the majority of its readers in not devoting the paper wholly to the reform for which it stands first, last, and all the time, but in giving something of the best that comes its way along all lines of thought and activity.[56]

Colby's description of the *Tribune* as a "good family and literary paper" reveals another, more subtle facet of her radical feminist editorial approach: she structured her newspaper so it would not be dismissed as a polemical tool of seditious women. Because it was grounded in the domestic roots of the cultural and political aspects of women's lives, unlike an organ of a party or cause, the *Tribune* was acceptable to both its target audience and to those who might oppose them. This was a key strategy on the part of the *Tribune*'s editor, because it produced a paper that, on the surface, could be viewed as appropriate reading material for women by their husbands and brothers—yet it carried within it the seeds of women's liberation.

Because of its many-layered focus, Colby's *Tribune* is qualitatively different than other singularly focused suffrage papers. By practicing a radical feminism that is at home among the daily activities of caring for children and family, washing and cooking, and conversing with women friends, Colby gives her readers permission to integrate a political analysis of women's roles into their daily routines. Thus, she keeps her feminist vision present in the minds of her readers through a sophisticated and comprehensive analysis of the daily realities of their lives—all the while informing them of the possibilities for freedom.

Clara Bewick Colby's carefully constructed radical feminist vision can be found in the material she selected for regular publication in the *Tribune*. These were topics that intersected with women's responsibilities of contributing socially and economically to the family unit, participating in shopping and commerce, understanding the legal ramifications of family relationships, and keeping up-to-date on current health issues. These columns often appeared as "departments" written by Colby's suffrage colleagues, or by Colby herself. These included the Department of Industry, which printed a ten-part series on beekeeping for women and a five-part series on silk culture;[57] the Department of Political and Social Science, which informed women of all things political, such as explaining the American political party system, the monetary system, currency, and banking;[58] the Department of Law, which was edited by Mrs. Ada M. Bittenbender—"Nebraska's lady lawyer"—and written to treat "the laws of our State which especially interest woman as a class, such as the laws of 'Decedents,' 'Marriage,' 'Divorce and Alimony,' 'Guardians and Wards,' citing cases illustrative of their working and effect." (This was one of the Tribune's longest-running departments; it examined topics in law relating to family issues, Homestead law, and real estate law.[59]) The Department of Hygiene and Medical Progress was edited by Jeannie McCowen, A.M., M.D.; it covered cutting-edge topics on physical and mental hygiene, and included discussions on epidemics and euthanasia.[60] Eventually it became the Department of Health, Beauty, and Dress, and attended not to the simple issues of what was fashionable but to the very serious issues of dress reform and care of the woman's body.

Other regular departments were focused not so much on women's political and intellectual life as on the social aspects of life encountered daily by women who were the primary caretakers of home and family. For example, a department titled "Household Hints" ran regularly throughout the 1890s. In the first issue of the *Tribune*, Colby printed tips on preserving flowers and lemons, washing stairs, doing laundry, as well as the placement of mirrors in the home. Other departments focused on family relationships important to the *Tribune*'s readers, such as "Baby's Corner," "For Our Young Friends," and "Utile Dulci" ("The useful with the beautiful").[61] These departments usually printed inspirational stories and lessons for children as well as polemical poetry and fiction. They were later consolidated and renamed "Children's Corner" as Colby's own children matured, and in 1895 were renamed again "Zintka Lanuni's Corner" to focus on anecdotes and stories relating to the exploits of Colby's adopted Lakota Sioux daughter. On the lighter side, Colby occasionally ran in the early issues of the *Tribune* a column of jokes titled "A Little Nonsense Now and Then is Relished By the Best of Woman Suffragists," showing that suffragists did not take themselves too seriously. Later, this material appeared intermittently under the title "Humorous."

Reading was an activity central to the lives of many rural women. Therefore, an important regular feature established in the *Tribune*'s first issues was "Books That Every Woman Should Read," which appeared in later editions of the paper in various incarnations such as "Literary Notes," "Books and Magazines," "Books for Women," and "Tribune Book Concern." Sometimes these columns were advertisements for premiums given upon paid subscriptions (these lists appeared when the

Tribune was most busy with other news); at others times, individual titles were extensively summarized and analyzed by Colby herself. These departments were close to Colby's heart—in January 1873 she had worked to establish the first public lending library for her new hometown of Beatrice, Nebraska, and a month later she was elected secretary of the Ladies Library Association.

Because of her extensive contact with her readers, Colby knew that they shared her deep appreciation for the written word. Indeed, Riley explains that Great Plains women were "readers, thinkers, and doers, in addition to being domestic practitioners and wage workers."[62] Daily reading—whether it was of newspapers, books, a daybook, or journal—provided stimulation, education, and entertainment. Reading was also a basis for exploring shared experiences with other women readers. Riley adds that reading allowed western women to become aware of "emerging ideas regarding women's roles and responsibilities as moral guardians. . . . These women considered reading an important and enjoyable undertaking in a land that denied them so many other aspects of 'civilization.'"[63] Riley explains further that "Although the stereotype of plainswomen seldom represents them sitting with books before them, thousands of them expanded their minds and horizons by reading. From the printed page, women derived many of their ideas and much of their information as well as finding much-needed companionship, entertainment, solace, and advice."[64]

The columns in the *Tribune* devoted to books and summaries of other periodicals reviewed reading material of which Colby felt her readers should be aware, so the texts she selected were not necessarily pro-suffrage or pro-woman works. For example, the *Tribune*'s first edition in 1883 reviewed texts relating to religion, liberation, and feminism: *Duties of Women* by Frances Power Cobbs; *Letters of Lydia Maria Child*; *Woman's Place To-Day* by antifeminist Rev. Morgan Dix; and a response entitled *Lenten Lectures on Women* by Lillie Deveraux Blake. In 1891, Colby indexed a number of "Books of Special Interest," including Mary F. Eastman's *The Biography of Dio Lewis*—the proponent of women's rights and physical culture who established an educational ideology of women and exercise known as the New Gymnastics; Harriet Riddle Davis's work of prose fiction *Gilbert Elgar's Son*; Helene Lange's *Higher Education of Women in Europe*; Thomas Hitchcock's *Unhappy Loves of Men of Genius*; Annie Nathan Meyer's *Woman's Work In America*, a collection of essays and letters written by women physicians between 1872 and 1890, which included an introduction by Julia Ward Howe; and Emma Robinson's *Which Wins, Love or Money?*.

Other literary features of the paper written or edited by Clara Bewick Colby included educational articles on women in history, and short stories. In nearly every issue, Colby printed poetry—sometimes poems by classical authors, sometimes poetry written and submitted by the *Tribune*'s readers. For example, the index to the *Tribune*'s volume 8 (1891) lists more than a hundred original poems by more than forty poets who were readers. Often, the *Tribune*'s readers submitted poetry that reflected their feelings about news reported in the *Tribune*. This was the case in 1891, the year the Colbys adopted a Lakota child named Zintka Lanuni and Colby published a number of poems submitted by her readers about her new daughter. In an effort to (literally) broaden the horizons of her readers, Colby often published travelogues, themselves a popular late-nineteenth-century genre, relating to her travels around the nation. Throughout the life of the paper, Colby wrote about her travels in the Black Hills of the Dakotas, Iowa, Kansas, Louisiana, Nebraska, Ohio, Oregon, Washington territory, and Wyoming. As Colby's access to print technology increased, some were even accompanied by drawings or photographs. She also published travelogues written by her suffrage colleagues, such as Margaret T. Skiff's description of Mount Vernon.[65]

The *Tribune*'s first issue of 1883 also formally established the long-running "Notes About Women," a lively potpourri of items of local, regional, national, and international importance to the women's movement and women's culture in general. From this issue alone, readers of the *Woman's Tribune* learned, among other things, that Vermont had two women acting as mail carriers; that married women of Portugal retain their maiden names; that the first law diploma ever bestowed upon an African American woman was by the University of Washington; and that the niece of composer Richard Wagner had just been appointed the first woman professor of music in Germany. Although they did not always appear under a formal department or heading, these notes appeared in nearly every issue of the *Tribune*, providing its readers with real-life examples of what "new women" could achieve. As a record of late-nineteenth-century social and historical events relating to women, the *Tribune*'s section "Notes About Women" was unsurpassed by any other publication before or since.

In addition to its regular departments, the *Woman's Tribune* routinely printed articles of interest to women's social and political lives. Its first issue included features on "Women in Politics," "Woman's Inventions," "Woman Suffrage in Congress," and "Woman Suffrage in England."[66] Articles in later editions addressed motherhood as a profession (9.26, 22 October 1892, p 201), canning (8.23, 6 June 1891, p 79), establishing homes for "erring girls who wish to reform" (10.23, 20 May 1893, p 89), a debate on the rise of department stores (14.5, 6 March 1897, p 17), the need for children's playgrounds (20.20, 27 June 1903, p 78), and "Marriage vs. A Profession" (7.3, 18 January 1890, p 18). These articles focused on issues relating to both women's culture and the need to raise the consciousness of the *Tribune*'s readers about vital feminist issues. One example of how Colby revealed her feminist educational program is reflected in discussions such as the one on "The Hyphenated Marriage Name," which analyzed whether women should take their husband's name after marriage:

> The time is coming when the women who on marrying will be unwilling to drop their father's name, a name in which they have, perhaps acquired personal fame—will be numerous and some fashion must be adopted whereby the dignity of the woman as an individual may be retained. The family becomes a new unit for society and there should be a joint name standing for both members of it. To hyphenate the two surnames makes a stately appellation equally adapted for social and business purposes and brings to each the prestige of the other. "Smith-Jones" like "Burne Jones," loses the mediocrity of both names.
>
> But immediately the question is asked what name will the children take, and this introduces a real difficulty, but one not at all to be compared with the present outrageous Anglo-Saxon custom of simply obliterating the woman's patronymic. The children should have a single name and a good arrangement would be for the boys to take the father's surname and the girls the mother's. This would have several advantages, as the name would always indicate the line of descent—a very important matter in genealogy. The single name for the unmarried indicating the condition of the man as we now know that of the woman would be a great protection to society, and be a great step in establishing equality between the sexes.[67]

Similar discussions frequently appeared in the pages of the *Tribune* as part of its ongoing feminist analysis of a woman's role in marriage. These columns may not have addressed popular social topics, but they were topics of which Clara Bewick Colby felt her readers should be aware.

Colby underscored the need for women to have knowledge of socially unpopular ideas in the *Tribune*'s edition of May 28, 1904, when she discussed a report released by the Free Employment Bureau of St. Louis. Here it was learned that "fully 70 percent of these [women seeking employment] have husbands from whom they have separated," and that these "young and prepossessing" women are most often separated due to their husbands' drunkenness. Colby writes, "[T]he time has certainly come when the self respecting woman, unless there are more than the usual considerations, will not tolerate the companionship of an inebriate. It is a pitiful story and whichever way it is read its lesson is that young women cannot look to marriage as the final settlement of all the problems of life but should be equipped for possible domestic shipwreck by a thorough knowledge of some industry whereby they may honestly earn their living."[68] These editorial writings, along with frank discussions of divorce and women's property rights within marriage, are illustrative of the kinds of topics Colby would openly address in the pages of her paper that were not routinely addressed in other suffrage publications because they were seen as too radical and unpopular. Colby's radical feminist vision was always for women to have the knowledge to be in control of their choices, and to attain a level of feminist awareness that could purposefully change their lives.

Colby also worked to increase the cultural awareness of her Anglo readership through her editorial focus on understanding social and political issues related to people of color. Because she usually reported news about people of color from a "woman's perspective," Colby's emphasis on diversity is yet another facet of her radical feminist activism. Truly, she viewed women as a comprehensive community united by the common conditions of their sex. As Jerry explains, "Diversity, which was the watchword of *The Woman's Tribune*, made it unique among reform newspapers."[69] In addition to a primary focus on reform based on gender, news and analyses of issues relating to people of color were frequently given space in the pages of the *Tribune*. For example, in the January 1, 1884, edition of the *Tribune*, Colby wrote an extensive obituary of Sojourner Truth that reprinted portions of Frances Dana Gage's account of Truth's "A'n't I a Woman" speech.[70] In a similar vein, Colby would also print speeches given or letters written by prominent people of color. In March 1884, Colby reprinted a discussion by Frederick Douglass relating to the storm of criticism that arose as a result of his marriage that year to white suffrage activist Helen Pitts, who was also his former secretary:

> Fred Douglass writes to a friend with regard to the criticisms on his marriage with a white woman.
>
> There are a million of people in this country of mixed blood—mainly the children and grandchildren of white men by colored women. I know of a colored woman here in Washington who is the mother of ten children by one of our most influential citizens, but no noise was made over the fact, simply because the woman was his concubine, and not his wife. It would seem that what the American people object to is not the mixture of the races, but honorable marriage between them. Is this reflection too severe? Perhaps it is, but does not the storm of criticism to which I have been subjected seem to justify it?[71]

In addition to drawing attention to issues faced by African Americans, Colby routinely addressed the oppression of women of color who faced American imperialism, including Native Hawaiian women, Cuban women, and Philippine women. For example, Colby published this strongly worded editorial ("In Behalf of Filipino Women") on the front page of the September 22, 1900, issue of the *Tribune*:

> Let this country be not less careful of the rights of the women of its distant and subject possessions than England is. The hardships of any country under military rule fall tenfold upon women. Whenever men of the dominant race have come in contact with the ignorant, trusting women of an inferior race it has been one long dark record of baseness and treachery. But the condition of the outcast woman is never absolutely hopeless until the law puts its brand upon her as one sealed to serve the passions of men. . . . The women of the United States should in every society or club take up this subject and add their protest. We ought to consider the Filipino women as a sacred charge. In their inexperience under these new conditions they will regard the law as their destiny and they will not have the courage, or the knowledge how, to appeal to the better element of American rulers which might be on their side. The strong word must be spoken for them and the suffrage leaders have done well to sound the alarm.[72]

Despite the fact that Colby replicated here some of the imperialist attitudes she so strongly condemned (in that she characterized Philippine women as "ignorant" and of "an inferior race"), her call for solidarity with Filipino women should not be underestimated as a radical political project. This editorial is an example of a political call to action where Colby explicitly frames radical politics within a maternal, domestic rhetoric to call middle-class Anglo American women to a reform cause. Her social project, then, could not be immediately dismissed by her readers, because it was framed as a "sacred charge" immediately relevant to their domestic vocation.

Closest to her heart, though, were issues relating to the oppression of Native American peoples. Certainly, her concern for American Indian interests was driven in part by her adopted Lakota daughter, and by her husband's work negotiating depredation claims against Indian tribes while Assistant Attorney General of the United States in Benjamin Harrison's cabinet. As E. Claire Jerry writes, "She always took a pro-Indian stance."[73] Examples of Clara Bewick Colby's pro-Indian reporting included an analysis of the battle of Wounded Knee in the January 31, 1891, edition of the *Tribune*, which put her in direct conflict with the federal government's account of the battle. Here Colby reported on Elaine Goodale's letter to Indian Commissioner Morgan that argued "the Indians did not deliberately plan resistance."[74] Establishing the rhetorical tone that would later be used to call Anglo women to fight for Philippine women, Colby summarized Goodale's report in a way that would most enflame her readers' domestic sensibilities:

> There had been friendly intercourse and hand-shaking between the Indians and the officers, and many of the men were unarmed. The demand for their arms was a surprise; their tepees had been searched and their guns, knives and hatchets found in them confiscated. Then began the searching of their persons—even of the women, whose knives (which they always carry for domestic purposes) were being taken from them. . . . Miss Goodale thinks that, while in part the killing of the women and children was unavoidable, yet much of it was deliberate and intentional. The scouts who buried the dead reported eighty-four bodies of men, forty-four of women and eighteen of children. The men were found mostly around Big Foot's tent, while the dead women and children were scattered along a distance of two miles from the scene of the encounter. Miss Goodale was not an eye-witness, but derives her information from Indian prisoners, half-breeds and parties who visited the battle-field. This only substantiates the general opinion that there

> was a very serious error on the part of the military authorities in charge at that time.[75]

In that same issue, Clara Bewick Colby first reported the adoption of her daughter Zintka Lanuni, a Lakota Sioux infant reportedly found by Colby's husband, Leonard, on the Wounded Knee battlefield. Clara Colby's relationship with her daughter Zintka, as she reported it in the *Tribune*, was to prove one of the most interesting ways Colby expressed her philosophies of race relations, domesticity, motherhood, and political activism.

Zintka was first introduced to the *Tribune*'s readers in a small article entitled "The Indian Baby," which Colby reprinted from an exchange from *The Republic* (Washington, D.C.):

> It seems it is not Mrs. Allison Nailor who has the Indian baby, but Mrs. Clara Bewick Colby, the editor of *The Woman's Tribune*, who is in Washington for the winter. Her husband, General L. W. Colby, who in charge of the Nebraska State militia has been engaged at the scene of the late Indian hostilities, has now returned, and writes Mrs. Colby that he has taken to their home in Beatrice, Neb., an orphan Indian girl, nine months old, who was found on the battlefield of Wounded Knee Creek four days after the battle. Her toes and the top of her head are a little frost-bitten, but nothing serious. The battle was on Monday and the baby was found on Thursday, with two others, who were then alive but have since died. General Colby writes: "She is my relic of the Sioux War of 1891 and the massacre of Wounded Knee, where Big Foot and his braves were slaughtered. [. . . She] is now being cared for by Mrs. Colby's sister, Dr. Mary B. White, until Mrs. Colby's return."[76]

About a month later, Colby reprinted another, more sensational exchange piece detailing Zintka's rescue from the battlefield.[77] Upon her return to Nebraska, Clara Colby, now forty-five years old, finally met her infant daughter three months after her rescue. Because of strong reader interest in her new daughter, she reported the meeting in an article titled "Home Again":

> So many correspondents have expressed an interest in Zintka Lanuni, the waif of Wounded Knee, that we are sure they will all expect a little mention of her at this time of home-coming. She has now but a slight cough and a fast fading scar on her cheek to show the result of her

> terrible four days exposure on the field of battle. As near as can be estimated, she is now nine months old. She gets around in her propeller in a very lively way, and if there is any tendency in her to the gravity of her race it has been held in abeyance by being a pet and plaything of all in the sister's home which has been her friendly shelter until this date. She is quite as winning and loveable as babies of her age are apt to be and her awakening intelligence is watched with more than the usual interest. Her name is commonly shortened to "Zintka," which is quite as musical as the English equivalent "Bird."[78]

From this moment, Zintka is a regular presence with her mother both on the suffrage lecture circuit and in the pages of the *Woman's Tribune.* Indeed, the very next mention of Zintka in the *Tribune* is in an article entitled "Chautauqua Notes" detailing a regional Chautauqua meeting in July, where there were probably few babies present and even fewer people of color. Colby describes Zintka's presence at the meeting as though it is natural to include an account of her presence beside accounts of speakers from around the world. But by the end of that article, Zintka has taken center stage in her own political campaign:

> Zintka Lanuni is the centre of attraction at the headquarters of the State Suffrage Association. She is a very healthy, happy, bright little thing, and so far is demonstrating that an Indian baby is as coquettish, playful and loveable as any other first-class baby. She is already winning the promise of future votes for the presidency of the United States. Perhaps a half a century hence the rights of her sex and her race may be fully vindicated in her.[79]

Colby structured for her readers descriptions of her new daughter in a way that was most familiar to her—in the language of politics. She had not yet gained a clear command of the vocabulary of motherhood, so she used language and concepts with which she had thorough knowledge: that of the woman's rights campaign. For example, Colby reports how, in addition to attending a number national meetings with her mother, this "first-class baby" was privileged with the gift of membership in the National American Woman Suffrage Association by Rev. Anna Howard Shaw, and she is mentioned as part of the *Tribune* "staff" allowed to accompany the editor on a train trip to Denver and later to the World's Fair.[80]

Until late 1894, news about Zintka in the *Tribune* could most often be characterized as "cute" or clever asides about this unusual infant who was the object of popular affection; some of these news items include Zintka's "rescue" story which is reprinted yet again, how she is fêted at social receptions, memorialized in poetry by the *Tribune*'s readers, and visited by Native American dignitaries.[81] But by her daughter's fourth birthday, as Clara Colby matured in her own role as a mother, Colby realized a unique bond had been created between her daughter and the other members of her "family"—the *Tribune*'s readers. Colby highlights this relationship in a column entitled "Editor's Notes by the Way," where she begins to move from the language of politics to the language of domesticity when describing her daughter:

> *Dear Readers:* [. . .] So many Tribune readers are warmly interested in the little maid that I will not apologise [*sic*] for saying something about her in these gossippy [*sic*] notes. At home she is intimately connected with the manufacture of the Tribune. In the desk where I write she has a drawer. Of the book shelves some are hers, and she has special corners in the den and library. Her greatest diversion is to arrange her papers, shorthand notes, etc., classifying them in the leaves of a magazine. She takes dictation, folds *Bulletins* and directs papers, imitating in a wonderful way all the usual features of each performance.[82]

For the first time, *Tribune* readers are allowed into Clara Bewick Colby's home to personally share two major aspects of her life: her daughter and her newspaper. Significantly, Zintka Lanuni's role as a daughter is conflated with Colby's other "child," her newspaper. Where Zintka had before been adjunct to Colby's work on the *Tribune,* she is now intimately connected to it. Moreover, the symbolism of Zintka's drawer in her mother's desk, her own bookshelves, and her "special corners" in the house mark an existence for Clara Colby that is symbolically but unmistakably "with child." From this point on, she describes her daughter's growing-up to her readers as a mother might illustrate stories about a growing child to the members of one's extended family.

From this more intimate approach to Zintka's presence in the *Tribune* is born her own regular department entitled "Zintka Lanuni's Corner" in the April 6, 1895, edition of the paper. Colby explains:

> The little "Lost Bird" is never so pleased as when running errands for the Tribune, folding papers, carrying copy; and whether helping or

> hindering, having a finger in every pie. She delights to be called the Tribune maid. So it is but fair to give her a little corner in it, all her own, where the poems and stories she is especially fond of may have [a] place, and to which she can invite the little folks of other families to send also their favorites for publication.[83]

"Zintka Lanuni's Corner" ran fairly regularly though the 1890s; however, it ran less frequently after the turn of the century, probably due to Colby's extended travels overseas and Zintka's entrance into adulthood. In the last few years of the *Tribune*, it is not present at all.

The subject matter of "Zintka Lanuni's Corner" most often contains charming poems for children (especially those featuring birds), stories about Zintka's pets and hobbies (and those of her friends and cousins), children's animal stories (again, often featuring birds), children's prayers, and news of Zintka's comings, goings, and sayings. Many items printed in "Zintka Lanuni's Corner" were submitted by readers of the *Tribune*—written especially for Zintka and her "Corner"—revealing a healthy relationship between the *Tribune* and its readers. While the pretty prattlings of a toddler and seemingly inconsequential children's stories might not seem to be appropriate material for a radical women's suffrage paper, in actuality, they illustrate nicely Colby's editorial philosophy that valued both the daily realities of her readers and their political activism; furthermore, they provide poignant points of intersection between the two. In her transparent writing about Zintka Lanuni, Colby publicly practiced her role as a working mother in the pages of the *Tribune*, thus demonstrating a progressive mode of motherhood that was child-centered and loving, always nurturing, and never impatient.

In this way, Colby's practice of motherhood in the pages of the *Tribune* was infused with radical politics for she was always aware of her daughter's race. Without doubt, the *Tribune*'s readers and Colby's colleagues in the Suffrage movement never forgot that Zintka was an Indian child who was out of place in white society. But instead of highlighting experiences that marked her daughter as a victim of race prejudice, Colby inverted what was seen by many as a negative social position into a positive situation that viewed Zintka as an essential link bringing together white people and people of color. In the pages of the *Tribune*, Zintka Lanuni is depicted as a tiny ambassador who engages productively with a variety of people of color who are welcomed into her home. For example, she meets with other Native Americans, including Chippewa, Puyallup, Mohican, Menominee, Lakota, and Sioux;[84] a Japanese Buddhist priest;[85] dignitaries from Madagascar;[86] and routinely plays with other children of color in her Washington, D.C., neighborhood. These moments are memorialized in "Zintka Lanuni's Corner," and presented to the *Tribune*'s readers with humor, style, and grace that underscored Colby's awareness of racialized social positions. For example, one entry noted how Zintka exclaimed to her visitors from Madagascar, "I am not white, neither!"[87]

Through her reporting on her daughter Zintka in the pages of the *Woman's Tribune*, Clara Bewick Colby demonstrated the seamlessness of her daily life with her political activism, and modeled this integration for others. But by presenting herself to her readers explicitly as a mother to a child of color, Colby lifted up her status as mother and simultaneously located it within a conscious understanding of the gendered intersections of race and class. Through this strategy, her readers became even more a part of her "extended family" as they, too, shared in Zintka's unique life. This editorial strategy built solidarity between Colby and her readers through their shared status as mothers, and in this way Colby expanded her readers' experiences with people of color through their shared association with her daughter.

Consequently, Colby's transparent descriptions of life with baby Zintka furthered the educational goals of the *Woman's Tribune*. The intersections of race, motherhood, and radical politics in Colby's personal life reflected those same intersections in her public life. As a result, Colby's credibility on these issues deepened, and granted her a unique kind of authority that was not given to other Suffrage activists.

Colby's positive reporting on Native issues, including those relating to her daughter, is perhaps one of her most interesting educational measures. Modifying the strategy of some reform editors before her who linked the tentative notion of suffrage for women with that of the movement for abolition and Negro suffrage, Colby modified that approach to link full equality for women (a measure she believed would succeed) with full equality for Native peoples (which was an unpopular movement at the end of the nineteenth century). She believed that the word "person" in the U.S. Constitution meant "human being," and that the Indian was therefore a person.[88] This attitude was reflected in one report Colby wrote unambiguously for "the Indian readers of the Tribune and their friends."[89] It detailed her husband's testimony to the United States Indian Commission and transcribed his argument that "the true theory of dealing with the Indians is to give them the same treatment that is demanded by white people."[90] Explicitly reporting news of interest for her Indian readers alongside news important to her white readers was one of Colby's most radical rhetorical tasks. By assuming that her audience of women in the West included Native women, Colby simultaneously worked for racial uplift and for a dismantling of the negative myths held about Indians by some Anglo settlers.

Her emphasis on diversity was unusual for a white woman's suffrage paper and reflected a dual commitment to providing a broad base of cultural education for women while building solidarity among all groups of women. In the October 22, 1892, edition of the paper are articles titled "Jewish and Columbian History," "Women of Japan," and "Ojibwa Courtship and Marriage." Colby also printed this note about Navajo Indian culture: "A singular thing about this tribe is that their women own all the property. No Navajo brave will even sell a pony without his wife's consent."[91] Unlike other suffrage editors, Colby's view of individual women was informed by her larger view of society, and by her openness to diversity. To be sure, her broadness of spirit was not always shared by her sisters in the suffrage movement. It is, however, simply one more example of the Nebraska editor's invitation to her readers to see all the experiences of women as diverse examples of the potential of the whole woman.

Clara Bewick Colby recognized that building a movement around a feminist ideology that truly included all women would not be an easy task. In spite of these difficulties, "Freedom for Woman" was the essential plank of her radical activism. As she wrote, "'Feminism' is the ancient bug-a-boo of 'Woman's Rights' under a foreign name which seems to invest it with new terrors and unknown possibilities of mischief."[92] Unlike many who viewed feminism as something to fear, Colby embraced it as the fundamental practice of her life as editor and publisher. In an article titled simply "Feminism," she outlined her philosophy of radical feminism as that which rests on the notion of freedom for women:

> Feminism is not to be judged by individual utterances. People of all parties, beliefs, and theories are standing on its one essential plank "Freedom for Woman." What women will do with freedom when achieved is her own affair. Freedom does not mean absolute liberty; no human being in social relations can have that. It does not mean equality; that is

> beyond law. But it means equal rights, equal opportunities, and equal voice in regulating social conditions. Is there anything terrifying in this? Why should the mother of the race be distrusted and feared?[93]

Just as she does in the content of her newspaper, Colby locates her philosophy of feminism in the power inherent in that simple phrase, "Freedom for Woman." Thus, Colby's definition of feminism turned from an exclusively didactic notion of women's freedom to a many-layered awareness of the daily realities of women's lives—and how they might intersect with radical politics.

The power of the *Woman's Tribune* was that its content supported women in their everyday lives and their "own affairs," yet also radicalized what were once seen as mundane "women's interests." The *Tribune* thus offered its readers new experiences and opportunities through the more comfortable intersection of daily activities and radical politics, allowing its readers to negotiate between political movement and the practical realities of women's lives. By practicing a feminism that was shaped by a feminist awareness of what was important to her readers, the content of Colby's *Woman's Tribune* reflected a workable definition of women's political lives integrated with their daily lives. Unlike other women's periodicals, which focused almost exclusively on suffrage politics or the social aspects of womanhood, the *Woman's Tribune* spoke to its readers in a holistic way. By locating feminist activism in the daily realities of women, Colby reshaped stereotypical feminine roles, politicized them, and used them as a base for social and political action. To this end, she used her command of the *Woman's Tribune* to provide examples of what "Freedom for Woman" could look like, to identify the women who would win that freedom, to teach women what they needed to know in order to win that freedom, and to explore the possibilities of the end results of that freedom.

Elizabeth Cady Stanton, Colby's close friend and suffrage colleague, praised the editor's feminist vision in a letter published in the *Tribune* on January 21, 1888:

> Dear Mrs. Colby:—A Merry Christmas and Happy New Year to you and the readers of the Tribune. The best wishes of the season for the success of the journal, in its new satin dress, good clear type, and its promise of weekly ministrations.

> I have just read it through, every word from beginning to end, and have thoroughly enjoyed its courageous tone, its radical thought and its evident determination to go to the root of the evils that block woman's path to freedom.
>
> I was especially pleased with the articles . . . all showing that women, having proved their right to vote, at least to their own satisfaction, are now beginning to think in what manner that right shall be exercised.[94]

Like Colby, Stanton believed in the radical notion that freedom for women would only be achieved once the "evils that block woman's path to freedom" were removed. Note, however, how Stanton identifies Colby's vision by creating an analysis of the *Tribune* that moves from a typical feminine discussion of the pretty presentation of the paper in its "new satin dress" and "good clear type" to a radical feminist political analysis in one fluid motion, without discomfort or interruption. Furthermore, Stanton acknowledges and affirms the feminine and domestic nature of the *Tribune*'s "weekly ministrations" in a way that elevates women's experiences and social roles as a site of power from which radical activism can move.

By moving easily from the domestic family realities of Christmas and New Year celebrations to radical politics, Stanton subtly underscores how feminism can be part of women's everyday lives. Stanton believed that the multiple roles of American women could not be made distinct or compartmentalized into separate public and private roles; this, too, was Colby's own vision for the content of the *Tribune*. In other words, Stanton believed with Colby that no woman could lead an individually separate public life as a radical feminist activist, and then return home to a hungry family waiting for dinner to be made, the house cleaned, and the laundry done. The *Woman's Tribune* and its editor spoke to the *whole woman*, not merely to a single "political" part. If a truly liberatory feminist practice were to become a reality, all these parts of a woman's life must be integrated.

Because she viewed "Freedom for Woman" as representing so much more than gaining the power of the ballot box, Clara Bewick Colby practiced in the pages of the *Woman's Tribune* a feminist ideal that would give women permission to be who they are as women and to live the way they lived as women. Only when a woman was able to integrate her domestic private roles and her political public roles could she move forward in support of the larger feminist project as a new woman. This, coupled with the "balance-wheel of Feminism"—the ballot—would allow feminist movement to progress. As Colby herself put it:

> The altruism of woman has ever subordinated individual desire to the social good and it may be trusted for the future, especially when her judgment becomes enlarged with civic service. The cure for the ills of social freedom is political freedom, for that means responsibility. Woman's ballot will be the balance-wheel of Feminism; the orderly marshalling of the forces of progress, laying on each woman's conscience the obligation to use her new powers for the good of all.[95]

In the pages of the *Woman's Tribune*, women readers found that they did not have to give up their families or their femininity. They did not have to divide the parts of themselves or give up what it meant to be a turn-of-the-century "woman" in order to also be a "feminist." The vision of the comprehensive new woman promulgated in the *Woman's Tribune* was one that could incorporate all the parts of women's lives, creating new definitions of what "woman" could mean in the dawn of a new century—a truly radical project that can be summed up in the words of those who wrote the *History of Woman Suffrage*:

> If the proverb that "the pen is mightier than the sword" be true, woman's skill and force in using this mightier weapon must soon change the destinies of the world.[96]

Notes

1. Eleanor Claire Jerry, "Clara Bewick Colby and *The Woman's Tribune*: Strategies of a Free Lance Movement Leader" (PhD diss., University of Kansas, 1986), 229.

2. Robert L. Griswold, "Anglo Women and Domestic Ideology," in *Western Women: Their Land, Their Lives*, ed. by Lillian Schlissel, Vicki L. Ruiz, and Janice Monk (Albuquerque: University of New Mexico Press, 1988), 18.

3. Ibid., 21.

4. Martha M. Solomon, "The Role of the Suffrage Press in the Woman's Rights Movement," in *A Voice of Their Own: The Woman Suffrage Press,*

1840–1910, ed. Martha M. Solomon (Tuscaloosa: University of Alabama Press, 1991), 6.

5. Nancy F. Cott, *The Bonds of Womanhood: "Woman's Sphere" in New England, 1780–1835* (New Haven: Yale University Press, 1977), 99.

6. Griswold, "Anglo Women and Domestic Ideology," 22. Griswold's emphasis.

7. Cott, *Bonds of Womanhood*, 100.

8. Judith Lorber, *Gender Inequality: Feminist Theories and Politics* (Los Angeles: Roxbury, 2001), 87.

9. Ibid., 90–91.

10. Griswold, "Anglo Women and Domestic Ideology," 21.

11. Ibid., 21.

12. Patricia Okker, *Our Sister Editors: Sarah J. Hale and the Tradition of Nineteenth-Century American Women Editors* (Athens: University of Georgia Press, 1995), 8.

13. While there existed a number of women-run periodicals in the mid-nineteenth century (e.g. Margaret Fuller's *The Dial*), in order to provide context for the *Woman's Tribune* I will focus here on early women's political periodicals that eventually turned to women's rights.

14. Elizabeth Cady Stanton, Susan B. Anthony, and Matilda Joslyn Gage, eds., *History of Woman Suffrage, Vol. I: 1848–1861* (2nd ed., Rochester, New York: Charles Mann, 1889), 45.

15. Ibid., I:47.

16. Lynne Masel-Walters, "Their Rights and Nothing More: A History of *The Revolution*, 1868–1870," *Journalism Quarterly* 53 (Summer 1976): 251.

17. E. Claire Jerry, "The Role of Newspapers in the Nineteenth-Century Women's Movement," in Solomon, ed., *A Voice of Their Own*, 22.

18. Ibid., 23–24.

19. *Woman's Tribune*, 1.3 (1 January 1884): 1.

20. Colby worked on the *Express* during 1876 and 1877 when her husband Leonard bought the paper as a vehicle for his political aspirations. (He was elected Nebraska state senator in 1876; the Colbys emigrated to Nebraska in 1871.) But even after Leonard's affiliation with the *Express* ceased, Clara continued to work with the paper, including editorship of a column titled "Woman's Work."

21. *Woman's Tribune*, 1.1 (August 1883): 1.

22. Stanton, Anthony, and Gage, *History of Woman Suffrage*, 3:671.

23. *Woman's Tribune*, 15.1 (3 January 1898): 2.

24. Jerry, "Clara Bewick Colby and *The Woman's Tribune*," 20.

25. Solomon, "The Role of the Suffrage Press," 3.

26. Ibid., 13.

27. Ibid., 13.

28. State Historical Society of Wisconsin (SHSW), MSS 379, box 8, folder 4, n.d., "No. 2."

29. SHSW 379.8.4, n.d., "No. 2."

30. In 1889 Leonard and Clara moved to Washington to further Leonard's political career and to give Clara better access to events of the national women's rights movement. From 1889 to 1892, Clara published the *Tribune* in Washington when Congress was in session (November to April) and published in Nebraska when it was not (May to October). From 1891 to 1893, Leonard served as First Assistant Attorney General of the United States under the Benjamin Harrison administration; when he completed his appointment, he returned to Nebraska while Clara continued to publish her paper year-round from Washington.

31. Linda Steiner, "Evolving Rhetorical Strategies/Evolving Identities," in Solomon, ed., *A Voice of Their Own*, 183–84.

32. Ibid., 185.

33. Jerry, "Clara Bewick Colby and *The Woman's Tribune*," 20.

34. Although she never achieved a readership that included half the nation's population, the quantity of women affected by Colby's journalistic endeavors is important to note. Journalism historians such as Marion Marzolf rank the *Woman's Tribune* among the top five leading suffrage papers, while Frank Luther Mott cites it among the top three. George P. Rowell's *American Newspaper Directory* cites circulation figures for the *Tribune* as routinely surpassing that of other suffrage periodicals. For example, Rowell states that in 1887 the *Tribune* achieved an annual circulation of more than 4,000 while other suffrage papers averaged from only 500 to 1,500 yearly. The *Woman's Tribune* reached peak circulation of 12,500 in 1888 when it was published daily during the meeting of the International Council of Women of the National Woman Suffrage Association held in Washington, D.C. Moreover, Clara Bewick Colby simultaneously published a companion tract, the *National Bulletin*, which achieved orders of up to 50,000 copies each issue.

35. *Woman's Tribune*, 1.2 (1 November 1883): 1.

36. James C. Olson and Ronald C. Naugle, *History of Nebraska* (Lincoln: University of Nebraska Press, 1997), 200.

37. *Woman's Tribune*, 3.1 (1 January 1884): 1.

38. Glenda Riley, *The Female Frontier: A Comparative View of Women on the Prairie and the Plains* (Lawrence: University Press of Kansas, 1988), 99.

39. Everett Dick, *The Sod-House Frontier, 1854–1890* (Lincoln: University of Nebraska Press, 1937, 1979), 233.

40. Ibid., 234.

41. Riley, *The Female Frontier*, 99.

42. Ibid., 97.

43. Steiner, "Evolving Rhetorical Strategies/Evolving Identities," 192.

44. Ibid., 192–93.
45. *Woman's Tribune*, 4.11 (October 1887): 2.
46. Riley, *The Female Frontier*, 150.
47. Interview with Laureen Riedesel, director of the Beatrice Public Library, 9 February 1999.
48. Jerry, "Clara Bewick Colby and *The Woman's Tribune*," 115.
49. *Woman's Tribune*, 4.1 (November 1886): 2.
50. Ibid., 8.23 (6 June 1891): 179.
51. SHSW 379.4.3.
52. *Woman's Tribune*, 1.2 (1 November 1883): 1.
53. Ibid., 1.3 (1 January 1884): 1.
54. Ibid.
55. Ibid., 2.1 (December 1884): 2.
56. Ibid., 15.1 (3 January 1898): 2.
57. Ibid., January 1884 through January 1885.
58. Ibid., May 1884 through 1886.
59. Ibid., 1.1 (August 1883): 1.
60. The department on "Hygiene and Medical Progress" (begun 1 June 1884 and appearing intermittently throughout the life of the *Tribune*) is particularly revealing of Clara Bewick Colby's commitment to providing an intellectually stimulating journal. The acceptance of the "germ theory" was only beginning to take hold at this time and penicillin would not be invented until 1929.
61. All these began in 1884, and ran intermittently. "Utile Dulci" is a Latin phrase from Horace's *Ars Poetica* (68–65 BC).
62. Riley, *The Female Frontier*, 174.
63. Ibid., 149.
64. Ibid., 174.
65. *Woman's Tribune*, 7.2 (11 January 1890): 14.
66. Ibid., 1.1 (1 August 1883).
67. Ibid., 17.9 (5 May 1900): 1.
68. Ibid., 21.16 (28 May 1904): 1.
69. Jerry, "Clara Bewick Colby and *The Woman's Trbune*," 118.
70. *Woman's Tribune*, 1.3 (1 January 1884): 4.
71. Ibid., 1.5 (March 1884): 3.
72. Ibid., 17.19 (22 September 1900): 73.
73. Jerry, "Clara Bewick Colby and *The Woman's Tribune*," 154.
74. *Woman's Tribune*, 8.5 (31 January 1891): 1.
75. Ibid., 8.5 (31 January 1891): 1.
76. "The Indian Baby," *Woman's Tribune*, 8.5 (31 January 1891): 36.
77. This was printed in the 21 February 1891 edition of the *Tribune* under the heading "Zintka Lanuni, The Waif of Wounded Knee," which out-

lined "the true story" (p. 59) of Zintka's rescue. Attribution was only given to "C. A."

78. *Woman's Tribune,* 8.19 (9 May 1891): 148.

79. Ibid., 8.27 (4 July 1891): 212.

80. "National American W. S. A.," *Woman's Tribune,* 9.4 (30 January 1892): 28. "Editorial Trip," *Woman's Tribune,* 8.35 (29 August 1891): 276–77. "World's Fair Letter," *Woman's Tribune,* 10.36 (19 August 1893): 144.

81. *Woman's Tribune,* 8.37 (12 September 1891): 289; *Woman's Tribune,* 8.41 (5 December 1891): 328; *Woman's Tribune,* 9.1 (9 January 1892): 3. These are only a few examples of the voluminous submissions of poetry celebrating Zintka herself and all manner of birds to the *Tribune* by its readers. *Woman's Tribune,* 9.15 (9 April 1892): 112; *Woman's Tribune,* 13.9 (28 March 1896): 36

82. *Woman's Tribune,* 11.41 (22 September 1894): 162.

83. Ibid., 12.14 (6 April 1895): 56.

84. "An Evening with Indians," *Woman's Tribune* 9.15 (9 April 1892): 112; "Zintka Lanuni's Corner," *Woman's Tribune* 13.9 (28 March 1896): 36.

85. "Zintka Lanuni's Corner," *Woman's Tribune* 12.38 (7 December 1895): 152.

86. Ibid., 13.15 (13 June 1896): 60.

87. Ibid.

88. Ibid., 10.16 (1 April 1893): 62.

89. Ibid., 10.16 (1 April 1893): 61.

90. Ibid., 10.16 (1 April 1893): 63.

91. Ibid., 9.26 (22 October 1892): 201.

92. SHSW 379.8.4, n.d., "No. 1."

93. Ibid., 379.8.4, n.d., "No. 1."

94. Woman's Tribune, 5.7 (21 January 1888): 2.

95. SHSW 379.8.4, n.d., "No. 2."

96. Stanton, Anthony, and Gage, History of Woman Suffrage, 1:49.

"Her Very Handwriting Looks as if She Owned the Earth"

Elizabeth Jordan and Editorial Power

JUNE HOWARD

In her autobiography *Three Rousing Cheers*, published in 1938 when she was seventy-three, Elizabeth Garver Jordan wrote: "I have been pianiste, reporter, newspaper editor, magazine editor, public speaker, playwright, dramatic critic, and novelist"—humorously adding, "which helps to explain why I have never done any one thing superlatively well. I even took a hand in the moving-picture game. But these different activities have given me an interesting life and a lot of those 'vital human experiences' clubwomen love to discuss."[1] As this passage suggests, Jordan deserves our attention not because of any single accomplishment or literary work but because of her creative participation in the crafting of a new kind of life for women.

Among the many roles that Elizabeth Jordan played, the one that she embraced most enthusiastically—and the one that most fully expresses her distinct contribution to this new womanhood—was the role of editor. In her autobiography, and in her papers at the New York Public Library, the years 1900–13 when she was editor of *Harper's Bazar* (as it was then spelled) emerge as a key period in her life, certainly the most fully documented period. She played other sorts of editorial roles as well. She was a book editor for Harper and Brothers for many years, edited a memoir by women's movement leader Anna Howard Shaw, and is now best known for her editing of two composite novels (that is, round robins in which each chapter is written by a different author). The first of those, *The Whole Family*, appeared serially in the *Bazar* in 1907 and 1908, during her editorship; the second, *The Sturdy Oak* (1917), was a fundraiser on behalf of the campaign for woman suffrage.

My research on Jordan began with *The Whole Family*.[2] In the course of that work I came to see her as constantly engaged in syncretism, constantly in practice bringing together values and practices that in the abstract seem opposed. She never rejects tradition and she never stops innovating; she is an unabashed individualist who is devoted to her family and friends and endlessly collaborative; she is a reverent admirer of high culture and always at work selling it, along with other, less elevated commodities. One of the two strands in this essay is a sketch of Elizabeth Jordan's biography, which is well preserved in the historical record but not very well known. I want to see this formidably energetic and creative woman restored to view. The other strand begins with her syncretism; it is an analysis of how the role of editor enables Jordan to maneuver among the intricately linked oppositions that structure modern understandings of "society." Distinctions like public and private, or commerce and culture, do not indicate separate spaces so much as they organize mental maps (and thus have material effects). Jordan consistently crosses and combines them, remapping spheres to make room for the professional woman. I describe my work on *The Whole Family* as a "microhistory"—by which I mean that it focuses very closely on a specific, small historical moment, but sees it as a site where large forces intersect. As the Italian historian Giovanni Levi puts it, to understand the simple act of buying a loaf of bread one must study the world's grain markets.[3] This brief essay cannot deliver a microhistory, of course, but the informing background of my discussion *is* that broad. I think Miss Jordan would have loved being on that big stage. She would have thought it quite right to take a bow not only as her own extraordinary self but also as a representative of a social movement and a historical moment—a participant in an enormous collaboration.

Elizabeth Jordan was born, in 1865, into a prosperous Catholic family in Milwaukee. She was educated—and this was important to her—at the Convent of Notre Dame in that city. The story of Elizabeth Jordan as a woman in print begins there, both because she began writing as a schoolgirl and because one of her early successes as a writer was the May Iverson series, set in a convent boarding school. These stories show female friendship as constantly mediated by the girls' reading and writing. As Jordan later wrote of herself, when she graduated at the age of seventeen what she wanted was to enter the convent as a novice and eventually become a nun. Her mother wanted her to continue her musical studies in Europe and eventually become a concert pianist. The compromise that her father worked out was for her to go into newspaper work, with an eye to pursuing another of her passions: literature.

Jordan started her career in journalism in an exceedingly feminine role: the humorist and journalist George Peck was a family friend, and her father secured her a position editing a new woman's page for *Peck's Sun* in Milwaukee. Jordan writes, "'Sunshine,' Mr. Peck insisted on calling the department; and he wrote a flowery introduction for it which conveyed the impression that I would personally supply light and warmth to the universe. I myself was not a sentimentalist. It is a miracle that the stuff I had to carry in 'Sunshine' did not permanently destroy my interest in newspaper work" (14). Feminist scholars have come to appreciate the importance of such discourse—but this was not the kind of serious journalism Jordan had in mind. Her father found her another local position, this time in an office, and she wrote occasionally for the *Chicago Tribune* and submitted articles to magazines. Soon, however, while ostensibly on holiday in the East, she interviewed for and won a position on Joseph Pulitzer's *World* in New York City.

Almost three decades of scholarship have shown us that, as a woman attempting a career in journalism, Jordan was adventurous but certainly not alone. By the time she arrived in New York in 1890, the field was populated enough that she could define herself not only against sunshine-spreaders but also against stunt journalism like that of Nellie Bly, who had preceded her at the *World*.[1] Her autobiography makes it clear, however, that she was quite willing to play the lady when it gave her an edge in the competitive arena of journalism. Nor did she hesitate, either from fear or from the suspicion that it was not serious journalism, to spend the night in a "haunted" house and write about the experience. In her early days, like many another fledgling journalist, Jordan was given trivial, frustrating assignments; in fact, her first exclusive story came when she was in exile doing articles about resort hotels on Long Island for the *World*'s Brooklyn edition. President Benjamin Harrison and his family, including "Baby McKee," a five-year-old-grandson who was the current darling of the press, came to vacation on Cape May, New Jersey. All reporters had been excluded from this elite, familial scene, until Jordan's combination of class privilege, confident professionalism, and personal warmth—aided, she admits, by some lucky timing—turned the key, and gained her a chance to watch Baby McKee's first swim in the Atlantic and to chat informally with Mrs. Harrison. This "beat," and her ability to write an account intimate enough to please her editor without making the Harrisons feel their privacy had been violated, earned her a raise and better assignments from that day on.

Jordan writes, in *Three Rousing Cheers*, that it was fortunate her mother had visited during her Long Island excursions and carried away an unrealistically pleasant image of newspaper work—for Jordan soon became "a daily frequenter of the Tombs, of Bellevue Hospital . . . , of the Police Courts and the city prisons." In her series "True Stories of the News" she researched the facts behind minor news items and wrote them up as if they were fiction. These half-page special articles, modeled on a Parisian innovation, contributed to the development of the "human interest" feature story and presaged the development of literary journalism.[5]

Throughout her work, in fact, Jordan meshed literature and journalism very closely. Her first published book, a collection titled *Tales of the City Room*, portrays a group of women journalists as they make choices that define their gendered professional identities. She wrote its ten linked stories in the city room of the *World* on Wednesday and Thursday nights, where she was supervising the reporters and artists who were producing the material for the Sunday supplement: she sat there waiting for their copy and put the time to use writing fiction. Several of her tales turn on tensions between an ethic of connection and more skeptical, self-interested attitudes—one, specifically on a conflict between loyalty to another woman and the imperative to get the story. Jordan's autobiographical character Ruth Herrick chooses not to print the fact that an abused wife acquitted of her husband's murder had admitted her guilt in a private interview—which, over Jordan's protests, was interpreted as indicating that Lizzie Borden had confessed to her. In fiction and her autobiography Jordan portrays it as a challenge to lose her "convent manner" and blend successfully into a workplace in which men swore constantly, yet remain completely respectable. Jordan even writes about sexual harassment, most openly in a final volume of the May Iverson series in which May becomes a journalist. By her own account, Jordan did find a way to be both a lady and a good fellow.

In New York, at Pulitzer's *World* during the period of its enormous success, Jordan was in the very center of "progressive publishing." The fact that she chose this career, as well as her pride in it, manifests the prestige that the role of the reporter had recently acquired; and her pride in the long hours she worked reflects the ethos of energy that characterized the emerging profession. This was—in a phrase from a memoir by one of the Harpers—"everybody's busy day."[6] Not only by her own account but by other people's as well, Jordan delighted in that atmosphere, and flourished in it. In *Ladies of the Press: The Story of Women in Journalism by an Insider* (1936), Ishbel Ross wrote: "Miss Jordan used to bedazzle the compositors by showing up in immaculate shirt-waists and slinging type with an experienced hand. When everyone else was sweating and in a state of collapse from heat and overwork, Miss Jordan would look completely self-possessed. . . . [She] was never bothered with minor women's page assignments, but combined the best features of the stunt age with sound writing. She tested the accommodations of jails and asylums, rode an engine cab, interviewed social leaders and covered the news of the town. She traveled through the mountains of Virginia and Tennessee on horseback, fording rivers, climbing gorges, forcing her way through thick forest, her only companion a Negro guide. She visited a lonely mining camp in the mountains, in which no woman had ever set foot. Armed with a Spanish stiletto she explored the camps of the moonshiners and did a series for the *Sunday World* that was copied widely."[7] The sort of writing Jordan did—not merely reporting the news but actively developing stories—was also characteristic of the innovative journalism of her era. In Ross's words one hears, as well, the racial, class, and regional hierarchies that Jordan operated within and the prejudices she actively endorsed.

The novelist Gertrude Atherton, who met Jordan during the 1890s and encouraged her ambitions in fiction, wrote: "Elizabeth Jordan, then the star woman reporter on the *World*, interviewed me . . . , and what she and other girl reporters told me of their vicissitudes and mortifications convinced me that this stratum of woman's endeavor was not for me. Miss Jordan had a masterful personality, and a Juno-like beauty that would give any girl confidence—she could hold her own; for that matter she was soon elevated to the editorship of the Woman's

Page; but all those other girls who told me their woes disappeared in a few years, worn out, body and soul."[8]

Atherton's concise verbal portrait captures vividly the impression Jordan seems to have made on people. She was a sizable woman of great energy and self-confidence. Alice Brown actually used the nickname "Juno" in their correspondence. (The letters, preserved like the others I quote here in the New York Library, are undated but come from late in their lives.) In one she addressed her friend as "dear Junoesque Juno," in another, as "Queen Bess." On one occasion Brown wrote to Jordan, "It was very heartening to see Elizabeth's envelope even, because her very handwriting looks as if she owned the earth, and one feels that all is well" (Jordan papers, Box 1, File 11, undated letter). Margaret Deland wrote to Jordan from Bermuda in 1920: "My dear what have you been doing? Flying about on the snow and wind to lunches + dinners + theatres + opera? Yes, I know you have. Nothing keeps you at home. Are you blooming + magnificent as always? Ah! My Elizabeth how I wish you were here. Have you written two new books + a thousand articles?" (Box 1, File 21, letter dated April 24).

The moment in 1900 when Jordan moved from the *World* to *Harper's* is very important in both strands of my story.[9] She had told her parents when she left Milwaukee that she would be editor of *Harper's Bazar* or *St. Nicholas* or the *Youth's Companion* within ten years, and indeed she made it—as she says in *Three Rousing Cheers*—"with hardly a day to spare". She felt she had "died and gone to heaven"—but, she also wrote, "I had my hours of fellow-feeling for the little girl whose mother had promised her heaven, and who, dazed by the effulgence of the picture drawn, wistfully asked if she could occasionally pass a Saturday afternoon with her little friends in hell. I had been living in an atmosphere where the news of the world broke over me like pounding breakers. The contrast of the academic calm of Harper's sometimes depressed me" (171).

What had happened was that Harper's, the bastion of genteel publishing, had gotten into financial difficulties, had taken loans from J. P. Morgan, and eventually went bankrupt. As William Dean Howells later remarked, "It was as if I had read that the government of the United States had failed." As a result, Harper's modernized abruptly under the leadership of Morgan's representative, George Harvey.[10] Elizabeth Jordan was part of that process. Her autobiography contains some wonderful stories about the stress of the transition, and there is equally interesting material in her unpublished correspondence. She writes in *Three Rousing Cheers* about the man in charge of the technical side of the art department who confided that she made him "noivous"—but she doesn't say that she also made William Dean Howells nervous, and she clearly did. Jordan saved even unimportant letters that prestigious authors like Howells wrote her, so we have a full record of his annoyance over being rushed to get proof back to her quickly, and his fear that she was going to act like exactly what she had been—a newspaper editor—and cut or edit his work without his approval.

At the same time, however, there is evidence in the correspondence that her connections with other women eased the transition between different publishing styles. Jordan was only the third editor of *Harper's Bazar*: Mary Booth edited it from its founding in 1867 until 1889, Margaret Sangster for the next ten years. Sangster was supplanted by Jordan when Harvey took over, but she wrote a series of warmly supportive notes to Jordan, expressing affection and confidence, and praising the new issues as they came out. Jordan managed to have her cake and eat it too—she was part of an aggressive, masculine, modernizing movement in publishing, but at the same time she embraced and was embraced by a nurturing women's community. Jordan represents herself—and the correspondence suggests that she was accepted as—the loving daughter of an older generation of literary women and activists. There is a warm letter from Susan B. Anthony dated from the very month Jordan took over as editor, saying that although she gets asked for photographs constantly she is sending some, because she loves to "help the cause along even by allowing my homely face at best—but still more so in newspaper cuts—to be shaddowed [sic]—+ especially am I willing that it should be seen in Harpers Bazaar—whose first editor—Mary L. Booth—I knew so well—and loved + honored so much—" (Jordan papers, Box 1, File 1).

Jordan was very proud of the fact that she knew so many prominent American women; *Three Rousing Cheers* asserts that she knew "most of them more or less intimately" (330). She writes with great affection and admiration about leaders of the women's movement such as Frances Willard and Anna Howard Shaw, and the story of her collaboration with the latter occupies an entire chapter of the autobiography.[11] Jordan considered Shaw "a born talker and probably the best woman speaker America ever had," but both knew she wrote badly (332). She needed to work with a skilled editor if her experiences as a pioneer in western

Michigan in the 1860s, and as a pioneer for women in the ministry, in medicine, and in the suffrage movement were to be recorded—and, not incidentally, to be published by Harper's. Jordan failed to persuade Shaw to accept her assistance until Dr. Shaw's busy schedule was suddenly interrupted by a broken leg. With characteristic humor, at once self-aggrandizing and self-mocking, Jordan writes that she "hardly gave her time to have the bones of her ankle set before I hurried up to the McAlpin Hotel, where she was stopping, to take up again the matter of that book" (330). Shaw disliked wasting time just as much as Jordan did, so every morning for three weeks Jordan and her secretary Charlotte Lambrecht came to the hotel. Jordan asked questions, Shaw talked, Lambrecht took the reminiscences down in shorthand, and they "laughed and cried with her; we were tense with interest during every hour" (333). Later Lambrecht typed up her notes and rearranged them in something like chronological order for Jordan, who created an outline, wrote the narrative, and read it, chapter by chapter, to Shaw for her approval. The memoir was published serially in *Metropolitan Magazine* and then in book form in 1915 by Harper's as *The Story of a Pioneer.* Shaw is listed as the author, but "with the collaboration of Elizabeth Jordan" also appears on the title page.

Of course, another name for this kind of editing is ghostwriting. That practice can be seen as a thoroughly commercial, perhaps even slightly disreputable practice that undermines our habitual reverence for individual authorship. Yet as described by Jordan, the production of the volume seems a remarkable exercise of recollection and candor on the one side, and of empathy and editorial craft on the other. Jordan wanted to convey her friend's spirit—to keep herself out of the book, which she knew was no easy matter when she was listening so passionately that she felt "as if I had lived her life with her" (333). Jordan praises both the other collaborators while making it clear that she herself deserves considerable credit for the book's success; she writes that Shaw "had been wonderful during her own telling of the tale—extraordinarily open-minded, always willing to follow leads and suggestions," but that she "was even more wonderful" during the reading: "From start to finish . . . she never interrupted it; and at the end she never suggested a change except a correction of some name or date. This seems too good to be true; but it is true, and it forms a unique record in collaboration" (334). On the commercial side of the arrangement, she frankly reports that both she and Shaw were paid generously for the serial, but that she "voluntarily and unnecessarily" (331) turned over all her royalties from the book to Shaw. As so often, Jordan manages to mesh two apparently contradictory positions: she is a self-supporting professional, and she earns something from the project, but her account also altruistically serves Shaw, the women's movement, and the reading public at large.

Jordan's narrative emphasizes her intimacy with Shaw, and she reports with visible pleasure that Shaw used the language of kinship to talk about their collaboration, always referring to the book as "'our child'" (336). The very basis of their connection is that they are both "public women." As Carroll Smith-Rosenberg has shown, politically radical New Women did not reject the loving female world and the female-guided family, but "wove the traditional ways of their mothers into the heart of their brave new world."[12] Jordan takes on the role of loving friend or daughter, inducing the hard-working Shaw to attend the theater, concerts, even the occasional vaudeville performance with her—which, again mixing the vocabularies of public and private, she describes as making herself "a committee of one" to bring new pleasures into Shaw's life. She interweaves family rhetoric with individualism, demonstrating pride in a degree of personal freedom (not only from the conventional family but from the political obligations that enmeshed Shaw) that even this "pioneer" for women's rights admires and implicitly compares to a man's. "One evening when we had seen a good play, and were sailing airily into the dressing-room of its distinguished woman star, Dr. Shaw said to me smilingly but almost enviously, 'What an independent cuss you are!'" (335). Here Jordan performs a similarly syncretic operation on behalf of an unnamed actress—the vocabulary of celebrity merges with that of high-cultural prestige, so the "star" is "distinguished." Jordan edits together family and citizenship, intimacy and publicity.

In a recent historical monograph, Margaret Finnegan argues that activist women of the early twentieth century appropriated the emerging strategies of consumer culture; suffrage, she tells us, was *sold.* Suffragists "incorporated modern methods of advertising, publicity, mass merchandising, and mass entertainment into their fight for voting rights. They adopted commercial standards of design and display. They equated consumer rights with consumer desire."[13] In the process they entered into a dialogue that alters the terms in which we understand gender, politics—and shopping. *The Sturdy Oak*, the composite novel about the New York suffrage campaign of 1916–17 that Jordan edited, certainly manifests this creative process. Both its content and its proceeds supported the movement.

The front of Finnegan's book is a clipping she found in Susan B. Anthony's papers: a drawing of suffragists on a train, titled "Campaign Literature." On their way to a convention, carrying signs proclaiming "Votes for Women," these ladies are eagerly reading fashion magazines, among them—its title prominently visible—the *Bazar*. The image, as Finnegan suggests, pokes fun at suffragists by implying an incongruity between their claim to political participation and their frivolous interest in clothing. Yet it also quite literally represents these privileged women laying claim to public space, implicitly pointing to the concomitant transformation of politics itself that was under way. The resonance of the image is deepened further when we note how *Harper's Bazar* itself represents a melding of cultivation and consumption. From the time of its first editor, Mary Booth, and certainly in Jordan's day, it was very much engaged with high culture and public affairs. This is to some degree still true for the Hearst-owned *Bazaar* later in the twentieth century—Carmel Snow, the magazine's celebrity editor during the 1940s and 1950s, famously described her reader as a "well-dressed woman" with a "well-dressed mind." (In the November 2001 issue, the new editor, Glenda Bailey, placed herself in the magazine's distinguished editorial tradition by invoking that very quotation.)

A related syncretism, I have suggested, is visible throughout Elizabeth Jordan's career. She constantly uses the rhetoric of the family to refer not only to women's networks but to all her close friends and her workplace community as well. She composed an elective family, a household consisting of two other women and an adopted daughter, as well as (for many years) her own biological mother. She wrote of her "best man friend" John à Becket: "During the first year of our acquaintance I had assured him I would be the mother he needed so sorely. He was much older than I but he accepted the relation, and called me 'Mother' to his last day. He always addressed my mother as 'Grandma,' and my 'adopted sisters' . . . as 'Aunt Harriet' and 'Aunt Martha.' He became knight errant to the family" (146). Jordan joined Harper and Brothers exactly at the moment—and exactly because—it ceased to be a family business, yet she wholeheartedly embraced Harper's as a home and its staff as a family.

Jordan's years as part of the Harper establishment put her in a powerful position as a cultural broker. She was by most accounts a very successful editor, seamlessly merging the commercial and the cultivated, the fashionable and the domestic, the dashing and the didactic. Margaret Deland wrote to her on one occasion: "I am convinced that you edit the *Bazar* for a missionary purpose, the encouragement of authors!" (Jordan papers, Box 2, File 4). That is, however, not the only perspective preserved in the correspondence. There are some painful letters from Mary Austin, who had hoped Jordan would negotiate an arrangement that would allow her to publish exclusively with Harper's in return for some financial stability. She was not satisfied with what Jordan offered her—and she found Jordan unsympathetic and overbearing. Austin particularly resented Jordan's interference with what she considered her artistic autonomy on something like the title of a piece. Here, as elsewhere, I have tended to emphasize here what we might call the utopian dimension of editing—the way in which it can allow human agents to work together in a common project that both fulfills them and pushes them beyond themselves. That is not always the way editorial power works; Austin sees it, instead, as gatekeeping. The moment of creative syncretism in the early twentieth century when Jordan edits the *Bazar* may be the exception rather than the rule.

Let me close with another critical view, from late in Jordan's life when the political situation—in terms of suffrage and much else—had changed profoundly. Susan B. Anthony's niece, who shared her name, apparently sent Jordan a manuscript to comment on—and was not pleased with the response she received. The archives preserve a letter, dated 1939, that opens with this rebuke: "Your letter and my manuscript came this morning—and thank you very much for the criticism. I am amazed at your interpretation of Aunt Susan's very words and speeches as Communist. Because, Miss Jordan, every word that I quote Aunt Susan as saying in the prologue is taken directly from some speech, article or book that she wrote. If her words coincide with those of the Communist then far from turning in her grave at the coincidence—she would be the first to leap up and say—'Why, I thought of that way back in the middle of the nineteenth century'" (Jordan papers, Box 1, File 1). This disagreement suggests the limits of Jordan's syncretism: some positions are too radical to be assimilated. It reminds us, too, of the complexity of the task of translating opinions across eras. What interests me most about the exchange, however, is the way Susan Anthony imagines her aunt undaunted by the accusation that she held dangerous views—in fact, to be proud of her prescience. She implies that what matters first, if not most, is continued relevance: in effect, being in print. I imagine the other women whose words are woven into this essay nodding in agreement.

My title (taken from Alice Brown's letter, quoted earlier) evokes both the exclusionary and the democratic dimensions of Elizabeth Garver Jordan's writing as if she "owned the earth." Contemplated at length, the phrase suggests class privilege and colonial domination—which are indeed the historical conditions of Jordan's self-assertion. At the same time it figures Jordan's refusal to accept any restriction of her sphere. Her syncretism tracks across public and private, individualism and family, to create a distinctively female version of the writer and editor. Her transformative labor helped make the category that frames this volume—"women in print"—available to us.

Notes

1. Elizabeth Jordan, *Three Rousing Cheers* (New York: D. Appleton-Century, 1938), 11.

2. June Howard, *Publishing the Family* (Duke University Press, 2001).

3. Giovanni Levi, "On Microhistory," in *New Perspectives on Historical Writing*, ed. Peter Burke (University Park: Pennsylvania State University Press, 1991), 96.

4. Relevant sources extend from Marion Marzolf, *Up From the Footnote: A History of Women Journalists* (New York : Hastings House, 1977) to the recent work of Linda Steiner—for example, "Gender at Work: Early Accounts by Women Journalists," *Journalism History* 23, no.1 (1997): 2–12, which draws on Three Rousing Cheers, and Agnes Gottlieb, "Grit Your Teeth, Then Learn to Swear: Women in Journalistic Careers, 1850–1926," *American Journalism* 18, no. 1 (2001): 53–72.

5. See Barbara Belford, *Brilliant Bylines* (New York: Columbia University Press, 1986), 152.

6. J. Henry Harper, *I Remember* (New York: Harper & Brothers, 1934), 28.

7. Ishbel Ross, *Ladies of the Press: The Story of Women in Journalism by an Insider* (New York: Harper & Brothers, 1936), 177–78.

8. Gertrude Atherton, *Adventures of a Novelist* (New York: Liveright, 1932), 222.

9. Women editors are now receiving substantial scholarly attention. For the nineteenth century, see Sherilyn Cox Bennion, *Equal to the Occasion: Women Editors of the Nineteenth-Century West* (Reno: University of Nevada Press, 1990) and Patricia Okker, *Our Sister Editors: Sarah J. Hale and the Tradition of Nine-*

teenth-Century American Women Editors (Athens: University of Georgia Press, 1995). See also *Blue Pencils and Hidden Hands: Women Editing Periodicals, 1830–1910,* ed. Sharon M. Haris and Ellen Gruber Garvey (Boston: Northeastern University Press, 2004), especially the foreword by Garvey, pp. xi–xxiii.

10. Howells's remark is quoted from J. Henry Harper, *The House of Harper: A Century of Publishing in Franklin Square* (New York: Harper & Brothers, 1912), 324. See also Christopher P. Wilson *The Labor of Words: Literary Professionalism in the Progressive Era* (Athens: University of Georgia Press, 1985).

11. The following paragraphs include slightly revised text from *Publishing the Family*. Please see that book for a fuller discussion of collaboration and composite novels, and especially of *The Whole Family.*

12. Carroll Smith-Rosenberg. *Disorderly Conduct: Visions of Gender in Victorian America* (New York: Alfred A. Knopf, 1985), 255.

13. Margaret Finnegan, *Selling Suffrage: Consumer Culture & Votes for Women* (New York: Columbia University Press, 1999), 2.

Making News

Marie Potts and the Smoke Signal *of the Federated Indians of California*

TERRI CASTANEDA

The first edition of the newspaper *Smoke Signal* was issued in January 1948. Published by the Federated Indians of California (FIC) and edited for nearly three decades by a Mountain Maidu woman named Marie Mason Potts, the *Smoke Signal* achieved national recognition in the early 1970s as a pioneering example of the political promise inherent in the budding American Indian press.[1] The *Smoke Signal* was by then in its calmer, waning years, but for the nation at large, the times were particularly turbulent. This was the era of civil rights demonstrations, and the American Indian Movement (AIM) seemed to make news on an almost daily basis. Biased coverage of such events as the Indian occupation of Alcatraz and the standoff between AIM and the FBI at Wounded Knee inspired American Indian journalists to develop newspapers independent of the dominant society and the mainstream press. Many of these publications, like *Akwesasne Notes* and the *Jicarilla Chieftan*, are still in circulation today. Although the *Smoke Signal* cannot be counted among them, it holds a special place in the history of print culture and the American Indian press for its early founding and its unprecedented, three-decades-long run. The story of its origin and impact on California

Indian culture and politics, like the biography of its venerable editor, takes us back much earlier than the 1940s to the devastating aftermath of the great Gold Rush of 1849 and California's subsequent statehood.

The populations indigenous to the territory now encompassed by the state of California represent a broad spectrum of cultural and linguistic diversity. Through waves of Spanish, Russian, Mexican, and U.S. domination, these groups have struggled against all odds to retain their native languages, their spiritual beliefs and practices, their lands and means of living upon them—indeed their very lives.[2] In many ways, this struggle continues today, as California's native peoples fight to retain their distinctive group identities and traditions—a cause that has consumed the personal and professional lives of countless individuals. Not surprisingly, the front lines of this ongoing battle to ensure cultural survival are heavily soldiered in the early twenty-first century by the descendants of those who made it their own cause and lifework a century ago, when Native Californians first began to respond pan-tribally to their common condition as dominated peoples.[3]

The ethnogenesis of the "California Indian" is a twentieth-century phenomenon, but as the outcome of a cumulative process, it is firmly rooted in the shared experiences of conquest and colonialism—the systematic genocide, the forced assimilation, and the loss of ancestral lands. By 1850, when California joined the Union, the combined effects of the Mission system, the Gold Rush, and more than three hundred years of exposure to invading settlers and foreign diseases had taken a tremendous toll on the state's indigenous peoples and cultures. But the ultimate blow was yet to be delivered. That came in July 1852, when the U.S. Senate, acting under pressure from California's legislature and senators, rejected eighteen treaties negotiated with various California Indian bands between 1851 and 1852. Ironically, just two years before, after approving California's entrance into the Union, the Senate had passed special legislation authorizing President Fillmore and his administration to create such relationships between the federal government and the aboriginal populations of the newest state. Although an inadequate measure of either the number or needs of Indians in California, the treaties would nonetheless have set aside 8,600,000 acres for their permanent use.[4] Unaware of the federal government's failure to ratify the treaties, many native groups moved off the territories they believed themselves to have ceded and onto the reserves they had been promised. Others, who knew nothing of the treaties to begin with, continued to defend their rights of occupancy, only to find themselves variously slaughtered, rounded up, or driven off their ancestral grounds as settlers and prospectors moved in to pursue the promise of lode-bearing lands. From the Cascades in the North, southward through the Sierra, and fanning out on either side into the foothills and bottomlands, the story was more or less the same. In northwestern California, where timberlands represented gold of a different sort, the means by which it was seized and harvested took an equally brutal toll upon tribal societies.

Displaced and disenfranchised, native peoples managed the ensuing poverty and fragmentation through a variety of means: migrating to the urban centers for low-paying wage work, hiring out to ranchers and farmers who had moved onto their aboriginal lands, or simply by eking out a bare living on the executive-order reservations, the rancherias, or the individual allotments eventually established by the federal government as way to solve the so-called "Indian Problem."[5] The treaty documents of the early 1850s were locked away, where they were forgotten for half a century. In 1905, through the combined pressure of several California legislators and public interest groups, the "lost" treaties were located in the Senate archives, declassified, and made public. As news of the rejected treaties came to light, public outrage and sympathy escalated. Humanitarian groups and white patrons, already working to improve the position of California's Indians, helped pressure the federal government to make reparations. In 1928, the California Indians Jurisdictional Act won the state's native populations the right to have their case heard before the U.S. Court of Claims. The previous year, anticipating passage of the act, California had appropriated funds and passed legislation empowering the state's attorney general to handle the Indians' suit on behalf of their lost treaty lands and rights.

On December 4, 1944, following unremitting complications, delays, and federal appeals, the Court of Claims finally handed down a decision in favor of the Indians: they were to receive a total of $17,053,941.98 for the 8,619,000 acres they had been promised. In arriving at the monetary figure, the court had capped the land value at $1.25 per acre—its worth in 1851—and made no provision for the increased value that such lands would have acquired in the eight decades intervening. The Act of 1928, although allowing a suit to be brought against the U.S. government, had been written in such a way as to protect the federal government against having to make significant cash outlays. This was accomplished by two means. First, the act guaranteed the federal government the right to subtract, from any Court of Claims award, the sum total of all expenditures made by the U.S. government to California Indians in the form of livestock, education, farming equipment and the like. These allowable "offsets" were calculated by valuing all goods and services delivered over the course of the preceding century, including the cost of rancherias and the executive order reservations that had been established in the late 1800s under pressure from the state.[6] By this measure, the original monetary figure set by the Court of Claims was reduced by more than $12 million, to just over $5 million. Divided among the 24,000 identifiable Indians who had been officially enrolled for the purposes of this suit between 1928 and 1933, the compensation, which amounted to some $200 per capita, seemed insultingly low.[7] Yet per capita distribution was not even a possibility under the act. This was the second measure by which the federal government had protected its own interests. The Act of 1928 had stipulated that any monetary award be paid into the U.S. Treasury and held in trust until a decision regarding the award's final disposition could be determined by Congress. Therefore, in 1945, a judgment fund was established to "hold" the award handed down by the Court of Claims. With an interest rate of only 4 percent and talk of applying the funds toward future social and medical welfare expenditures on behalf of California Indians, the stage was set for continuing controversy. Considering the poor track record the United States had already established with state's native population, few could have been surprised when California Indians and their advocates within state government and the private sector expressed anger and disappointment at the outcome of the suit.

On March 25, 1946, thirty-two California Indian leaders gathered at the California State Capitol to air their grievances before a legislative subcommittee on Indian Affairs.[8] Several recurring themes dominated the meeting: resentment over failure of the Jurisdictional Act of 1928 to justly compensate them for their stolen lands, means by which they could achieve per capita distribution of the $5 million judgment fund, and support of legislation pending on the national level to create an Indian Claims Commission. This latter legislation was particularly significant because it would create a means by which California's Indians could sue for the 91 million acres of California land not covered under the treaties and therefore not subject to recovery or compensation under the Act of 1928.[9]

Many of the individuals present at the meeting also chose this occasion to publicly renounce their affiliation with a white missionary named Frederick G. Collett, complaining that the organization he had founded in the early part of the century, the Indian Board of Co-operation, had served them neither well nor honestly. Several of these outspoken Indians had been strong supporters of Collett for two decades; some had even traveled with him to Washington as delegates of the "Indian Auxiliaries" of his Indian Board of Co-operation. But Collett's ethics and motivations had been called into question almost from the start.[10] In the first two decades of the century he had moved quickly to establish himself in both Washington and California as *the* representative authorized to speak for all Indians in California. By encouraging Indians to form tribal or regional auxiliaries, he created extensive networks and strongholds throughout northern and central California. By this means, he was able to collect yearly and even monthly "dues" from individual Indians, most of whom were landless and destitute. Critics charged that by posing himself and his agents as legal advisors or brokers to the Indians, he was able to intimidate them into paying dues by suggesting that unless they belonged to his Indian Board of Co-operation, they would be unable to share in any benefits that might come from his lobbying efforts. Collett's fund-raising tactics became particularly ruthless after the long awaited passage of the Act of 1928, which called for an official roll of all California Indians. Misrepresenting the Indian Board of Co-operation roster and petitions, which they were asked to sign, as an official roll for use in distributing any funds that might result from a favorable judgment, he effectively extorted power of attorney from thousands of Indians. Through such means, Collett was able to introduce bills they had neither asked for nor approved of, but from which he and his attorney friends in Washington would illicitly profit.[11]

Responsibility for enrollment under the Act of 1928 was assigned to Frederic A. Baker, an official agent of the U.S. government. But even as Baker or one of his own representatives moved throughout the state, helping Indians to apply for membership on the official Roll of the Indians of California, Collett continued to capitalize, especially among rural-dwelling Indians, on the limited understanding of many natives of the enrollment process. Long after the official Roll of California Indians was completed and approved in 1933, Collett maintained his base of financial support and political power by such unethical tactics as convincing impoverished Indians to turn over to him their monthly

California Old Age (and later, Social) Security payments. This sacrifice, he told them, was necessary in order for them to retain their membership in the Indian Board of Co-operation. Supposedly, this was the only way they could be guaranteed a share of the monetary award that would be forthcoming by virtue of his work on their behalf in Washington.[12]

Among those who attacked Collett's means and motives at the March 1946 meeting in Sacramento were William Fuller (Central Sierra Miwok), Ethan Anderson (Pomo), John Porter (Central Sierra Miwok), Martha Lemay (Nisenan Maidu), Stephen Knight (Pomo), Bertha Stewart (Tolowa; representing the Del Norte Indian Welfare Association or DIWA), and Arthur Treppa (Pomo). A few of Collett's staunchest supporters, who were also in attendance at this meeting, spoke up in defense of both him and the latest iteration of his Indian welfare organizations: The Indians of California, Inc. Nonetheless, the principal outcome of this meeting was a political alliance of the California Indian leadership intent on leaving his ranks. Although they wanted legislation introduced to allow per capita distribution of the $5 million judgment fund resulting from the Court of Claims award, their larger motive in allying themselves together was to file suit against the U.S. government before the Indian Claims Commission for loss of their ancestral lands—meaning the whole of the state of California, minus the territory covered by the Act of 1928. In contradistinction to Collett's organizations and methods, their group would be run by Indians for Indians. No membership dues would be collected, and delegates to Washington would be elected by the Indians themselves, rather than appointed by a white executive secretary, attorney, or board of directors. The name they chose for themselves was the Federated Indians of California (FIC).[13] Two officers were elected to govern the group: Chief William Fuller as President and Bertha Stewart as Secretary.

The FIC's first order of business was to make its presence, purpose, and principles of self-governance known to the Indians in California.[14] From March 1946 through the end of 1947, Bertha Stewart used direct-mail letters to announce meetings, report developments in their claims case, and solicit new membership to their cause. This technique met with considerable success.[15] Among the earliest recruits to the FIC's rapidly growing ranks were three women who would soon play critical roles within the organization: Marie Mason Potts, Kitty Potts Flores, and Pansy Potts Marine.[16]

As the FIC expanded its numbers and reach, the need to distribute the growing responsibilities and duties among its members grew as well. In December 1947, when the FIC selected its slate of officers for the coming year, Kitty Flores, a Maidu, was elected to the newly created position of publicity agent. Only twenty-two years old, Flores was the youngest of five daughters born to Marie Potts, but neither her youth nor newlywed status hampered her ability to get the job done expertly. She immediately began arranging for the group to make a public appearance with Governor Earl Warren as a way of garnering publicity and public sympathy for their claim against the federal government. Scheduled to coincide with a Centennial Celebration of gold discovery in California (1948), the FIC membership was invited to travel to the grounds of Sutter's Fort in Sacramento, site of the State Indian Museum, to participate in what she promoted as "a peace pipe ceremonial."[17] Understanding the press coverage to be gained from appearing in native costume, Flores encouraged members to bring tribal regalia or some other component of their aboriginal dress in order to enhance their Indian identity and public appeal.[18]

On February 9, 1948, both *The Sacramento Union* and *The Sacramento Bee* carried stories about Governor Warren's smoking a "peace pipe" with the Federated Indians of California. But more importantly, they quoted Warren's support for their claim against the U.S. government.[19]

> The Indians of California have been good, loyal citizens; they bear us no ill will. They have just grievances and I hope the day is not far off when the Indians of our state will receive justice. In Washington, there are some unscrupulous lawyers who follow litigation in the courts involving Indians like low-grade ambulance chasers. It is my purpose and desire to see that these real Americans are not victimized any further in this state. They have suffered too many injustices already.[20]

Thus the state of California went on record in favor of the FIC's claim case—and Kitty Flores lost no time in making sure this news was carried statewide.[21] Transcribing the *Union* and *Bee* articles verbatim into the body of a letter explaining the land claims history of California's Indians, she forwarded the two stories to newspaper editors throughout the state. Shortly afterward, she turned her attention to reporting these stories and events in a newspaper of her own creation: *The Smoke Signal* of the Federated Indians of California.[22]

Only four pages long, the second issue of the *Smoke Signal* (February 1948) was full of news important to California's Indian population; but for Flores, this was only a beginning:

> We wish to thank our readers for their response and enthusiasm for the first issue of the *Smoke Signal*. The staff is always at your service, for only through you, the readers, can we hope to make a bigger and better *Smoke Signal*. This is your paper and we want to encourage you to send us your suggestions and opinions. . . . We hope more of our people can be benefited by our Signal, for it is through your cooperation and good will that we can send our *Smoke Signal*s from mountain to mountain, across valleys and canyons, to the Indians far and near, until the truth can be brought to our people, one and all.[23]

"The truth," to which Flores makes reference in this latter statement, was further emphasized in a publisher's statement that appeared immediately after: "The *Smoke Signal* is edited and controlled completely by California Indians, published for the Indians of California. Feel free to write to The *Smoke Signal* c/o the Federated Indians of California, 2727 Santa Clara Way, Sacramento 17, California." The implication was clear: the *Smoke Signal* was the only newspaper Indians in California could count on to honestly and accurately represent their legal rights and entitlements. The FIC had been founded upon this principle, but they faced a tremendous challenge when it came to countering what they believed to be fraudulent procedures and misleading information offered in meetings, bulletins, and periodicals sponsored by "The Indians of California" and "The California Indians, Inc."[24] The Federated Indians and their own lawyer, retired enrolling agent Frederic A. Baker (who donated his legal time and expertise, as opposed to charging a fee or working on a contingency basis), were both adamant in their belief that these competing pan-tribal organizations were nothing more than misguided Indians subject to manipulation by white "racketeers" who sought to benefit monetarily by representing, before the Indian Claims Commission, the legal class named in the jurisdictional legislation of 1928 as the "Indians of California."[25] Conceived as a newspaper containing a broad spectrum of news and information relevant to all Indians within the state, the *Smoke Signal* was clearly designed to institutionalize the FIC's authority and establish its superior credibility over other organizations and print media that were neither owned nor controlled by California Indians. The paper's very name reinforced this distinction. As Kitty Flores explained in the first edition of the paper: "The *Smoke Signal* was adopted because this means of communications was formerly used by our ancestors."[26]

Kitty, along with her husband, Lt. Kesner Flores, established a strong presence for the publication during its inaugural year. When Kitty resigned in March 1949 to move to Camp Roberts Army Base, where Lt. Flores had been transferred, Chief William Fuller thanked them both for the work they had done on the *Smoke Signal*'s behalf.[27] Together, they had contributed articles, editorials, and illustrations, including the artwork for the masthead. When Kitty died in April 1951 from injuries sustained in an automobile accident, Bertha Stewart memorialized her in the *Smoke Signal:*

> Kitty's contribution to the Federated Indians will never be forgotten. . . . It was her inspiration and ingenuity plus a lot of courage and hard work that brought into being this little publication of the Federated Indians. . . . Her cheerful personality and winning smile will long remain in our hearts, while her courage and resourcefulness will remain as an inspiration to continue our fight to get justice for the Indians of California.[28]

Kitty Flores left no descendants when she died, but her vision of a California Indian newspaper lived on in the *Smoke Signal* for many years to come, in the capable hands of her successor—her mother, Marie Potts, who had been tapped to fill the position of publicity agent immediately following Flores's resignation and move to Camp Roberts in 1949. Potts had already served as an essential member of the *Smoke Signal* staff, along with one of Kitty's older sisters, Pansy Marine. The newspaper had been a family affair from the first; it would remain so to the very end.

Marie Mason Potts was born in 1895 at Big Meadows in Plumas County, California. This idyllic-sounding place, along with the neighboring territories of Hebe Meadow and Mountain Meadow, represents the ancestral homelands of the Northern or Mountain Maidu. Long before the coming of settlers to their lands, the Maidu practiced a traditional mode of subsistence called foraging, exploiting the natural bounty of wild resources found in the northern reaches of the Sierra Nevada, just south of Mount Lassen. They wove beautiful basketry containers of red bud, maple, spruce root, and willow. Simple cedar-bark homes sheltered them from the snow and cold winter winds. Their children learned to fish, hunt, and process acorn and other plant foods while at their parents' side. In contrast to less isolated Indian groups who had experienced white contact as much as two hundred years before, the world of the Mountain Maidu maintained a semblance of its aboriginal form well into the latter half of the nineteenth century, when even this mere semblance was eventually destroyed.

In many ways, Marie Potts's early biography typifies the life experience of many California Indians born in the late 1800s. She was fortunate to enjoy, for a few short years of her early life, a relatively traditional northern Maidu childhood, surrounded by the love and teachings of her family. Her grandfather, whom she remembered with great fondness, was known as "Big Meadow Bill" and held a position of leadership among his people. With no need for an official certificate to establish her precise date of entry into the world, her birth was recalled by reference to the subsistence activity of the season. So in later years, when census takers, enrolling agents, and schoolmasters needed a month and date to satisfy the inflexible standards of governmental bureaucracy, September 30th was supplied to them—the closest translation for "apple-picking time." But her life was shaped by the encroaching white world well before this invention of a precise birth date. Potts's father, a white man and prospector whom she apparently never knew, had raped and then abandoned her mother, in the fashion so typical of the countless gold miners who wreaked havoc throughout California Indian territory.[29] These circumstances of birth made sure that the dehumanizing label of "half-breed" would follow her into every sphere of life the federal government could possibly penetrate—and the Bureau of Indian Affairs (BIA) reached well beyond the limits imaginable to the non-Indian world. Originally housed within the Department of War, one of the BIA's many charges was to oversee the Indian boarding schools that the government designed to strip from Indian children all traces of their tribal identity. But in carrying out their mandate, these schools also served as critical venues for the formation of pan-Indian consciousness and political activism.[30] The *Smoke Signal* would come to reflect much of that mixed legacy; two generations of boarding school experience were indelibly imprinted upon its pages.

At the tender age of five, Marie Potts was taken to the Greenville Indian School, where her sister Lizette and her brother John were already enrolled. The older children had been assigned the last name of "Mason" when they entered the school several years before, so Marie was enrolled under that name as well.[31] More than fifty years later, when she talked to schoolchildren and adults about traditional Maidu culture, Potts always began her lecture by recalling that first day at the Greenville School. Unable to speak English, she stood in confused silence as the matron stripped her of her clothing. Nearby, steam rose ominously from hot water being drawn into a large tub like those used to cook acorn mush back home. Assuming she was about to meet a similar fate, she ran for her life, naked and terrified, until an older cousin, also a student at the school, managed to overtake her, miles away, on a borrowed bicycle.[32] Wrapping his shirt about her, he hauled her back to the institution that would become her home for more than a decade.

So successful was the assimilationist machinery of the Indian school system and the disenfranchisement of native California peoples from their lands, that in the late summer of 1912, at age seventeen, Marie Potts readily complied with the Greenville School superintendent's suggestion that she continue her education in Pennsylvania, at the Carlisle Indian Industrial School. To her dying day she insisted it was her true and independent desire to do so. And, in fact, she had few options open: Big Meadows, her ancestral homeland and birthright, was now submerged under Lake Almanor, a reservoir built two years before to generate electricity for the city of San Francisco.[33] Although she had already been granted admission to Carlisle, on August 28, 1912, its superintendent wrote to the Greenville School authorities, informing them that funding for students to come that year from points as far west as California could not be justified under that year's transportation budget.[34] Clearly determined to go, nonetheless, Marie paid for her own train fare out of funds earned by working in the nearby town of Susanville.[35] There, she had waited tables over the summer at a restaurant bearing a sign that read "No dogs or Indians."

On September 5, 1912, the Greenville superintendent wrote to his counterpart at the Carlisle Indian Industrial School to inform him that his newest student would be arriving by train within two weeks. She was traveling in the company of Miss Selena Twoguns, a Carlisle alumna who wished to go back East. "You will find Marie a bright girl," he wrote, "and I trust you will let her take up the things she is best fitted for."[36] Much of what Marie Mason Potts turned out to be "fitted for," at least in the final decades of her life, involved reasserting the Maidu and northern California Indian cultural identity that the Indian boarding school system had worked so hard to erode.

When Potts took over as editor of the *Smoke Signal*, she was fifty-three years old. The years intervening between her Carlisle education and her move to Sacramento in 1942 had been spent in relatively conventional pursuits. After graduating in the spring of 1915, she moved back to Plumas County, where on December 30th she married former Greenville schoolmate Hensley Potts, a Maidu from a neighboring tribal group.[37] At the time, he was employed at Engel's Mine, earning a respectable $3 per day.[38] Later on, he worked as a cowboy for ranchers in the area. The couple made their home in towns that dotted the landscape of their aboriginal territory—places like Taylorsville, Quincy, and Susanville. For many years, they operated a hunting and fishing camp at Chester, on the northwestern shores of Lake Almanor. Over the course of their marriage, Marie Potts gave birth to seven children: two boys who died in infancy, and five daughters, all of whom survived to adulthood. In 1947, when she joined the Federated Indians of California, there was little in the thirty years of her life just past to hint at the highly public future the next three decades would bring. But at seventeen, when she paid her own way out to Pennsylvania, Marie Mason must have shown every sign of resourcefulness her position with the FIC would require: a keen sense of humor, the ability to speak and write her mind, a love of travel and adventure, a talent for seeking out the truth, and a personality that thrived on creativity and social contact.

In 1942 Marie Potts departed Lassen County and moved in with her daughter Pansy, who had become seriously ill that year.[39] Their home at 2727 Santa Clara Way, just a few blocks west of the California State Fairgrounds, was tucked away on a quiet street in the popular Sacramento neighborhood of Oak Park. In November of 1947, it became headquarters of the Federated Indians of California, when Pansy, who served as an assistant secretary to Bertha Stewart, offered six months' free rent for a small office in the back of the house.[40] The group's decision to accept the offer was likely an easy one. From a purely geographical standpoint, Sacramento was centrally situated within the state. Even more important was its proximity to the capitol and legislature—two political resources the FIC had already learned to tap.

For thirty years, their modest bungalow served as "grand central station" for the Federated Indians of California. The *Smoke Signal* nearly always carried news of various members' comings and goings. Many of these visitors to the FIC office were already relatives, friends, and neighbors, but just as frequently, Marie Potts and Pansy Marine welcomed virtual strangers through their door. But these out-of-town FIC members did not remain strangers for long. They were usually put to work on the *Smoke Signal*, which, though it was published irregularly (typically following a monthly or bi-monthly schedule), still required a tremendous commitment of time and energy. Virtually every issue contained comments such as this from the March 26, 1949 paper: "A recent visitor at the F.I.C. office was Charles Bowen, of Crescent City, who got a taste of some of the work done here. We wish to thank him for the help he gave in rushing the *Smoke Signal*." Managing the newspaper with an all-volunteer staff required keen organizational skills and the ability to delegate tasks. Marie Potts was evidently gifted with both.

The *Smoke Signal* was printed on a mimeograph machine to keep its costs low enough for the Federated Indians to publish and for its readers to afford. But this made the mechanics of production both primitive and labor-intensive: the final copy, once decided upon, had to be painstakingly retyped, line by line, onto the waxy, unforgiving mimeograph stencils from which the final copy was to be printed. Typing errors were annoyingly difficult to correct. Line illustrations—for the process did not permit photo-halftones—were likewise manually cut into the stencil with a pointed stylus. Getting these properly blocked in, either before or after the typist went to work, was a critical part of the layout process. The *Smoke Signal* featured a fairly simple two-column format, but a great deal of attention was clearly given to the placement of lead stories. The front page typically carried at least two such articles, with continuations carried onto other pages throughout the body of the paper. This practice made sure that those readers who finished nothing more than the cover articles would at least be superficially exposed to the rest of the *Smoke Signal*'s content; but it also made the preparation of the stencils more complicated, since the copy for many stories could not simply be typed on the stencils from beginning to end.

Once the stencils were complete, the newspaper was mimeographed onto both sides of 8 ½ by 14-inch sheets—first one side, then the other. These pages then had to be collated, stapled, folded in half, and then stapled again. One final step in this process remained:

delivering the *Smoke Signal* to its readers. Subscriber addresses were typically written or typed directly onto the newspaper in the late 1940s and early 1950s. A decade or so later, adhesive labels (typed in duplicate sets of three or four) made the job of addressing the paper a bit less tedious and time-consuming. The FIC eventually acquired a bulk-mail code, which they stamped directly onto the newspaper; but in the very early days, someone had to lick the stamps and affix them on every copy that went to the post office.[41]

Circulation fluctuated over the years, and hard numbers are difficult to estimate. Considering the membership had grown to just over 4,000 by February 1948, one month shy of the FIC's second anniversary, expenses associated with the newspaper must have seemed as overwhelming as the job of producing it. The first four issues of the *Smoke Signal* (January, February 8th, March 7th, and March 23rd of 1948, labeled "volumes" 1–4), were mailed out free to the entire membership. This practice was in keeping with the FIC's desire to distinguish itself from F. G. Collett's group, wherein mere membership required an outlay of cash. But by the second issue of the paper, its material costs (stencils, paper, ink, postage, typewriter rental, and repairs to the donated mimeograph machine) were taking such a serious toll on the coffers of the FIC that readers were polled about a possible subscription fee:

> Since the funds in the treasury of the Federated Indians of California Indians are not sufficient to sustain the expenses involved in both the sending of delegates to Washington and the publication of the *Smoke Signal*, we have been advised that in any event the delegates would be given preference in the disposition of funds. Many of our readers have suggested, in order to eliminate a constant drain of the treasury by cost of publication of the *Smoke Signal*, that a dollar donation be given for a year's subscription. . . . We are submitting this suggestion to our readers for your approval. Let us know what you think of this suggested method of relieving our desperate situation by filling in and returning the following form to the *Smoke Signal*, 2727 Santa Clara Way, Sacramento 17, California.

The following month, the editor was pleased to report that results of the survey demonstrated unanimous support for the idea, prompting the board to vote at their March 7th meeting in favor of a $1 subscription fee, effective April 1, 1948.[42] Membership in the FIC remained free and open to all California Indians, but whereas previously every single adult member automatically received a *Smoke Signal*, now groups of individuals, such as households and tribal organizations, might share a subscription to the paper. Their collective savings were passed along to the FIC, since the staff could reduce their own time and material costs as well, no longer being compelled to send out thousands of each run. During both the Korean and Vietnam Wars, circulation rose significantly, because the FIC sent the *Smoke Signal* free to overseas California Indian servicemen and women, as well as to returning veterans, whose names they obtained from their families (who responded to a request in the *Smoke Signal*) and from the Bureau of Indian Affairs. The Vietnam War not only increased the paper's circulation, it also ushered in a period of civil unrest and American Indian activism that led to the development of ethnic studies programs in colleges and universities around the country. By the late 1960s and early 1970s, the *Smoke Signal* could be found among the current periodicals at some of the foremost academic institutions in the nation—from the University of Chicago to the Smithsonian to the University of California, Berkeley.[13] The cost of a yearly subscription had risen by this time to $2.50, and then to $3.50, per year; but this still represented a bargain many legislators, professors, students, and California Indians could not afford to pass up.[14]

From its earliest days as a vehicle for disseminating news about the status of various California land claims, the *Smoke Signal* had been conceived as a full-fledged newspaper, rather than simply a newsletter for the Federated Indians. By the March 7, 1948, edition (vol. 3), it carried a masthead featuring the volume number, publisher's address, and the date of issue. The newspaper's title was not typed but embedded into a hand-rendered image that ran the full width of the front page. This illustration featured a stereotypical Plains Indian sending smoke signals across the valley to his unseen counterpart in the distant hills beyond. Standing with his back to the reader, he draws a blanket over the fire to form white, puffy letters of smoke that hover in three centered lines across the darkened sky: The *Smoke Signal* of the F.I.C. Scattered patches of grass in the foreground give way on the right-hand side to the hand-printed FIC motto: "In Unity there is Strength"—a reference to the FIC's late 1940s campaign to displace pan-tribal suits sponsored by Collett and Foster, so California Indians could sue (perhaps more successfully) as a single, self-governing entity. The paper retained this motto on its masthead long after California Indian land claims were settled and a new call for unity, this time on a national scale, gave the motto currency within the context of the civil rights movement and American Indian activism. Though redrawn over the years from the original stencils rendered by Kitty and Kesner Flores, the basic design of the masthead remained in place for the life of the paper. In a sense, the home-grown artwork made manifest the *Smoke Signal's* aspiration to be read and received as equal to any daily newspaper published by more conventional means. Of course, the principal means by which the *Smoke Signal* established itself as a legitimate California Indian newspaper was by cultivating an authentic sense of community and cultural belonging among its readership—one that was clearly grounded in their lived experience and common political condition.

The *Smoke Signal* offered its readers a broad spectrum of political news and commentary, calendars of regional and statewide social events, humor, notices of births and deaths, editorial columns, and the like. The nature and tone of the newspaper's content kept pace with changing times and evolving issues. A key news source in the late 1940s and early 1950s was the Bureau of Indian Affairs. In April 1948, Kitty Flores had notified the BIA in Washington of the *Smoke Signal*'s existence and mission:

> Dear Sirs: The Federated Indians of California publish a small monthly paper in which they endeavor to inform the California Indians on activities in Washington concerning the Indians. The *Smoke Signal* has enjoyed the cooperation of the Indian Agency at Sacramento, California, and also that of Mr. Walter V. Woehlke, Superintendent. Through this channel your circular letter dated April 13, 1948, was sent to the *Smoke Signal*. Since it is our policy to enlighten the Indians on such misleading information we intend to publish the contents of your letter in our coming issue. If it is possible we would appreciate any further information affecting Indians.[45]

Kitty had not only "enjoyed the cooperation" of the state BIA office; like many Indian boarding school graduates, she found steady employment with the Bureau, working in its per capita payment section until Lt. Flores was transferred to Camp Roberts in 1949. After this, the FIC offices at 2727 Santa Clara Way continued to receive and publish BIA bulletins, in whole or in part, for the edification of its readers. This turned out to be one of the paper's most valuable services.[46] Much of the paper's readership, particularly in the 1940s and 1950s when land claims issues were at the forefront of California Indian affairs, was comprised of precisely the kind of people Collett had always targeted as easy prey—remotely dwelling, impoverished, uneducated Indians who had no means of decent subsistence, no transportation into urban areas, and no access to local (much less long distance) telephone service. An early mailing list reveals that more than half the paper's subscribers received mail at locations that lacked street numbers or addresses; a personal name, followed by their camp or community name was all that was needed for postal delivery. For Native Californians such as these—from Requa to Tehachapi to Stewart's Point—the *Smoke Signal* was a voice, a forum, a beacon. For some, it was literally a lifeline. The following letter is typical. It was sent to Marie Potts from a man in Weldon, in southern California, in December 1950. It serves to illustrate the means by which the newspaper and its editor reached across the miles and cultural divide of countless California Indian bands and tribes to disseminate important information and to help disenfranchised individuals gain access to their legal entitlements. Foremost among these during the *Smoke Signal*'s first fifteen years of publication was the opportunity to participate in the official process by which they could gain compensation for their ancestral lands:

> Marie Potts, I am writing to you this please send me. Five application Roll. Blank please to me at Weldon P. O. Kern Co., Calif. These could not read The name are ___, ___, ___, and___ . . . Send the application to me. Or. You add to them Your truly, c/o ______ Camp. [*sic*][17]

Marie Potts was far more than an editor to correspondents such as these; she wrote to them personally, providing appropriate forms, instructions, and contacts. And she gave them two other things as well: simple human compassion and confidence that a fellow Native Californian, who understood and had access to the system, was on their side. These were both invaluable commodities, neither of which any Indian was likely to receive—at least in those days—by sending a letter directly to the BIA, whether it was written in broken or perfect English. Potts's daughter, Pansy, also provided *Smoke Signal* correspondents with much the same. Together, they helped to enroll countless California Indians who might otherwise have been excluded from sharing in per capita distribution of any awards that might result from the land claims being heard by the Indian Claims Commission. True, these awards were unjustly small when they came. But for people like this man, who lived in conditions most people would not consider suitable for their pets, a check of $150 was not only theirs to receive by rights of ancestral occupancy but might mean several months of food or enough firewood to last through the winter.

As editor of the *Smoke Signal*, Marie Potts received other kinds of correspondence as well. The following is excerpted from a letter of June 15, 1952, written by Francis T. Allen, Sr.:

> Dear Madame, This is to let you know that I have received 2 issues of the *Smoke Signal*, for which I am very grateful. I graduated from Sherman Inst. in Riverside, Cal in 1924. Am an Ex Combat Infantry man, saw action in Germany, was wounded in action April 30th 1945, just 8 days before the War ended, was discharged Honorably Sept 30, 1945. Was awarded the Purple Heart, the Combat Infantry-man's badge and 2 bronze stars, and the Good Conduct Ribbon. Am now sick with bad kidneys, am in the Deschon Veterans Hospital at Butler Penn. Am sending $2.00 to help the Organization; let me hear from you soon? Respectfully Yours.[48]

The letters of these two readers demonstrate the power of the print media to shape cultural knowledge and identity. While we have few clues as to the tribal origin or ancestral tongue of either man, we do know they came from different generations and had vastly different experiences of what it meant to live under these United States. One had minimal education and literacy skills; the other had attended a premier institution for Indian education and assimilation—a boarding school called the Sherman Institute.[49] One writer traveled to foreign nations to defend his country during World War II; the other experienced the alienation of no longer having a nation, a tribe, a band, to secure the borders of his own lost lands. The *Smoke Signal* served to foster and reify the diaspora to which they both belonged.[50] The paper cut across gender, class, and geographical lines to help disparate California Indian tribes and individuals to awaken to their common condition as a colonized people and to the potential political power that they represented as a pan-tribal collectivity. It also articulated and supported the values and beliefs they shared relative to mainstream society. This process first took root at the turn of the century, when philanthropists and reformers began to lobby the state and federal government on behalf of California's native population, and to promote opportunities for those native peoples to organize collectively. With passage of the Act of 1928, their common status as "California Indians" and "Indians of California" was formally declared in a statutory sense, but the cultural logic of their collective standing had yet to take a concrete form. The *Smoke Signal* helped to shape that cultural logic and to give self-expression to a "California Indian" identity that otherwise had no meaningful subjectivity outside a purely jurisdictional space and set of entitlements.

This process of ethnogenesis—of developing and institutionalizing a pan-California Indian identity and sense of collective cultural belonging—played itself out on the pages of the *Smoke Signal* not only in news reports of relevant bills in Congress or the state legislature but also in feature stories, social announcements, and news articles. For instance, in 1948 the *Smoke Signal* began publishing a serialized history of California Indians written by Fred Baker, the FIC's attorney, who had been in charge of enrollment under the Act of 1928 and had worked for the state Attorney General when that suit was being tried in the Court of Claims.[51] In plain, everyday language Baker's "History of the California Indians Claims" clarified and synthesized complex legal rulings and issues that are poorly understood to this day. His articles—written exclusively for the *Smoke Signal*—gave California Indians knowledge, and therefore power, to better direct their efforts and attorneys, and helped them to develop a sense of ownership with regard to their own historical past.

Although Fred Baker was a frequent contributor to the paper, other voices—Indian voices—were more regularly heard from the pages of the *Smoke Signal.* One of those voices was that of the FIC's president, William Fuller, whose prayer commemorating the organization's third birthday appears on the front page of volume 3:

> Oh Spirit, hear me, you who gives life to all the world! I stand before you, with heart heavy, for the burdens of my people have been great. I am but one of your many children and I come to take cover of your wisdom. Make me wise, that I may lead my people through the evils and hardships that may arise. Give me strength, oh Great Spirit, not to be superior to my brothers, but to ward off the evils, which face us today. Give of your protections, Great Spirit, from the powers of evil and lead us out of the dark into the light of betterment. I thank you for my people and may your blessings bring peace to all your children through the world.[52]

Fuller, like other prominent members of the statewide and regional chapters of the FIC, was also heard from within the context of board meeting minutes. From the beginning, the FIC had endeavored to keep its members fully engaged and informed. The minutes of their meetings were professionally recorded and included the names of all members in attendance, as well as their tribal or intertribal group affiliations. These were summarized and published in the *Smoke Signal*, for the benefit of the FIC membership and the California Indian population at large. These minutes of the FIC's meetings constitute an important historical record of the political sentiments, unique contributions, and resolute commitment demonstrated by the organization's most active members over the course of several decades.

Part of the *Smoke Signal*'s success in developing postcolonial and pan-California Indian consciousness relates to the fact that it also addressed more than merely the political dimensions of that emerging community. From the very first, it announced social and educational events, whether sponsored by the FIC (or one of its regional chapters) or by other Indian organizations. One such entity was the first "All Indian" VFW Post, which formed around the same time as the FIC, in Bryte, California (now West Sacramento). Their dance socials and patriotic parade float entries were regularly featured in the *Smoke Signal*. An ongoing need for funds to send delegates to Washington sparked increased opportunities and motivation for Indians to gather socially. FIC fund-raisers helped to cement community in rural areas and on reservations, but they were immeasurably important as community-builders in urban areas, where assimilated Indians of diverse backgrounds now had a collective cause and purpose in coming together on a regular basis. These occasions clearly facilitated a revitalization of ancestral culture, in terms of both social values and expressive arts. As people sought to share their ancestral traditions cross-culturally within the urban Indian community, they often rebuilt interest and bases of knowledge for their own kin groups. As these events proliferated in both cities and small communities across the central and northern parts of state, where the FIC drew its greatest membership, an image of shared California Indian culture began to unfold on the pages of the *Smoke Signal*. Potluck suppers featured traditional delicacies like smoked salmon and acorn biscuits, while State Fair exhibits—which Marie Potts organized, advertised, and reported in the *Smoke Signal*—showcased baby baskets, ceremonial regalia, and other cultural artifacts. These award-winning educational displays also featured performances by California Indian dancers and basket weavers. In response to growing cultural pride and steady public demand, Potts actively recruited participants to these activities, helping to develop an interest in the preservation and revitalization of cultural forms nearly lost to a younger generation. Between the announcement of these popular activities in one issue of the paper and their actual coverage in another, Indians and non-Indians alike soon came to recognize and celebrate the common themes, practices, and materials that animated and eventually came to symbolize or typify "California Indian" culture. These were not "subsistence activities" or "rituals" documented by historians and ethnographers in the pages of an academic text; these were everyday practices and communal celebrations of cultural traditions and identities interpreted and reinvented by contemporary Native Californians. They took place on reservations, in rural towns, and in urban centers; they were translated into news stories by the actual participants themselves, not for the mainstream press but for publication in a newspaper created and controlled by California Indians. When the *Smoke Signal* offered "a bowl of acorn soup to Mr. Lloyd Joseph, who is convalescing in the Mare Island Naval Hospital," its readers could smile and feel a small tug of cultural pride at this play on the proverbial remedy of homemade chicken soup.[53]

Readers could also rally around the sarcasm and humor that were ever-present in this California Indian paper. The ignorance of white people and their stereotypic notions provided a natural foil and abundant material for some of the *Smoke Signal*'s more hard-hitting social commentary. A character named "Injun Louie" made a regular appearance in both cartoon and editorial form. Wearing only a loincloth and a couple of scraggly feathers in his headband, he typically hung out in teepees—a decidedly non-California Indian mode of housing. Appearing most often in single-frame cartoons where he was occupied with such activities as dreaming about the housing improvements he could make if only his land claims payment would come through, or angrily holding forth an unsigned treaty to a befuddled Uncle Sam, Injun Louie's alter-ego(s) wrote impassioned political commentary in perfectly broken English.[54] The following excerpt, from a November 1949 column titled "Injun Louie No Unnerstan," expresses the FIC's frustration with the failure of either the BIA or FBI to sanction claims case lawyers whom they felt were engaged in fraudulent and unethical practices:

> Injun Louie hear big talk bout free Country. Too free for bad mans. Injun Louie no like. Big Law-bosses do bad things, discriminate against Injun Louie. Injun Louie say bad business to Law-bosses. Law-bosses say, "no can punish Law-boss" Him my brother Why for we have law when Law-bosses uphold bad Law-bosses? . . . Injun Louie no can unnerstan. When Injun Louie have bad brother, Injun Louie help punish bad brother. When White Law boss have bad brother, White Law-boss uphold his bad law-boss brother. . . . Injun Louie have one law for bad brother and bad mans. Take bad brother hunting, Bad brother no come back. . . . Injun Louie jus don unnerstan.[55]

Injun Louie was a brilliant creation. He took the white stereotype of the Indian—half-dressed, half-witted, and illiterate—and transformed him into a biting caricature of the dominant society. Originally drawn by Kitty and Kesner Flores, who signed their work as "2KS," Injun Louie's winking visage also graced the postcards by which the FIC notified subscribers that it was time to renew: "Me always say-um 'Truth never hurtum nobody.' If us 'war-whoops' want-um truth on Injun facts, jus' readum THE SMOKE SIGNAL. . . . Reck-uh-member this all writ by California Injuns for-um Injuns . . . [signed] Injun Louie." Readers related to the multifaceted Injun Louie, who received more than a few letters addressed to him at 2727 Santa Clara Way.

It may seem a stretch to reconcile the comical figure of Injun Louie with the smoke-signaling Indian that graced the masthead of the newspaper, but the two figures embodied different translations of a singular symbol. The Plains Indian stereotype became institutionalized during this period in several powerful venues. The mass media, and particularly the movie industry, exercised unprecedented hegemony with regard to the production and popular consumption of American Indian imagery. Ironically, another important site for the institutionalization of such stereotypical imagery was the Indian boarding school scene. Here, students came to identify with Hollywood's Plains Indian imagery as an embodiment of the strength they found in collective identity. School authorities systematically oppressed individual cultural and linguistic affiliation to such an extent that they fostered a new tier of Indian kinship. With its wholesale approach to "Americanizing" Indians, the very same assimilationist machinery designed to launder tribal identity actively promoted the development of a pan-tribal identity and postcolonial consciousness. Two editors and generations of *Smoke Signal* management had been shaped by these molten forces: Pansy Marine, as well as Kitty and Kesner Flores, had attended Sherman Institute, while Marie Potts had graduated from the Carlisle Indian Industrial School a generation before. For them, the figure of the Plains Indian could embody both the insultingly indiscriminate "Indian" stereotype of Hollywood and the political power of American Indian pan-tribalism. It was ironic, and paradoxical, but nonetheless true. There was no contradiction inherent in their use of this multivalent symbol—they knew how to work its every angle, whether to evoke the levity that comes from a bit of self-parody, to rally California Indians to collective action, or simply to poke fun at mainstream society's gloss on the complexities of American Indian culture and identity. Injun Louie was endowed with incredible talent for working this latter front.

Potts also liked to scatter Indian-related jokes throughout the paper.[56] She maintained a now tattered manila file labeled simply "Humor" in which she stored items clipped from mainstream publications like *Reader's Digest.* The pages of the *Smoke Signal* are liberally peppered with these. "An Indian was being interviewed for a position. Among the questions asked was 'Do you know a foreign language?' His reply was, 'Yes. English.'"[57] Such snippets provided levity and filled small, otherwise unusable space in the newspaper. Sometimes the "joke" was embedded in a news report. These two examples date from 1950:

> It has finally been revealed through the Smithsonian Institute that scalping was taught to the Indians by the white man. (Uncle Sam's skeleton in the closet.) What a shattering blow to the western movie fans! What a blow to the teachers who have been teaching American history. What's more, what a blow to our egos, who have earned fame through this misrepresentation.

> A tourist was being packed out on a hunting trip in Shasta County by an Indian guide. It seems that after a day's trip the tourist who had two rifles with him complained about his pack being too heavy and asked the Indian guide what he could do about it. The Indian told him to leave one of his rifles in the hollow of the tree and they would pick it up on their return. The tourist, rather hesitant, asked if it would be safe in the tree as the rifle was quite valuable. "Why, sure it will be safe," replied the Indian, "There hasn't been a white man in these mountains for years.[58]

Witty jokes, cartoons, and editorials, whether penned tongue-in-cheek by Injun Louie, or in standard journalistic prose, contributed as much toward the building of California Indian political solidarity and cultural identity as the *Smoke Signal*'s more serious copy. Humor helped to galvanize the readership's growing sense of pan-tribal cultural belonging and distinction.

In 1961, Marie Potts's work on the *Smoke Signal* caught the attention of Helen Peterson, editor of the National Congress of the American Indian (NCAI) *Bulletin*. In May of that year, Potts became the NCAI's first "editor-trainee." She spent the entire month at the NCAI headquarters in Washington, helping out with production of the *Bulletin* and honing her editorial skills. Potts had already been active with the NCAI for several years, but this position placed both her and the *Smoke Signal* in the national spotlight of Indian affairs. The May 1961 *Bulletin* features a large photograph of her holding Maidu and other California Indian basketry. It was accompanied by an introductory column authored by Peterson, "Marie Potts Guest Editor This Issue," and by a lengthy article written by Potts herself. The subject of this latter piece was the American Indian Chicago Conference (AICC), to be held at the University of Chicago that June.[59] Potts had been involved in this conference's planning for many months, and she was able to write with passion and personal experience about many of the subjects with which the conference would be concerned:

> The Indian people often regard their lands as their last hold upon the continent that once was all theirs! The Indians ceded vast tracts of land, often against their wishes in return for guarantees that they might live forever, unmolested, upon the remaining lands. . . . The Indians view of the land is different from that of the non-Indian. Indians feel a social relationship to the land while non-Indians regard the land in commercial terms. Indians are concerned about the development of their human and natural resources and cannot see why people must be dispossessed of their land or other natural resources to help them 'get on their feet.' . . . It is the base of their existence, of tribal organization and Indian identity.[60]

While Potts was absent in Washington and Chicago, *Smoke Signal* subscribers missed her presence sorely, and they wrote the FIC office to complain about not having received a newspaper since March. In a special, undated, one-page edition, she made her apologies and let readers know that she had not been idle, explaining her busy schedule over the course of the last few months. By the time she closed with "I hope you will accept my explanation for . . . why you haven't been seeing the *Smoke Signal* floating around," some of the Sacramento-based FIC members and readers likely felt a twinge of embarrassment that they had not taken up the slack in her absence.[61]

Over the course of the next decade, Potts's schedule became increasingly hectic as she began to focus on national Indian affairs. She became a western regional vice president for the NCAI and rarely missed an annual meeting. *Smoke Signal* readers were treated to comprehensive summaries of both the conferences and the attendant road trips, which Potts had quickly become expert at managing.[62] Back in 1962, just one year after her Washington internship, she had finally learned how to drive. By then she was sixty-seven years old and a great-grandmother several times over. In 1953, she and Bertha Stewart had practically hitchhiked to Washington as delegates for the FIC. But from here on out, she was the tireless and adventurous driver, taking others along for the ride. In the winter of 1969, when one of Pansy's sons became involved in the Indian occupation of Alcatraz, she drove herself and a Sacramento contingent of Federated Indians over to San Francisco in order to cover the event in the *Smoke Signal.* She printed the occupiers' "Proclamation to the Great White Father and All His People" on the front page of the December 1969 *Smoke Signal.* Inside, she recounted her boat ride out to the former island penitentiary and listed various supplies the Indians could use. Readers were encouraged to stop by the FIC office and sign one of the thousands of Alcatraz petitions that had been distributed around the nation: "Your signature may be the miracle," she wrote.[63]

In the coming months and years, the *Smoke Signal* carried news of other Indian activism, including occupation of the land that would soon become home to the tribally controlled college outside Davis, California, where Marie Potts's papers and the records of the FIC are now archived. The mainstream press in San Francisco, Los Angeles, Sacramento, and Davis also carried stories of D-Q University's hard-won founding, but they ran under racist headlines that talked about "Long Noses" on the "War-Path."[64] Such language was in banner print all over the nation in reference to Alcatraz, Wounded Knee, and the American

Indian Movement (AIM) in general. American Indian journalists took note.

In 1970, Charles Trimble (Oglala Sioux) invited a group of American Indian journalists to meet in Spokane, Washington, to discuss the formation of what would eventually become the American Indian Press Association (AIPA). In attendance at that first meeting were Carol Wright *(Native Nevadan)*, Mary Baca *(Jicarilla Chieftain)*, Gwen Owle *(Cherokee One Feather)* James Jefferson *(Southern Ute Drum)*, James LaPointe *(Rosebud Sioux Herald)*, Father Tom Connolly *(Northwest Indian Times)*, Rupert Costo *(The Indian Historian)*, and Marie Potts.[65] By the time a constitution and bylaws had been adopted more than a year later, some of these individuals had left the group (Rupert Costo, for instance) and others had joined (like Russell Means, of the *Cleveland Crier*). Together, these pioneering American Indian journalists cofounded the AIPA. Although their primary purpose was to change the way the media represented American Indians, secondary goals were established as well. One of these was to "improve the technical and editorial quality of newspapers and other periodicals directed at Indian readership."[66]

Marie Potts, the senior member of the group, was quick to achieve this for the *Smoke Signal* through her work with and among her younger, cofounding peers. In a letter to Rupert Costo, who had written from the *Indian Historian* office in San Francisco in early March 1971, Potts replied:

> I am sorry to hear that you are resigning from the Indian Press Association. I have known about your feeling about BIA and its connection with the organization. I am not happy about it either. My feeling is that the Federated Indians of California has always been free of the BIA. Our paper, the *Smoke Signal*, has also been a free and independent paper. We do print a lot of BIA news because it concerns Indian people, but as far as having any control over us, as long as I am the editor, I'll keep free of them. *I am in it for the news and that only. I am learning something from the other writers. I never had any training as a writer, so I'm learning little by little* [emphasis added].[67]

While Costo disapproved of the AIPA's decision to affiliate with the BIA in order to receive financial and operating support, he had great admiration for Marie Potts and, that very same month, named her as an Honored Indian Historian.[68] This tribute was quickly followed up with another by the AIPA itself, which recognized Potts's pathbreaking work by establishing and naming a journalism award for her. It was unveiled on November 16, 1972, at their first annual convention, in Denver. The *Rocky Mountain News* reported on both the meeting and "The Marie Potts Achievement Award," which went that year to Jerry Gambill, managing editor of *Akwesasne Notes*: "The award includes a $500.00 prize and is the AIPA equivalent of the Pulitzer Prize. Mrs. Marie Potts, the award's namesake is the seventy-seven-year-old editor of "*Smoke Signals*" [*sic*]. . . . She was instrumental in founding the AIPA."[69] In addition to prize monies, recipients received a framed award certificate featuring a portrait of Mrs. Potts.[70]

Potts's association with professionally trained journalists and editors is evident in the subtle transformation that took place in the *Smoke Signal* during the early 1970s. The AIPA provided its members with regular press releases and clipping services. Potts either ran these stories verbatim, with credit to the AIPA, or integrated them into her own copy. Around this time she also began to make use of her editorial authority to record information about traditional Maidu and other Indian cultures indigenous to the state. These ethnographic vignettes were usually a paragraph or two in length and appeared immediately beneath the masthead, in single-spaced type. Whether writing about the Maidu Bear Dance, basket weaving, acorn processing, or her grandfather Big Meadow Bill's protection of the mountains' natural resources, Potts opened for her readers a new window onto both herself and the changing times in which her generation of California Indians had lived:

> BASKETS WERE A NECESSITY for some Indian tribes a few years ago. Today, they are collector's items or museum pieces. Although there is a great demand for baskets, there are very few basket weavers today. The slump in basket weaving became apparent when the young people were carted off to boarding schools. Weaving was taught in the home as soon as children were able to handle the tools and unless you continue to work at it day after day the technique is soon lost. At the boarding schools students were taught other methods of earning a living that were less time consuming than basket weaving. We are trying to pick up the threads now but we find it very difficult to find materials with so much of the land occupied as private property, public parks, national forests and huge construction projects destroying so much of the materials. . . . A few weavers take orders and demand some down payment because

> so often the customer will not accept the item when it is finished. They yell "too much." The weaver only averages a few cents an hour for her work.[71]

In the early years of the paper, Marie Potts had rarely revealed her actual editorial presence—writing and production was accomplished by "the staff." By the early 1960s, she sometimes made oblique reference to herself through such as statements as "your editor attended a meeting of . . . ," but these glimpses were rarely offered in an authoritative context. Instead, she exercised her editorial power more anonymously, by personally controlling the paper's final copy or by writing unsigned political columns. In the mid-1960s, however, things slowly began to change. For instance, writing about Columbus Day, under the heading "Patriotism," she offered a rare bit of personal history and cultural critique to whites and Indians alike:

> On October 12, I displayed the American flag, not because I was overjoyed that Columbus discovered America, but because I am a patriotic citizen. Now that I am in my second childhood, I recall songs taught us by our beloved teachers in the Indian schools that I attended. How we used to sing with such gusto and enthusiasm, almost bursting our lungs. One of the songs in particular came to me as I was hanging the American flag. It went like this: "Columbus sailed across the sea, to find this land for you and me. . . . And many brave men since that time, have helped to make your home and mine. . . . We'll thank Columbus and the rest but love our Washington the best." *Since recalling this song I wondered if our teachers ever gave a thought to how inappropriate the words of the first verse were in relation to us* [emphasis added].[72]

Despite such insightful writing, her self-acknowledged editorial presence tended to be revealed in small, unassuming comments, as in her observation in December 1969: "The cool evenings, I love to sit by the fire and read from end to end all the Indian newspapers."[73]

By the final decade of her life, Marie Potts had grown confident of her official editorial role and capacity to offer a valuable and sought-after perspective. In the July/August 1972 paper, when California Indians were still waiting to receive their per capita payments from the Indian Claims Commission ruling and writing to her to find out why, she sympathized with complaints about the long wait but scolded those Indians who seemed to have forgotten why they were due these payments to begin with: "It would sound better if they would ask 'when will we get our ancestor's money?'"[74] And when the Bicentennial rolled around, Potts queried the lack of American Indian participation in the planning process and remarked upon the way this neglect paralleled their exclusion from U.S. history, when in fact, they were the first Americans.[75]

Potts had experienced, firsthand, a remarkable slice of that U.S. history, and it showed in the paper she produced. Even her years at the Carlisle Indian Industrial School (1912–15) were reflected in the *Smoke Signal.* They can be seen in the stylistic adaptations, literary conventions, and layouts she sometimes borrowed from the boarding school's weekly paper. Inspirational quotes, poetry, social banter, political propaganda, and cultural commentary filled the pages of the *Carlisle Arrow*. Marie Mason had figured, as either a newsmaker or a writer, into many of its issues, and into at least one edition of its monthly counterpart, *The Red Man.*[76] More than forty years later, the Carlisle figured into the *Smoke Signal*: in its own use of inspirational quotations; in its social columns where news of the FIC membership included the frequent mention of Carlisle alums; in a column titled "Poetically Speaking (with Apologies to the *Carlisle Arrow*)," wherein Potts borrows the scaffolding of an *Arrow* poem as the basis for her own appeal to readers to join the FIC; and in the November 1949 edition of the paper, where the entire last page of the *Smoke Signal* is devoted to "A Thanksgiving Soliloquy (with Apologies to Shakespeare)." Here, she reprinted all twenty-seven lines, just as they had originally been written to entertain and Americanize the school's young Indian readers. ("Is this the leg of turkey I see before me / The 'ball-bat' upward standing?" asked the first lines of the poem.) At the end, Potts took care to include both the author's name and her source:

> —O. H. Lipps.
> Superintendent
> Carlisle Indian School
> from the THANKSGIVING MENU
> Thursday, November 26, 1914.

She had saved it all those years.

The *Smoke Signal* was a pioneering publication in many ways. Its longevity, its wide distribution, and its singular success in bringing California

Indian culture and politics into sustained national focus rank among the most important of these. But in other ways, the *Smoke Signal* clearly drew upon historical precedents, like the Indian school press, which was a direct outgrowth of earlier missionizing and governmental publications designed to bolster the religious conversion and assimilation of American Indians. On- and off-reservation school presses flowered in the first two decades of the twentieth century, when schools like Hampton, Sherman, Chilocco, and Stewart followed the lead established by Carlisle. Having issued its first publication, *Eadle Keatah Toh*, in 1880, Carlisle was not only the pioneer but also the dominant Indian school press by the turn of the century.[77] Beyond the obvious role the *Red Man* and the *Arrow* played in providing a rough template for layout and some of the *Smoke Signal*'s content (particularly humor and coverage of social events), there were other ways in which the Carlisle Indian Industrial School would have left its imprint upon the young Marie Mason. The school's publications were first and foremost instruments to foster assimilationist ideology among current and former students, and to demonstrate the success of that agenda to white subscribers coast to coast. But they also provided students with practical work experience that could translate into jobs after graduation. In fact, one of the Carlisle's primary vocational training programs for boys turned on the operation and maintenance of the modern printing press. As early as 1885, with the inauguration of the *Indian Helper*, Carlisle's weekly newsletter boldly proclaimed what those who matriculated at the school soon came to learn firsthand: "Printed Every Friday, at the Indian Industrial School, Carlisle, Pa., by the Indian Printer Boys."[78] Potts's own ability to participate in the Carlisle's publishing activity was limited by virtue of her gender to the writing of occasional copy and to the act of reading itself. But the Carlisle milieu, the mass appeal of the Indian school paper as an exotic news and literary genre, and the hegemony of the Indian school press itself during the early decades of the twentieth century—all helped to define and direct the historical trajectory of the *Smoke Signal.*

The newspaper built upon another tradition as well—a tradition geographically closer to home and animated by the very same concern that drove creation of the *Smoke Signal*: California Indian land claims legislation.[79] As early as 1921, newspapers designed to convince Indian readers to join one or another land claims suit began to roll off the presses in the Golden State. In the earliest days, these papers were either edited and/or published by white men.[80] The first newspaper aimed at a pan-California Indian readership was the *California Indian Herald*, sponsored by the California Indian Board of Co-operation (1923–24).[81] George Wharton James edited the paper's first three issues.[82] After his death, Frederick G. Collett took over this responsibility. Collett had formed the Indian Board of Co-operation (IBC) in 1910. Twelve years later, he began publishing the *California Indian Herald* as a way to promote California Indian rights, to further his personal vision of how treaty reparations ought to be accomplished, and to defend his own organizational, fund-raising, and spending practices. For example, he sought to clarify the point that "until 1919, when auxiliaries were formed, Indians had not contributed financially" to the IBC's efforts on their behalf.[83] (Collett had clearly made up for lost time in that regard, because the very first issue reported a count of more than sixty-one auxiliaries representing eight thousand Indians who, between November 1922 and the close of January 1923, had contributed dues in an amount totaling $2,083.50.) Most of the *Herald*'s inaugural edition was devoted to defending Collett against his detractors, in part by offering to readers a full audit of monies and expenditures. Although the *California Indian Herald* also advanced understanding of various California Indian cultures by featuring scholarly and popular articles by well-known figures like John Collier and Gertrude Bonnin, the virtues of any given issue were usually undermined or overwhelmed by Collett's defense of himself and the IBC against their many critics and detractors.[84]

For more than a decade following the final edition of the *Herald*, there were no periodicals or serials dedicated to California Indians as a pan-tribal collectivity or potential readership. But in April 1935, the *California Indian News* debuted. Published out of Los Angeles by the Yanga Council of the California Indian Rights Association, Inc. (CIRA), this monthly periodical featured a permanent cover illustration drawn by Elmer Curlie, a Navajo student enrolled at Sherman Institute in nearby Riverside. Subscription rates began at $1 per year (or a dime an issue), and climbed by 1939 to $2 per year (or twenty-five cents an issue). Like the Federated Indians who would organize some ten years later, CIRA characterized itself as a progressive group, run by and for Indians. Like the *Herald* and, later, the *Smoke Signal*, the *California Indian News* was dominated by issues related to land claims and to Frederick G. Collett. The California Indians Jurisdictional Act had been law for more than seven years by the time CIRA formed and printed its first issue. The corporation's founders were unimpressed with the progress that had been made in that case and organized for the express purpose of reclaiming from Collett and other "white racketeers" a modicum of control over the Court of Claims suit.[85] An article of July 1936 by Tom Largo (CIRA president) offered readers a detailed reminder of "Why We Organized." Among the many charges Largo leveled against Collett was one that would become a chorus for the founding members of the FIC:

> Collett was getting, according to his own admissions, $425.00 a month all of this time, and we have reason to believe it was much more. He was also raising money from us for his attorneys, and working constantly to force them on us, without the right to fire them, so they could collect 3 percent of our award when they could do us no good.[86]

The California attorney general continued to handle the Court of Claims case to the very end, despite Collett's ceaseless efforts to amend the Act of 1928 to allow for the introduction of private attorneys into the suit.[87] But CIRA knew they were dealing with a complex and formidable foe, and they used the press as a weapon against him. The first edition of *California Indian News* was packed with headlines and articles calling Collett's credibility into question: "A Collett Trick Exposed," "Disbarment of Collett," "Our Attorney's Trip to Washington," and "Concerning our Per Capita Payments." In July 1936, volume 2(1), readers were offered similar fare: "Someone Tried to Sell Us Out" and "Another Collett Trick Exposed." Four years later, in April 1939, volume 5(1), headlines were more or less the same: "Collett's Latest Bogey Man." "Collett's Latest Scheme to Exploit Us-S-1402," "Here is the Collett in Collett's Bill," "Gardners Sue Collett for Borrowed Moneys," "Collett Loses Again," and "It Was Full of Tricky Statements" (a reference to Collett's most recent communiqué to the Board of Co-operation membership). This pattern of hammering Collett in the press, and thereby hoping to hit him hard in the pocketbook, continued for the life of the newsletter—leaving no doubt as to the number-one priority of *California Indian News*.

CIRA ceased publication of *California Indian News* in 1942, following eight years in print, but it stands as a milestone in many regards. Its polished appearance and professionally printed format was underwritten by extensive advertising. Interspersed among its attacks on Collett were occasional bits and pieces on the folklore of California and other Southwestern Indian cultures. News from CIRA regional councils, updates on legislation related to the Court of Claims case, and political endorsements for southern California judges and politicians running for state or national legislative seats were far more typical fare. Readers could also count on a regular slate of commentary written by CIRA's attorney, officers, and representatives in Washington, including letters from delegate Rupert Costo (Cahuilla), who would later publish *The Indian Historian* and *Wassaja*. His letters to *California Indian News* appeared as regular columns and included detailed reports of his extensive lobbying and investigative work.[88]

California Indian News also deserves historical mention because it represents the introduction of women into the California Indian press. The inside back cover of the April 1939 issue featured a photograph of three CIRA delegates who had testified that year before the Indian Affairs Committee: Julia Gardner (Paiute—whose husband Allan had edited the magazine during its first year), Tom Largo of Pasadena (who had remained "Sachem" or president from the beginning), and Stella Von Bulow (Luiseno from Pechanga). In addition to serving, since 1935, as both a delegate to Washington and as CIRA's secretary, from 1936 to 1942, Stella Von Bulow was editor of *California Indian News*. It seems likely that both she and the newsletter, itself, served as inspiration for the birth and editorship of the *Smoke Signal*. Kitty Flores, the *Smoke Signal*'s creator and inaugural editor, had been enrolled at Sherman during CIRA's heyday, making it hard to imagine any circumstances under which she would not have read or been exposed to *California Indian News*. As a California Indian woman editor and active presence in Washington, Von Bulow surely served as a mentor for countless Indian women across the nation. Marie Potts, Flores's mother, retained at least three issues of the periodical in the files of the Federated Indians of California. Whether these were carried home by her own daughters while they were enrolled at Sherman Institute, mailed to her independently at the time of publication, or passed along to her in later years, we will probably never know. But one thing seems clear: Von Bulow's seven years at the editorial helm of *California Indian News* would certainly have disabused Potts of any notions she might have held over from her Carlisle days that the press was strictly Indian men's work. And considering her determination to enroll at Carlisle in the first place, it is difficult to imagine with any real conviction that stereotypes of gender or ethnicity would have kept her from realizing her own goals or capabilities. Nonetheless, Stella Von Bulow modeled with great success the rare figure of both the female editor and the American Indian editor. The combined weight of each status in a single individual was remarkable in her time, and it enhanced the credibility with which the *Smoke Signal* and its two female editors would have been received and read, especially in the newspaper's earliest years.

Helen Peterson (Oglala Dakota) added to this credibility, and to Potts's professional knowledge and network of journalists and activists, when she generously invited Potts to Washington as the NCAI's first editor-trainee. Marie Potts carried on this tradition by bringing other women editors into the same pioneering fold over the span of not one but *two* generations, mentoring both actively and making them exemplars to women throughout the state and nation.[89]

In 1968, Kay Black (Seneca) became editor of the California Indian Education Association (CIEA) newsletter, the *Early American*. Black lived in Modesto, just a short drive down California's Central Valley from Sacramento, where Potts had already set a brilliant example of how to use the state legislature and the print media to bring public pressure to bear on behalf of the Indian community. Potts was an active member of CIEA, but, by far, her greatest contribution to the organization was her cultivation of a California Indian readership that was primed, by two decades of the *Smoke Signal*, to have another periodical dedicated to issues of direct importance to their community.[90]

Darlene Brown (Miwuk), who from 1972 to 1974, and again in 1977, edited the *Tribal Spokesman* (newsletter of the Intertribal Council of California), was another woman whom Potts took under her wing. Together they traveled to Denver for the 1972 AIPA conference. On January 26, 1973, Brown wrote Potts a thank-you letter on ICC letterhead and enclosed a scrapbook commemorating the occasion of the first Marie Potts Journalism Achievement Award. Included with photographs of Potts, Trimble, Costo, and other attendees at the conference were news clippings from various publications, including the December 1972 and January 1973 *Tribal Spokesman*, which featured Potts and the award presentation.[91] What a memorable experience this would have been for Brown, surrounded not only by the biggest names in the American Indian press but by countless American Indian women editors, many of whom Potts knew well, such as Jeanette Henry Costo (Cherokee) editor of the *Indian Historian* and *Wassaja*, as well as AIPA cofounders Mary Baca *(Jicarilla Chieftain)* and Carol Wright *(Native Nevadan)*. These were heady times for American Indians, for Indian women, and for Marie Potts herself. She bridged the assimilationist era of the boarding school press and the civil rights activism of American Indian nationalism. Although born at the close of the nineteenth century, at age seventy-seven she personified the feminist ideals and ethnic pride of the 1970s. Enculturated in an oral tradition, she used literacy to inspire and empower those whose traditional world had been brutally ripped from beneath them. Schooled to excel in "domestic arts" like lace making, laundry, and cooking, at age fifty-three she had crossed into the masculine world of print. For thirty years thereafter she continued to map new territory for the Indian newspapers and women editors who have followed in her stead.

The final edition of the *Smoke Signal* was published in January 1978. Potts had suffered a stroke several years before and never fully recovered. Her friends, neighbors, nephews, and grandchildren helped her to carry on production of the paper; the final years of the *Smoke Signal* were clearly made possible because of them.[92] When she passed away on June 24, the *Smoke Signal* died with her. But the legacy of the newspaper and its editor endures. In the early 1970s, Marie Potts self-published a small book with photographs and sketches.[93] Her *Brief History of California Indians* was dedicated to her three daughters, Josephine, Kitty Marie, and Pansy, "who have taken the 'Never to look back' journey."[94] Her authorship is revealed only by the penname "Inyahnom Kulam," which translates as "Indian Woman" in Maidu.[95] She adapted portions of this early (undated) text for use in her 1977 book, *The Northern Maidu*, published by Naturegraph Press. Today, *The Northern Maidu* is widely used by elementary school teachers all over California to help children learn about the changes imposed on California's indigenous populations with the coming of white people to their ancestral lands. Many California Indian men and women personally lived (and died) these changes. Few wrote books or newspaper editorials about them. Remarkably, Marie Potts was clearly able and compelled to do both.[96]

The state of California honored Mrs. Potts on May 16, 1975. The ceremony was officiated by Mario Obledo, Governor Jerry Brown's Secretary of Health and Welfare, who dedicated to her the second floor of State Office Building No. 1, as well as the land upon which the building sits. A portrait of Marie Potts hangs in the second floor gallery as a permanent tribute to her and the work she accomplished on behalf of the state's indigenous people.[97]

Just months before she died in March 1978, the California State Indian Museum named Marie Potts as its first "Honored Elder." On this very ground, some thirty years before, three generations of Potts family members had gathered with other Federated Indians to make their land claims case against the federal government known to the people of California. The *Smoke Signal*, as well as mainstream newspapers from across the state, had then carried stories of Governor Warren smoking the proffered peace pipe in public support for their case. When the Indian Claims Commission finally handed down its judgment in 1964, the paltry price of forty-seven cents an acre marked a sad and bitter close to their case. But the FIC and the *Smoke Signal* continued to fight for California Indian rights and recognition, with Marie Potts at its helm until the very end.

When she died in 1978, her life had come nearly full circle. Potts was in the Janesville area of Lassen County to attend the Maidu spring ceremony of annual renewal, or Bear Dance, which she and her friend Gladys Mankins had helped to revive. When she became ill, she was taken to the hospital in nearby Susanville, and it was here that she passed away. This was the very same town where she had spent the summer of 1912, waiting tables at a restaurant where dogs and Indians were prohibited. The fruits of that labor would carry her out to Pennsylvania and the Carlisle—where boys printed newspapers and girls learned to mend and stitch. Ironically, it was the experience of this assimilationist cauldron and pan-Indian milieu that would help her, years later, to assume a position of leadership with the Federated Indians of California, to foster California Indian culture and political activism among the state's diverse indigenous peoples, and to reclaim and write about her own Maidu identity. For more than a quarter-century, Marie Mason Potts had made news. As editor of the *Smoke Signal*, she charted the course of California's first Indian-owned and operated newspaper. But more than that, by her long life and hard work she also helped to define, embody, and institutionalize an enduring national presence for California Indian culture and politics.[98]

Notes

This paper is based upon archival research and interviews with several of Mrs. Potts's descendants, friends, and associates. I owe a special debt of thanks to Richenda Wilkinson, D-QU librarian, who has become a valued friend and colleague. Several of Mrs. Potts's grandchildren, including Marvin Lee Marine, Judy Marine, SusieBear, and Joe Marine (all children of Pansy) have generously shared memories and stories of "Nana." Special thanks go to Peggy Fontenot (daughter of Jean Potts O'Taylor), who has not only enriched my sense of her grandmother, but introduced me, as well, to the tradition of California Indian Big Times. I am also indebted to Barbara Landis, Cumberland County Historical Society (repository for many of the Carlisle's archival records); Kathleen O'Connor, NARA—Pacific Regional Branch; Charles Trimble, John G. Neihardt Foundation; Craig Bates, Curator of Ethnography, Yosemite National Park Museum; Linda Johnson, California State Archives; Tanis Thorne, UC Irvine; Jerry Johnson and Gerald Heine, CSU Sacramento; and the late Francis (Fritz) Riddell.

1. The American Indian Press Association was a short-lived, but important organization of American Indian journalists, organized by Charles Trimble. Trimble recalled Potts with great fondness: "She was a wonderful woman, and a favorite of all those in attendance at that original meeting [1970], and in subsequent meetings. Helen [Peterson] told me that Marie hitchhiked to DC to help her at the National Congress of the American Indians. I don't know if she actually hitchhiked or just caught a ride with friends, but it was a great story. Marie was just loved by all." (Personal correspondence, August 23, 2000.)

2. Russian colonization of the Pacific Northwest included territory now encompassed by northern California.

3. These family legacies reveal the complex layering of culture that shapes much contemporary California Indian identity: an intergenerational family tradition of leadership, artistry, or activism, set within a larger context of tribal ties to one or more of the many autochthonous groups whose ancestral lands comprise California, contained within the still larger context of the inclusive ethnic grouping now commonly referred to as "California Indian." For an introduction to the earliest forms of pan-tribalism in California, see Edward D Castillo, "Twentieth-Century Secular Movements," in *Handbook of North American Indians, vol. 8: California,* ed. Robert Heizer, 713–17 (Washington, D.C.: Smithsonian Institution, 1978).

4. It also would have effectively removed them from the everyday conflict and violence resulting from contact with settlers and gold miners.

5. Rancherias were scattered, small "reservations" of one or more acres of very poor land, which might accommodate housing for landless

Indians, but rarely enabled traditional subsistence. These were purchased after 1880 from public land sales. The Dawes Severalty Act of 1887, an important (and devastating) piece of Federal legislation called for the dismantling of large communal land holdings through establishment of an allotment system. Under this plan every head of household received a 160-acre portion of their tribal holdings. After a period of time, these could be (and were) sold in fee simple. For more information on this legislation, see: Edward Castillo, "The Impact of Euro-American Exploration and Settlement" in Heizer, *Handbook of North American Indians, Vol. 8: California*, 99–127.

6. Seven executive order "military reservations" were established between 1853 and 1887. Indians were rounded up and driven onto these reserves, which had been created to both "care" for the Indians and clear them off of lands that settlers wanted. The story of the establishment and forced peopling of these reservations is the story of California Indian genocide, resistance, and survival. See Heizer, "Treaties," in *Handbook of North American Indians, Vol. 8: California*, 701–4.

7. This per capita figure would be reduced even further, as the rolls were reopened for revision, resulting in a count of 36,095 officially set in June of 1955. See Omer C. Stewart, "Litigation and Its Effects," in Heizer, *Handbook of North American Indians, Vol. 8: California*, 705–12.

8. Notice announcing the meeting had been sent to various Indian groups throughout the state. Don Allen and John Evans, both members of the California State Assembly were present to discuss bills and hear grievances (FIC Administrative Records, Marie Potts Collection, D-QU Archives).

9. Enacted into law in August of 1946, the Indian Claims Commission Act established a specialized judicial venue and process to handle Indian Claims cases, thereby relieving the Court of Claims, which was backlogged with lawsuits from tribes across the country.

10. The *California Indian Herald*, newspaper of the California Indian Board of Co-operation was begun as a way to deflect the accusations of Collett's many detractors, who ran the gamut from the Indian Office and its field agents to independent philanthropic groups, such as the Indian Rights Association. Volume 1, no. 1 of the *Herald* (January 1923), included a complete accounting of funds prepared by an outside auditor, as well as an explanation of how the Indian Auxiliaries related to the IBC. Dues collected from these auxiliaries (introduced in 1922 as a way to increase funds and perhaps demonstrate Indian involvement in an entity otherwise governed by white people) were a major source of contention among both Indians and whites by the mid-1930s. Nonetheless, the IBC, which included in its governing structure many influential politicians and social reformers, was among a handful of groups, including the Indian Rights Association (see vol. 1[4]:16 of the *California Indian Herald*) who brought unrelenting pressure to bear on Congress such that after a long

string of failed legislative efforts, the Act of 1928 finally won California Indians the right to sue for broken treaty promises. For further information about the *California Indian Herald,* see Daniel F. Littlefield, Jr. and James W. Parins, *American Indian and Alaska Native Newspapers and Periodicals, 1826–1924* (Westport, CN: Greenwood Press, 1984), 47–50.

11. See April 1935, vol. 1(1), of *California Indian News,* published by the Yanga Council of the Indian Rights Association (CIRA) of Los Angeles.

12. T. Castaneda, "Photodocumentation as Ethnographic Portraiture: Interpreting Winnifred Codman's Field Report on Aging Indians in New Deal California," paper presented at the California Indian Conference, Chaffey College, Rancho Cucamonga, October 2000.

13. This name was suggested by Stephen Knight (Pomo) of Ukiah (FIC Administrative Records, Marie Potts Collection, D-QU Archives).

14. The Jurisdictional Act of 1928, in both its language and its outcome, created lasting precedents and problems. First, it recognized and formally named a set of culturally disparate and diverse aboriginal groups as constituting a single legal class: "Indians of California." Second, it created a virtual cottage industry among lawyers who sought to benefit from the Indians' legal troubles and the ambiguity surrounding the U.S. government's failure to establish a formal legal relationship with them when California joined the Union in 1850.

15. For instance, in January 1947, the FIC held a meeting in the Sacramento Convention Center to which they had invited all interested Indians. Between 250 and 300 individuals attended. On February 1, 1947, Stewart mailed out a three-page, legal-sized, document titled "Report and Comments on the Sacramento Meeting and Events Following". She also regularly wrote letters to various Indian groups and representatives under cover of the FIC, explaining legislation or other political developments of interest to them (FIC Administrative Records, Marie Potts Collection, D-QU Archives).

16. By March 1947, Kitty was assisting Bertha Stewart as recording secretary and in May, Pansy Marine was elected to the FIC's Executive Committee.

17. The ironic success of these events in garnering both Indian and white support for the FIC is discussed in T. Castaneda, "Making Their Presence Known," paper presented at the California Council for the Promotion of History, Annual Meeting, Lake Tahoe, September 2000.

18. Flores to FIC members (Jan. 29, 1948). FIC Admin. Records, Marie Potts Collection, D-QU Archives.

19. By this time, not only Collett's group but the "California Indians, Inc.," an organization established by Bay Area attorney Reginald Foster, had also entered the Claims arena and the FIC needed Warren's support, more than ever, for their plan to unify all California Indians under their own suit.

20. *Smoke Signal* (hereafter *SS*), vol. 2, p. 4. Earl Warren, as former attorney general of California, knew the Indians' case all too well, since he was one of a series of attorneys general, who had tried the Indian suit before the Court of Claims. The federal government and the state of California had both opposed the presence of independent attorneys working on contingency (and therefore on the promise of sharing some of the resultant award) on behalf of the first claims case. The jury is still out on whether or not independent attorneys might have been more motivated, capable, and efficient in winning the 1928 case. On the one hand, many Indians did not want to see the award reduced by attorney fees. On the other hand, one has to recognize that private attorneys would have had some advantage over the succession of attorneys general whose attention was divided among other state matters and who likely passed much of the work off to less experienced assistant attorneys general. As soon as the judgment was handed down in favor of the Indians, Collett and the attorneys with whom he had collaborated in Washington submitted a bill to have a million dollars worth of the judgment fund (one-fifth of the total award!) split among those attorneys who had worked to get passage of the Act of 1928. Clearly, the state and the Indians who opposed private attorneys had their own well-reasoned positions.

21. Warren's support for the FIC was important, because even before the Indian Claims Commission became law, several entities with pan-tribal membership (but in contradistinction to the FIC—run by white leadership and private attorneys) began mobilizing, like the FIC, to file suit as that ambiguous and arbitrary collectivity already recognized by the federal government (based upon the Act of 1928) as "California Indians."

22. The paper seems an obvious outgrowth of the Publicity Agent's position. Article 6, Section 5, of the FIC's Constitution and Bylaws, adopted January 12, 1948, states: "It shall be the duty of the publicity agent to furnish all newspapers and radios and other news distributing agencies with reports of all meetings and notices of meetings of said organization. It shall be the further duty of the publicity agent to otherwise publicize the activities of this organization in so far as may be possible" (Marie Potts Collection, D-QU Archives).

23. *SS*, vol. 2, p. 3.

24. These groups were run by Frederick G. Collett in the first instance (Indians of California, Inc.) and San Francisco Bay Area attorney Reginald G. Foster, in the second (California Indians, Inc.).

25. Frederic Baker was later able to trace the formation of Reginald Foster's group to a Nevada corporation and group of attorney investors who had indeed formed for the express purpose of capitalizing on California Indian Land Claims cases to be tried before the Indian Claims Commission. While the ethics of this corporation's genesis may have been questionable, Baker was never able to convince the FBI of the corporation's illegality or sufficiently

document what he viewed as fraudulent practices (Frederic Baker Päpers, Marie Potts Collection, D-QU Archives).

26. *SS*, vol. 1, no. 3 (January 1948).

27. "Summary of Meeting," *SS*, vol. 8, no. 9, p. 2

28. *SS*, vol. 10, no. 3 (March/April 1951), p. 1.

29. Potts discusses this in a *Sacramento Bee* article (Sunday, April 22, 1973) titled "Memories: Marie Potts Recalls White Man's Treatment of Indians." At the time of that interview, Potts was teaching basket weaving classes at CSU, Sacramento and offering a YWCA sewing class out of her home at 2727 Santa Clara Way, but she was hardly a retiring or domesticated voice at seventy-eight years old. Her condemnation of the settlers' efforts to "remove" Indians from their own lands was more impassioned than ever.

30. For an in depth discussion of Indian boarding schools, see David Wallace Adams, *Education for Extinction: American Indians and the Boarding School Experience, 1875–1928* (Lawrence, KS: University of Kansas Press, 1995).

31. Student Attendance Records, Greenville Indian School, Record Group 75, Coded Admin. Records, Boxes 118–119, NARA, Pacific Regional Branch.

32. Quoted from "Chen-Kut-Pam," a film produced about Mrs. Potts in 1970 for use in elementary schools. The title translates as "one-with-sharp-eyes"; Chen-kut-pam was her Maidu name.

33. Construction had begun in 1910, financed by a partnership that would later evolve into the Pacific Gas and Electric Company.

34. M. Friedman to W.S. Campbell, August 28, 1912, RG 75, Greenville Indian School, Coded Admin. Records, Box 70[1912], NARA, Pacific Regional Branch.

35. When asked many years later about the "outing system" at Carlisle, where students were taken by locals into their homes to live, Potts revealed what might well have been an underlying motivation for her own matriculation at Carlisle: "No, they just accepted the students from Carlisle. That was a big deal out there. Everybody wanted students from Carlisle. Carlisle was something worth, you know . . . you just mention Carlisle and you were in." (Transcription of Riddell and Bennyhoff Interview, May 17, 1972: 9. Francis A. Riddell Collection, California State Archives.)

36. W. S. Campbell to M. Friedman, September 5, 1912, RG 75, Greenville Indian School, Coded Admin. Records, Box 70 [1912], NARA, Pacific Regional Branch.

37. The Maidu are composed of three linguistic groupings: Mountain (or Northern) Maidu, Konkow or Western (also written Concow) Maidu, and Nisenan (or Southern) Maidu. Marie Potts referred to Hensley as Konkow during her own lifetime, but at the time this paper was being written, some of his descendants who are enrolled with the Strawberry Valley Band in Brownsville,

California, believed that he was, in fact, of Nisenan descent and like so many other Indians, simply misclassified by the BIA during the early part of the century. The area of California in which it appears he was born and raised, is on the cusp of both the Nisenan and Konkow languages. Mountain Maidu, Konkow, and Nisenan Maidu each contain many dialects.

38. *Carlisle Arrow*, January 21, 1916, p. 5.

39. Potts apparently took this opportunity to effect a separation from Hensley. Although they never reconciled, in years to come, when he was terminally ill, Potts allowed him to move into Pansy's home where she cared for him during his final days (Fritz Riddell, recorded interview with T. Castaneda, June 2000). Pansy recovered from her first bout of tuberculosis, only to have it claim her life nearly two decades later.

40. Rent was billed after the first six months at $6.00 per month. This increased only marginally over the next thirty years.

41. Marvin Lee Marine, one of Pansy's sons, told me that he still remembers how exciting it was to "graduate" from less skilled aspects of production—stapling, licking, and stamping postage—to writing address labels and the like. Preparing the paper for mailing occasioned a partylike atmosphere, with family and friends gathering to socialize while they worked. Potts's grandchildren and other young people who participated in these events would have also been enculturated into world of California Indian activism during this time as well as exposed to their elders' discussions of bygone times and traditions.

42. Had the entire FIC membership subscribed, many of the organization's financial problems might have been solved, including its ability to pay the expenses of their delegates—but considering the financial situation of many Indians in the state, the numbers were still impressive. The minutes of board meetings in 1948 reveal that members subscribed at the rate of 189 in March; 74 in April; 49 in May; and so forth. During the 1960s, the number of subscribers seems to have grown still larger to include state agencies associated with social welfare, public libraries, universities, and elementary schools ranging from the local to the national (MP Collection, D-QU Archives).

43. The circulation records for the *SS* include subscription requests and renewals as well as check stubs from these and many other institutions.

44. It is clear that the readership of the paper in its first decade of existence was primarily landless, rural and urban Indians for whom the claims cases were critical. But by the late 1960s and early 1970s, the paper had also become popular as a source of cultural information for sectors of the white population for whom Indian affairs in California were either a source of romantic appeal, scholarly interest, or social welfare and political concern.

45. KF to BIA (April 30, 1948), *SS* Admin. Records, MP Collection, D-QU Archives.

46. What is more important to know is how much the BIA connection may have domesticated the FIC. David Risling, Jr. (Yurok/Karuk; Hoopa Reservation), whose father was a prominent member of the Foster-led group, "The California Indians, Inc.," has reminded me upon a number of occasions, that the FIC "had the BIA." The clear implication was that this road ran both ways—as in the BIA "had" the FIC. My own research leads me to believe that there was in fact a great deal on both the positive and negative side that came out of these connections. But the fact remains that the *SS* retained editorial control and in the mid-1950s spoke out strongly against termination of rancherias, sale of public allotments, and against any BIA policy that they believed was not in the best interest of Indians. And the FIC, as well as Frederic Baker, was extremely disapproving of the way the BIA held a second vote among the Pit River Indians in order to obtain a majority "yes" vote in favor of accepting the land claims settlement. Frederic Baker wrote to Marie Potts that he had grave doubts as to the legality of the vote—this from a man who had worked for and within the inner circles of the BIA and the federal government for most of his career. He was the only attorney for Docket 31 or 37 who opposed the settlement. See *SS*, vol. 23, no. 1 (Jan/Feb/March 1964), p. 2.

47. *SS* Admin. Records, MP Collection, D-QU Archives. Personal names and the surname identifying the camp address were deleted for privacy.

48. Ibid.

49. Potts's own daughters, including Pansy Marine and Kitty Flores were educated at Indian boarding schools, including Stewart (in Carson City, Nevada) and Sherman Institute (in Riverside, California). The *Smoke Signal* often carried news of Sherman reunions in Sacramento and the surrounding regions.

50. A huge corpus of literature addresses the role of print (and other mass) media in creating and/or maintaining collective identity in the contexts of diaspora, nationalism, postcolonialism, and immigration. For instance, see Walter Benjamin's classic essay "The Work of Art in the Age of Mechanical Reproduction," in *Illuminations* (New York: Schocken Books) 1978: 221–52; Benedict Anderson's *Imagined Communities* (London: Verso/NLB) 1983; and the collected works in *Nation & Narration*, Homi Bhabha, ed. (New York: Routledge) 1990. *Print Culture in a Diverse America* (edited by Danky and Weigand, Chicago: University of Illinois Press, 1998) features a number of important essays which speak to this same set of cultural processes within the social and historical context of American minorities and associated serials. In particular, the works by Rudolph J. Vecoli, Violet Johnson, and Yumei Sun cast new light on the relationship between the immigrant press and the process of ethnogenesis.

51. His insider's knowledge and his own lifetime of working with and for the Indians in the state, earned him the trust and respect of many *Smoke*

Signal readers, who sometimes wrote to him for legal help. In his capacity as pro bono attorney for the FIC, he counseled these correspondents for free.

52. *SS*, vol. 3 (March 7, 1948), p. 1.

53. By August 1967, when David Risling, Jr. Chairman of the Ad Hoc Committee on Indian Education reported on a Modesto organizational meeting of what would later come to be called the California Indian Educational Association (CIEA), *Smoke Signal* readers were accustomed to having their palettes teased mercilessly: "The familiar flavors of the evening feast of turkey, baked salmon, acorn soup, seaweed, elk and venison stew, smoke trout and salmon, surf-fish, fried bread, wild tea and other American dishes brought back many fond memories of days gone by, and the relaxed, happy feeling of food fellowship was a fitting finale to a long, busy and stimulating day" *SS*, vol. 26, no. 5, (Aug. 1967), p. 2.

54. *SS*, vol. 8, no. 9 contains a cartoon entitled "Still Dreaming," which shows Injun Louie leaning against his teepee thinking about a new house and car, while Louie, Jr., napping inside, sees visions of toy airplanes and a new bike. Signed JP (for John Porter), this is the second cartoon of Injun Louie drawn and initialed by John Porter, who would later sign his artwork with "JHP." I suspect that John Porter and Marie Potts may have both shared the editorial voice behind Injun Louie, but the physical image was first introduced through the drawings of Kitty and Kesner Flores.

55. *SS*, vol. 8, no. 13 (Nov. 1949), p. 5.

56. Potts' love of laughter and wit is documented in the December 4, 1914 edition of the *Carlisle Arrow* in a story about a party hosted by Marie Mason in honor of her friend Blanche Jollie's birthday. "The first thing required of the guests was for each to give a hearty laugh" (vol. 11, no 14, p. 68).

57. *SS*, vol. 25, no. 1 (Nov/Dec 1965; Jan/Feb 1966), p.7.

58. *SS*, vol. 9, no. 4 (April 1950), pp. 5–8.

59. The AICC paid for Potts to travel to and attend a task force meeting in Reno in early April and to a steering committee meeting in Chicago in late April.

60. *NCAI Bulletin*, vol. 6, no. 1 (May 1961), p. 3

61. *SS*, n.d. (Summer 1961).

62. Potts had loved to travel since her boarding school days in Carlisle, Pennsylvania, when under the "outing system," she had lived for summers and other periods with families in the surrounding countryside. Vacations and trips with these "country parents" had taken her to Ocean City, NJ, Philadelphia, PA, Morristown, NJ, and other places along the Eastern Seaboard. Later, in life, she traveled with friends as their babysitter: "We went to Alabama, so I got to see that part of the country: Texas, New Orleans, and Alabama. And we came back through Nashville, Tennessee and Missouri and then back through Little Rock and saw that. And I have seen Carlsbad Caverns twice now. I've

climbed Mount Lassen five and six times. But I think we have just as much scenery right here in California. We don't have to go over to Europe to see the things. There is enough right here" (Transcription of Riddell and Bennyhoff Interview, May 17, 1972: 6–7. Francis A. Riddell Collection, California State Archives).

63. *SS*, vol. 28, no. 7 (Dec. 1969), pp. 1–2.

64. Enlarged reproductions of these news stories line the corridors of the college, a constant reminder of the institution's embattled past and the social milieu in which it was born.

65. Personal communication (Charles Trimble, Aug. 23, 2000).

66. Constitution and bylaws of the AIPA, MP Papers, MP Collection, D-QU Archives.

67. MP to RC, MP Papers, MP Collection, D-QU Archives.

68. The AIPA accepted this offer from the BIA because it had been denied nonprofit status as 501(c) 3 and was unable to collect from the already struggling American Indian press sufficient subscription dues or other funds to keep the organization afloat as an independent entity. This ultimately led to the AIPA's demise (personal communication, Charles Trimble, Aug. 23, 2000).

69. *Rocky Mountain News*, Friday, Nov. 17, 1972 (clipping from MP scrapbook owned by Marine family).

70. In 1974 the Marie Potts Award went to *Wassaja* . See *SS*, vol. 29, no. 6 (Dec. 1974:6).

71. *SS*, vol. 31, no. 4 (July/Aug. 1972), p. 1.

72. *SS*, vol. 25, no. 4 (Aug/Sept/Oct 1966), p. 2.

73. Potts was truly an avid reader. Anthropologists Francis Riddell (a friend of Potts' from her Susanville days, who also attended public grammar school with her daughter Pansy) and UCLA professor James Bennyhoff interviewed Potts in 1972, over a casual lunch in Riddell's home. She remarked that she used to stay up late trying to get through all the Indian newspapers to which she subscribed or with which the *Smoke Signal* had exchange agreements. In recent years, she had given up this practice: "My table at home is just littered with papers. Honest to Pete, I just—I just can't keep up with it . . . I just have so many Indian newspapers and I want to read them all, and I just can't get around to them all. I used to sit up until two o'clock at night, but I quit that. I read what I can and let the rest of it go." Revealing her political sensibility, she commented that she still read the press releases of Senators Cranston and Tunney in full.

74. *SS*, vol. 31, no. 4 (July/Aug. 1972), p. 1

75. *SS*, vol. 31 [*sic*], no. 6 (Aug./Sept. 1975), p. 1.

76. See the *Carlisle Arrow* for the years 1912–15 (especially vol. 11, no. 12, pp. 210 and 221, which features two full-length articles written by Potts). Volume 7 of *The Red Man* (May 1915) includes a photo of Potts (Marie Mason)

and the entire graduating class. Potts's marriage to Hensley was reported in the pages of the *Carlisle Arrow*, as well. (See page 5, Jan. 21, 1916, edition.)

77. For an excellent summary of this and related trends in the American Indian press, see the introduction offered in the invaluable guide by Daniel F. Littlefield, Jr. and James W. Parins, *American Indian and Alaska Native Newspapers and Periodicals, 1826–1924* (Westport, CN: Greenwood Press, 1984). Their second volume, *American Indian and Alaska Native Newspapers and Periodicals, 1925–1970* (Westport, CN: Greenwood Press, 1986) offers an introduction which includes a discussion of how the Indian school press was virtually unchanged in its paternalistic approach until well after World War II. Scholars of the American Indian press will also want to consult the edited volume by James P Danky and Maureen E. Hady, *Native American Periodicals and Newspapers 1828–1982: Bibliography, Publishing Record, and Holdings.* (Westport, CN: Greenwood Press, 1984).

78. See Littlefield, Jr. and Parins (1984, p. 181), as well as the website of Barbara Landis, archivist for Cumberland County Historical Society's Carlisle material: http://home.epix.net/~landis/main.html.

79. Today, casino gaming is in many ways fostering the same kinds of processes as did land claims, during the early twentieth century: the proliferation of native periodicals primarily themed on gaming issues (but also providing a platform for other cultural and political stories); a new period of cultural revitalization (as casino monies help to finance other tribal concerns like repatriation of cultural patrimony, language revitalization programs, and the creation of tribal museums); and the lobbying of many groups for federal recognition or re-recognition in part, to qualify for casino operations, but also as a means of rebuilding their cultural communities.

80. The Mission Indian Federation issued a paper as early as 1921; however, it did not last long in its earliest iteration and never aimed to have the statewide, pan-California Indian scope or objectives of later papers. See Littlefield and Parins (1984, 157–58).

81. Its inaugural subscription rate was seventy-five cents a year; however, this was raised to $1.25 in 1924, during the short-lived paper's final year of publication. The *California Indian Herald* proclaimed in vol. 1(4):15, that "35,000 copies" had been distributed as of December 1923.

82. For more information about James's editorial background and interests, see Littlefield and Parins (1984, 46).

83. See *California Indian Herald*, vol. 1(1): 11. It is important to note that while Indians had not previously contributed financially on a regular basis, even at this point of publication, the officers of the corporation were all white. Court hearings would later press home the point that the Indian auxiliaries and delegates—even after significant financial contributions—had no control over the corporation (through voting or any other mechanism).

84. For instance, informative articles by two noted California Indian ethnographers, T. T. Waterman and C. Hart Merriam, were published in the *Herald*. Of particular note with regard to the legislative effort building in Washington to allow Indians to sue in the Court of Claims, was Waterman's piece titled "Justice for the Indians of California," *California Indian Herald*, vol. 2(7).

85. William Fuller, former IBC delegate, prominent member of CIRA, and future president of the FIC, apparently favored the use of this term to characterize the attorneys and attorney-types (e.g. Collett and another man named Purl Willis) who swirled around the Indians with sympathetic outrage and bottomless collection plates during the first half of the twentieth century. See *California Indian News*, vol. 5(1):11.

86. See *California Indian News*, July 1935, p. 5.

87. Although CIRA disliked Collett from the first, they had initially backed the concept of private attorneys, in keeping with similar efforts by the Mission Indian Federation. Having the opportunity to have their case tried by attorneys of their own choosing, they argued, was a basic right of citizenship, made all the more important by the fact that California's attorney general, U. S. Webb, seemed ineffectual and uncommitted. But CIRA soon learned that Collett was simultaneously introducing legislation to allow for payment of attorney fees and other expenses incurred by non-attorneys (such as himself), all to be paid out of what was clearly going to be a much smaller settlement than initially hoped for by California Indians. By the late 1930s, CIRA had fully reversed this position and stood behind the new attorney general of California, Earl Warren, who in accordance with the original terms of the act, would not cost the Indians any of their potential claims award.

88. It is worth noting here, that some California Indian periodicals arose in direct opposition to the pan-Indianism that animated others. One of these was the *Yurok News*, which began on May 20, 1949. Editor Robert Spott declared, "Whether you are signed up with the Collett group; the Bay Area Group [Foster]; or the Federated Indians of California, it makes no difference so far as your Tribal Organization is concerned. None of them are going to come up here and see that we have a decent burial ground for our dead; None of them are going to come up here and put up a fight for our fishing rights; None of them are going to come up here and do any of the many things that need to be done for our people. These things we must do for ourselves." Centered below, in the middle of the page, were the following words typed in all caps: "The Yurok Tribal Organization is not signed up with any of the statewide groups, nor their attorneys." Land claims issues, in many ways, sidetracked attention and action from more immediate needs.

89. It is important to recognize that newspaper stories about Potts (especially her AIPA association) as well as mention of her in other publications, offered countless American Indian women a rare and invaluable role model.

For instance, see the book *Let My People Know: American Indian Journalism* (James E. Murphy and Sharon M. Murphy, Oklahoma Press, 1981). For two decades now, it has taught students, aspiring editors, and American Indian journalists the nation over, that by the early 1970s, Potts was considered to be the "dean of Indian Journalists" (p. 103), despite the fact that hers was a cottage-based enterprise (also see p. 103.)

90. Black and Potts collected and frequently cited each other's publications; its seems fitting that the records of both the *Smoke Signal* and the *Early American* are now archived together at California's tribal college, where young Indian women, and men, can gain access to the primary documentation associated with these publications and be inspired to carry forward the legacy both women worked to create.

91. This scrapbook is in the possession of Pansy Marine's descendants.

92. Some of the most frequently mentioned names include: grandchildren Susie Yanes, Judy Marine, Joe Marine, Marvin Lee Marine, nephew Merton Mason, friend Leona Begay, and Jeanne O'Taylor, Potts's daughter.

93. Potts thanked her granddaughter, Peggy Ann O'Taylor (Fontenot), for the sketches of sweathouses, dolls, and baskets. Fontenot is still sketching today and carrying on the business of interpreting Native California culture to visitors at Petaluma Adobe State Park in California. Several of Pansy's children dance in the Sacramento area as members of the "Maidu Dancers and Traditionalists."

94. Pansy died on May 14, 1965, leaving six children and her role in the *Smoke Signal's* production for her mother to carry on alone. In August, when Potts finally managed to get herself back to the business of the *Smoke Signal*, her grief was still raw and painfully palpable in the tribute she paid to her daughter: "Without her it has been real hard to get down to brass tacks and get on the ball. We were like a pair of plow mules that had pulled together for years. When one is gone it is difficult for the other to pull the plow alone. No more jawing back and forth, no criticism, no moral support. What's the use!!" (*SS*, vol. 24, no. 2, p. 6).

95. Potts sometimes translated this parenthetically and signed her name "Marie Potts," for those who bought her book. The copy I examined was originally owned by her friend Jack Dyson and is today archived at the Yosemite National Park Museum in the curatorial offices.

96. The historical sensibility that animated both her books and her editorials is further revealed in the archival records of the Federated Indians of California, which—like the 1914 Thanksgiving Menu from the Carlisle Indian Industrial School, Potts collected and preserved for more than thirty years at 2727 Santa Clara Way in Sacramento, California. These records are now

permanently housed in the Archives and Special Collections of the Sequoyah Library, D-QU Tribal College, Davis, California.

97. On March 12, 2002, six California Indian women's portraits were added to this gallery wall, in a continuing tribute to Native California women. As Larry Myers (Pomo), executive secretary of the California Native American Heritage Commission remarked at the ceremony and reception honoring the contributions of Vivien Hailstone (Yurok/Karuk), Reba Fuller (Central Sierra Me-wuk), Margaret Dalton (Miwok), Jane Penn (Cahuilla), Kathryn Saubel (Cahuilla), and Tillie Hardwick (Pomo) "Marie Potts has been here by herself for a long time—her spirit must be lonely. It's time we gave her some company."

98. Today, *News from Native California* serves some of the same readers and needs as the *Smoke Signal.* Published by Heyday Press in Berkeley, California, its contributing editors include many Native Californians. Countless tribal newspapers dot the contemporary landscape of the California Indian Press, as renewed interest in the diverse linguistic and cultural traditions once threatened by assimilation are brought to the fore of political and economic efforts. Visitors to the library at D-QU Tribal College will find one of the most comprehensive, indigenously-oriented current periodicals sections in the West.

Unbossed and Unbought

Booklegger Press, the First Women-Owned American Library Publisher

TONI SAMEK

> Without an alternative culture there can be no alternative press.
>
> Alexander Cockburn

> You can't be neutral on a moving train.
>
> Howard Zinn

In July 2001, the Committee on Professional Ethics of the American Library Association (ALA) adopted a special explanatory statement of the ALA's Code of Ethics titled "Questions and Answers on Librarian Speech in the Workplace." The document states that, "Through the Library Bill of Rights and its Interpretations, the American Library Association supports freedom of expression and the First Amendment in the strongest possible terms. This freedom of expression, however, has traditionally not been thought to apply to employee speech in the workplace." Subsequently, in response to the hypothetical question—"Since librarians have a special responsibility to protect intellectual freedom and freedom of expression, do librarians have a special responsibility to create a workplace that tolerates employee expression more than other professions?"—the document declares: "Yes. . . . If librarians are denied the ability to speak on work related matters, what does that say about our own commitment to free speech? We need to demonstrate our commitment to free speech by encouraging it in the workplace."[1] (For the full text of the Library Bill of Rights, see Appendix A.)

In the context of contemporary Western library and information studies, the phrase *intellectual freedom* is widely understood to mean "the right of every individual to both seek and receive information from all points of view without restriction." Intellectual freedom "provides for free access to all expressions of ideas through which any and all sides of a question, cause or movement may be explored."[2] Democratic societies such as the United States and Canada endorse this concept because it stands for people making their own choices and governing themselves. In the library profession, the rhetoric of intellectual freedom dates back to the late 1930s. Beginning in the late 1960s, however, advocates of an alternative library philosophy based on a new library concept of *social responsibility,* which included the librarian's right to freedom of expression, lobbied the American Library Association to extend the concept of intellectual freedom to include library practitioners as well as library users. These advocates of an alternative library philosophy believed that while, as professionals, librarians have "the responsibility for the development and maintenance of intellectual freedom," as citizens, librarians also have the fundamental right to freedom of expression.[3] This research paper explores the role that Booklegger Press—founded more than thirty years ago by a public librarian in San Francisco, California—played in the history and development of this alternative library philosophy.

Wallace Koehler's survey of library and information literature, association codes of ethics, and librarian values identifies intellectual freedom as a widely held professional principle.[4] His survey shows that *intellectual freedom* is an umbrella term that covers many others, including such principles as service, equality of access, information literacy, preservation of the record, literacy, professional neutrality, diversity of opinion, confidentiality, and cultural diversity. However, several key terms related to intellectual freedom are markedly absent from Koehler's findings—for example *censorship, self-censorship,* and *social responsibility,* all of which are commonly considered professional antivalues and are germane to any discussion of intellectual freedom.

Traditionally, the act of censorship includes efforts to ban, prohibit, suppress, proscribe, remove, label, or restrict materials. Censorship violates the notion of intellectual freedom because it hinders people's ability to make informed decisions.[5] To effectively promote intellectual freedom (as the ALA's Library Bill of Rights directs), librarians must also combat censorship. To do so effectively, librarians must extend their defense of intellectual freedom beyond the purview of library collections.

The act of *self-censorship* occurs when librarians consciously choose not to include an item in the library collection for fear that it will provoke a challenge from the community. In this age of electronic information, this form of self-censorship inevitably means limiting the library user's access to online information, including the Internet. Self-censorship shows the discrepancy between library rhetoric and the realities of daily practice. And, because of the profession's heavy reliance on mainstream review media, publishers, and vendors, self-censorship also plays out on a more unconscious level. Consequently, materials produced by the alternative press, and materials which reflect alienated social sectors, are often underrepresented by libraries. Self-censorship has broad-reaching implications as reliance on mainstream sources favors not only "safe" or "acceptable" establishment cultural interests but economic, social and political ones as well. Library activist Sanford Berman has identified other "widespread and serious" kinds of "inside" censorship that contribute to a library culture steeped in "limited access to ideas and opinions and cultural expression" as well as what he terms "throttled" speech. These include circulation-driven weeding of materials, fines collected for revenue only, fees for services that discriminate against poor or fixed-income people, cataloguing that impedes access, restrictive shelving practices, and workplace repression of free speech on professional or policy issues, including electronic monitoring.[6]

In *Our Enduring Values: Librarianship in the 21st Century*, Michael Gorman observes that the concept of the library as an advocate of intellectual freedom is not without controversy.[7] There is a conflict between those in the profession who take a purist moral stance on library neutrality (i.e., providing information on all sides without taking sides, and no social agenda) and those who advocate that the profession should take a stand on social issues, such as international relations, hunger, poverty, corporatization, *and* freedom of expression for librarians. Supporters of the latter often use the phrase "social responsibility" to illustrate their position.

In general, advocates of social responsibility see librarians as active agents of social change. These advocates represent divergent voices, largely on the margins of librarianship, that have questioned the absolutism of the library ethic of intellectual freedom. Their (primarily leftist) voices have generally concurred that the core value of library neutrality (on which the ethic of intellectual freedom is based) is unrealistic in the context of library practice. They find fault, for example, with the idea of library "neutrality" in the traditional functions of collections and services, charging that libraries are vehicles of dominant ideology to the exclusion of marginalized groups like the homeless, youth, gays and lesbians, women, ethnic minorities, and radicals of all kinds. But they also challenge the profession to promote intellectual freedom and combat censorship within its own ranks—for example, library employee freedom of speech in the workplace on professional and policy issues, and freedom of the library press. In particular, however, these voices have represented a range of viewpoints on a continuum that spans from an anarchist stance to varying degrees of a progressive library perspective. The Progressive Librarians Guild, for example, defines its purpose as follows:

> Progressive Librarians Guild [PLG], an affiliate organization of the Social Responsibilities Round Table of the American Library Association, was formed in January 1990 by a group of librarians concerned with our profession's rapid drift into dubious alliances with business and the information industry, and into complacent acceptance of service to the political, economic and cultural status quo. . . . Current trends in librarianship assert that the library is merely a neutral mediator in the information marketplace and a facilitator of a value-neutral information society. Members of PLG do not accept this notion of neutrality, and we strongly oppose the commodification of information. We will help to dissect the implications of these powerful trends, and fight their anti-democratic tendency.[8]

On the other hand, librarians who take an absolutist stance on intellectual freedom appear to stand united. As library historian Wayne A. Wiegand noted in 1996, the ALA's Library Bill of Right's codification of intellectual freedom as an absolute goes largely unchallenged by librarians. Scholarship on "race, gender, class, Third World, and sexual orientation" he argued, indicates that librarian and information rhetoric mistakenly treats terms like "democracy," "family values," and "tolerance" as one-dimensional.[9] A similar concern was on the mind of Celeste West, a San Francisco Public Library librarian and the founding editor of Booklegger Press, some thirty years ago.

Celeste West, born in Portland, Oregon, in 1942, discovered the power of libraries early on. After finishing her master's degree at Rutgers, she returned to Portland where she worked at Portland State University's library. When West moved to San Francisco various strands of her personal and professional lives began to meld. From her work at the Bay Area Reference Center in the 1960s to her present (2002) position as chief of the San Francisco Zen Center Library, West has focused on providing information that directly addressed people's information needs. Working alongside educators, journalists, religious workers, and others involved in shaping the nation's culture, librarians of the 1960s were trained to create "balanced" library collections representing many points of view and to provide access to these materials. Both goals required that librarians take a "neutral" stance and disregard, or suppress, their own political views and moral persuasions. But as the sixties wore on, Celeste West grew increasingly uncomfortable with this bland, normative creed. She began to argue that it was not possible for librarians to take apolitical, nonaligned positions in their professional work. The chances of encountering an "unbiased" librarian, she said, were about as great as meeting an "objective" journalist. The notion of an unbiased individual was, to her, an impossible construct. An examination of library collections in the 1960s led her (and others) to speak out about the imbalances and deficiencies in acquisitions. In particular, she advocated a place on library shelves for the alternative press.[10]

During the 1960s, the "underground" or alternative press flourished as the voice of the American counterculture and documented the experience of alienated sectors of society such as disenchanted youth, women, ethnic minorities, poor people, working class people, trade union workers, and political radicals. Many of the viewpoints and experiences of these otherwise marginalized groups had never been recorded elsewhere. Those editors who assembled and published nonmainstream opinions were frequently subjected to harassment by both individuals and groups. Sometimes they were sued or subjected to boycotts.

By drawing attention to librarians' neglect of the alternative press, West and other advocates of a new library ethic of social responsibility also drew attention to the discrepancy between professional rhetoric and the realities of library practice. There was decidedly a gap between the two. As early as 1939, the profession had carefully crafted a Library's Bill of Rights that directed librarians to "fairly represent" materials on "all sides of questions on which differences of opinion exist" and to oppose censorship of "books and other reading matter" because of "the race or nationality or the political or religious views of the writers"; but in practice, in the 1960s West and her cohorts repeatedly found the alternative press to be inadequately represented in library collections.[11]

The implications of this neglect were threefold. First, because library users did not have adequate access to the products of the alternative press, they did not have access to the viewpoints expressed therein. Thus, libraries failed to provide access and exposure to the wide spectrum of viewpoints necessary for thoughtful debate and a variety of contending ideas. Second, because the alternative press was not being adequately preserved as part of society's cultural record, many voices from the 1960s would be lost to future generations. Third, because of the absence of alternative perspectives, the mainstream media was overrepresented in most library collections.

West was especially irritated by the third point. She argued that to be silent and support the status quo, as most librarians did, was de facto to take a political stance. The social responsibility movement not only encouraged librarians to be fair in their work; it also educated librarians to recognize the political context of their work. This new outlook seemed threatening to many in a profession that prided itself on its "neutral" stance. Furthermore, in their attempt to preserve the traditional role of librarians and maintain the status quo, some in the professional library establishment sought to discredit the social responsibility movement. The ensuing debate over "neutrality" introduced a professional identity crisis that characterized the mood of American librarianship in the 1960s. It was in the midst of this crisis that an alternative library philosophy developed hand-in-hand with a call for freedom of expression for librarians.

When Celeste West had attended library school at Rutgers University in the late 1960s, times were unusual. "We would go to classes only 4 days a week and everyone would take off to New York for 3 days of multi-media blow-out. . . . Yes, we marched on the Pentagon. Saw Columbia fall. On getting their degrees, some of the men had to take jobs in Canadian libraries to escape the Vietnam War."[12] The climate of the 1960s, including the emergence of the alternative press movement and a rising feminist consciousness, endowed library school subjects such as intellectual freedom a new urgency for West and some of her cohorts. Some students began to reexamine the impracticality of library "neutrality" when it came to library collections—and in the context of library rhetoric as well. As West put it, it began to "dawn on us that *Libraries to the People* [a popular slogan of the library social responsibility movement] meant *us* too!"[13]

Momentum for an alternative library press was slow to build. But by the mid 1960s, social protest movements in larger society were mirrored in American librarianship. Through their involvement in the causes and issues espoused by the era's alternative press, many librarians became more socially aware, and more active. Some librarians were intrigued by the novelty of the messages in the alternative press, others by the freshness of the medium itself. When, for example, publications like the *Oracle* (San Francisco), the *East Village Other* (New York), the *Fifth Estate* (Detroit), the *Paper* (East Lansing), the *Los Angeles Free Press* (Los Angeles), and the *Berkeley Barb* (Berkeley) began attracting national recognition because they questioned the objectivity of the establishment press in the mid-1960s, a subset of American librarians took note. They established their own mechanisms for publishing a wide variety of alternative library literature. (See Appendix C for examples of alternative library press.) This new wave of library titles created a fresh forum for activities on behalf of freedom of expression within the library profession. The new publications printed viewpoints "not tolerated" by mainstream library periodicals such as *Library Journal, Wilson Library Bulletin,* and *American Libraries,* and their contributors challenged the conformity of the professional discourse.[14] But this challenge was to prove controversial.

On the one hand, ALA's 1967 version of its Library Bill of Rights (See Appendix B) instructed librarians to combat censorship and to protect freedom of expression. On the other hand, some alternative voices in library publishing were outright censored, and others were simply ignored. Furthermore, as Sanford Berman expressed it, the publishers of "core alternative library literature" were often "heavily shit upon" by the establishment. He believed that alternative library publishers were targeted precisely because the literature they produced tightened connections between the alternative library movement and other movement groups, and had the potential to make libraries "more like the social catalysts they should be" rather than the vehicles for establishment ideology "that most of them [were]."[15] Celeste West's first major library publishing experience with the vanguard alternative library publication *Synergy* (1967–73), a precursor to Booklegger Press, is a case in point.

In the late 1960s, the San Francisco Public Library's experimental Bay Area Reference Center (BARC) provided support reference services to seventeen North Bay Cooperative Library System libraries scattered across six counties. BARC looked to noncommercial book publishers to find information on new areas of interest and in 1967 began to publish a monthly newsletter titled *Synergy* to serve as a reference tool and disseminate news of the project. *Synergy*'s "Update" section listed outstanding new additions to the San Francisco Public Library reference collection. Another section of the newsletter included a bibliography of topical importance "not obtainable through usual channels."[16]

In 1967, San Francisco was of course a hotbed of social activism. Everyone in America had heard of the sex-drugs-and-rock culture of Haight-Ashbury and the almost daily demonstrations provoked by opposition to the Vietnam War. From the city's 65,000-person antiwar demonstration, held concomitantly with the Spring Mobilization Committee's New York City protest, to the influx of thousands of people for the "Summer of Love" activities, the Bay community manifested social change.[17] As editor of *Synergy*, West frequently commented on the relationship between San Francisco's transformation and the local library scene. She described the city as "a trend-mecca—whether it be communal living, campus riots, gay liberation, independent film making . . . you name it and we've got it." But what San Francisco had, she argued, was not (and in future would not be) reflected in library collections unless and until someone took the time to assemble "the elusive printed material." Therefore, *Synergy* began examining the nature of library card catalogs, indexes, and selecting tools because its staff believed that such tools were mostly "rear-view mirrors" that provided little or no bibliographic access to the public's current information needs.[18]

Synergy's staff believed that because librarians were not sufficiently trained to create access to and/or learn about where to find many forms of information, they were unable to fulfill their professional mandate to present balanced/multiple points of view. The passive nature of library practice, grounded in the myth of "neutral" service, understated this information access problem. *Synergy* consistently included information about noteworthy topics that were largely ignored by the mainstream media, and by conventional librarians. The April-May 1968 issue, for example, criticized conventional library literature's lack of attention to subjects like astrology, Native Americans, the women's liberation movement, ecology, the drug revolution, library service to prisoners, the occult, the family, the underground press, and criticism of "the establishment." In subsequent issues, *Synergy* provided coverage of these and other topics. But *Synergy* stood for more than just information access. Under West's direction, it called on librarians to become "pivotal agents to enforce"[19] the Library Bill of Rights, to support a free press, and to develop a new professional attitude by shifting from "conserving and organizing" information to "generating or promoting it."[20] *Synergy* defined an alternative library culture that worried less about the library as a keeper of the cultural record, and more about the library as an active agent for change.

In his book *A Trumpet to Arms: Alternative Media in America,* David Armstrong notes that alternative media serve as "the central nervous system in the body politic of the adversary culture. Through that culture's media are transmitted ideas, values, and visions that make up the shared language that radicals and dissidents use to communicate with each other and engage the dominant culture in dialogue."[21] Between 1966 and 1972, he observes, the underground media flourished in the United States, "united chiefly in their opposition to the Vietnam War and their advocacy of drugs, rock music, and sex." "Issues first explored in the underground media—chiefly feminism, gay liberation, and environmentalism—grew to full-fledged movements with media of their own, part of the expanded notion of what came to be called alternative media. In the early seventies, alternative media, witnesses to the governmental repression of underground media and movements, backed away from the confrontational style of the underground. They examined the commercial exploitation of drugs, sex, and rock more fully and critically than did the underground, and they explored the confluence of the personal and political." By the early 1980s, Armstrong continues, the alternative media were: "tools for community action and organizing"; having an "activist rather than passive relationship with their constituents"; seeking "to create change rather than affirming things as they are"; and "not neutral." Instead they were "highly partisan media enterprises that make no attempt to disguise their partisanship." In fact, *Synergy* displayed such basic alternative media characteristics by the late 1960s. But the roots of such media, as Armstrong says, extend back to 1776 when Thomas Paine published his epoch-making pamphlet *Common Sense.* "Social and political activists in today's alternative media," Armstrong writes, "claim Paine as an honored predecessor, together with the abolitionists, suffragists, Transcendentalists, muckrakers, socialists, and others who have made extensive use of media to promote their visions of a better world."[22]

According to David Farber, the "long subterranean history" of the 1960s alternative press confirms that diverse published opinions have for many years been pushed to the margins of public discourse.[23] In a similar vein, Ruth Marie Eshenaur writes that the alternative press is rooted in the protest journalism of the colonial New England papers, the abolitionist press of the antislavery movement, the populist and socialist papers of the late nineteenth and early twentieth century, and the1950s "underground press."[24] Kenneth Cmiel likewise views artistic modernism and Rousseau's "mid-eighteenth century attack on politeness" as other influences in the history of protest journalism.[25]

For a number of years, as part of its effort to provide information about the alternative press and alternative library activity, *Synergy*'s staff lobbied for the "Great Unreviewed," which its editor claimed constituted "60%+ of all books published."[26] Because standard reviewing journals like *Kirkus Reviews, Publishers Weekly,* and *Choice* did not cover the alternative press, *Synergy* tried to fill the void. It encouraged subscribers to read intensively in their areas of specialty and to get involved in self-publication. But by the summer of 1973, problems arose.

In August of that year, the *SRRT Newsletter* announced that California State librarian Ethel Crockett was terminating federal funding for *Synergy*. Crockett maintained that Title I of the Library Services and Construction Act funded demonstration projects for not more than two years. Since *Synergy* had already received five years' funding, she told it to seek financial assistance elsewhere.[27] But while Crockett initially claimed she notified BARC of the funding cut on April 26 and followed it up on May 4 with a memorandum to "Persons Interested in the Future of *Synergy*," she later admitted that somehow the "information was not given to the *Synergy* staff, so that the announcement that funds would, indeed, be cut off after this June 30 came as a shock." Celeste West maintained that the abrupt notice left little time to save *Synergy* and, disgusted with the funding flap and tired of hassles, she resigned. In her resignation letter, West asked "WHAT DOES THE STATE LIBRARY HAVE IN ITS CROCK O' RELEVANCE?" She said that she believed *Synergy*'s many bibliographies and reviews on topics such as feminism, native Americans, unions, children's liberation, occultism, head comix, radicals in the professions, free schools, and independent publishing were very "relevant" to the contemporary library world.[28]

The San Francisco Public Library talked publicly of taking over the magazine, but BARC feared censorship. BARC members recognized that publications of the library profession were not free. In general, library publishing was monopolized by a blend of associations and institutions, and was controlled by particular publishing interests. Even the vanguard alternative library title *Synergy,* for example, was not only financially dependent on a federal grant; each issue also required San Francisco Public Library's approval before publication. The library had previously "bollixed five different reprint offers which might have brought in money," West wrote, "choked creativity on the bone of prior censorship," and suppressed editorials with which it did not agree. "The battle of intimidation, she wrote, "was endless." "I'd cry First Amendment and IF [intellectual freedom]—they'd rail with you're lucky we allow this maverick at all. It got so when we'd submit the mag for administrative approval, it was practically edited with a paper cutter."[29] West maintained she had to kidnap the final *Synergy* issue from the printer just to get it published. Other staff members complained of "odd military-school-like reprimands" and threats that they would be denied legal salary increases.[30]

In hindsight, West argued (though without providing evidence) that Crockett's real objection to the high-impact periodical was not a question of money. Instead, she asserted, California governor Ronald Reagan had appointed Crockett state librarian, and in West's view, had directed Crockett "to kill" *Synergy*. The magazine was, after all, the flagship alternative library publication. *Synergy* fostered an attitude for change in the profession, gave rise to a wave of alternative library literature, provided a ground for library activists to express their opinions and make connections, and (in West's words) "upped the ante on library periodicals" at a time when most librarians remained "purveyors of Reader's Digested Status Quo print." "There was a rationale," she asserted, "for saying the mag was too political and was run by a bunch of leftys. Straight Reaganomics. There is money, but it is for some things and not for others." The San Francisco Public Library, she concluded, "did not want to rock the boat in Sacramento."[31] In the end, "We all watched *Synergy* get suppressed and snuffed."[32] Ironically, in its final year of existence *Synergy* received its second H. W. Wilson Periodical Award and sold 2,000 copies a month.

Although *Synergy* was a lost cause, Celeste West was not ready to abandon the idea of a free library press. In fact, prior to the demise of *Synergy,* she had already found a way to publish free of institutional restrictions. In 1972, West, Elizabeth Katz, and a few others had formed an independent publishing house called Booklegger Press. The first Booklegger Press publication, *Revolting Librarians* (1972), was a daring anthology of provocative essays edited by West and Katz.[33] The 158-page book (with a cover price of $2) took the field by storm with its diverse collection of library workers' free voices on a wide range of topics: the image of librarians, library schools and education, professionalism, mainstream bias and representation in Library of Congress subject headings, undemocratic library work practices, paraprofessional issues, homophobia, alternative libraries, alternative education, young adult services, libraries for migrant workers, and the library press. Contributions to the book comprised approximately forty essays, articles, poems, fictional stories, and fables by librarians aimed at their peers as well as at library administrators and managers.

Revolting Librarians was a print "index" to a new library culture.[34] The book's "political use"[35] of print culture was intended to foster a "universe of discourse."[36] For example, it encouraged activist librarians, "and implicitly, though indirectly," librarianship, "to debate the burning issues of the day, to protest injustices . . . to illuminate the paths to progress . . . to define and promote shared meanings," and to encourage freedom of expression.[37] Print culture scholar Rudolph J. Vecoli asserted that "rather than simply serving as transmitters of information, communication media" are "forces actively constructing social reality and identity in the minds of their audiences."[38] Drawing on Antonio Gramsci's concept of ideological hegemony, Vecoli said that "communication is viewed as the means whereby the ruling element manufactures and secures consensus to its view of the world among subaltern groups. Since such hegemonic conceptions are subject to challenges by oppositional views, the media become the site of ideological contestation of a struggle over meaning."[39] Contributors to *Revolting Librarians* addressed themselves to library administrators and managers, not merely to workers. Indeed, a key purpose of the book was to "oppose the influence of the dominant culture" of librarianship and its publications—"that is, to subvert the hegemony."[40]

The reader response to *Revolting Librarians* reflected the book's political aim. For example, Charles W. Conaway's *Library Resources & Technical Services* review said the book deserved "at least selective reading by all librarians and particularly by administrators and library educators, the groups with whom the revolting librarians have the most difficulty in communicating."[41] Eugene Darling's review in the *Library Union Caucus Newsletter* said "we have in this book some very vivid and accurate pictures of what's wrong with libraries."[42] *Library Journal* editor John Berry wrote simply, "Get the little red book!"[43]

In three years, Booklegger Press sold 15,000 copies of *Revolting Librarians* "with virtually no promotion." It was an "underground smash."[44] In late 1973, in direct response to both the success of *Revolting Librarians* and the abrupt cancellation of *Synergy*, West launched a new library journal, free of institutional restrictions under the Booklegger Press banner. *Booklegger Magazine*, like *Revolting Librarians*, was intended it to take on the library establishment and assist librarians in taking power over their working lives. *Synergy*, West wrote in 1976, "was born in the advocacy and celebration of the 60s. Some say she perished in politics (a horrific tale) but she simply pulled up her socks and became Booklegger."[45]

The first issue of *Booklegger Magazine* was published in the winter of 1973 under the direction of staff members West, Wheat, and Sue Critchfield—"the three musketeers of library lit"—with the help of friends.[46] Over the next three years, the kitchen-table publishing collective oversaw the production of sixteen issues. *Booklegger Magazine* successfully carried on the *Synergy* and *Revolting Librarians* dialogue. It was a viable alternative library journal that dealt purposefully with issues and concerns that might have been otherwise ignored or fallen victim to de facto censorship. In the late 1960s, during her University of Chicago library education, for example, *Booklegger Magazine* contributor Jackie Eubanks became disheartened that library schools lacked courses in publishing and the book trade, and that the collections and acquisitions courses were too often "concentrated entirely on the "freedom-to-read issue" and seen "entirely from a civil libertarian standpoint."[47] In her opinion, librarianship's commitment to the dissemination of information, as expressed in the Library Bill of Rights, was largely ineffective.

If librarians really wanted to convey information to the public, they needed to get involved in publishing. Eubanks viewed the formation of Booklegger Press, and its production of *Revolting Librarians* and *Booklegger Magazine*, as a coup. As she wrote: "To counteract censorship by distribution of information is to move towards intellectual freedom."[18]

Booklegger Press was a strong supporter of intellectual freedom. It was also a passionately feminist effort. *Booklegger Magazine* was intended as a deliberate, meaningful stroke on the landscape of library publishing as well as the landscapes of feminism and social reform. The magazine was launched just one year after Congress passed the Equal Rights Amendment in and the same year that *Ms.* magazine began publication. At the time, "a particular set of experiences in the southern civil rights movement and parts of the student new left" had "catalyzed a new feminist consciousness." With this new feminist consciousness came "an oppositional ideology" based on "a political analysis of women's repression" created in social spaces such as "dozens of journals and newspapers," magazines, feminist caucuses, and feminist publishing houses. In and among these spaces, women "could share and develop these new ideas and actions." Sara Evans noted in her book *Personal Politics: The Roots of Women's Liberation in the Civil Rights Movement and the New Left* that by the early 1970s, "a range of institutions—from corporations to families—began to experience angry insurgency from within.[19] The library institution was no exception.

Throughout its run, *Booklegger Magazine's* area of coverage included the women's movement and general issues of concern for female library workers, such as the gender imbalance between library workers and administrators or managers, workplace democracy, challenges to traditional managerial practices within the library workplace, and feminist publishing. From its outset, the *Booklegger* staff had joined forces with the ALA's Social Responsibilities Round Table, which served as an umbrella for numerous discontented library groups. Initially, Booklegger Press and the Round Table organized a Task Force on Women Preconference to generate discussion on the 1974 ALA annual conference theme "The Woman Librarian: Her Job Situation." Subsequently, Booklegger Press participated in other joint projects in support of library-based women, most notably sharing its office space, and a feminist agenda, with a group called Women Library Workers. These efforts resulted in lobbies on the ALA to go on record endorsing the ratification of the Equal Rights Amendment, to create salary equity, to eradicate sexist terminology from ALA publications, to press libraries to provide child care services for employees, and to initiate regular staff evaluations of library administrators.[50]

Other Booklegger Press ventures specifically addressed women and film. In the mid-1970s, for example, Booklegger published two such books: *Women's Films in Print: An Annotated Guide to 800 16mm Films by Women* (1975), compiled by Bonnie Dawson, and *Positive Images: A Guide to 400 Non-Sexist Films For Young People* (1976), written by Linda Artel and others. Like other Booklegger Press publications, these two provided representation for nonmainstream or marginalized voices, as well as for nonmainstream artistic/film productions. *Women's Films In Print* is widely considered one of the best early, annotated women's filmographies.[51]

Aside from addressing women's issues, *Booklegger Magazine* also addressed subjects ranging from cooperative housing and alternative education to patient's rights and library materials for prisoners. The magazine featured a series of semiregular columns entitled "Media Maze," "Grapevine," "YA" [young adults], and "Kids," which created a new forum for librarians to discuss nonmainstream approaches to various library services and materials. The magazine included annotated bibliographies on various alternative press publications and on a variety of countercultural, marginalized, and neglected topics as well as reviews of books published by the independent and alternative press. Occasionally entire issues of the magazine were dedicated to a particular theme. For example, numbers 2/3 (a double issue) focused on democracy in the library workplace; number 13 (a split issue with *Emergency Librarian*) focused on American and Canadian librarian perspectives on library education; and number 5 focused on the publishing industry.

In later *Booklegger Magazine* issues, the staff featured both appreciative and critical letters to the editor. Analysis of this reader response indicates that *Booklegger Magazine* filled gaps in library literature, by providing library workers with an arena for voicing dissent against established practices, and was one of a handful of library resources that gave librarians access to bibliographic information on, and reviews of, the alternative press. But despite positive reviews like one in *American Libraries*, which reported, "This phoenix . . . deserves to fly," the future of the magazine was threatened by its limited circulation and marginal financial underpinnings.[52]

In the spring of 1976, West wrote, "We are read by 500 souls, need 5,000 more to make a dent in payroll, even publishing quarterly.

[The first fourteen issues were published bimonthly and the final two issues were quarterlies.] This means ads, reviews, promo. Next time you go to the bank, ask them to buy us a page in LJ [*Library Journal*] ($945). After being put off for 2 ½ years, we finally understand that an alternative voice in library lit[erature] has to *pay its dues* to get a serious review in LJ's *Professional Reading* or *Magazines* [columns]. Once we got a 3-line teaser; one line was the address and that was totally incorrect. The Library-Industrial Complex doesn't fight competition: it just ignores it to death."[53] This viewpoint was not unfounded. In 1975, for example, Eric Moon, president of Scarecrow Publishing, wrote, "There are more restrictions on freedom of expression around ALA than in some domains of the Literary Industrial Complex."[54] Just a few years earlier, Scarecrow Publishing had picked up a controversial monograph project by Sanford Berman entitled *Prejudices and Antipathies: A Tract on the LC Subject Heads Concerning People.* Scarecrow took on this project just shortly after ALA's Publishing Services Editor Richard A. Gray dropped the book he had originally invited Berman to write, on the grounds that it was "severely critical of "an old and venerable institution"—the Library of Congress.[55] Somehow Gray had changed his original view, as expressed in a letter to Berman, that "a good lively controversy" was just what ALA needed "to counteract the prevailing tone of dullness in professional literature."[56]

By fall 1976, with *Booklegger* teetering on the edge of financial disaster, West assessed the damage and called upon her readership for help:

> "Please HELP! *Booklegger Magazine* must suspend publication until we can raise the funds to continue publication. . . . We never expected to turn our rag to riches. So we lived on love alone: its hope that libraries would become New Age consciousness centers, with librarians as change agents, enjoying themselves. We kept warm being part of the library free press and opening a forum for library workers' dissent—and dance. We watched feminism begin to thaw libraryland as Women Library Workers set up offices with us. We explored new worlds with the resource lists we printed. We loved getting the word out about the independent press, unbossed and unbought. . . . Optimistically, we had ridden a publishing venture with none of the stored energy of investment capital, grants, or contributions. From subscriptions we could just manage to pay an editorial staff subsistence wages and meet minimum operating costs. In ignorance, and because of time and money crunch,

> we slighted two key staff operations: promotion and financial management. Absence of concerted, well-funded promotion meant lack of growth. The absence of financial savvy muddied all kinds of waters. We were all ends and no means."[57]

To be sure, the woes West described above were not unique to Booklegger Press. In an article titled "pressing women's issues: four feminist presses," for example, Suzanne Little noted that in the early 1970s, numerous "maverick" women's presses (e.g., Diana Press, Daughters, Inc., and The Women's Press Collective) "rose, only to languish, victims ultimately of financial hardship and, in some cases, lack of publishing expertise."[58] But as Little concluded, these presses were publishing books and periodicals "no one else" would and were "building a women's revolution at the same time."[59]

A one-page entry titled "The Library Free Press," published in *Booklegger Magazine* in 1974, noted: "Our profession has finally birthed its own alternative press, with the voice of change publishing ideas, hopes, demands. There are at least five totally independent, adventurous library mags. [*Booklegger Magazine, Emergency Librarian, Sipapu, The Unabashed Librarian: A Letter for Innovators,* and *The Young Adult Alternative Newsletter.*] They are not slick with ad money and please-everybody. They are home-grown, in touch, labors of love. Staffs are *paid* in freedom of expression and its warm response."[60] The birth of this press, however, was hard won. Just two years after "The Library Free Press" entry appeared in *Booklegger Magazine,* for example, West wrote in a letter to Berman and his wife Lorraine that, "I had my first—I'd guess you call it nervous breakdown—at the end of the year. . . . I knew *Booklegger* was falling, falling & I couldn't hold on any longer. Valerie burnt out and I was a few months later. Now things can't get any worse and I feel peace at last."[61] West seem to have known that she was caught in a dangerous trap for some women publishers—"she was intelligent, sophisticated, well educated, conscientious—and she was a martyr."[62] *Booklegger Magazine* ceased publication in 1976.

Review articles indicate that the Booklegger staff intended to resume publication in late 1977 or 1978 under the title *Booklegger—Feminist Review of Books*, but the staff was plagued by both lack of funds and energy. Whereas in 1973 West had almost instantaneously bounced back from the loss of *Synergy* with the immediate introduction of *Booklegger Magazine,* between 1976 and 1978 the Booklegger Press was silent.

It was not the first women's press to lose its voice. As Marilyn Weller wrote in 1980, "publishing is a tough business, and publishing women's books is even more tenuous."[63]

In 1978, West and Wheat published *The Booklegger Guide to: The Passionate Perils of Publishing,* which included reprints of their articles from earlier *Booklegger* issues. West and Wheat identified the "bookazine" as the seventeenth issue of *Booklegger Magazine* (No. 17, Vol. 4, Summer 1978).This book addressed the challenges that self-publishers faced and could pose to the mainstream or "establishment" publishing industry. It included articles on the publishing industry, self-publishing, and the alternative (or free or independent) library press. Carol Seajay (editor of the Feminist Books Network) reacted to *The Passionate Perils of Publishing* by describing it as "the best and most complete analysis of publishing and feminist publishing that I've found."[64] The work divided into six chapters, written by either West or Wheat, and directed at those people who wished to self-publish and/or obtain information that was not produced by the mainstream publishing industry. The book pointed to resources on self-publishing and the independent or alternative publishing industry (including contact information for feminist book publishers), criticisms of the mainstream publishing industry, and the alternative library press. In the introduction to the final chapter, which is an annotated bibliography of alternative library publications, Wheat paid tribute to *Synergy*, *Booklegger Magazine,* and its Canadian counterpart *Emergency Librarian* as the catalysts for an explosion of alternative library literature.

Following *Booklegger Magazine*'s first issue, the bimonthly Toronto journal *Emergency Librarian* appeared as the "sister ship" publication in Canada. Edited by Canadian librarians Sherrill Cheda and Phyllis Yaffe, *Emergency Librarian* was the product of a surge of feminist interest at the 1972 Canadian Library Association conference. Together, *Booklegger Magazine* and *Emergency Librarian* became the first "women-owned and published library magazines . . . in a profession run by women but still ruled by men."[65] And as the mouthpieces for some of the profession's leading feminist voices, they blended the 1960s women's, alternative press, and library movements. Other alternative library titles that were launched in the years 1967 to 1978 include the *Liberated Librarian's Newsletter* (1969–75); *Women Library Workers* (1969–79), which continued as *WLW Journal* until 1994; *Sipapu (*1970–95); *Women in Libraries* (1970–); *Prejudices and Antipathies: A Tract on the LC Subject Heads Concerning People*

(1971); *Alternatives in Print* (1971–80); *Unabashed Librarian* (1971–); *Revolting Librarians* (1972); *Librarians for Social Change* (1972–84), which continued as *Social Change and Information Systems* (1985–); *Current Awareness-Library Literature* (1972–80); *Young Adult Alternative Newsletter* (1973–79); *The Living Z: A Guide to the Literature of the Counter-culture, the Alternative Press, and Little Magazines* (1975); *On Equal Terms: A Thesaurus for Nonsexist Indexing and Cataloging* (1977); and *VOYA, Voice of Youth Advocates* (1978–).

Nothing more issued from the Booklegger Press until 1985, when *Words in Our Pockets: The Feminist Writers Guild Handbook on How to Gain Power, Get Published & Get Paid.* The book was edited by Celeste West; it published in hardback by Dustbooks and in paperback by Booklegger Press. West and Wheat designed *Words in Our Pockets* to provide an arena for marginalized groups such as feminists and lesbians to stake a claim against the establishment book trade. Their list of collaborators included authors, novelists, poets, playwrights, workers, farmers, librarians, academics, teachers, health care workers, filmmakers, publishers, editors, and journalists. Only one article in the collection deals specifically with the library: "The Library As A Feminist Resource" by Joan Ariel. In the eleven-year publishing gap, West had withdrawn from the library community. The content of the book, for example, reflects a progression away from the earlier Booklegger themes, away from librarianship, and toward a more specific focus on feminist and/or lesbian publishing. During the long gap, however, a number of alternative library titles were launched elsewhere, including *New Pages* (1980–), *Feminist Collections* (1980–), and *Alternative Library Literature* (1984–).

Subsequent Booklegger Press projects addressed the poetry of the pioneering lesbian poet Elsa Gidlow (1898–1986) and the lesbian community. These books are *Makings for Meditation: A Collection of Parapoems Reverant and Irreverant* (1973); *Ask No Man Pardon: The Philosophical Significance of Being Lesbian* (1975); *Sapphic Songs: Eighteen to Eighty, The Love Poetry of Elsa Gidlow* (1982); and *Elsa, I Come With My Songs: The Autobiography of Elsa Gidlow* (1986). West herself wrote and published three books through Booklegger Press that deal with issues relating to the lesbian community: *Book of Lesbian Etiquette* (1985); *A Lesbian Love Advisor* (1989); and *Lesbian Polyfidelity: A Pleasure Guide for the Women Whose Heart is Open to Multiple Concurrent Sexual Loves, or How to Keep Non-Monogamy Safe, Sane, Honest and Laughing, You Rogue!* (1996).

With the publication of *Lesbian Polyfidelity,* the name Booklegger Press was changed to Booklegger Publishing. Currently, Booklegger

Publishing has an Internet presence, where one can access reviews of Booklegger titles (see Appendix D), find library and information studies on student papers that quote West on such topics as self-censorship, learn about West's current role at the San Francisco Zen Center,[66] and trace links to websites such as the Women's Institute for Freedom of the Press.[67] Thus, thirty-five years after West first took on the editorship of *Synergy*, the predecessor to *Booklegger Magazine,* and thirty years after the founding of Booklegger Press, her influence has extended well beyond the alternative library community of the late 1960s and early 1970s. Irene Reti of HerBooks once said, "I had this sense of lesbian culture being very tenuous, something that had to be built. I had to contribute."[68] In just such a manner, Booklegger Press heralded and helped to birth a new library culture.

Booklegger Press, the first women-owned American library publisher, became a key communication tool for some of librarianship's leading alternative voices in the 1970s, countered mainstream library publishing, challenged limitations to freedom of expression within librarianship, introduced a wave of alternative library publishing that persists to this day, served as an open forum for library workers' dissent, and advanced women's library causes, as well as those of other alienated library groups, such as gays and lesbians, politically active library school students, individuals interested in library unions, and alternative library publishers. But dating back to the days with *Synergy,* West and her cohorts did more than spur interest in the alternative press. These librarians also urged library professionals to address social issues and to recognize the social and political contexts of their work. Ultimately, this threatened a profession that prided itself on its "neutral stance" by raising that critical question: *Was librarianship "neutral" when it came to the provision of access to any form of information?* Most importantly, though, advocates of an alternative library philosophy based on a new library concept of social responsibility—a concept that included the librarian's right to freedom of expression, challenged members of the profession to extend the ethic of intellectual freedom to include library practitioners as well as users, and to defend it beyond the limited purview of library collections. In David Armstrong's view, "uncompromising journalism was the most dramatically successful use of media to spark social change in American history."[69] Celeste West and her Booklegger Press cohorts intended their publishing as a vehicle for change in American library history.

Contemporary American alternative library philosophy—shaped by alternative monographs (e.g., *Zoia! Memoirs of Zoia Horn, Battler for the People's Right to Know*), monographic series (e.g., *Alternative Library Literature*), publishers (e.g., CRISES Press), electronic serials (e.g., *Library Juice*), print journals (*Progressive Librarian: A Journal for Critical Studies & Progressive Politics in Librarianship*), websites (e.g., *Anarchist Librarians Web*), newsletters (e.g., *Social Responsibilities Round Table of the American Library Association Newsletter*), and listservs (e.g., PLGNET-L)—are all indebted to the pioneering efforts of Booklegger Press. But while contemporary alternative library philosophy continues to examine the library in its social context, extend the reach of the professional discussion beyond the status quo, and provide a forum for freedom of expression within the library and information studies press, the late 1960s call for freedom of expression for librarians on professional and policy issues has yet to be adequately addressed by the ALA.

On the horizon is a continued and vociferous call from Sanford Berman (and supporters) for the ALA to add a seven-point directive to its Library Bill of Rights (first proposed in March 1999), which reads as follows: "Libraries should permit and encourage a full and free expression of views by staff in professional and policy matters."[70] Unless the Library Bill of Rights is amended as such, librarians remain in a "catch-22" situation. According to the ALA's Committee on Professional Ethics' document "Questions & Answers on Librarian Speech in the Workplace," librarians are not afforded freedom in terms of employee speech in the workplace. They do, however, have "a special responsibility to protect intellectual freedom and freedom of expression" and "to create a workplace that tolerates employee expression more than other professions."[71] At the heart of the matter is the issue of library culture. As John Buschman and Mark Rosenzweig noted in 1999, "If librarians do not feel they have intellectual freedom in their work, or feel they have the right to dissent only if they are individually and collectively exposed to risk without adequate support, then the larger public freedom the profession seeks to protect is undermined."[72] Meanwhile, nothing is on the ALA books regarding freedom of the library press.

West asserted that a key requirement to effectively promoting intellectual freedom and combating censorship, including freedom of expression for librarians, is freedom of the library press. Based on her experience, the traditional approach to librarianship, in which the librarian serves as a mediator between the public and the cultural record, is insufficient. She believed that the librarian must also, at times, be prepared to generate information. And so she did. "Nothing is ever always," West reflected in 1982, "and I have learned to be a publisher, as well as a librarian and a journalist."[73]

Author Note

The first part of this paper includes excerpts from the following of my publications:

"Pioneering Progressive Library Discourse." In *Revolting Librarians Redux: Radical Librarians Speak Out.* Jefferson, NC: McFarland & Company, Inc. 2003.

"*Synergy,* Social Responsibilities and the Sixties: Pivotal Points in the Evolution of American Outreach Library Service." In *Bringing Libraries to the People: Histories of Library Outreach.* Jefferson, NC: McFarland & Company, Inc. Forthcoming.

Intellectual Freedom and Social Responsibility in American Librarianship, 1967–1974. Jefferson, NC: McFarland & Company, Inc., 2001.

"Introducing Intellectual Freedom Courses into the Canadian LIS Curriculum." *Feliciter* 47, no. 1 (2001): 40–43.

"Intellectual Freedom within the Profession: A Look Back at the Alternative Library Press." *Counterpoise: For Social Responsibilities, Liberty and Dissent* 4, no. 1/2 (2000): 10–16.

Many thanks to School of Library and Information Studies, University of Alberta student Stephen Carney for his research assistance on aspects of this paper. And special thanks to Jim Danky and Wayne Wiegand for their most generous editorial support and friendship.

Appendix A

ALA's Library Bill of Rights

Adopted June 18, 1948. Amended by the ALA Council February 2, 1961; June 27, 1967; and January 23, 1980, inclusion of "age" reaffirmed January 23, 1996.

The American Library Association affirms that all libraries are forums for information and ideas, and that the following basic policies should guide their services. Books and other library resources should be provided for the interest, information, and enlightenment of all people of the community the library serves. Materials should not be excluded because of the origin, background, or views of those contributing to their creation.

1. Libraries should provide materials and information presenting all points of view on current and historical issues. Materials should not be proscribed or removed because of partisan or doctrinal disapproval.
2. Libraries should challenge censorship in the fulfillment of their responsibility to provide information and enlightenment.
3. Libraries should cooperate with all persons and groups concerned with resisting abridgment of free expression and free access to ideas.
4. A person's right to use a library should not be denied or abridged because of origin, age, background, or views.
5. Libraries which make exhibit spaces and meeting rooms available to the public they serve should make such facilities available on an equitable basis, regardless of the beliefs or affiliations of individuals or groups requesting their use.

Appendix B

ALA's Library Bill of Rights, *1967 version*

The Council of the American Library Association reaffirms its belief in the following basic policies which should govern the services of all libraries.

1. As a responsibility of library service, books and other library materials selected should be chosen for values of interest, information and enlightenment of all the people of the community. In no case should any library materials be excluded because of the race or nationality or the social, political, or religious views of the authors.
2. Libraries should provide books and other materials presenting all points of view concerning the problems and issues of our

times; no library materials should be proscribed or removed from libraries because of partisan or doctrinal disapproval.

3. Censorship should be challenged by libraries in the maintenance of their responsibility to provide public information and enlightenment.
4. Libraries should cooperate with all persons and groups concerned with resisting abridgement of free expression and free access to ideas.
5. The rights of an individual to the use of a library should not be denied or abridged because of his age, race, religion, national origins or social or political views.
6. As an institution of education for democratic living, the library should welcome the use of its meeting rooms for socially useful and cultural activities and discussion of current public questions. Such meeting places should be available on equal terms to all groups in the community regardless of the beliefs and affiliations of their members, provided that the meetings be open to the public.

Appendix C

Selected Alternative Print Library Press Chronology

The original version of this chronology appeared in *Counterpoise* 4(1/2) (January/April 2000): 10.

This chronology highlights some key contributions to the alternative print library press in the United States from its origins in the late 1960s to recent times. While all but four of the alternative print library titles included in the chronology are American, *Emergency Librarian* (Canadian), *Librarians for Social Change* (U.K.), *Information for Social Change* (U.K.), and *Bis* (Sweden) are included to illustrate that the alternative library press is not restricted to the U.S.

1967–73	*Synergy*
1969–75	*Liberated Librarian's Newsletter*
1969–79	*Women Library Workers*—continued as *WLW Journal* until 1994
1970–95	*Sipapu*

1970–	*Women in Libraries*
1970	*Top Secret*
1971	*Prejudices and Antipathies: A Tract on the LC Subject Heads Concerning People*
1971–80	*Alternatives in Print*
1971–	*Unabashed Librarian*
1972	*Revolting Librarians*
1972–84	*Librarians for Social Change*—continued as *Social Change and Information Systems* (1985–)
1972–80	*Current Awareness-Library Literature*
1973–76	*Booklegger Magazine*
1973–79	*Young Adult Alternative Newsletter*
1973–98	*Emergency Librarian*—continued as *Teacher Librarian* (1998–)
1975	*The Living Z: A Guide to the Literature of the Counter-culture, the Alternative Press, and Little Magazines*
1977	*On Equal Terms: A Thesaurus for Nonsexist Indexing and Cataloging*
1977–78	*Collectors' Network News*
1978–	*VOYA, Voice of Youth Advocates*
1980–	*New Pages* [now electronic]
1980–	*MSRRT Newsletter*
1980–	*Feminist Collections*
1982	*Alternative Materials in Libraries*
1984–	*Alternative Library Literature*
1985–	*Social Change and Information Systems*
1990–	*Progressive Librarian*
1993–	*Librarians at Liberty*
1994–	*Information for Social Change*
1994–	*Alternative Publishers of Books in North America*
1995	*Zoia! Memoirs of Zoia Horn, Battler for the People's Right to Know*
1996	*Alternative Literature: A Practical Guide for Librarians*
1997–	*Counterpoise: For Social Responsibilities, Liberty and Dissent*
1998	*Poor People and Library Services*
1998–	*HERMÈS: revue critique*
1998–	*Bis: Utgiven av föreningen Bibliotek i Samhälle*
2003–	*Dismantling the Public Sphere*
2003–	*Revolting Librarians Redux*

Appendix D

Booklegger Press/Booklegger Publishing List of Publications

Artel, Linda, et al. *Positive Images: A Guide to 400 Non-Sexist Films For Young People.* San Francisco, 1976.

Dawson, Bonnie (Compiler). *Women's Films in Print: An Annotated Guide to 800 16mm Films by Women.* San Francisco: Booklegger Press, 1975.

Gidlow, Elsa. *Makings for Meditation: A Collection of Parapoems Reverant and Irreverant.* San Francisco: Booklegger Press, 1973.

————. *Ask No Man Pardon: The Philosophical Significance of Being Lesbian.* San Francisco: Booklegger Press, 1975.

————. *Sapphic Songs: Eighteen to Eighty, The Love Poetry of Elsa Gidlow.* San Francisco: Booklegger Press, 1982.

————. *Elsa, I Come With My Songs: The Autobiography of Elsa Gidlow. San* Francisco: Booklegger Press,1986.

West, Celeste. *Revolting Librarians.* San Francisco: Booklegger Press, 1972.

————. *Book of Lesbian Etiquette.* San Francisco: Booklegger, 1985.

————, ed. *Words in Our Pockets: The Feminist Writers Guild Handbook on How to Gain Power, Get Published & Get Paid.* San Francisco: Booklegger Press, 1985. (Hardcover Published by Paradise, California: Dustbooks, 1985).

————. *A Lesbian Love Advisor.* San Francisco: Booklegger Press, 1989.

————. *Lesbian Polyfidelity: A Pleasure Guide for the Women Who's Heart is Open to Multiple Concurrent Sexual Loves, or How to Keep Non-Monogamy Safe, Sane, Honest and Laughing, You Rogue!* Nicole Ferentz, Illustrations. San Francisco: Booklegger Publishing, 1996.

West, Celeste, and Valerie Wheat. *Booklegger Guide to: The Passionate Perils of Publishing.* San Francisco: Booklegger Press, 1978.

West, Celeste, et al. *Booklegger Magazine.* San Francisco: Booklegger Press, 1972–1976. (Vol. 1–4; Issues 1–16).

Notes

1. "Questions and Answers on Librarian Speech in the Workplace: An Explanatory Statement of the ALA Code of Ethics," Adopted July 2001, American Library Association, Committee on Professional Ethics. See http://www.ala.org/alaorg/oif/libspeechq&a.html. Last modified: Monday, 03-Dec-2001.

2. "Intellectual Freedom and Censorship Q & A," American Library Association, Office of Intellectual Freedom web page. See http://www.ala.org/alaorg/oif/intellectualfreedomandcensorship.html. Last modified: Thursday, 10-Jan-2002.

3. Canadian Library Association, Statement on Intellectual Freedom, Adopted June 27, 1974; Amended November 17, 1983 and November 18, 1985. See http://www.cla.ca/about/intfreed.htm.

4. Wallace Koehler, "Core Values as Defined by the LIS Discipline." See http://faculty-staff.ou.edu/K/Wallace.C.Koehler-1.Jr/.

5. *Intellectual Freedom Manual,* 5th ed. (Chicago: American Library Association, Office for Intellectual Freedom, 1996), xx.

6. Sanford Berman, "'Inside' Censorship," *Progressive Librarian* 18 (Spring 2001): 49–50.

7. Michael Gorman, *Our Enduring Values: Librarianship in the 21st Century* (Chicago, American Library Association, 2000), 89.

8. Progressive Librarians Guild. Statement of Purpose. See http://libr.org/PLG/#statement.

9. Wayne A. Wiegand, "Introduction," in *The Library Bill of Rights,* ed. Wayne A. Wiegand. *Library Trends* 45, no. 1 (Summer 1996): 1–6.

10. "A Conversation with Celeste West," *Technicalities* 2, no. 4 (April 1982): 3–6. (Hereinafter cited as "A Conversation.")

11. *Intellectual Freedom Manual,* 7.

12. "A Conversation," 3–6.

13. Celeste West, "Working Loose," *Booklegger Magazine* nos. 3–4 (March/April 1974, May/June 1974): 2.

14. Joe W. Kraus, "The Progressive Librarians' Council," *Library Journal* 97, no. 13 (July 1972): 2351–54. See also Rosalee McReynolds, "Trouble in Big Sky's Ivory Tower: The Montana Tenure Dispute 1937–1939," *Libraries & Culture* 32, no. 2 (Spring 1997): 163–90.

15. Sanford Berman to Mr. Brian Kirby, March 1971, Libraries to the People, 1971–1973. ALA's Sanford Berman Papers, University of Illinois at Urbana-Champaign, University Archives.

16. Richard Cronenberg. "SYNERGIZING Reference Service in the San Francisco Bay Region," *ALA Bulletin* 62, no. 11 (December 1968): 1379, 1384.

17. Edward P. Morgan, *The Sixties Experience: Hard Lessons About Modern America* (Philadelphia: Temple University Press, 1991), xix–xx.

18. Celeste West, "Stop! The Print is Killing Me," *Synergy* 33 (1971): 3.

19. Celeste West, "Congloms: Stalking the literary-industrial complex," *American Libraries* 13, no. 5 (1982): 299.

20. "A Conversation," 3–6.

21. David Armstrong, *A Trumpet to Arms: Alternative Media in America* (Los Angeles: J.P. Tarcher, 1981), 16.

22. Armstrong, *A Trumpet to Arms*, 20; 21; 21–22; 15.

23. David Farber, ed., *The Sixties: From Memory to History* (Chapel Hill, NC: University of North Carolina Press, 1994), 269.

24. Ruth Marie Eshenaur, *Censorship of the Alternative Press: A Descriptive Study of the Social and Political Control of Radical Periodicals (1964–1973)* (Carbondale, IL: [s.n.], 1975, 5.

25. Farber, *The Sixties*, 269.

26. West, "Stop!," 3.

27. *Synergy* (1973), ALA's Sanford Berman Papers. See also Edward Swanson, "Synergy Protest" *American Libraries* 4, no. 7 (July/August 1973): 408; Noel Peattie, The Fortunes of *Synergy*," *Sipapu* 4, no. 2 (July 1973): 8–10.

28. "*Synergy* Editor Resigns," *American Libraries* 7, no. 4 (July/August 1973): 412.

29. "A Conversation," 3–6. Congress passed the ERA in 1972,but the Amendment died in 1982 when it failed to be ratified by three-fourths of the states.

30. Ibid.

31. "Celeste West on Synergy," *Sipapu* 4, no. 2 (July 1973): 71.

32. *Booklegger Magazine* 1 (Nov./Dec. 1973): 1.

33. Celeste West, Elizabeth Katz, eds., *Revolting Librarians* (San Francisco: Booklegger Press, 1972).

34. Violet Johnson, "Pan-Africanism in Print: The *Boston Chronicle* and the Struggle for Black Liberation and Advancement, 1930–50," in *Print Culture in a Diverse America*, ed. James P. Danky and Wayne A Wiegand, 58 (Urbana: University of Illinois Press, 1998).

35. Danky and Wiegand, *Print Culture in a Diverse America*, 4.

36. Michael Fultz, "'The Morning Cometh': African-American Periodicals, Education, and the Black Middle Class, 1900–1930," in Danky and Wiegand, *Print Culture in a Diverse America*, 130–31.

37. Ibid.

38. Rudolph J. Vecoli, "The Italian Immigrant Press and the Construction of Social Reality, 1850–1920," in Danky and Wiegand, *Print Culture in a Diverse America*, 19.

39. Ibid.

40. Ibid, 26.

41. Charles W. Conaway, *Library Resources and Technical Services* 18, no. 3 (Summer 1974): 294–95.

42. Eugene Darling, "Are Librarians Revolting?," *Library Union Caucus Newsletter* 2, no. 1 (January 1973): 5.

43. John Berry, "Little Red Book," *Library Journal* 98, no. 4 (Feb. 15, 1973): 515.

44. "A Conversation," 3–6.

45. Sue Critchfield, "Grapevine," *Booklegger Magazine* 16 (Autumn 1976): 52.

46. Sue Critchfield, "The Collective Unconscious" *Booklegger Magazine*5 (July/Aug. 1974): 1.

47. Noel Peattie and A. D. Winans, "RISE UP SO EARLY IN THE MORN," *Sipapu* 7, no .2 (July 1976): 4.

48. "A.I.P. Adventures by Jackie Eubanks," *Booklegger Magazine* 1 (Nov./Dec. 1973): 7.

49. Sara Evans, *Personal Politics: The Roots of Women's Liberation in the Civil Rights Movement and the New Left"* (New York: Alfred A. Knopf, 1979), 23, 18, 222, 227, 222, 22.

50. "Strategy, Structure, and Specialization," *Library Journal* 99, no. 14 (August 1974): 1901–1902.

51. Dawson lists the 800 films under 370 women filmmakers, including a film-title index. Where possible she provides the cost of the film and includes a list of film distributors and contact information.

52. "What the Critics Said . . . ," *Booklegger Magazine* 8 (March/April 1975): 24.

53. Celeste West, Martha Ammidon Powers, and Valerie Wheat, "What Would You Say?" *Booklegger Magazine* 14 (Spring 1976): 2.

54. Eric Moon, "Letters to the Editors," *Booklegger Magazine* 7 (Jan./Feb. 1975): 4.

55. Richard A. Gray to Sanford Berman, October 6, 1970, ALA's Social Responsibilities Round Table (SRRT) Papers, Box 11.

56. Richard A. Gray, Senior Editor (ALA) to Sanford Berman, May 12, 1970, SRRT Correspondence, 1969–75, ALA's Sanford Berman Papers.

57. Celeste West, "GOING . . . GOING . . . dawn?," *Booklegger Magazine* 16 (Autumn 1976): 3.

58. Suzanne Little, "pressing women's issues: four feminist presses," *Small Press* (February 1988): 23–27.

59. Mariyn Weller, "Women's Own Media," *Equal Times: Boston's Newspaper for Working Women* 5(98), October 13–26, 1980.

60. "The Library Free Press," *Booklegger Magazine* 2 (Jan./Feb. 1974): 24.

61. ALA's Sanford Berman Papers, Booklegger Press/Booklegger Magazine (Celeste West/Sue Critchfield), 1972–84. Letter from Celeste West to Sandy and Lorraine Berman, Feb. 22, 1977.

62. Laura Furmam, "'A House Is Not a Home': Women in Publishing," in *Sisterhood Is Powerful: An Anthology of Writings from the Women's Liberation Movement*, ed. Robin Morgan, 67 (New York: Random House, 1970).

63. Weller, "Women's Own Media," October 13–26, 1980.

64. Carole Seajay, [editorial], *Feminist Bookstores Newsletter* 2(5/6) Fall 1978.

65. "A Conversation," 3–6.

66. San Francisco Zen Center. See http://www.sfzc.com/index.html.

67. Women's Institute for Freedom of the Press. See http://wifp.org/index.html.

68. "Feminist Publishers," *Matrix* (August 1990): 25.

69. Armstrong, *A Trumpet to Arms*, 15.

70. Sanford Berman, "Free Speech for Librarians," *The Unabashed Librarian* 118 (2001): 17.

71. Questions and Answers on Librarian Speech in the Workplace: An Explanatory Statement of the ALA Code of Ethics." Adopted July 2001. American Library Association, Committee on Professional Ethics. See http://www.ala.org/alaorg/oif/libspeechq&a.html Last Modified: Monday, 03-Dec-2001.

72. John Buschman and Mark Rosenzweig, "Intellectual Freedom within the Library Workplace: An Exploratory Study in the U.S.," *Journal of Information Ethics* 8, no. 2 (Fall 1999): 39.

73. "A Conversation," 3–6.

Part 2

Women in a World of Books

Alice Millard and the Gospel of Beauty and Taste

MICHELE V. CLOONAN

In 1896 two ambitious, creative, middle-class Chicago sisters in their early twenties set off for Europe to further their educations.[1] Emily Parsons went to Berlin to study piano, while Alice Parsons studied art in London. Emily returned to Chicago to teach and perform the piano. Alice would eventually teach and perform as well, in southern California, where she also lectured on the "gospel of beauty"[2] as it pertained to books and the decorative arts. As Alice Millard, she became one of the most important American booksellers of the twentieth century, advising, teaching, and influencing such affluent disciples as William Andrews Clark, Templeton Crocker, Caroline Boeing Poole, and Estelle Doheny. She also introduced Californians to the British fine press movement through the exhibitions she curated and the accompanying catalogs that she wrote. Millard was a connoisseur and a judge of taste—a promoter of highbrow culture, even (according to Lucille Miller, Estelle Doheny's secretary and librarian) in "philistine Pasadena."[3] Since there were no other American women when she started out who sold books at the high end of the trade, Millard's role, and her influence, is even more remarkable. This paper will examine Alice Millard's influence as an arbiter of highbrow taste in the face of prevailing middlebrow values. The notion of "taste" in reading and book collecting that Millard promoted will be considered against writings on the subject.

Alice Millard's own taste was formed as much by Chicago, where she came of age, as by Europe, which she frequented throughout her life. She blended American and British sensibilities in her approach to collecting and selling art and books. Her career embodies the discourse on taste and culture in Britain and America reflected in the nineteenth-century writings of artists and critics such as James Jackson Jarves, T. J. Cobden-Sanderson, Charles Eastlake, and Matthew Arnold.

Chicago in the 1890s was a microcosm of American culture. It was home to architects Louis Sullivan and Frank Lloyd Wright (who later built two homes for Millard), the social reformers Jane Addams and Ellen Gates Starr and their Hull-House, and the newly founded University of Chicago.[4] (Wright, Addams, and Starr were all influenced by the Arts and Crafts Movement.) In 1893, Chicago hosted the Columbian Exposition, the most splendid American fair to date with its 150 buildings dubbed the "White City." At the same time, the decade also witnessed the aftermath of the Haymarket Square riot,[5] the Pullman strike of 1894, and financial panics. Mr. Dooley, the fictional Irish saloonkeeper created by *Chicago Post* columnist Finley Peter Dunne,[6] provided a running social commentary on the times. His commentaries reflected the often uneasy tension between the haves and have-nots, a tension found frequently in the contemporary fiction of Chicago-realist writers Hamlin Garland and Frank Norris in the 1890s, and Upton Sinclair and Theodore Dreiser a decade later.[7]

The social tensions of the late nineteenth century are also explored in *The Gilded Age* (Mark Twain and Charles Dudley Warner) and *Democracy* (Henry Adams). Both novels describe political and social corruption, though the rough-hewn manners and mores of Americans are satirized particularly by Twain in *The Gilded Age*. How did these mores reflect the cultural taste of Americans? How did the material excesses that these authors portrayed suggest an American tendency to commodify culture? Or even to measure the "worth" of all things by their monetary value? There is no better source to begin our inquiry with than Fanny Trollope's *Domestic Manners of the Americans*, a work that Mark Twain himself admired.[8]

Fanny Trollope came to America in 1827 with two of her children "to seek temporary shelter from hardship and troubles at home."[9] She was hoping to improve her family's fortunes, but the only enterprise she succeeded at was lambasting the Americans in her first book. And succeed the book did:[10] In its first year of publication, 1832, it went through four English and four American editions. The book was enthusiastically received in Europe, but Americans were understandably furious with the author. Trollope would be caricatured in print and illustrations for decades.[11] The term "Trollopize" was even coined to suggest harsh criticism.[12]

Trollope's sin? *Domestic Manners of the Americans*, though undeniably witty, is harshly critical of Americans. Trollope faults the brand of democracy that Americans practiced, repudiating Jefferson's "mischievous sophistry that all men were born free and equal" (57). She also criticizes Americans who "with one hand [were] hoisting the cap of liberty, and with the other flogging their slaves" (168).

Besides criticizing Americans—justifiably—for the institution of slavery, Trollope derides them for being uncouth, unmannered, and uncultured. To cite but one example of many, she relates a conversation she had concerning English literature with a Mr. Flint, then editor of the *Western Monthly Review*:

> And Shakespeare, sir?
>
> Shakespeare, Madam, is obscene, and, thank God, WE are sufficiently advanced to have found it out! (72)

Trollope's narrative is liberally peppered with such anecdotes; indeed, she seemed to believe that the New World was evidence of the collapse of the standards of the Old World. As a Briton, Fanny Trollope could be expected to look down on what she obviously felt was a breakaway republic, and it is clear that she could not overcome her own class consciousness. She concludes her book by observing that

> . . . if refinement once creeps in among them, if they once learn to cling to the graces, the honours, the chivalry of life, then we shall say farewell to American equality, and welcome to European fellowship one of the finest countries on the earth. (318)

The critic Russell Lynes has dubbed the period in which Fanny Trollope was writing—the late 1820s through the early 1830s—the "Age of Public Taste."[13] The period was ushered in by the election of President Andrew Jackson, "Old Hickory," in 1828. By the 1830s almost everyone in America could afford carpets, wallpapers, and certain textiles because of the invention of new weaving looms and wallpaper-printing machines. The home-decorating industries flourished and magazines such as Peterson's *The Lady's World of Fashion* and *Godey's Lady's Book* introduced European style to the emerging American mass market.

The development of a taste for fine art in America was much slower to evolve. Art unions opened and closed, while by the 1840s, P. T. Barnum operated the most popular museum of the day—a dubious attainment, given the nature of Barnum's exhibits.[14] Paintings that had prurient or sensationalist features were popular; others were ignored. From the 1850s to the Civil War, several American "art missionaries," the best known of whom was James Jackson Jarves, tried to introduce the American public to European art by purchasing paintings in Europe and placing them in American institutions such as athenaeums and universities. Jarves also wrote about art in such volumes as *Art Hints* and *Art Studies*. The results he achieved were mixed: the Boston Athenaeum could not muster support to purchase his collection, and Yale wound up with it by default. Still, Jarves had influence. After the Civil War, comprehensive and historical collections were gathered in museums such as the Metropolitan in New York.[15] Later, collectors such as William C. Corcoran and William T. Walters were able to open museums to house their enormous collections.

Meanwhile, on the other side of the Atlantic, critics and artists were beginning to speak out against the injustices brought about by the Industrial Revolution. These voices would eventually find a large audience in America. In England, John Ruskin, perhaps the most influential art critic of the nineteenth century, wrote prolifically about art and social reform for a wide audience. Great art, Ruskin believed, should convey great ideas. To understand art, one needed a discerning eye. Wealthy industrialists had little training in art and so could only imitate earlier art patrons. Further, industrialists ran factories and mills that exploited child labor and caused all manner of social ills. Ruskin felt that reform could take place if society returned to medieval craftsmanship and the naturalistic style of the Gothic era, an aesthetic that—though naïve—was embedded in his moral convictions. (He was also shortsighted in opposing efforts to raise the standard of design in industry.) Ruskin's writings inspired designer, craftsman, and social reformer William Morris and others to champion the Arts and Crafts Movement in the 1880s. Unlike Ruskin, Morris had the genius to fuse ideals with practical activity.

William Morris was a prolific craftsman and writer. In 1861 he founded the manufacturing and decorating firm of Morris, Marshall, Faulkner & Co., which produced furniture, tapestry, stained glass, furnishing fabrics, wallpaper, carpets, and more. For Morris, art was the expression of one's joy in the labor. His last venture was to produce letterpress-printed books on handmade papers. Morris started his Kelmscott Press in 1891 and in the scant five years before his death, the press produced dozens of books that continue to influence book design to this day. Ironically, as a socialist Morris wanted to produce art for the masses, but only the well-to-do could afford his expensive handmade products.

Charles Eastlake was another British aesthetic crusader. Eastlake's uncle, Sir Charles Eastlake, was president of the Royal Academy. Eastlake the nephew was a talented architect and watercolorist who turned his attention to interior design. His first book, *Hints on Household Taste* (1868),[16] was a best seller on both sides of the Atlantic. Like Ruskin and Morris, Eastlake was concerned with both aesthetics and morals. He favored the "sincere" over the "showy" and insisted that there is "a right and a wrong notion of taste in jewelry . . . and in many other fields which stand apart from a connoisseurship of what is commonly called 'high art'" (12). He concludes that if the public "encourage[s] that sound and healthy taste which alone is found allied with conscientious labor, whether in the workshop or factory, then we may hope to see the ancient glory of those industrial arts which . . . should owe their highest perfection to civilized skill" (264).

Ruskin, Morris, and Eastlake were born to wealth, as was the American social reformer Jane Addams. In founding the social settlement Hull-House, she aimed not only to educate Chicago's poor but also to bring beautiful objects into their lives. Addams had visited the first settlement house, Toynbee Hall in London, in June 1888 and within a year began Hull-House. Her cofounder, Ellen Gates Starr, later studied bookbinding with William Morris' protégé T. J. Cobden-Sanderson and then taught it at Hull-House. This is but one of many links between Americans and the British Arts and Crafts Movement. Such links, in

Chicago and elsewhere, influenced American tastes and sensibilities for more than a generation.

Let us now turn our attention back to young Alice Parsons, who at the beginning of this essay was headed to London. Her development as a book expert and taste-maker can be partially gleaned from her background. But little is known about her early life, and Millard left few letters and no diaries. Therefore, the process of "triangulation"—so well described by Jean Strouse in her biography of J. P. Morgan—is necessary.[17]

Alice Covell Parsons was born in Jefferson City, Missouri, on May 4, 1873.[18] She had two sisters, Emily and Clara, and a brother, Walter. Little is known of her childhood, though a surviving grandnephew believes that Alice Millard's father was an alcoholic and that her mother may have left him and moved the children to Chicago.[19] At some point the Parsons converted to Christian Science, which Millard practiced for the rest of her life.[20] Her family was not wealthy, and her nephew and others believe that she was a schoolteacher before, and possibly after, she went to Europe. That is the extent of what is known about her prior to her departure for Europe in 1896.[21]

Unfortunately, information about Millard's experiences during her first stay in London has also been lost. But we can glean something of them from her return to Chicago. One day she went to McClurg's bookstore looking for volumes on the Pre-Raphaelite painters. George Madison Millard sold or gave her J. W. Mackail's newly published *Life of William Morris* (1899). As Ward Ritchie describes it, "Millard soon became a regular visitor at the bookstore, seeking guidance from her new-found mentor."[22]

In fact, there was more to this mentorship than George Millard had provided the many others who sought his advice and judgment. In 1901, Alice Parsons accompanied the bookseller on his annual European book-buying trip—and returned as Mrs. George Millard. The two were married in the Christopher-Wren-designed St. Bride's Church in London, an appropriate venue for this bookish couple, since the St. Bride Printing Library—which opened in 1895—was just across the way.

Richie and Rosenthal have each described the May-December relationship of Alice and George Millard: she was twenty-eight and he was fifty-four or fifty-five at the time of their marriage.[23] By all accounts it was a happy one, fueled in part by their shared interests. According to Ritchie as well as family accounts,[24] Alice Millard continued to travel with her husband, meeting the William Morris family, the Cobden-Sandersons, the booksellers Pickering & Chatto, Maggs, Quaritch, and many others involved in the creation and/or selling of books. These men became teachers and role models for Alice Millard. Many years later she would do business with them as an established bookseller herself.

George was, no doubt, Millard's teacher in matters pertaining to the book world, and she seems to have spent the early years of their marriage absorbing all the knowledge she could. It seems likely that she also educated herself through extensive reading. We can draw some conclusions about what she read by studying the list of books in the inventory of her possessions made shortly after her death, as well as by looking at the books she owned that are still in her family, many of which have inscriptions and other marks of bibliographical evidence.[25]

There are four generalizations that can be made about the Millard library: 1) George and/or Alice was interested in fiction and poetry—nearly every nineteenth-century British and French writer of importance appears on the inventory. 2) The Millards maintained a strong reference collection. The inventory contains many books on bibliography, fine art, decorative art, and design, dating from the 1880s until shortly before Alice Millard's death in 1938. 3) The Millards held on to many of their reference books. For example, the Mackail book that Alice acquired from George in 1899 was on the inventory. Millard might have kept it for sentimental reasons, but it would still have been as useful a reference tool in the 1930s as it was when it was first published. 4) Millard probably read books on design, the arts, bibliography, and bookbinding, since she continued buying books in these areas to the end of her life.

It is probably safe to conclude that Millard was reading reference books published in the 1880s, 1890s, and the first decade of the twentieth century while she and George were living in Chicago. Some of these authors and titles from the inventory are: Owen Jones, *Grammar of Ornament*; William Thackeray, *Critical Essays in Art*; William Morris, *Gothic Architecture*; T. J. Cobden-Sanderson, *The Ideal Book or Book Beautiful*; Sydney Cockerell, *Some German Woodcuts*; and works by the young Bernard Berenson as well as books on bookbinding by William H. J. Weale and Joseph Cundall. Missing from the inventory are Matthew Arnold and Charles Eastlake. It is possible that Millard read their works when she was studying in London.

The happiness of the Millards' relationship was marred only by the tragic birth of their daughter Roxana on January 22, 1904. In accordance with Alice's Christian Science beliefs, the child was born in their home on the South Side of Chicago. Apparently there were complications with the delivery, and later on it was evident that the child was mentally retarded. For a time they relied on home care, but eventually—after the Millards moved to California, and probably after George died—Roxana was placed in the first of the institutions in which she resided until her death in the 1980s.[26]

In 1906 the Millards moved into a house in Highland Park designed for them by their friend, Frank Lloyd Wright. Their two-story Prairie-style house was the setting for many Millard parties.[27] Alice Millard's friendship with Wright continued in California, where he designed another house for her after she and George moved to Pasadena in 1914.

By then, George Millard was in his late sixties and ready to retire from McClurg's. The Millards decided to start a rare-book firm in California, calling it George M. Millard Rare & Fine Imported Books—a name Alice continued to use after her husband's death. They started such a business based on George's reputation alone: he was well known in the book world in part because Eugene Field had written about the Saints and Sinners Corner at McClurg's, a gathering place for writers and other artists. Not long after the couple's arrival in southern California, the *Los Angeles Times* featured a long article about George with a title and subheads that give evidence of his reputation: "'New Nook for His Hobbies. Saints and Sinners' Corner Relocated Here. Genius and Friend of Chicago Literati Comes. Has Established Unique Book Corner in House.'"[28]

Alice is not mentioned in the *Times* article—not surprising, given the era. Yet she seamlessly continued running the book business immediately after George's death in November 1918. That, along with the fact that women are still not common in the high end of the rare book trade, is further evidence of her expertise and importance—another illustration of biographical triangulation. Millard created a unique and distinctive place for herself, a position she held for some time. In effect, there was no other woman doing what she was doing. Later on, two pairs of women antiquarian booksellers established themselves: Frances Hamill and Margery Barker of Chicago (1928), and Leona Rostenberg and Madeleine B. Stern of New York (1944). These younger women had something that Alice did not: money.

Alice Millard was different from these other women in another way, too: she didn't just sell books, she created "undeniable opportunities for those who wanted to possess fine things."[29] She was able to achieve some financial success because she sold antiques and art as well as books and could place a higher markup on decorative objects than she could on books.[30] She genuinely seemed to love having opportunities to teach her clients how to appreciate her wares. And she had tremendous flair. She advertised in fashion magazines, reported on her European buying trips to the local newspapers,[31] and lectured to her fellow members in the Friday Morning Club.

Her style was quite different from that of her husband, as is revealed in the letters each wrote to the collector William Andrews Clark, Jr. that are now preserved in the library that bears his name. Where George was gentle and deferential, Alice was bold, even daring. When she felt that a particular collector should own a particular book or object, she did not hesitate to make that point vehemently. She helped Clark select not only books but furniture and literary portraits as well. Seven letters that she wrote to him characterize the nature of her working relationship with Clark.[32] Throughout the letters Millard seems to take advantage of what she judged was Clark's competitiveness as a collector. In a letter dated November 23, 1923, she writes that if Clark doesn't want a certain Dryden portrait, "I shall offer it to Mr. Huntington." A year later (May 3, 1924) she writes him regarding an edition of Walton's Angler, "Mr. [Templeton] Crocker had wanted it, but he's abroad," and consequently she is offering it to Clark instead.

At the same time that Millard employs these rather transparent business tactics, her letters contain meticulous descriptions of the items that she is offering for sale. Her deep knowledge of books and art is always evident. As the inventory of her library shows, Millard continued to buy reference books throughout her life, many of them published in the 1920s. To read her correspondence is to imagine her beginning all of her research in her own studio/library.

Another important client was Estelle Doheny, who was serious, reserved, and a deeply devout Catholic. The two women never had much personal rapport.[33] At the time they became acquainted, Doheny was collecting literary first editions. Millard sensed that this woman of enormous wealth should be collecting more of the highbrow items that were Millard's stock-in-trade. If Millard could educate Mrs. Doheny, she would have the opportunity to create a great American private library—and of course to reap significant financial rewards.

Others have described at length Mrs. Doheny's initial rejection of Alice Millard's wares.[34] Little by little, however, she captured Mrs. Doheny's imagination. The first significant purchase that Doheny made from Millard was the *Aeneid* manuscript written on vellum by William Morris. Mrs. Doheny, unsure of her own tastes, was naïve and undiscriminating; Millard even suggested the design of Mrs. Doheny's bookplates.[35] Alice, on the other hand, seemingly was never unsure of her own taste. She seemed to infuse her confidence into others. Eventually, Alice Millard transformed the reluctant Mrs. Doheny into a discerning collector. Mrs. Doheny became interested in works illustrating the art and history of printing, and books and manuscripts that had religious content. Other significant purchases included Colonna's *Hypnerotomachia Poliphili* and one volume of the Gutenberg Bible. Although Mrs. Doheny purchased books and manuscripts from other dealers, Alice Millard provided the foundation for her great library.[36]

We know from photographs that Alice Millard was physically striking. We also know it from accounts of her by Ward Ritchie and Frank Lloyd Wright. Millard's stunning looks and intelligence were coupled with a formidable side, which at times intimidated the young Ward Ritchie. Ritchie knew her for the last ten years of her life, during which time he printed catalogs for her exhibits. He has written of their first meeting in 1928 that

> I too was captivated by her charm and ardor. . . . She was crowned with a glorious burst of white hair delicately tinted bluish. Here eyes too were blue as were her clothes. [Her appearance] belied her aggressive forcefulness. She had one distressing habit of pulling back her lips as if snarling at one as she made a telling statement. . . . [Yet] [t]here was an elegance she created in her fashionable attire, her surroundings, and her impeccable taste and style of living.[37]

Ritchie also wrote—in a draft letter to her—that "in the beauty of your little museum I first found my delight in the lovely thing that a book can be, and I remembered your talking with such reverence for those books which you showed me that I could not help wanting to know them and to love them as you did."[38]

Wright, who knew her for over thirty years, called her "slender, energetic—fighting for the best of everything for everyone." As the architect recalled,

> The Millards lived in a little wooden dwelling I had built for them at Highland Park near Chicago. I was proud now to have a client survive the first house and ask me to build a second. Out of one hundred and seventy-two buildings this made only the eleventh time it had happened to me. . . . Alice Millard, [was] artistic herself, with her frank blue-eyed smile beneath her unruly hair.[39]

Wright then describes the building of La Miniatura, the first of four houses he designed for his Los Angeles clients. (The house was completed in 1923.) Millard risked all of her assets to build the house, which—typical of many Wright projects—had significant cost overruns. With La Miniatura, Wright was experimenting with his new technique known as the "knit block" or "textile-block," and there were tremendous technical difficulties with the construction. Wright had selected a site for the house on a ravine, so in addition to all the other difficulties, leaks and floods were a constant worry for Millard throughout her residence in the house.[40] One of Millard's closest friends felt that the house was too much of a drain on her slender financial resources, and he gave up the legal guardianship of Roxana in protest.[41]

Still, the creation of La Miniatura is one of the most significant collaborations in Millard's career and is starkly revealing of her personality, demonstrating her risk-taking and understanding of the importance—socially and professionally—of allying herself with a famous and controversial architect. Had George Millard survived, he might not have selected such a daring design.[42] In addition to the house itself, Wright's son Lloyd designed, in 1926, a small museum below the living quarters; Alice referred to it as her "Little Museum of the Book." The museum housed much of Millard's collection of books and antiques, and it was the setting for the exhibits that she curated of newly arrived treasures or the books owned by friends and customers. The first exhibit, titled "Order Touched with Delight," was devoted to the work of her old friend T. J. Cobden-Sanderson. Millard assembled 166 items from nineteen collections.[43] Another exhibit, "Civic Relief," demonstrated the history of printing. She organized it for students in the Printing Department of the Frank Wiggins Trade School.[44] This exhibit was drawn from her own collection and included work from some of the earliest printers, continuing through to the 1930s. Some of these printing students later produced their own catalog, *From Gutenberg to the Twentieth Century*.

Millard's little museum furthered all of her aims. Her exhibits attracted visitors, which sometimes translated into sales. The backdrop of Frank Lloyd Wright and his architecture added to the allure of Millard and her books. And the Little Museum of the Book gave her the opportunity to influence cultural taste. Collectors and dealers knew of Millard as herself a collector and purveyor of fine art and desirable books. If she showed a copy of a book in an exhibit in her museum, it must be collectable. In such a circumstance, it was (she probably hoped) an easy matter for her to influence the taste of her colleagues, friends, and customers.

Alice Millard was active in the book trade until just a few weeks before her death from cancer in July 1938, at the age of sixty-five. (The cancer was discovered only after she was injured in a car crash, by which time the disease was far advanced.) She left behind a treasure trove of objects and books, most of which had to be sold for the benefit of Roxana. A group of her friends purchased items from her history of the book collection and donated them to the Huntington Library as "The Alice and George Millard Collection Illustrating the Evolution of the Book."

Alice Millard's taste was rooted in the Arts and Crafts Movement, and her longtime friend T. J. Cobden-Sanderson particularly inspired her. His *The Ideal Book or Book Beautiful*, first published in 1900,[45] has become something of a manifesto to printers, designers, and bookbinders. Cobden-Sanderson asserts that there are many elements of a book's design that contribute to its beauty; and that no single element should stand out more prominently than any of the others. All elements should contribute equally to the beauty of the whole. Millard seems to have modeled her life on that premise. The life of the mind was not enough for her; beautiful things must be part of it too. Her religious beliefs played an important part in the life that she created for herself. As a Christian Scientist, she embraced a positive outlook that included self-healing.

Beauty and perfection were the hallmarks of culture, according to Matthew Arnold: "Culture is, or ought to be, the study and pursuit of perfection; and that of perfection as pursued by culture, beauty and intelligence."[46] Arnold's cultural optimism had enormous appeal to

American intellectuals such as Ralph Waldo Emerson, and it continued unabated into the twentieth century. (Arnold published *Culture and Anarchy* in 1869; he died in 1888.) Late-nineteenth-century Americans became interested in fineness, taste, and culture as antidotes to vulgarity. Dictionaries and grammar and etiquette books were popular. In the twentieth century, some of the people who edited the book review sections of newspapers and magazines, and started organizations like the Book of the Month Club (e.g., Stuart P. Sherman, Irita Van Doren, and Henry Seidel Canby), were also Arnoldians.[17]

In an article on book ownership in the 1920s, Megan Benton discusses the debate that was taking place about the meaning and function of books.[18] Critics like Canby—editor of the *Saturday Review of Literature*—felt that real booklovers cared about books for the "right" reason: for the merits of a book's content alone. Benton says that "bookaflage"—using books to create a personal environment that suggests or pronounces one's cultural values—"proved as constructive a strategy for self-definition for those beleaguered elite who struggled to preserve traditional cultural hierarchies as it was for those who wished to transcend such boundaries."[19] Those who championed "serious" book stewardship, Benton continues, "used book ownership to assess others' cultural identity" (271). These two book cultures have been characterized as highbrow and middlebrow. The highbrow-middlebrow debate is extended by Joan Shelley Rubin as she evaluates the books selected for the Book of the Month Club and how they were selected.[20] Critics have derided the Club as decidedly middlebrow.

How does Alice Millard fit into the two book cultures and the highbrow middlebrow debate? Alice's clients were highbrow, if considered solely from a socioeconomic viewpoint. The Clarks, Crockers, and Dohenys were among the wealthiest families in California, if not in America. But from the standpoint of taste, some of them were firmly middlebrow. Mrs. Doheny was an unimaginative collector buying first editions when Alice Millard met her. She was clearly seeking assistance in developing her own taste, and Millard served her purposes.

Millard would most likely have argued with Canby that the books she collected and sold were characterized by the merits of their texts and by their beauty. Millard's tastes were highbrow but not avant garde. Her library did not contain works by Ezra Pound, Amy Lowell, Virginia Woolf, or James Joyce. Her Arnoldian optimism seems not to have been clouded by the End of American Innocence, as May describes the years 1912 through 1917, or later, by the Great Depression.[51] Perhaps by the end of her life she could best be described as a standard-bearer of a culture that had begun its "descent" to middlebrow. One example is her continued preference for antique over modern furnishings. In a letter to Frank Lloyd Wright (March 13, 1929), she discusses the interior of "San Marcos in the Desert," which would later be named Taliesin West: "Just because it is in the desert I can't see why it has to be handled with fabrics modern in spirit. To me, the beauty and dignity of your patterned blocks is so enhanced by quiet rich old fabrics—or plain velvets, and I am sure that these things could be bought, wholesale, abroad, very inexpensively."[52] Needless to say, Wright was one person whose taste Millard could not influence, but Alice was always looking for opportunities to share her vision and to sell her goods.

Lucille Miller's memoir of Alice Millard includes several observations that are useful to any consideration of Millard as an arbiter, even a missionary, of taste. To Miller, Millard seems "to be *all* intellect, all soul, all mind. . . . [S]he believed in IDEALS. . . . The ordinary, the commonplace, the second-rate, were not for her. Ugliness and vulgarity gave her actual pain." Alice was "a born teacher. She needed disciples, she needed an audience." But at the same time, "Alice was a Voice crying in the Wilderness—the Wilderness of the Depression; the Wilderness of provincial class-conscious Pasadena; the Wilderness of her struggle to survive in business as a woman alone, without capital. . . . But she was undaunted and undismayed. She . . . expounded her Gospel of Beauty to any who would listen."[53]

Similarly, Kevin Starr notes that Millard sold her important wares to collectors eager "to bring the world into southern California, to seek out the symbols and artifacts of older civilizations so as to possess and re-express them locally."[54] Starr's observations are reminiscent of the social critics of the nineteenth century who lamented the lack of culture in America. A review of Eastlake's *Hints on Household Taste* that ran in *Harper's Bazar* noted that "Suddenly the voice of the prophet Eastlake was heard crying in the [American] wilderness. . . . Repent ye, for the kingdom of the Tasteful is at hand!"[55]

Starr's appraisal of Millard's clients can also be appreciated within the more general context of collecting. In "A Rationale of Collecting," G. Thomas Tanselle describes motivations for it when he writes that "one's sense of self-awareness is increased by being able to place one's own endeavors in a framework that comprehends the full panoply of related pursuits." He adds, "For some people, the pleasure of amassing objects is increased by knowing that the activity supports scholarship, science, and art; for others, the satisfactions are entirely personal, but the results are nevertheless of public benefit. Collecting is a prime example of behavior in which private desire and social gain are mutually supportive."[56]

There is a growing literature about collecting by biographical and cultural studies scholars. Tanselle and Nicolas Barker are of the former school; Susan M. Pearce and Werner Muensterberger exemplify the latter. Alice Millard's career as a bookseller can be evaluated within both contexts: she appealed to the social and psychological needs of her clients as well as the bibliographical needs of their collections. She catered to the social and psychological by creating La Miniatura, an elite and inviting setting. Her knowledge of books, and her desire to build important collections for her clients, appealed to the bibliographical acumen of some of her clients.

Alice Millard's role as an arbiter of taste can also be given a sociological reading. In *Distinction: A Social Critique of the Judgement of Taste*, Pierre Bourdieu surveyed Parisians and "provincials" representing various social classes and educational levels.[57] He examined not just judgments of taste but also aesthetic attitudes. In this work, as well as in his other writings, Bourdieu concludes that culture bestows status and power. Although the survey on which *Distinction* is based was carried out in France during the 1960s, it might just as well apply to the robber barons of the nineteenth century or the bourgeoisie of Pasadena in the 1920s. While Alice Millard might have functioned as a commercial facilitator of a particular community of taste, she also facilitated the need within the bourgeoisie for cultural validation, as Starr implies.

Another finding in *Distinction* has relevance here. Bourdieu asserts that all cultural practices and judgments of taste—from museum visits to reading—can be linked primarily to educational level and, secondarily, to social origin. Although Bourdieu is referring to the French educational system, an appropriate comparison can be made to Millard and her circle. Few women of Millard's generation went to college; indeed, it was an era in which many colleges were just beginning to admit women and also in which many women's colleges were being established. Millard herself probably never went to college. Yet through her own initiative—not to mention her acute mind and boundless curiosity—she became highly educated. Not all of her clients were formally educated either; yet many of them were wealthy. In the United States, new money and new education created enormous opportunities for acquiring cultural capital. One way to display this new capital was through collecting. Millard may have implicitly understood this need through her own desire for education, a desire that probably led her to study in Europe as a young woman.

The Gospel of Taste is always subject to revision, as a reading of Bourdieu's *Distinction* demonstrates. Still, Alice Millard preached an Anglo-American gospel that has endured in the rare-book world. The areas in which she collected and sold—early printed books, fine-press books, and books about books—have proven to be of lasting interest. It is clear that she preached an enduring gospel.

Notes

1. The author acknowledges, with thanks, the research assistance of SuKim Chung, Nina Schneider, and Michael Porta, all UCLA graduate students when this paper was researched and written. Special thanks to Peter Thompson for making available family photographs of Alice and George Millard.

2. Lucille V. Miller, "Remembering Alice Parsons Millard." Typescript, Pasadena, CA, April 1984, 12 pp., in the Huntington Library, San Marino, CA. This phrase is on p. 12.

3. Ibid., 6.

4. Chicago had many direct links to the British Arts and Crafts Movement. Wright, Addams, and Starr were all members of, and the latter two were founders of, the Chicago Arts and Crafts Society in 1897. Starr had studied bookbinding with T. J. Cobden-Sanderson in London. Several professors at the University of Chicago were active in the society as well as in the Art Industrial League, which was founded by Professor Oscar Lovell Triggs in 1899. Finally, Walter Crane, T. J. Cobden-Sanderson, and others lectured in Chicago.

5. The riot took place on May 4, 1886; Alice Millard was born May 4, 1873. One wonders what impact the riots may have had on the thirteen-year-old Alice Parsons, occurring as they did on her birthday.

6. Jacques Barzun, *From Dawn to Decadence, 1500 to the Present* (New York: Harper Collins, 2000), 593. Meanwhile, in New York City, the journalist Jacob Riis wrote *How the Other Half Lives.* Published in 1890, this book (together

with its accompanying photographs) created an uproar that resulted in some reforms.

7. Chicago realism has had staying power, as illustrated by the novels of James T. Farrell, Nelson Algren, and Richard Wright.

8. Fanny Trollope, *Domestic Manners of the Americans;* ed. by Pamela Neville-Sington (London: Penguin, 1997), "Introduction," xxxvi.

9. Her husband had serious debts and was suffering from mercury poisoning. Ibid., "Introduction," viii.

10. Fanny Trollope went on to write five more travel books and thirty-five novels, and she also helped launch the writing careers of her two sons Anthony and Thomas. (Thomas went to the United States with his mother, while Anthony was left behind.)

11. It is amusing that the title of the first of Anthony Trollope's *Palliser* novels is *Can You Forgive Her?* The Americans apparently could not.

12. Trollope, "Introduction," xxxiii.

13. Russell Lynes, *The Taste-Makers* (New York: Harper & Brothers, 1955), 6.

14. Ibid., 19.

15. Some critics believe that the museum has manufactured history by trying to summarize it without context. By taking art out of context, museums are criticized for actually dehistoricizing art. See, for example, Didier Maleuvre, *Museum Memories: History, Technology, Art* (Stanford, CA: Stanford University Press, 1999).

16. Charles L. Eastlake, *Hints on Household Taste in Furniture, Upholstery and Other Details,* 2nd ed. (London: Longman's Green, 1869). Quotations are drawn from the second edition.

17. "Biography inevitably includes elements of triangulation—locating an unknown point on a triangle by reference to its two known points—but the known points for the aging Morgan rarely yield straight lines." Jean Strouse, *Morgan: American Financier* (New York: Random House, 1999), 629.

18. From her 1926 passport at the Huntington Library in the Millard, Alice (Parsons) Papers, #2024.

19. Interview with Peter Thompson, Chicago, May 28, 1998.

20. Robert Rosenthal states that Millard had adopted Christian Science in 1904 but presents no evidence to support that claim. Mary Baker Eddy established the religion in 1879, when Alice was six. Mrs. Parsons probably learned about the religion in Chicago. See Rosenthal's "Los Angeles & Chicago: Two Cities, Two Bibliophiles," in *A Bibliophile's Los Angeles: Essays for the International Association of Bibliophiles on the Occasion of Its XIVth Congress, 30 September—11 October 1985,* ed. John Bidwell and Carol A. Sommer (Los Angeles: William Andrews Clark Memorial Library, 1985), 7.

21. Peter Thompson, Chicago, May 28, 1998, and a conversation between the author and Ward Ritchie in December 1995.

22. Ward Ritchie, "Alice Millard as I Remember Her," *AB Bookman's Weekly* 95.7 (February 13, 1995): 648. According to one of Alice Millard's friends, the copy of the book that was in her library at the time of her death was inscribed "Alice Parsons from George Millard, 1901," so the book may have been a gift. See *The Alice and George Millard Collection Illustrating the Evolution of the Book. Acquired for the Huntington Library by a group of their friends* [n.p.: 1939] printed by the Ward Ritchie Press, 2.

23. Ritchie, "Alice Millard as I Remember Her," 648; Rosenthal, "Los Angeles & Chicago," 7–8. There are inconsistencies in the ages that are given for George Millard. Roxana Millard's birth certificate states that George was fifty-seven at the time of her birth in January 1904. That would put his birth date at 1846 or 1847. He was born in Greenfield, MA, but the town clerk's office there could not locate a birth certificate for him. He appears in the *Massachusetts 1850 Census Index* (Bountiful, UT: Accelerated Indexing Systems, 1978), 585.

24. A letter written January 30, 1978, to Betty Hunt Thompson, Alice Millard's niece, by Thompson's eighty-eight-year-old cousin, Mabel Hilton Stock, another niece, gives a short description of the Chicago years following the birth of Roxana Millard. The letter mentions that the Millards traveled to Europe together for George's book-buying trips. (One-page typescript letter, Millard, Alice [Parsons] Papers, #2024, Huntington Library.)

25. The Inventory is contained in five "order books." When I began my research, Millard's great-nephew Peter Thompson owned them; they are now in the Huntington Library. I have also examined Alice and George Millard books that are owned by Thompson.

26. The expense of institutionalizing Roxana was high, as Alice Millard concedes in two letters dated April 6 and May 3, 1928, to Frank Lloyd Wright. The letters relate to overruns in the cost of building a museum addition to Millard's Pasadena home, La Miniatura, and the necessity of safeguarding money for Roxana. The original letters are housed at the Frank Lloyd Wright Archives at Taliesin West in Scottsdale, AZ. The author examined the microfiche copies at the Getty Research Institute, M003A02 and M003A04. For a complete listing of the Wright/Millard correspondence, see *Frank Lloyd Wright: An Index to the Taliesin Correspondence*, 5 vols. (New York and London: Garland, 1988).

27. See, for example, Marianne Tidcombe, *The Doves Bindery* (London: The British Library; reprinted New Castle, DE: Oak Knoll Books, 1991). Tidcombe gives an account of T. J., Annie, and Stella Cobden-Sanderson's visit with the Millards in Highland Park in October, 1907.

28. Sydney Ford, *Los Angeles Times*, Section 2 (Sunday, February 22, 1914), 9.

29. Rosenthal, "Los Angeles & Chicago," 12.

30. Millard describes her finances in some detail to Frank Lloyd Wright in the letter cited above. Also, the inventory of her goods is included in her papers at the Huntington Library. The prices Millard paid for things as well as what they sold for after her death can be compared.

31. To whit: "Rare Books on Exhibition. Pasadena Woman Acquires Choice Works During Summer Trip to Europe." *Los Angeles Times* Section 2 (November 26, 1924), 3.

32. These letters are at the William Andrews Clark Memorial Library at UCLA.

33. Lucille Miller describes their relationship in her memoir.

34. See both Rosenthal and Miller.

35. See Msgr. Francis J. Weber, "Carrie Estelle Doheny: The 'Other' Collection," *Hoja Volante* 216 (February 2002): 5.

36. Mrs. Doheny donated her library to St. John's Seminary in Camarillo, CA, in 1940. The Church decided in 1987 to sell the library. See "The Estelle Doheny Collection," 7 vols. (New York: Christie, Manson & Woods, 1987–89). Between 1987 and 1989 Christie's auctioned the library in eight sales. In the seven-volume auction catalog, one can identify the Millard books.

37. Ritchie, "Alice Millard as I Remember Her," 654, 658.

38. Ward Ritchie, draft of letter to Alice Millard, n.d., ca. 1936, in the Ward Ritchie Press Archives, ca. 1930–78, Box 88, 1934–39, A–O, in the William Andrews Clark Memorial Library, UCLA.

39. Frank Lloyd Wright, *Frank Lloyd Wright: An Autobiography* (New York: Duell, Sloan, and Pearce, 1943), 241.

40. In a letter to Frank Lloyd Wright of January 10, 1935, Alice Millard details all of the problems with the house that occurred during a recent rain storm: six inches of muddy water in the dining room, the ensuing damages to all the furnaces, and so forth. (Getty Research Institute, M035B02.)

41. Alice Millard spells this out in the letter to Frank Lloyd Wright cited above. She refers to Colonel John Hudson and Mrs. Poole. Caroline Boeing Poole was a close friend and client of Alice Millard.

42. In a letter to W. A. Clark of November 16, 1922, Alice describes her late husband as "very cautious and conservative" in the way he did business. It is fair to assume from that description that George probably would not have agreed to the enormous cost overruns that resulted from Wright's novel design.

43. The Huntington Library owns some of Alice's exhibition catalogues.

44. Rosenthal, "Los Angeles & Chicago," 18.

45. T. J. Cobden-Sanderson, *The Ideal Book or Book Beautiful: A Tract on Calligraphy, Printing & Illustration and on The Book Beautiful as a Whole* (Doves Press, October 19, 1900); this brief pamphlet has frequently been reprinted.

46. Matthew Arnold, *Culture and Anarchy* (New York: Macmillan, 1925), 69.

47. For a discussion of Arnold's twentieth-century influence, see Joan Shelley Rubin, *The Making of Middlebrow Culture* (Chapel Hill: University of North Carolina Press, 1992).

48. Megan Benton, "'Too Many Books': Book Ownership and Cultural Identity in the 1920s," *American Quarterly* 49.2 (June 1997): 268–97.

49. Ibid., 271.

50. Rubin, *The Making of Middlebrow Culture.*

51. Henry F. May, *The End of American Innocence: A Study of the Years of Our Own Time, 1912–1917* (New York: Alfred A. Knopf, 1959).

52. Alice Millard to Frank Lloyd Wright, March 13, 1929, typescript, 2. (Getty Research Institute, M005E06.)

53. Miller, *Remembering Alice Parsons Millard,* 5, 6, 12.

54. Kevin Starr, *Material Dreams: Southern California Through the 1920s* (New York: Oxford University Press, 1990), 334.

55. Lynes, *The Taste-Makers,* 100.

56. G. Thomas Tanselle, "A Rationale of Collecting," *Studies in Bibliography* 51 (1998): 1, 25.

57. Pierre Bourdieu, *Distinction: A Social Critique of the Judgement of Taste,* trans. Richard Nice (Cambridge, MA: Harvard University Press, 1984).

Women and Intellectual Resources

Interpreting Print Culture at the Library of Congress

JANE AIKIN

Librarians are world-class detectives, able to take a query on any subject and trace the answer to its source or to locate information on any topic, specific or broad. Their tools are uniformity and systematization: by shaping common intellectual approaches to their print collections, they impose an order that both assists searching and presents readers and scholars with knowledge as an organized system. While users have by and large not much noticed their efforts, the organization of collections and the relationships traced among their disparate parts have the potential to make a search successful or unsuccessful, to disclose new avenues of thought, and to shape ideas. Connections traced among fields and among subfields and topics inevitably mirror contemporary ideas; yet the system must adapt readily to new subjects and events. During the late nineteenth century American librarians were creating cataloging, classification, and subject-heading systems to index the printed output of a rapidly growing publishing industry. At the same time, they were pressing their claims to expertise and professional status with the officials who hired candidates for library positions.[1] Leaders of the profession had already established formal training programs and (in 1876) the

American Library Association (ALA), but they sometimes encountered resistance from city officials or library board members seeking to hire their favorites.

At the nation's largest repository of printed material, the Library of Congress, patronage and professionals clashed before the turn of the twentieth century, coincident with pressures to reorganize the library's collections and to record them more adequately. Unlike other makers of systems, the library's staff could draw on its large collections to make sure that their classification and cataloging comprehensively reflected the range and scope of both historical and contemporary print culture. The task called for many expert workers, and unlike most libraries, the Library of Congress was able to increase staffing because a new building, completed in 1897, required an expanded work force. Leaders of the ALA recognized that controlling the Library of Congress was important to expanding the influence of their profession. They also knew that the most successful professionalization projects to date had been in predominantly male professions. But in the library profession, women far outnumbered men. The men who led the ALA conceded that women would have a role in the profession, but they generally assumed that role was, and would continue to be, subordinate. Some women thought otherwise. As librarians sought in the late 1890s to gain control of the Library of Congress, women presented their own claims to professional status by applying for Library of Congress positions. Their presence inevitably affected the culture of print in the nation's largest library and libraries nationwide.

In 1893, Bessie A. Dwyer, a twenty-year-old Texan, became the first woman appointed to the Library of Congress staff. It had taken the library a long time to begin hiring women; even before the Civil War, women worked for the federal government.[2] However, the library remained outside the federal civil service system because it was affiliated with the legislative branch. To a degree, this worked to Dwyer's advantage, since senators and congressmen routinely sought positions and advancement for their constituents. On her behalf, Texas congressmen Roger Quarles Mills and James Slayden sent letters to Librarian John Russell Young at different times to request her transfer and promotion.[3] Nevertheless, by 1897 Dwyer earned only $900 per year, one of the smaller salaries in the Library of Congress.[4]

Miss Dwyer's title was "assistant"—the simple, nondescript title applied to the work of much of the staff in an institution that in the mid-1890s remained undifferentiated with respect to organization and chaotic with respect to arrangement. But it would be a mistake to equate Bessie Dwyer with her undistinguished title. She worked in the Copyright Office, and she was unhappy there; she sought political support to try to obtain a transfer in 1898, and her written request pointedly reminded John Russell Young that she had been the library's first permanent woman employee. When Young asked library superintendent David Hutcheson to employ her in the Reading Room, Hutcheson responded that she was not strong enough to do the work. But perhaps due to political pressure, Young transferred her anyway.[5]

Dwyer resigned in 1903 to take a library position in the Philippines. The chief clerk's memo stated that because she provided the chief financial support for her family, her widowed sister Marie, with whom she lived, was temporarily appointed in her place.[6] While Dwyer had attended business college, Marie U. Nordstrom was educated at a convent in London and learned both French and German. These qualifications made her more suitable for Reading Room service than her sister, and she probably commanded the same political influence, but she entered the service at a time when politics had lost ground to merit. Assigned as a stack assistant at $720, Nordstrom remained in that position until she resigned in the mid-1920s.[7]

The experiences of these two women reveal some of the significant changes that occurred in the library's administration and staffing around 1900. Shortly before the collections were moved from the Capitol to the new building in 1897, President McKinley replaced Librarian Ainsworth Rand Spofford with an old friend, John Russell Young, and Congress voted increased funding, including sixty-six new positions. The library profession pressed Young to hire trained librarians, which he did for several important posts, but senators and representatives secured the lesser positions for their favorites. In spite of Young's efforts to obtain a qualified staff, the exercise of political influence seems evident in the case of the new women employees. Among the forty-four women appointed between 1893 and April, 1899, only six possessed either library school training or significant library experience: Alice S. Griswold, a graduate of the Drexel Institute Library School, Anita H. Stephens of the Washington City Free Library, Eva J. Lawton of the Weather Bureau Library, Alice F. Stevens, who had taken the Amherst Library School summer course, Effie J. Curtiss, librarian at Iowa Agricultural College, and Malina A. Gilkey, a veteran of the Boston Athenaeum, the

St. Louis Mercantile Library, and the Washington City Free Library.[8] They were the only women in the Library of Congress who had actually worked with print culture in a library setting.

As noted in the case of Nordstrom, political influence did not necessarily secure women high salaries. Only three of them entered at salaries of more than $720 or $900: Myrtle Mason, who received $1,000; and Malina Gilkey and Virginia C. Thompson, both of whom commanded $1,200. Mason had been a professional musician. Thompson was a widow and former federal postmistress who had received political assistance in obtaining her previous position. The remaining women employees served as messengers, assistants, typists, and clerks. Ten of them had attended high schools or academies; five had some college training, and two went to business school. Four had been teachers; six had worked as government clerks, one was a typist, and one listed business experience.[9] These women were unlikely to have absorbed much of the contemporary culture of print through either training or education, and their positions reflected that lack of knowledge.

Had John Russell Young continued as Librarian, the staff would likely have remained largely nonprofessional and highly politicized, but he died unexpectedly in January 1899. To replace him, President McKinley nominated Herbert Putnam, director of the Boston Public Library. Putnam almost immediately obtained from Congress a large budget increase, and he moved quickly to change the composition of the library staff.[10] Accustomed to clearing hiring decisions only with a supportive board of trustees, the new librarian was not inclined to allow Congress to inflict ill-qualified constituents on the library. He observed that the appropriations act of 1897 dictated the employment of persons possessing "special aptitude" for library work—which Putnam interpreted to include substantial knowledge of print culture.[11] Since his ambitions for the library included not only making it an exemplary institution but also the leader of the American library community, Putnam was adamant about setting high standards for staff. To attract them, he had three assets: the library's nearly one-million-volume collection of record of American print culture, which also included European printed materials; a magnificent new building; and the enthusiastic support of the library profession.

The librarian was acutely aware that by 1900 about three-quarters of all qualified librarians were women and that library schools were not turning out graduates fast enough to meet the needs of American libraries.[12] Many of the library's new positions would therefore be filled by women, and he wanted the most able. "In a small library, as in an elementary school, a woman may be preferred," he observed. "In a library with a constituency of women and children . . . a woman in charge may have better understanding of their needs, may meet them more sympathetically, and endure with better patience the constant repetition of questions which women and children ask." But this was by no means sufficient for the Library of Congress. "The larger library is more nearly like a university," Putnam declared. "The work is highly differentiated, and the personal characteristics of the employee are relatively of less importance than the thoroughness of their bibliographic knowledge. . . . If in the smaller libraries a woman may bring qualifications which are to be preferred, in the larger ones there is no position from which her sex need exclude her."[13]

In the next sentence Putnam qualified his statement, noting that men were better suited for executive positions. He thought that women might possess less education and less knowledge of print culture than men and were therefore lower paid; or they perhaps produced less work or their talents were less wide-ranging. What he found in many women employees, he later stated, was a lack of perspective, a want of knowledge of business ethics and practices, a tendency to inflexibility, and a lack of initiative. But none of these qualities, he observed, were impossible for women to acquire, and he thought that the inequality between male and female employees would disappear over time. On only one score did he express doubts about female ability: the possibility that hard work would cause "a stress which they are physically unable to bear, and which, accordingly their conscience transfers to their nerves. Their nerves were not meant to bear it, and inevitably give way under it."[14]

Putnam's attitudes were similar to those of other contemporary male librarians, and even to those of women in the profession. However, unlike some, he thought women's strengths complemented men's abilities and that they contributed essential attributes to library service—for example, their patience with detailed and demanding tasks such as cataloging.[15] But the qualifications he specified were daunting at a time when graduation from high school was considered a significant accomplishment. Knowledge of history and belles lettres, the history not solely of politics and government but also of the sciences, the arts, and literature were requisite; in literature it was not criticism or composition that was important but factual knowledge. He stated that a library position would not offer opportunities to exercise literary talent, but rather work that would tax the mind. To illustrate his point, he reeled off a series of questions from library school entrance examinations: "What was the Holy Roman Empire? For what ideas do the following men and women stand before the world: Robert Owen, Froebel, Demosthenes, Frances Willard, etc.? What is suggested to your mind by the following: Selencidae, Argon, Naseby, Weissmannism, The Gloucester, Brünnhilde, Filioque, Unearned Increment, Le Salon Carré, etc.? Who were the Schoolmen? What are the great periods in the history of English literature and the men most prominent in each?"[16] That the individuals and works were largely of European and American origin was no accident, for Putnam intended the Library of Congress's collections to be securely based in the European-American tradition. He also expected to acquire the best and most authoritative works on any given subject—but emphatically *not* such materials as dime novels, popular songs, comic books, and patent medicine almanacs—all of which arrived on copyright deposit but were stored away and not cataloged for the national library's collections.

Putnam therefore sought candidates with a good general education and if possible, a college degree. A reading knowledge of at least French and German was important, and ideally also Latin. Even university graduates, he noted, ought to take at least a short library school course, and he also advised foreign travel. Experience in a library was not, in his view, equivalent to formal training because in small libraries the work was too elementary and in large libraries the work was too highly specialized to foster broad knowledge. Those who worked in small libraries were not likely to come in contact with the wide range of printed materials that larger institutions would contain.[17]

Putnam's position qualifications varied according to the requirements of the different divisions. For the Reading Room, for example, he sought persons with tact, courtesy, and patience; for the Copyright Office, business experience; for the specialized areas, expertise in such areas as musicology, law, cartography, and the visual arts.[18] But overall he wanted employees who had an excellent education, cultivated minds, a continuing interest in knowledge and scholarship, and cosmopolitan tastes.[19] Because colleges based their offerings solidly in canonical print culture, with courses exposing students to well-known authors, historians, cultural critics, and ancient and modern languages and literatures, as well as the standard works and theories of the sciences, social sciences, and the arts, their students were excellent candidates. So valuable did he consider college training that Putnam decided that when a candidate had a college degree but no library training, he would hire that individual and provide the training.

At the turn of the century, a limited number of occupations were open to women, and an even more limited number were available to those who desired a regular salary that in some measure recognized their academic training. Teaching at the secondary or college levels was one of the few vocations that demanded both a broad educational background and perhaps specialization in a branch of knowledge. But some well-educated women might dislike the cutthroat rivalry of male-dominated college faculties, or the close community of women's institutions. They might have fewer of the maternal instincts generally ascribed to teachers and public librarians; or they might find teaching too stressful. As Melvil Dewey characterized librarianship, "there is hardly any occupation that is so free from annoying surroundings or that has so much in the character of the work and of the people which is grateful to a refined and educated women." College women who wanted work that kept them in touch with print culture materials of the "high culture" variety and with scholarly pursuits therefore might find specialized library work congenial—and especially the ever-expanding print culture collections at the Library of Congress.[20] As it turned out, they found the prospect of library work very attractive indeed. Women applied, and in large numbers, for the available positions (Table 1).[21]

Table 1. Women Staff in the Library of Congress, 1899–1914

Year	Number of Staff[a]	Number of Women Staff[b]	Percent	Number of Women Professionals
1899	133	44	33	7
1902	256	143	55.8	69
1905	303	148	48.8	81
1910	317	153	48	81
1914	343	163	47.5	75

[a] Staff totals calculated from appropriations legislation for fiscal years; i.e., 1899 figures are for the fiscal year ending June 30, 1899.

[b] Includes only permanent staff who stayed in their positions at least one year.

For the lowest-paid positions, at $360 per year, candidates for Catalogue Division positions had to have at least one to two years of high school (Table 2). At successive salary steps, more education, foreign languages, and library education and experience were requisite. A $720 position, essentially the beginning professional level, demanded at least two years of college or equivalent education, reading knowledge of foreign languages, and either a year's library experience or a library school degree.[22]

The entry salary was comparable to that of other libraries: in 1899 graduates of the Pratt Institute library school received salaries ranging from $416 to $2,000 per year, with an average of $686. Head librarians

Table 2. Qualifications for Catalog Division Staff, 1900

Salary	Desired Qualifications
$360	Good common school education plus one two years in high school
$540 and $600	High school education Some knowledge of French, German and Latin Short course in library science or equivalent in actual service
$720	At least two years' college or equivalent Reading knowledge of French, German, and Latin Library school course of two years and at least one year's experience; or three or more years' service in a library
$900	College course or equivalent Reading knowledge of French, German, and Latin Library school course of two years and at least one year's experience; or, three or more years' service in a library
$1,200	Four-year college course or equivalent Reading knowledge of French and German, and sufficient knowledge of the classical and one or two modern languages other than French and German for library purposes Three to four years' actual experience in a reference library, particularly in classification and cataloging
$1,500	Four-year college course or equivalent A year or more of postgraduate work along some particular line Considerable knowledge of books and literature Knowledge of French and German; sufficient command of the other modern languages and of Latin and Greek for library purposes From three to six years' actual experience in one of the larger reference libraries, such experience to have been particularly in the work of cataloging and classification Possession of physical stamina

Source: J. C. M. Hanson to Herbert Putnam, 26 February 1900, Library of Congress Archives, Manuscript Division, Library of Congress. Other division chiefs established similar criteria for the particular requirements of those divisions.

averaged $808; beginning catalogers received $667. Librarians in land-grant institutions earned $600, while women librarians in the western states were paid $40 to $70 per month. The Library of Congress's $720 salary was therefore just above the average for entering professionals in a seller's market.[23]

Positions above the beginning professional level required much more education, experience, and language training. The positions paying $1,200 and $1,500 did not require a library degree but did stipulate library experience, and for them Putnam intended to lure professionals from other library positions. He was sometimes able to hire highly qualified staff at lower salaries by holding out the promise of promotion. For example, Harriet Wheeler Pierson and her cousin Mary MacNair, both catalogers, worked at the New York Public Library, then directed by John Shaw Billings. Putnam's appeal to Billings for assistance in building up a staff led to an offer of $720 positions to both, but he later increased the offer to $900.[24] Both in their mid-twenties, Pierson and MacNair were college graduates, and they had completed the two-year course at the most prestigious library school, Melvil Dewey's New York State Library School in Albany. Each had four years of experience when she joined the Library of Congress staff, and Pierson listed knowledge of French, German, and Latin. MacNair, in addition to these languages, worked with Dutch, Spanish, and Italian. By 1906 each earned $1,200; MacNair had taken charge of the cataloging of periodicals, and she became the editor of the library's subject heading list and later its bibliography of doctoral dissertations.[25] Pierson assumed responsibility for the bibliographic control of society publications, and by 1914 both women were also revisers who checked and corrected others' work.[26]

In their roles as bibliographers and subject heading specialists, Pierson and MacNair entered areas requiring knowledge of the publication patterns of various types of printed works; of commercial and scholarly publishers; and of indexing "in relatively permanent form new events, movements, discoveries, which themselves are only in the process of formation," as Putnam put it.[27] Their workplace, the Catalogue Division, was the largest division in the library, and more women librarians worked there than in any other unit. It was highly stratified: the division chief had two chief assistants, one for the old classification being phased out, and one for the new classification system, plus four revisers of cataloging, each a specialist in a particular field of knowledge. There was also a curator of the Official Catalog, a supervisor of copying and clerical work, and by 1902, a head of the card section.[28] In 1901 Malina Gilkey was appointed head of the copying section and promoted to $1,400; Jessie Watson and Jane Bowne Haines became revisers at $1,200, and Mary Griswold the curator of the Official Catalogue, also at $1,200. Revisers distributed books among the twenty-four regular catalogers, according to subject specialization and type of material; e.g., government publications, periodicals, society publications, current foreign books, rare books, or copyright books. Catalogers also performed specialized tasks. In 1904, for example, when the library undertook to produce cards for all titles in the ALA's forthcoming second edition of its *ALA Catalog,* a list of recommended books for libraries, the catalogers worked evenings to complete the work.[29] And when Catalogue Division chief J. C. M. Hanson chaired the ALA committee formed in 1901 to produce a code of cataloging rules, Emma Runner and her assistants Mary Melcher and Julia Gregory selected the examples for each rule and proofread the text. While they did not select many examples related to women, neither did they ignore them: the rule for "Conventions, conferences" featured "Boston. Women's rights meeting, 1859"; the rule for "Affiliated societies" included the General Federation of Women's Clubs Norumbega Women's Club of Charlestown, Massachusetts; and the rule for "Architectural designs and plans" listed the drawings of "Holman, Emily Elizabeth."[30] Such entries silently indicated the need to take women's activities into consideration when organizing library collections.

Putnam wanted above all an efficient system of ordering and cataloging books, and he associated no other library activity so completely with technical competence. Deliberately breaking with the European national library tradition of brief book catalog listings, he and Hanson chose to provide detailed bibliographic descriptions on cards, plus extensive subject and added entries to maximize access to the book and pamphlet collections. They also specified rigorous authentication of authorship, close classification, and a high standard of excellence. "There is no limit to the knowledge useful for a cataloger," Putnam emphasized. "There is scarcely any information, fact, or intellectual experience which may not be brought into play in the course of a year's work in cataloging. The mere linguistic difficulties are formidable; the accessions of the Library of Congress include books in more than a hundred different languages."[31]

Catalogers had to be familiar with the full range of reference works that could assist their work, from national bibliographies and biographical compendia to subject bibliographies, directories, educational institutions' catalogs, alumnae registers, and similar items. The lack of published reference works complicated their work. In 1900, there was only one ongoing periodical index, *Poole's Index*, that covered those periodicals that librarians seeking "the best reading" for their users were likely to acquire. There was as yet no *Reader's Guide to Periodical Literature* and no *Book Review Digest*. There was an irregularly published *English Catalogue of Books*, but no *British National Bibliography*. The forerunner of *Books in Print* was just being established, and *Who's Who in America* had just appeared. The *Publisher's Trade List Annual* had been published since 1873 but it was simply a compilation of publishers' catalogs and lacked an index. Lacking reference sources that organized crucial information pertaining to the world of print, it was a challenging task for librarians to verify publication data and establish authorship accurately.

In general, cataloging commanded high respect in the profession as one of the most demanding tasks librarians performed. A single book could require long research to identify the author, examine the contents, distinguish among editions, or otherwise determine the bibliographic statement; and Library of Congress catalogers were trained to spend the time needed, from half a day up to "perhaps several weeks."[32] A contemporary, Celia Hayward, tells of cataloging Archbishop Whately's book, *Historic Doubts Relative to Napoleon Buonaparte*. "Reading the book technically," a cataloger's technique that focused on extracting essential information without actually reading the work, she discovered that *Historic Doubts* was not an appraisal of French history but instead doctrinal theology. In the back of the book she encountered an appendix titled *Historic Certainties Respecting the Early History of America*, by the Rev. Aristarchus Newlight, a pseudonym. Was *Historic Certainties* also by Whately? In a biography of Whately written by his daughter she found the perplexing information that it was edited by Whately but written by Bishop Ferguson, while the index contained a reference to a letter written by Whately regarding the identity of the pseudonymous Newlight. "I confess," she concluded, "that I look with stony disapproval on the author who hides himself behind one pseudonym today, appears under his own name tomorrow in a fit of self-confidence, or whatever it is, and concocts a new pseudonym for the day after." The British Museum entered books under the names that appeared on their title pages, but

American catalogers rejected the practice because, given an author with one or several pseudonyms, it meant scattering the entries for the works of that author throughout the catalog.[33] In their organization of print culture, American catalogers wanted readers to be able to identify any author without question and to be able to find all of that author's works listed together.

An area similarly in dispute was the entry of names. The ALA's catalog rules committee and the (British) Library Association were at odds: the British favored retaining the first entry while the Americans changed entries to reflect an individual's life and career. The American edition of the *Catalog Rules* instructed American catalogers to enter married women under the most recent name "unless she has consistently written under an earlier one (either her maiden name or the name of a former husband)." Entries had to include the husband's surname, her own forenames, and her maiden name, thus: "Jackson, Mrs. Helen Maria (Fiske) Hunt." Kate Douglas Wiggin, however, was entered as "Wiggin, Kate Douglas (Smith), 'Mrs. G. C. Riggs'" because she had once used the name of a former husband. And Mary Ward, who used "Mrs. Humphry Ward" on the title pages of her books, had the entry "Ward, Mary Angela (Arnold), 'Mrs. Humphry Ward.'" Given the need to at least create one card to cross-reference each name, a contemporary dryly remarked, "It would be a great boon to catalogers if women were sworn to celibacy before entering the literary profession."[34] A passion for accuracy and exhaustive coverage enforced cross-referencing; but the outcome was a system that effectively kept women's oeuvre intact in the world of print culture.

Similar challenges entered the work of Hester Coddington, former head cataloger at the University of Wisconsin, and Emma Runner, a cataloger from Cornell University. Salaried at $1,200, both were described as "catalogers doing subject work," meaning the task of assigning subject headings. As one of the most intellectually sophisticated tasks of cataloging, this work required enough knowledge of a subject to select suitable key words or phrases to describe each book so that users could find appropriate titles under subject in the card catalog. The goal was to assign every book to the most specific heading directly suggested by its title or contents, and with absolute consistency. "The increasing specialization in all branches of knowledge makes the determination of subject headings correspondingly difficult," Putnam explained. "Looking to the future growth of the Library, the development of its subject catalogues and classification must necessarily be sufficiently minute to permit the grouping of titles bearing directly on one topic under the name of that topic, not under the name of a large group of related subjects. For example, the student interested in the question of *Reciprocity* should find the titles collected under *Reciprocity* and should not be forced to search through all the titles under *Tariff* or *Commerce*." Cross-references were added to lead researchers to related subjects; thus the subject cataloger had to have sufficient knowledge to refer from *Finance,* for example, to *Bimetallism, Currency Question, Money, Silver Question,* and so on and from *Labor Question* to *Apprentices, Communism, Convict labor, Cooperation,* and *Eight-hour movement.*[35]

Librarians' care to systematize index terms, verify names, and formulate rules were aimed at giving users an efficient system for identifying the books, pamphlets, and journal articles they needed. But while no single individual in the Catalog Division selected all the subject headings, the *Subject Headings Used in the Dictionary Catalogues of the Library of Congress* (1910–14) reveals a good deal about the staff's thinking—careful and exact, but also revealing contemporary views of social class, gender, and other subjects.[36] There was a subject heading for "Woman" that included specialized subheadings such as "anatomy and physiology," "diseases," "dress," and "history and condition." However, "Man" embraced the entire human species with subheadings such as "origin of," "migrations of," and "erect position of." Neither "Feminism" nor "Sex discrimination" was listed, but under "Woman" appeared a subdivision for "Rights of Women." Readers could find material relating to "Education of women," but under "Profession, choice of" inquirers were referred to "Woman-Employment." A long series of special headings revealed the exceptional nature of "Women as artists," "Women as authors," "Women as inventors," and the like. The headings "Young men" and "Young women" included cross-references to the prescriptive topics of "self-culture" "YMCA," "YWCA," and "success." In matters of science, however, the subject cataloger could not allow embarrassment to become an issue: "Womb," see "Uterus."[37]

Subject work required detailed knowledge of both the old and new Library of Congress classification systems to ensure consistency of application. In 1900, these systems were used nowhere other than the library.[38] Subject catalogers had to be aware of precedents that guided the choice of headings and the definitions that distinguished established subject headings from similar terms that were not used. Experienced catalogers were needed since library-school training could not provide the ability to assimilate a new system quickly, and in the process, assess the adequacy and accuracy of its intellectual coverage against experience with other systems. A former teacher who had attended the universities of Chicago, Wisconsin, and Illinois and specialized in foreign languages, including Italian, Spanish, Portuguese, Dutch, the Scandinavian languages and Russian, Hester Coddington was a translator as well as a librarian. Emma Runner had received a bachelor's degree from Cornell University, where she had cataloged special collections using her knowledge of French, German, Italian, Spanish, Latin, Greek, Russian, Portuguese, and Dutch. With their backgrounds and experience squarely based in the cultures and materials the library was actively collecting, within two years both women were receiving $1,400 salaries.

Even the lesser positions demanded a high level of expertise in an institution the size of the Library of Congress. When Elizabeth Howard West, who had taken a master's degree in history and a library training course, applied for a position, she was offered work as a shelflister at $720.[39] "The work of shelflisting, which in an ordinary library is not especially technical, is in this Library, owing to the character of the material handled, considered a technical work requiring no mean abilities," chief clerk Allen Boyd assured her. West accepted the appointment. But in keeping with the policy of channeling expertise to areas where it was most needed, she was soon transferred to the Manuscript Division, where she used both her history and technical training to calendar the Martin Van Buren papers and to work with the Spanish colonial New Mexico collection.[40]

Similar to the intellectual demands of cataloging in Putnam's estimation were the functions of the Division of Bibliography. Its staff compiled lists of references on topics of current interest—particularly those under discussion or investigation by Congress. They also edited Library of Congress publications, engaged in cooperative bibliographic work with other libraries, and recommended acquisitions. They answered lengthy inquiries, in person or by mail, and when appropriate they referred inquirers to other institutions or other federal departments.[41] The division was a partial forerunner of today's Congressional Research Service, and the staff had to provide expert guidance on such complex public policy issues as colonization, mercantile marine subsidies, the Trans-Siberian Railway, comparative legislation, international arbitration, land tenure, and proportional representation—all of which were subjects of the division's bibliographies during the first few years of the century. Among the small staff were two former teachers, Florence Hellman, a University of Wyoming graduate, and Lucy Arrick, who had attended Columbian University.[12]

The Division of Bibliography, however, was removed from the public and therefore apparently considered a suitable place of employment for women librarians. The Reading Room, on the other hand, included only junior or less qualified female professionals. A glance at entry salaries shows that women in Reading Room positions entered at $360 or $720, and most never made more than $900 as stack attendants. Only men worked at the central desk to accept requests for books and answer questions from the public.[13] As highly educated and trained as they were, Putnam did not place women librarians in the position of serving publicly as print culture authorities for Library of Congress users.

Users, in fact, were probably not aware of the extent to which the library depended on women staff. Yet by 1902 women held over half the positions (Table 1), and they worked in every division of the library except the Law Library, where the first woman was hired in 1906, and in the small (four-person) Smithsonian Division. They collaborated with male supervisors and colleagues, and generally with a shared sense of mission and ambition.[14] Men and women librarians with equal responsibilities performed the same tasks for the same salaries.

Some 171 women entered the Library to do professional work before 1915. As a group, these women were overwhelmingly white, single (more than 90 percent) and relatively young, with only forty (27 percent) born before 1870.[15] They generally roomed or boarded within the city limits, and usually alone. Only forty-nine (29 percent) are known to have lived in households with relatives.[16] Most were not Washington, D.C., natives, nor were they from Virginia or Maryland. Rather, women from many states moved to Washington to work at the Library of Congress.

Their education and training is carefully documented. One hundred seventeen (68 percent) were graduates of two-year, one-year, or short courses in library schools. One hundred six (62 percent) had attended, graduated from, or taken postgraduate training in, universities and colleges. Sixty-four women had both library degrees and college training. Those without either college or library school training were educated at academies, normal schools, private schools or high schools.

Eighty-five (50 percent) had some previous library experience, while nineteen had been teachers, nine had served in other government offices, and twelve held a variety of other positions. More highly educated and trained than the majority of their contemporaries—even those in such professions as teaching—the female professional staff's abilities testified to Putnam's and the library profession's command of the institution. They also testified to the female presence in institutionalized print culture.

With their excellent qualifications, women might expect advancement to higher salaries. In 1902, division chiefs were paid $2,000 or $3,000, and the most highly paid chief assistants made $1,800. In keeping with the gender stratification of the library profession, males generally filled these upper-level positions. Women were not selected as division chiefs, although they might be "in charge" for short periods.[17] They seldom became chief assistants. The highest-paid woman was the secretary of the library, Margaret D. McGuffey, at $1,800. She served as a communications officer as well, for all correspondence came to the librarian's office and was routed to the chief assistant librarian or the division chiefs for their responses. From their memos, Putnam formulated replies, which went out over his signature. McGuffey coordinated responses, tracked delinquent items, and communicated daily with Putnam during his absences on matters requiring decisions. Trained as a librarian, she was the former chief of the Issue Department at the Boston Public Library, thus bringing technical knowledge, supervisory ability, and experience with Herbert Putnam to the secretary's post. He placed her temporarily in charge of the Order Division in 1908. Significantly, in an early picture of library officers and chiefs, she is the only woman.

In the supervisory or deputy positions that paid $1,200 to $1,800, the library did not approach the proportion of women in the profession as a whole, but a growing number of women were able to obtain these positions as time passed, especially in cataloging, classification, and ordering. In the Catalog Division in 1901, for example, the highest-salaried woman made $1,200, and among the seven librarians paid that salary, five were female. Eighteen men with salaries ranging from $1,400 to $1,800 were the highest-paid division assistants. In 1905, the number of women in mid-level cataloging positions had increased: by then, twelve women earned $1,200 to $1,500. Since a total of thirty staff made $1,200 or more, however, men still dominated the upper-level positions.

Library-wide, by 1910 some twenty-six women received between $1,200 and $1,500 (Table 3). Of the thirty positions paying $1,200 or more in cataloging, women held seventeen. Four years later, in 1914, there were twenty-nine women professionals making $1,200 or more in a salary structure that remained essentially unchanged, although the number of salary grades had increased. By far the greatest number of professional women were still in cataloging, where they held twenty of the twenty-nine positions salaried at $1,200 to $1,800. Thus while the ratio of supervisory to nonsupervisory staff remained much the same library-wide between 1902 and 1914, the proportion of women supervisors grew to 27 percent by 1914.

Table 3. Supervisory Positions Held by Women Professionals at the Library of Congress, 1899–1914[a]

Year	No. of Staff[b]	No. of positions below $1,200 (%)	No. of positions $1200 and above	No. held by women (%)
1899	133	86 (65%)	47	2 (4%)
1902	256	181 (71%)	75	9 (12%)
1905	303	207 (68%)	96	17 (17.7%)
1910	317	223 (70%)	94	26 (27.7%)
1914	343	236 (69%)	107	29 (27.1%)

[a] Staff totals calculated from appropriations legislation for fiscal years; i.e., 1899 figures are for the fiscal year ending June 30, 1899.

[b] Includes only permanent staff who stayed in their positions at least one year.

The fact that the library placed an increasing number of women in middle- to upper-level positions, close to the leadership, is a perspective that cannot be gained from the *Annual Report of the Librarian of Congress,* which seldom mentioned staff members by name, or from secondary accounts of the library's history, which feature primarily the men in upper administrative positions. The progressive salary schedule, with greater responsibilities at each step, provided these women librarians with both a higher standard of living and with managerial experience that were infrequently available to women in the early twentieth-century economy. Also important was the federal policy of paying women the same salary as men for the same work. Women librarians in federal service generally earned salaries that were higher than salaries in other types of libraries, assuming they had the qualifications to command more money."[18] When Mary Salome Cutler Fairchild surveyed women librarians in 1904, she found that in the government libraries, women held five of the twenty-nine administrative positions (17 percent).[49]

During the first quarter of the twentieth century, the Library of Congress was the most important institution shaping American cataloging practices and therefore the most influential organizer of print culture in libraries.[50] Herbert Putnam started the card service in 1901 to provide what the library community had long needed: high-quality, inexpensive cataloging for recently published American trade books. The service immediately and significantly impacted other libraries. It helped standardize, for example the order process: publishers who smelled profits soon began printing Library of Congress card numbers in their catalogs and bibliographies to make it easier to order both books and cards. For librarians, cards greatly reduced cataloging tasks, because they could simply file Library of Congress cards for their new books.[51] Users also benefited, for they could expect to find books under the same author and subject headings in different libraries, making it easier for scholars and students to tap their holdings. The library's cataloging homogenized approaches to printed materials throughout the country. But it was difficult during the early years for other libraries to copy the Library of Congress's practices: library schools could not make a quick transition to teaching Library of Congress cataloging because the printed catalog code did not become available until 1907. The subject heading list was not published until 1911, and the library's classification scheme appeared only slowly, volume by volume. The place to learn Library of Congress practice was the library itself, which meant that considerable staff resources were devoted to training.

Once trained, a staff member was a valuable resource, but retention soon became a problem. Because the rapid expansion of the Library of Congress was unprecedented in the profession, and because it was able to tie that world securely together through the establishment of standard systems of cataloging, classifying, and interlending for the entire record of print culture, professional mobility became a significant factor. The Library of Congress was the national authority for the profession—and in a broad sense for the entire population—because it amassed and disseminated the definitive record of American print culture by means of its printed copyright catalog and worldwide card service. Librarians who had mastered the systems employed in the nation's largest repository found opportunities elsewhere because they were able to carry Library of Congress practices to other institutions.

And if other libraries' need for trained staff provided the pull factor, the business cycle supplied a push. In the middle years of the first decade of the century, an economic downturn affected federal workers, whose salaries remained low while inflation increased. As the effects spread to workers more generally, the rising prices seemed to threaten the survival of the middle class.[52]

With few promotions available and living costs rising, Catalogue Division chief Hanson reported that he was essentially running a training school "where persons come for two or three years of experience at a low salary intending to accept the first promising offer from outside." He noted that several catalogers with between seven and twelve years of experience, who had advanced only to the medium grades, had accepted positions elsewhere. At one time in 1904, three women catalogers, all of whom made $720, were competing for a position at the Brooklyn Public Library. Hanson assured Putnam that two of them were unlikely to move unless they received a promise of promotion, but the third took the job.[53] At that time, the highest salary paid to women librarians not in administrative positions was $946, but experienced librarians at the Pratt Institute Library were beginning to exceed lower-range Library of Congress professional salaries: they received $1,000 to $1,300.[54] And as a portent of what salary increases elsewhere might mean to the library, Putnam found that other library directors were increasingly reluctant to recommend well-qualified men because salaries were inadequate.[55] He continued to regard every staff member who left as "an outpost and a continuing associate in a work which is not confined to Washington, but which seeks to be understood and utilized throughout the country at large." But pride in growing Library of Congress influence on the profession and on print culture was of less moment to the division chiefs than their decreasing productivity.[56]

Among the thirty women who left the Library from 1901 through 1905, the average number of years served was 2.7, and none worked there longer than five years. From 1906 through 1910, when forty-two women left, the average length of service increased to 4.7 years, but nearly one-fourth of these women remained at the library only one or two years. Library schools suggested that professionals stay at least two years in each position before moving on, and the majority of those who left heeded that suggestion. But also, it became more difficult to move quickly to another federal job when, in 1906, Congress passed a law forbidding federal employees from transferring to another agency until they had served three years.[57]

Of the ninety-nine professional women who left the Library before 1915, forty-six (46 percent) moved to positions in other libraries, ranging from the New York Public Library to the Georgia Institute of Technology, to the Universities of Chicago and Wisconsin, the Library Association of Portland, Oregon, and the Van Wert, Ohio, Public Library. Eleven married, three died, six took nonlibrary jobs, four stopped working entirely, and one moved away from Washington.[58] The standard career-progression model ascribes to economic motivation individuals' decisions on whether to stay or leave. But for these women who left their jobs, a better model should include noneconomic motives, allowing for individual decision making on preferred alternatives to work and on interrupting their careers.[59] Scholars have noted, for example, that well-educated women of the period were predominantly middle class rather than upper class, and if they prepared for a career to be able to support themselves or dependents, they might not have been able financially to interrupt their work.[60] There is evidence, however, that some of the women of the Library of Congress "dropped out" for periods both short and long; Margaret McGuffey, for example, went abroad in the summer of 1909 and decided to spend the winter in Italy, "as an intermission in library work." Julia Blandy asked for a temporary separation in 1903, when she wanted to travel. She reentered the service briefly, but resigned in 1905 to seek a library position elsewhere.

Adding the number who remained in library work to those who retired or died in service reveals that 104 of these professional women—nearly three-fourths—remained committed to library work. This is a large number—but perhaps not so remarkable for the early generation of educated women, many of whom chose not to marry. It is perhaps more surprising that the greater number left rather than completing their working lives at the library, and, moreover, that many left after relatively short periods. Brief tenure suggests the allure of the library's training during the early years of the century, in accordance with the career-progression model prediction that individuals acquire experience in one position in order to be able to move to another. The model also suggests that individuals may plan such changes in advance. These women may have intended to stay only briefly and then seek another position, possibly at a preferred location near family or friends.[61]

The forty-four women who stayed at the library were in general among the earliest to enter the service, and many of them did not leave the work force until well into the 1920s, the 1930s, and even the 1940s.[62] Their long careers at the library occurred because of unusual institutional circumstances: they arrived as the staff expanded so much that women were needed to provide the expertise Putnam required.[63] Their long tenure had important implications for women who came later because the promotion ladder worked slowly. The older women achieved promotion early and remained in their well-paying positions.

The younger women faced the challenge of finding new opportunities. Several records bear the chief clerk's comment that employees resigned "through discontent," to seek higher-paying jobs. "The salary is too low and you are too slow to promote," wrote Sara L. Young when she submitted her resignation. A college and library school graduate and an experienced cataloger when she entered in 1914 at $780, she received $960 four years later. Elizabeth G. Hopper, who entered service in 1910 at $720, obtained two promotions, rising to $960 before she resigned in 1918.[64] Hopper had a Cornell University bachelor's degree and had been a cataloger in the Cornell Library. Both women accepted positions in other federal libraries: Young became chief cataloger at the Department of Labor, and Hopper the assistant chief of the Periodical Division of the Department of Agriculture Library.[65] Had they stayed at the Library of Congress, they would almost certainly not have attained either chief or assistant chief positions.

Hazel Bartlett was more patient. A Wellesley graduate and an apostle of print culture, she arrived at the library in 1911 after working at *Youth's Companion*, the popular magazine that promoted reading for children, youth, and families. Her beginning salary was $600; by 1913 she was earning $900 and in 1914, $960. It took another five years to achieve promotion to $1,200 but by 1921 she received $1,400, and by the 1940s she was the assistant chief and head reviser of the Descriptive Cataloging Division.[66] Her long career, as well as those of others who chose to remain at the library in lesser positions, seems to reveal the lasting attraction of its extensive collections, marble halls, and national prestige.

Other decisions these women made reveal the heterogeneity of women's career progression in the early 1900s. Those who found the "family claim" strong returned home, perhaps obtaining new positions there.[67] Of those who married, nearly all disappeared from the work force. Some women, who came with aging parents or siblings to the nation's capital simply disappeared the family presumably having relocated. Some remained in Washington, working at other federal agencies. For others, there were library jobs elsewhere, and still others left the field to take up different work. But it is impossible to evaluate the typicality of this group without comparable data on other women professionals.

The advantage to studying a large bureaucracy is that it reveals important differences among layers and functions and a more varied picture of professional work.[68] In the case of the Library of Congress, the importance attached to print culture institutions and collections during the period becomes clearer when its large resources, complex organization, and intricate systems are delineated. The frequent omission of lower-status employees from the analysis of political and administrative systems has led to a failure to appreciate such complexities and to evaluate more fully the influence of gender on collections, services, and bibliographic organization. It has also led to a tendency to describe the work of the profession—and particularly women's work in the profession—in terms less sophisticated than both deserve. The library attracted highly educated women who were able to attain upward mobility and positions of authority in subject or technical areas—an important part of the profession's growing infrastructure. Their experiences in a large organization differed significantly from those of the many librarians in small public libraries. Their presence argues for a library profession more diverse at an early date than scholars have generally described.[69]

It also argues a presence for women in a metaworld of print culture. Once authors wrote and publishers published, books entered the domain of a set of arbiters: the indexers, the catalogers, the bibliographers, the abstracters, the collection developers who tried to channel them to the readers who needed them. Women librarians helped develop the systems for organizing printed works. Their work enabled books to be used and reused as needed, drew attention to landmark works, provided useful guides and maps of subjects and fields, and pointed to related subjects. Their analyses of print culture and their ideas about systematizing it appear in their publications—bibliographies, lists of subject headings, and manuals of practice for dealing with many different types of material. That they were so clearly devoted to the stuff of their work conveys the importance of understanding its context, content, and intellectual demands.[70]

Notes

1. This analysis draws on the theories of Magali Sarfatti Larson, Terence Johnson, and Eliot Freidson regarding professionals' objectives of enhancing their authority, controlling their work, and the market for their services, but also on Paul Starr's recognition that socioeconomic relations, culture, and institutions influence professional sovereignty. Andrew Abbott's interest in tracing the links between a profession and its actual work is relevant as is Barbara Melosh's emphasis on the altruistic goals of improving client services and practices. See Magali Sarfatti Larson, *The Rise of Professionalism: A Sociological Analysis* (Berkeley: University of California Press, 1977); Terence J. Johnson, *Professions and Power* (London: Macmillan, 1972; Eliot Freidson, *Professional Powers: A Study of the Institutionalization of Formal Knowledge* (Chicago: University of Chicago Press, 1986); Paul Starr, *The Social Transformation of American Medicine* (New York: Basic Books, 1982); Barbara Melosh, *The Physician's Hand: Work Culture and Conflict in American Nursing* (Philadelphia: Temple University Press, 1982).

2. Jane A. W. Turner was employed by the Smithsonian Institution as early as the late 1850s as a clerk in charge of recording foreign exchanges, but when the Smithsonian's collection was transferred to the Library of Congress in the mid-1860s, she remained at the Smithsonian. Librarian Ainsworth Rand Spofford stated in 1868 that the Library had not yet employed women; see U.S. Civil Service Commission, *Women in the Federal Service* (Washington, D.C.: Civil Service Commission, 1938), 3–6, 9.

3. R. Q. Mills to John Russell Young, 10 September 1897; James Slayden to Young, 13 October 1898, John Russell Young Papers, Library of Congress Archives, Manuscript Division, Library of Congress. Hereafter abbreviated LCA.

4. Until the passage of the Reclassification Act in 1923 (42 Stat 1488), salaries for civil service positions were set mainly at the discretion of department heads. The Library of Congress's salary schedule follows an 1854 law (10 Stat 276) that provided a classification for clerks' salaries and the 1883 Civil Service Commission plan constructed for examination purposes. See U. S. Civil Service Commission, Position Classification Division, *History of Position Classification and Salary Standardization in the Federal Service, 1789–1941*, 2nd ed., Washington, D.C., The Commission, 1941.

5. Bessie A. Dwyer to John Russell Young, 10 June 1898; David Hutcheson to Young, 20 September 1898, Young Papers, LCA.

6. Chief Clerk's Letterbook, 9 November 1898, p. 1, LCA. This appointment also may have involved political support since the U.S. was establishing new institutions in its recently acquired territory. Another professional, Anita Stephens, resigned in 1910 to accept "an appointment in the Philippines."

Employing another family member to maintain family support was not unusual in federal offices.

7. The data on Library of Congress employees comes from the Chief Clerk's records and the Librarian's Letterbooks, LCA, the Federal Personnel Records Center, federal censuses, city directories, and C. C. Williamson and Alice L. Jewett, eds., *Who's Who in Library Service* (New York, Wilson, 1933). Because working conditions in the library (and in federal service) were changing by 1914, this study covers women professionals from 1893 through 1914. Women who stayed less than one year are excluded.

8. Young's policy was to try to get members of Congress to suggest qualified candidates. He did not contact library schools to obtain lists of graduates since he thought that "to do so would be an invasion of the prerogatives of Congress." John Russell Young to Hon. C. W. Fairbanks, 17 Sept. 1898, Librarian's Letterbooks, vol. 27, p. 444–46, LCA.

9. The LCA records dating to Young's tenure cite political sponsors but frequently omit individuals' qualifications. Politicians often cited personal need as the reason constituents wanted jobs.

10. Jane Aikin Rosenberg, "Patronage and Professionals: The Transformation of the Library of Congress Staff, 1890–1907," *Libraries & Culture* 26 (Spring 1991): 251–68.

11. Jane Aikin, "'Referred to the Librarian, With Power to Act: Herbert Putnam and the Boston Public Library," p. 27–37 in *Occasional Papers,* no. 212, Graduate School of Library and Information Science, University of Illinois at Urbana, Champaign, May 2002.

12. By 1900 the four library schools were producing only between ten and twenty-five students annually who had taken the full course; Jane Aikin Rosenberg, *The Nation's Great Library: Herbert Putnam and the Library of Congress, 1899–1939* (Urbana: University of Illinois Press, 1993), 31–33.

13. Herbert Putnam, "What it Means to be a Librarian," *Ladies Home Journal* 17 (February 1900): 22.

14. Putnam, "What it Means," 22; Herbert Putnam, "The Prospect: An Address Before a Graduating Class of Women," *Library Journal* 37 (December 1912): 651–58; Mary Salome Cutler Fairchild, "Women in American Libraries," *Library Journal* 29 (December 1904): 161–62. There were less than half a dozen cases of resignation or leave due to illness among the Library's women professionals. If illness related to job stress, as McReynolds hypothesizes, it is possible that professionals experienced less stress than workers of lesser rank. See Rosalee McReynolds, "The Sexual Politics of Illness in Turn of the Century Libraries," *Libraries & Culture* 25 (Spring 1990): 211–12.

15. Barbara Brand, "Sex-Typing in Education for Librarianship, 1870–1920," in Kathleen Heim, *The Status of Women in Librarianship: Historical, Sociological and Economic Issues,* (New York: Neal Schuman, 1983), 36; Mary

Niles Maack, "No Philosophy Carries so Much Conviction as the Personal Life: Mary Wright Plummer as an Independent Woman," *Library Quarterly* 70 (January 2000): 6.

16. Putnam, "What it Means," 22; Brand, "Sex-Typing in Education," 34–39.

17. Putnam, "What it Means," 22; Herbert Putnam, "Education for Library Work," *Independent* 52 (November 22, 1900): 2775.

18. Putnam, "Education for Library Work," 2776.

19. For contemporary debate over this issue, see Demarchus C. Brown, "The Librarian a Scholar or Not?" *Public Libraries* 13 (May 1908): 169; Aksel G. D. Josephson, "Is Librarianship a Learned Profession?" *Public Libraries* 1 (1896): 195–96.

20. Melvil Dewey, *Librarianship as a Profession for College-Bred Women*, Boston, Library Bureau, 1886; Mary Emogene Hazeltone, "Opportunities for College Women in Library Work," *Wisconsin Library Bulletin* 12 (July 1916): 290; Maack, "'No Philosophy Carries,'" 8.

21. By 1902 there were more than 1,800 applications on file, but they were not tabulated by sex. John Russell Young frequently noted women's interest in library work; see Rosenberg, "Patronage and Professionals."

22. Professional employees are defined as persons employed at or above $720, with a few exceptions for individuals who entered at lower salaries but were otherwise professionally qualified.

23. "Salaries, Hours and Vacations of Library School Graduates," *Public Libraries* 5 (1900): 254; Joanne Passet, *Cultural Crusaders: Women Librarians in the American West, 1900–1917* (Albuquerque: University of New Mexico Press, 1994), 46; Georgia Metos Higley, "College, Community and Librarianship: Women Librarians at the Western Land-Grant Colleges," in Suzanne Hildenbrand, ed., *Reclaiming the American Library Past: Writing the Women In* (Norwood, NJ: Ablex, 1996), 65; see also Joanne Passet, "'You do not have to pay librarians': Women, Salaries, and Status in the Early 20th Century," in Hildenbrand, *Reclaiming the American Library Past, 207–19*. The federal benefits of thirty days' annual leave plus thirty days' sick leave may also have attracted applicants.

24. According to Brand, women were seldom included in directors' informal recruitment contacts. However, Putnam frequently appealed to other library directors and to library schools for help in filling professional positions; see Brand, "Sex-Typing in Education," 47, and Jane Pejsa, *Gratia Countryman: Her Life, Her Loves, and Her Library* (Minneapolis: Nodin Press, 1995), 88–90; 118–19.

25. The subject heading list was already under way; the dissertation bibliography was published 1919–35.

26. Harriet Wheeler Pierson, *Rosemary: Reminiscences of the Library of Congress* (Washington, D.C.: n.p., 1943), 3–4.

27. *Annual Report of the Librarian of Congress* 1939, 321 (hereafter abbreviated *ARLC*). The two women are among the most cited authors on cataloging; see Donald J. Lehnus, *Milestones in Cataloging: Famous Catalogers and Their Writing, 1835–1969* (Littleton, CO: Libraries Unlimited, 1974).

28. *ARLC*, 1901, 227–28.

29. Rosenberg, *Nation's Great Library*, 55. The library staff normally worked seven-hour days six days per week (in two shifts to cover 9 A.M. through 10 P.M.) with a half holiday on Saturday during July and August; see *ARLC*, 1901, 206–7.

30. *Catalog Rules: Author and Title Entries*, compiled by committees of the American Library Association and the (British) Library Association (Chicago: American Library Association Publishing Board, 1908), xi.

31. *ARLC* 1901, 225; Herbert Putnam, "The Woman in the Library," *Library Journal* 41 (December 1916): 880.

32. David A. Smith, "Processing Services 1905: Putting the Library's House in Order and the Country's Cataloging in Gear," *Library Resources and Technical Services* 29 (July/Sept 1985): 254–55.

33. *ARLC*, 1901, 225; Celia A. Hayward, "Woman as Cataloger," *Public Libraries* 3 (1898): 122.

34. *Catalog Rules*, 12–13; J. C. M. Hanson, *A Comparative Study of Cataloging Rules Based on the Anglo-American Code of 1908* (Chicago: University of Chicago Press, 1939), 32; Marie Ganley, "Some Problems in Cataloging," *Public Libraries* 6 (1901): 141.

35. *ARLC*, 1901, 233.

36. To compile its own list of subject headings, the library adopted the ALA's slender 1895 list and incorporated ideas from other current lists. By 1914, it had grown to two fat volumes. The issue of bias in subject assignments did not enter the library profession's deliberations until later in the twentieth century; see, for example, Hope A. Olson, "Difference, Culture and Change: The Untapped Potential of *LCSH*," in *The LCSH Century: One Hundred Years with the Library of Congress Subject Headings System*, ed. Alva T. Stone (New York: Haworth Press, 2000), p. 53–71.

37. *Subject Headings Used in the Dictionary Catalogues of the Library of Congress*, 1st ed. (Washington, D.C.: Government Printing Office, Library Branch, 1910–14).

38. *ARLC*, 1901, 231–32. However, as early as 1906 use of the Library of Congress classification began to spread to other libraries.

39. Shelf-listing involves locating a book logically with reference to other similar books by applying a classification number and an author code.

40. Tom Cutrer, "Elizabeth Howard West," *Texas Libraries* (Summer 1990): 36; Employment Records 1906–07, 126, LCA.

41. *ARLC*, 1901, 242.

42. Now George Washington University.

43. Josephus Nelson and Judith Farley, *Full Circle: Ninety Years of Service in the Main Reading Room* (Washington, D.C.: Library of Congress, 1991), 12–20. The one exception was the attendant for a more isolated unit, the Reading Room for the Blind.

44. See, for example Harriet Wheeler Pierson and Mary Wilson MacNair, *Francis Henry Parsons,* Washington, D.C., 1927.

45. The sole exception was Violetta Clarke Baker, an African American woman born in 1869 in Canada and married to Henry E. Baker, a government patent examiner. She had attended high school, business school, and the Amherst College Library School, and she held positions as a teacher and in other federal agencies.

46. Percentages are calculated from totals that exclude missing cases. Although birth dates are missing for twenty-one women, this was a younger, more independent group than women in federal service overall. About two-thirds of the women professionals entering the library before 1901 were under thirty-five years of age, but Aron's sample study found that in 1900 44 percent of women federal clerks were under thirty-five, and two-thirds lived with family members. See Cindy Sondik Aron, *Ladies and Gentlemen of the Civil Service: Middle-Class Workers in Victorian America* (New York: Oxford University Press, 1987), 46, 55.

47. During Putnam's tenure there was one case of a woman chief assistant (Card Division, 1902–11), two cases of women "in charge" (Order and Bibliography Divisions) and one woman chief (Bibliography)—but she did not attain that position until 1938.

48. Marion Parris, "Women in the Civil Service," in *Vocations for the Trained Woman,* ed. Agnes F. Perkins (Boston: Women's Educational and Industrial Union, 1910), 7.

49. Fairchild, "Women in American Libraries," 160.

50. Lehnus, *Milestones in Cataloging,* 87.

51. Libraries usually did not accept all Library of Congress cataloging practices, but most eventually did use its cards. See Rosenberg, *Nation's Great Library,* 51–54.

52. Daniel Horowitz, *The Morality of Spending: Attitudes Toward the Consumer Society in America, 1875–1940* (Baltimore: Johns Hopkins University Press, 1985), 67–72; Paul Van Riper, *History of the United States Civil Service* (Evanston, IL: Row, Peterson, 1958), 243–44.

53. J. C. M. Hanson to Herbert Putnam, 5 Jan. 1904, LCA; *ARLC* 1907, 45–46. It took about two years to train a cataloger. Hiring experienced catalogers provided Hanson the means of staffing higher-level positions without long training, but well-qualified workers often left before they could be promoted. The library's experience in this regard was similar to that traced by Joni

Hersch, "Optimal 'Mismatch' and Promotions," *Economic Inquiry* 33 (October 1995): 611–24.

54. Fairchild, "Women in American Libraries," 157–62; Maack, , "'No Philosophy Carries,'" 32.

55. Frank P. Hill to Putnam, 5 January, 11 February, 1904; 18 December 1905; 18 April 1907; Putnam to Hill, 19 December 1905, LCA.

56. *ARLC,* 1904, 15.

57. Passet, *Cultural Crusaders,* 213; 34 Stat 449, June 22, 1906.

58. Data is missing for the remaining cases.

59. Nachum Sicherman and Oded Galor, "A Theory of Career Mobility," *Journal of Political Economy* 98 (1990): 169–92; Seymour Spilerman and Trond Peterson, "Organizational Structure, Determinants of Promotion, and Gender Differences in Attainment," *Social Science Research* 28 (1999): 203–27.

60. Barbara Sicherman, "Colleges and Careers: Historical Perspectives on the Lives and Work Patterns of Women College Graduates," in *Women and Higher Education in American History: Essays from the Mount Holyoke College Sesquicentennial Symposia,* ed. John Mack Faragher and Florence Howe (New York: W. W. Norton, 1988), 136.

61. Sicherman and Galor, "Theory of Career Mobility," 185.

62. No pension plan was in effect for the federal work force until 1920, and it was not until the 1930s that mandatory retirement at age seventy was imposed.

63. The records do not provide evidence of a quota system, but the percentage of women staff remained fairly stable during the period.

64. In 1921 Elizabeth Kemper Adams advised college and library school graduates working in large cities not to accept less than $1,400. See Elizabeth Kemper Adams, *Women Professional Workers: A Study Made for the Women's Educational and Industrial Union* (New York: Macmillan, 1921), 364.

65. Workers not promoted but with a high probability of promotion are most likely to seek other jobs; see Sicherman and Galor, "Theory of Career Mobility," 188. Misfits between qualifications and salary levels made the Library vulnerable to such mobility.

66. Promotion is uncertain but with longevity the chances of such promotions increase; see Sicherman and Galor, "A Theory of Career Mobility," 187–88. The library appears to have followed the principle of seniority promotion to an extent; phrases such as "there are three ahead of her for promotion" and similar comments appear in the Chief Clerk's records, LCA.

67. Jane Addams, "The College Woman and the Family Claim," *The Commons* (September 1898): 3–7.

68. See Phyllis Dain, "Women's Studies in American Library History: Some Critical Reflections," *Journal of Library History* 18 (Fall 1983): 456 on broadening the study of women in libraries.

69. The traditional view of women librarians is Dee Garrison's *Apostles of Culture: The Public Librarian and American Society, 1876–1920* (New York: Free Press, 1979). For current scholarship, see Suzanne Hildenbrand, "Library Feminism and Library Women's History: Activism and Scholarship, Equity and Culture," *Libraries & Culture* 35 (Winter 2000): 51–65. On women's upward mobility in large organizations, see Spilerman and Peterson, "Organizational Structure." Jeffrey Waddoups and Djeto Assane, "Mobility and Gender in a Segmented Labor Market," *American Journal of Economics and Sociology* 52 (October 1993): 399–411 found that a high level of education and a tight labor market affected women's upward mobility positively in the high status professional and managerial segment while household related variables affected it negatively: being single was a significant advantage for women seeking advancement.

70. Suzanne Hildenbrand, "Women in Library History: From the Politics of Library History to the History of Library Politics (Bibliographical Essay)" in Hildenbrand, *Reclaiming the American Library Past*, 16; LeeAnne Giannone Kryder, "Self-Assertion and Social Commitment: The Significance of Work to the Progressive Era's New Woman," *Journal of American Culture* 6 (Summer 1983): 25–30.

A "Bouncing Babe," a "Little Bastard"

Women, Print, and the Door-Kewaunee Regional Library, 1950–52

CHRISTINE PAWLEY

In the summer of 1950[1], Wisconsin Free Library Commission (WFLC) consultant Anne Farrington wrote to her friend and colleague Gretchen Schenk, "All day today I've struggled to write an article for ALA [American Library Association] Bulletin and one for Minnesota Libraries. Being in a very low state of mind . . . all that came forth was this ditty. I have cleaned it up somewhat but am afraid I have allowed it to become a bit maudlin at the end—effects of listening to the radio news with one ear and the resulting depression of spirit I guess."[2] Adopting the title "Pregnant with Possibilities," Farrington went on to describe the Wisconsin Door-Kewaunee Regional Library Demonstration as a child—a "premature, out-sized, Paul Bunyan of a baby, conceived by a combination of circumstances growing out of frustration, idealism and pig-headed perseverance of a group of librarians, commission and commission staff members, and fellow-travelers. The baby, she wrote, "is now a booming six-month-old infant of unpredictable tendencies." But whether the infant would prove to be a "bouncing babe" or a "little bastard" was anyone's guess.

Farrington's use of a metaphor of maternity was an apt one for the period. Historians describe the 1950s as a decade in which many American women experienced a distinct contraction in lifestyle options. Not long after the end of World War II, Rosie the Riveter and her sisters were laid off and sent home to make room for hundreds of thousands of returning veterans. Despite the vital role they had played in manufacturing and commerce, women were suddenly redundant in the labor market. An informal practice of "domestic containment" persuaded, instructed, pressured, and sometimes coerced them to rededicate their lives to homemaking and childrearing.[3] Cheerfully or reluctantly, many women returned to their kitchens and nurseries.

Yet some women broadened their range in the 1950s. One such opportunity offered itself in Wisconsin between 1950 and 1952 through the Door-Kewaunee Regional Library Demonstration, a state-sponsored experiment in rural library service. In the postwar period, poor rural library service in many parts of the United States was a matter of concern to librarians and public policy makers. Despite the turn-of-the-century establishment of a wide-ranging traveling library system and an increase in small-town public libraries, fifty years later those living in fifty-three out of Wisconsin's seventy-one counties still lacked free library access. But by the late 1940s, a movement to provide demonstrations of best library practice in rural areas had gained momentum, and in September 1949, the WFLC succeeded in obtaining state funding for a regional library project in the contiguous counties of Door and Kewaunee, which together form the Door Peninsula, an area of great natural beauty that juts into Lake Michigan—the "thumb" of Wisconsin's mitten-shaped outline.

The purpose was to demonstrate the library's value as "an important educational and informational asset . . . [and] to prove and perfect more efficient and economical procedures."[4] Library supporters hoped that once rural residents experienced the very best public library service possible, they would be willing to support this level of service on a permanent basis, through local taxes. The plan provided for six (later seven) existing library "units" (i.e. permanent library buildings), plus two new bookmobiles, each capable of carrying at least one thousand volumes. While recognizing that past studies had showed that children and women tended to be the most frequent users of public libraries, the WFLC hoped that by providing a wide range of reading materials, the demonstration would attract more men to the library.[5]

For three years, residents of Door and Kewaunee counties experienced vastly improved library service. For the first time, local libraries not only cooperated in selecting, purchasing, and cataloging materials but also provided the kinds of public services—including reference, reader's advisory, and children's story-telling—that urban residents might take for granted but which rural residents rarely, if ever, experienced. The regular bookmobile service also offered a range of choice in reading materials that the region's farm families had never before enjoyed. Overall, library circulation figures soared by 160 percent. But in November 1952, at the end of the three-year trial period, when voters were asked to pass a referendum authorizing the project's continuation, only Door County voted in favor.[6] So while the Door County bookmobile continued for another forty years, the Kewaunee bookmobile service came to an abrupt halt.

While the project lasted, it was women who both invested most, and perhaps also received most. Although the majority of bookmobile users were children, 95 percent of adult users were women—including many farm women, married and often with large families. Another group—also mainly women—who placed high value on the bookmobile service were the teachers of one- and two-room rural schools. A third group whose lives were transformed by the project were the librarians (again mostly female) who administered it locally, who interacted with the library's patrons, and who infused the process with energy, hope, and commitment. Each of these groups of women used the library project in different ways to push out the boundaries of their traditionally gendered domains—librarianship, teaching, and homemaking—and to challenge prevailing definitions of how they might fulfill their roles.

Despite wartime industrial expansion in the Kewaunee County cities of Algoma, Kewaunee, and Sturgeon Bay, the most common postwar occupation was still agriculture.[7] In the late 1940s, farmers continued to dwell in enclaves of the ethnic groups that had migrated there in the nineteenth century. In southern Kewaunee County were groups of Czechs and Poles. Belgians lived in and around the Door County community of Brussels, while farther north lived groups of Scandinavians, including Icelanders on Washington Island, which lay at the very tip of the peninsula. Germans were scattered throughout both counties. The region also experienced an influx of seasonal visitors. The picturesque coastal villages of northern Door County had long provided a desirable summer cottage location for wealthy business and professional families from urban centers like Chicago and Milwaukee.[8] These summer visitors introduced to northern Door County a value for middle-class leisure pursuits that included reading; but the residents of southern Door County and Kewaunee County, mainly agricultural, did not necessarily share the same values. At the same time, cherry and apple orchards employed seasonal workers—mostly Hispanic migrants who also transplanted their families to the Door Peninsula for a few weeks during the summer. Thus the region as a whole was culturally more heterogeneous than the blanket term "rural" conveys. While the northern districts gradually took on the characteristics of an upper-middle-class tourist destination, the southern districts retained their independent, conservative values, resisting "outsider" values and resenting both the prosperity and "other" quality that characterized the northern peninsula. And it was rural families of the type that predominated in the south that the WFLC particularly wanted the demonstration to reach.

For the librarians, teachers, and homemakers, the library project provided scope and pretext for expanded horizons. Some undertook a level of political action and organizational decision making that was still unusual for women at mid-twentieth century. Other women experienced opportunities to interact socially and professionally not only with other women, but with men, both locally and at the state and national levels. Officials and researchers based in Madison made frequent trips to the peninsula. So did WFLC Secretary Walter S. Botsford and Chairman John Chancellor, University of Wisconsin rural sociology professor John Barton and graduate student Eugene Rector, all of whom came not only to observe but to support and advise. The Door-Kewaunee Demonstration attracted interest from all over country—and all over the world. American visitors came from as far away as Alabama and Vermont, New York and California. International visitors came from Burma, Germany, New Zealand, the Philippines, and Sweden.

The demonstration enabled women who were full-time homemakers to step outside the then normal routines of domestic chores, child care, and church activities. Through social encounters at the bookmobile, and through reading the printed materials they took home with them, women experienced a subtle enrichment of their lives. Library books and magazines provided the means to breach the bounds of domesticity. Yet at the same time, and in some ways, women chose to embrace the ideology of domesticity through the language they used to describe and justify their activities, and through their reading choices.[9]

Ostensibly, it might seem likely that the three different groups—librarians, teachers, and homemakers—led clearly distinct lives. Compared with most Door Peninsula residents, librarians were educationally privileged. In addition to a bachelor's degree, they also had graduate-level professional training. Schoolteachers, too, had benefited from several years of education beyond the norm. After graduating from high school—itself an unusual achievement in the 1930s—aspiring teachers attended the Door-Kewaunee Normal School in Algoma for two years before receiving certification. It might be assumed, therefore, that teachers and librarians would feel themselves somewhat set apart: elite members of the community, whose role was to provide expert reading guidance to the children and rural families they served. And indeed, that may well have been the perception of some farm families. However, interviews with former librarians and teachers suggest that they saw their identities as overlapping those of their rural patrons—both adults and children. Though they recognized that not everyone necessarily valued reading to the extent that they did, in their own eyes they felt they retained an authentic rural identity that to some extent justified their intervention in the local community. In particular, some recalled their own grade-school education in one-room rural schools, where all eight grades were instructed by a single teacher, and where they suffered, they felt, from a chronic shortage of reading materials. At the same time, however, librarians recognized that some of the ethnic groups that composed the farming community had distinctive characteristics that they themselves did not share.

Library staff fulfilled administrative, professional, clerical, and technical roles. Headquartered in Sturgeon Bay (the seat of Door County) were project director Jane Livingston, reference librarians and catalogers, technical services staff who processed materials, clerical staff who dealt with day-to-day administration, and bookmobile personnel, consisting of a librarian and driver. Livingston was a Wisconsin native who had worked in a Michigan county library system for several years. However, on a visit home, she found herself recruited for the directorship of the Sturgeon Bay Public Library, largely on the basis of her Michigan experience. The Sturgeon Bay library board was interested in the concept of a county-wide system that would open up reading opportunities for rural residents, and wanted to hire a director who could facilitate such a program.

In August 1945, Livingston moved to Door County. At that time, rural residents were permitted to use the Sturgeon Bay library for an annual fee of fifty cents, but either this apparently modest sum was too much for many families, or perhaps they were simply not interested in patronizing the public library, for few took advantage of the arrangement. With the support of county school superintendent Curtis Tronson, Livingston set about stumping the county, making speeches, and drumming up support for a county system that would not only coordinate service among the existing libraries but also provide books for rural readers through a bookmobile. Success depended on her ability to convince local politicians, and she undertook this task with tireless energy. Stanley Greene, originally a library board skeptic, changed his mind about the potential value of a county system after he attended a Wisconsin Library Association meeting in Madison. But not all community leaders were able or willing to make such a journey, so to win over county supervisors, Livingston and Tronson arranged for the evidence to come to Door County. At the 1949 Door County fair, they set up a bookmobile demonstration, using a state-owned vehicle that they borrowed for the duration of the fair. "We snared every [supervisor]," Livingston commented. "All we did was tell them we wanted to show them what it was. We didn't put any pressure on them. . . . But we got most of them." However, they missed one supervisor from the north of the Door Peninsula. "On Monday morning the bookmobile was still here. . . . So we took off and went up there and stopped at his house." Fortunately for Livingston and Tronson, the man's wife was a library supporter. "He's off out in the woods up there, but you can get through," she told them. Following her directions, Livingston and Tronson drove the bookmobile off the highway into the woods and finally located—and persuaded—the elusive supervisor. From then on, "he was always one of our supporters," Livingston recalled. "I think it impressed him that we chased him down. . . ."[10]

In addition to the headquarters staff, each of the local library units—in the towns of Algoma and Kewaunee in Kewaunee County, and in several villages of northern Door County—employed their own library staff. While the project director and some of the headquarters employees were professionally qualified, most of the women who staffed the regional units were not. But boundaries between staff with professional qualifications and those without were far from rigid. All library personnel, no matter what their qualifications, took part in key decisions. Materials selection, for instance, was devolved to local units and bookmobile staff on the grounds that those in closest contact with readers should be responsible for choosing what to buy. Like many women of her time, Olivia Traven, the librarian at Bailey's Harbor, had not gone to college. Yet lack of a library degree was no barrier to Traven's contributing as fully to the demonstration as those with more formal qualifications. Highly active in local affairs as a vocal woman's club member and library volunteer, she possessed solid writing and leadership abilities, so that when the previous Bailey's Harbor librarian resigned, she seemed the natural choice to take over the running of the library. For Traven, the library provided the outlet for her considerable skills and energy that she had always longed for, at the same time enabling the community to benefit from her commitment and creativity for twenty years.[11]

Librarians included not only those locally employed but also Wisconsin Free Library Commission field workers based in Madison. A key figure was Anne Farrington. Her staff associates saw the red-haired and slightly built Farrington as dynamic and idealistic, as well as practical and pragmatic. Born in southwestern Wisconsin, Farrington had also worked in Michigan, eventually becoming county librarian for Van Buren County.[12] In 1949, the Wisconsin Free Library Commission hired her to liaise with local staff in Door and Kewaunee counties, the area already selected for the regional library experiment. This move prompted a happy coincidence: Jane Livingston was a former colleague of Farrington's from her Michigan days. Although the two women had previously been no more than acquaintances, now they became friends as well as close collaborators.

Farrington loved Door County. She bought a cottage on the shore near Sturgeon Bay and spent as much time there as she could. "Anne had such great hopes for things," recalled Livingston. "I can remember sitting looking out over Green Bay and watching the sunset and talking with her about things we were going to do. She was just that kind. . . . [She] inspired people to want to do things." The librarians used Anne's cottage as a social and strategic center. "We would all go over to Anne's for dinner," remembered another former librarian. "She would say, 'I'll provide the place—you bring the food. I'm not much of a cook!'"[13] In this domestic setting, then, these relatively undomestic women reveled in their professional freedom.

Together, they formed themselves into a close-knit group—"almost like a family," this librarian related. To be sure, sometimes the "family" failed to function effectively. In August 1952, as participants were gearing up for the coming electoral struggle, Farrington addressed a staff meeting: "Those of you who have been here for the 'duration' know something of the trials and tribulations, the unforeseen crises, and the element of real tragedy which have gone into this program."[14] One such "tragic" aspect was the discovery that one library staff member—a bookkeeper—had been embezzling funds. At this news, other staff reacted with outrage. "It was like a betrayal," Livingston remembered.

Teachers constituted another group that was heavily invested in the experiment. School facilities in the two counties were very limited in the late 1940s. Of the farm men and women in Door County, barely one-quarter had more than an eighth-grade education. In Kewaunee County, this was true of only 18 percent.[15] At the close of the 1940s, most of the area's rural children attended their local country school for all eight grades. In 1950, of a total of 114 schools, seventy-five were rural one-room schools and another twenty-two were rural graded schools. Four parochial schools, both Catholic and Lutheran, also served rural areas. But rural children's school performance persistently failed to match that of their urban counterparts. Even rural children who attended urban schools were less likely to succeed in the eighth grade than were urban children.[16] Rural schoolteachers were often young women who had themselves been pupils in a similar school before going on to high school and preparing to teach by attending the Door-Kewaunee Normal School. At the age of twenty or even younger, they might find themselves in charge of as many as forty children in a one-room school containing all eight grades. In school, children sat in columns according to their grade and studied on their own for long stretches. Typically, lessons aimed specifically at their grade lasted no longer than ten minutes. Teachers struggled to maintain the high degree of organization required to satisfy the needs of such a wide range of ages, while older children often found themselves helping younger students—a practice that carried both advantages and disadvantages.[17]

The classroom contained little physical equipment beyond basic furniture. A meager shelf of well-worn books at the back of the room might provide the only reading materials apart from the district-designated textbooks. "We had very few library books in our school . . . and we [had] probably read all those books at our school already," recalled a former student.[18] And few public libraries served the two counties. The cities of Sturgeon Bay in Door County, and Algoma and Kewaunee in Kewaunee County, each had its own library. Six northern Door County villages—Bailey's Harbor, Egg Harbor, Ephraim, Sister Bay, and (offshore) Washington Island—also had small libraries that were, for the most part, run by volunteers, open for restricted hours, and poorly stocked. But southern Door and Kewaunee counties had no rural libraries at all, though rural residents could use the city libraries for a fee.

The Door-Kewaunee Regional Library Demonstration suddenly changed all this. Now, from January 1950 to the end of December 1952, classroom reading opportunities were transformed by regular visits from the two county bookmobiles. Staffed by both a librarian and a driver, these consisted of heavy-duty vans carrying hundreds of books, pamphlets, and periodicals arranged by age and subject level. For the first time, rural teachers had regular access to an educational resource that simply arrived on their doorstep. "If it hadn't been for that bookmobile I suppose those children wouldn't have had the opportunity to read many books," pointed out a former rural teacher, "because I don't think any of them had a library. . . . Well, there wasn't a local library. You would have had to drive to a library and most of those people didn't have time to do that."[19] The children, too, eagerly anticipated the bookmobile's arrival. As a former student recounted, "[We were] very very excited. . . . I'm sure we were hard to contain for the teacher, because it was such an event for us to think that they were bringing books out to us." This student remembered that the books were arranged "by grade level. There were encyclopedias way on the top shelf and then they went on down with the lower grades on the bottom so they could reach them and see them." More importantly, perhaps, she also recalled the "warm, cozy" feeling of the bookmobile, and even the smell: "I don't know, it was a good—yeah it was—there was just something about it that I liked the way the bookmobile smelled."[20] Some teachers limited the number of books children could choose; others encouraged children to pick as many books as they could carry away. Some organized a secondary circulating system, so that children had access to a constantly changing collection of books chosen by their classmates. Teachers and children became accustomed to the bookmobiles' regular appearances. Teachers could count on a supply of print materials to enhance their classroom activities. Children looked forward to tapping the seemingly endless supply of stories.

But in the summer of 1952, as the referendum approached, the teachers grew anxious about the library's survival. Passage seemed likely in Door County, but in Kewaunee County, opposition to paying for public library services had always been stronger. In September, fifty-eight Kewaunee County rural teachers (almost all women) issued a notice "To Voters of Kewaunee County" in the local newspapers: "Do you know that the part of your tax dollar which was spent for the Bookmobile has been a great factor in aiding and broadening of the education of the Kewaunee County rural children? We, the rural Teachers of Kewaunee County wish to thank you through this publication and sincerely hope you continue such a fine program at the Referendum vote in November."[21]

This mild example of collective action was hardly indicative of a radical political consciousness, but after Kewaunee County defeated the referendum on 4 November 1952 by a vote of 4,239 to 3,459, some teachers took the more assertive step of addressing the Kewaunee County supervisors' meeting. Door County supervisors, following the results of the referendum mandate (which carried the county by 5,149 to 3,459), quickly designated $30,000 to establish a county library. But in Kewaunee County, even after a teachers' delegation argued for two hours in favor of some kind of rural library, they failed to convince a majority of the Kewaunee supervisors. The debates dragged on for another six months, but in June 1953 the supervisors took a final vote of 11 to 9 against the county library, and the service was pronounced dead.[22] As the Kewaunee County bookmobile made its final rounds in December, teachers, schoolchildren, and their mothers said a last goodbye to its driver and librarian, some in tears, others furious—most in dismay and disbelief.[23]

Of the three groups of women—librarians, schoolteachers, and library patrons—the latter are the most difficult to discern through the mists of time. They were less likely than teachers and librarians to be mentioned in surviving institutional records, and because of their status as "ordinary citizens" it was also rare for their letters and diaries to survive in archives. However, the records of their library choices help to reconstitute a picture of their reading practices. About six hundred charges represent books and magazines selected by a group of about two hundred married women.[24] The majority (69 percent) were rural residents who used either the bookmobile service at its crossroad, school, or village stops, or who patronized the small village libraries. Probably these women's lives conformed to what seems to have been a common pattern for rural married women at the time: an endless series of farm and domestic chores that included child care, gardening, cooking, cleaning, laundry, and perhaps still overseeing poultry and milking. (Some, it would seem, drew the line at making soap.)[25] The traditional, ethnically based families in which many farm women lived in the postwar period were male-centered and male-dominated. Men ran not only the family farm but also made the major decisions in that key local institution, the church. Women in German Lutheran farm families, for instance, were expected to focus their energies almost exclusively on home and children. Even at church, they provided "the equivalent of domestic labor to make the church function."[26]

But the 1940s saw structural changes in the lives of farm women, the result of an accelerating industrialization of agriculture. On the one hand, the mechanization and concentration of some traditional spheres of women's farming, like poultry and egg production, meant relinquishing this activity to men. On the other, mechanization of fieldwork made it possible for women to "help out" in activities formerly reserved for men, and a general shortage of hired male labor made it increasingly likely that they would spend more time in the fields. But farm women were not exempt from the domestic ideology of the 1950s, and fieldwork was contrasted unfavorably with "homemaking," an activity that was represented as being not only as natural to women but also preferred by them.[27]

By 1950, most Wisconsin farms were electrified, though many still lacked indoor plumbing—as did many village homes of the period. With electrification, farm and village women joined city dwellers as potential consumers of such household appliances as refrigerators, freezers, stoves, and water heaters. Some women learned to drive, while others depended on their husbands or older children to take them to town, to church, or to visit a neighbor. Another destination was the monthly meeting of the local homemakers club. These organizations, sponsored by the state-funded county extension agency, provided not only a social venue in which rural women met regularly as a group but also a means of expanding their learning opportunities and organizational abilities. Homemakers clubs focused primarily on domestic skills and activities, and so seemed to reinforce the era's conservative message of "domestic containment." But at the same time, club activities recognized the bifurcated nature of farm women's lives and represented an effort to reduce this burden. Home agents drew rural women's attention to the new, so-called labor-saving devices being commercially produced for the household.[28] Farm journals likewise drew women's attention to household consumer products, and some editors even suggested—a radical idea!—that domestic technology might have priority over the purchase of new machinery for the farm.[29] Thus county extension agencies, farm publications, and commercial advertising joined in urging farm families to mechanize household tasks, just as they were mechanizing other farm tasks. So—at least in the idealized world of printed publications and farm women's own educational institutions—the domestic lives of rural women began to approach those of their urban counterparts.

The reading materials chosen by rural women library patrons reflected the era's preoccupation with gender and domesticity. A rough classification of charges indicates that, conforming to the urban patterns uncovered by previous research, these rural readers preferred popular fiction—especially novels with a domestic theme, written by women.[30] A favorite was Kathleen Thompson Norris, a prolific novelist of Irish Catholic descent who wrote stories that idealized family life and the role of women as mothers of many children. Close behind Norris were other best-selling women novelists: Faith Baldwin, Frances Parkinson Keyes, Mazo de la Roche, Emilie Loring, and Daphne Du Maurier. In choosing predominantly domestic fiction, the women seemed to express their value for leisure and entertainment in a gendered form.

The nonfiction that the women patrons borrowed also echoed the domestic themes that dominated not only their favorite fiction but also the homemaking club meetings, women's magazines, and the advertisements in local newspapers. By far the most popular consisted of craft books with titles like *Painting Patterns for Home Decorations*, *How to Beautify and Improve Your Home*, and *Use and Care of Furniture*. Cookbooks and manuals of food preparation, too, were popular, including the best-selling *Betty Crocker's Picture Cookbook* and *Home Freezing for Everyone*. Women checked out sewing and knitting titles like *The Complete Book of Knitting and Sewing for the Home*, in addition to books about gardening like *Garden Flowers in Color* and *Grow Your Own Vegetables*. Among charges of periodicals, the most popular were *Good Housekeeping*, *House and Garden*, and the *Ladies Home Journal*.

The women also charged out materials for their young children. About 30 percent of their charges consisted of children's stories and readers. Evidently mothers wished to pass on to children their own love of reading as a recreational activity. Moreover, the borrowing of women who chose several books at once suggests that they made reading choices for other family members. For example, Mrs. J. of rural Door County charged out seven books on one bookmobile visit. Two were children's titles—Maj Lindman's *Snipp, Snapp, Snurr and The Big Farm*, and Phil Strong's *Honk the Moose*. The rest were novels: as well as Faith Baldwin's *High Road* Mrs. J. picked a crime story—Eleazar Lipsky's *People Against O'Hara*, and a western—Frank Robertson's *Wrangler on the Prod.* Perhaps she had eclectic reading tastes; perhaps she was choosing books for other family members, including her husband. A casual comment in a local newspaper suggests that women were indeed expected to pick up—and perhaps select—books for others, especially men and children. After recommending that readers borrow a particular title available in the public library, the newspaper editor suggested to the implied male reader, "Perhaps you can get your wife to bring it home for you, too!"[31]

On the other hand, some women had very specific informational needs when they chose books at the library. In November 1950, Mrs. B. of the city of Algoma chose six titles that suggested a theme, including *Understanding Your Boy*, *Life with Family*, and *Keeping Your Child Normal: Suggestions for Parents, Teachers and Physicians; with a Critical Estimate of the Influence of Psychoanalysis.* Mrs. B.'s preoccupation with parenting and family books reflected an application of expert study and recommendations to what in previous eras had been largely a matter of private, individual choice based on class, religion, or ethnic tradition.[32]

For these three groups of women, the library demonstration carried with it possibilities of change. For the librarians, it represented the chance to put into practice the most innovative ideas of the time in the company of committed and like-minded colleagues. For the rural teachers the bookmobile provided not only a much-appreciated break from the daily challenge of educating too many children of too many different ages in too many subjects but also a stimulus to the teaching and learning that went on in their classrooms. To the married women readers, it provided access to diversion and pleasure as well as information—their own, as well as that of their children. The bookmobile also provided a site for social interaction, where neighbors could meet and chat, not just with each other but with the bookmobile staff, who became familiar figures, literally the embodiment of the library and its values, throughout both counties.

After 1952, the Kewaunee County bookmobile ceased its rounds, and the Kewaunee bookmobile librarian left the district for a post elsewhere in Wisconsin. The rural schoolteachers went back to the old teaching methods—at least until consolidation caught up with them later in the decade and the small country schools were closed. In Madison, WFLC officials lamented the failure of the referendum, and Anne Farrington, who had worked so hard to make the demonstration a success, did not live much beyond the end of the project. Even as the county-wide referenda were being conducted in the fall of 1952, she was suffering from the debilitating effects of colon cancer, and year later, in August 1953, she was dead. By then, the demonstration, too, had died a premature death. To voters, cost appeared to be the principal obstacle. However, to the program's participants, its worth was intangible. "The most valuable part of the program to me personally," wrote one staff member, "has been the sharing of professional training and experience in the monthly staff meeting." "I am proud to be a member of this staff," wrote another. "I have utmost pride and confidence in our director," wrote a third.[33] For these library workers, the rich social and professional interactions that the demonstration afforded outweighed all other benefits.

Nor did 1952 really mark the end of the story. True, rural Kewaunee County still lacks local library service, but in Door County, the county system proved to be a "bouncing babe" after all. Like a character in one of her library's romances, in 1954 Jane Livingston married library board member Stanley Greene (by then the mayor of Sturgeon Bay), thus cementing with a personal alliance a political one that served the interests of Door County readers for decades. An attempt by county supervisors to put an end to the bookmobile service in 1967 (when the old 1950 vehicle finally came to the end of its life) met with such a storm of protest that they gave in and bought a new van that maintained service until the mid-1990s. In the 1970s Bailey's Harbor librarian Olivia Traven helped to spearhead a successful drive for a new county library headquarters in Sturgeon Bay—the only woman on the fund-raising committee—and went on to become the first president of the Friends of Door County Libraries. And in 1981, eighteen women of the Homemakers Club of Forestville, a southern Door County village (population around four hundred), tired and resentful of the fact that while northern

Door had seven library branches, southern Door had none, took matters into their own hands and founded the first branch library in the still mainly agricultural southern part of the county.

Without the help of male "fellow-travelers"—library supporters like Stanley Greene, Curtis Tronson, WFLC Commission Secretary Walter Botsford, John Chancellor, and rural sociologists Gene Rector and John Barton—the women's efforts would doubtless have had less impact. But what was remarkable about the role played by women in the transformation of the local print culture on the Door Peninsula was not only the phenomenon of female local leadership, but also the women's adaptation of the language of domestic ideology to express and to achieve their aims. Rather than representing an acceptance of traditional home-centered roles for women, this use of domestic metaphor and choice of domestically oriented reading demonstrated a degree of resistance to past restrictions and an excitement about new possibilities, albeit within domains already established as female. At least in Door County, it was the women's actions that won legitimacy for the "little bastard," which knitted the disparate group of library staff members into a "family" and extended conceptions of homemaking beyond the instrumental fundamentals of cooking, cleaning, and child care into a more creative expression of individual taste and judgment through the provision and use of advice books.

Participation in print culture also provided a pathway for women into the traditionally male-dominated arena of policy making. The Kewaunee teachers who wrote and signed a public political document, and who represented their colleagues at the county supervisors' meeting, were publicly speaking out for perhaps the first time in their lives. Jane Livingston provided her library staff with a model of determined action that eventually won over the conservative-minded male politicians of Door County. And in the end, it was a group of homemakers who exercised practical judgment and political acuity when they introduced permanent library service to the agricultural southern peninsula. For all these women, print provided the rationale, as well as the means, for making their voices heard. Ultimately, print helped them to acquire influence over the distribution of print resources in this area of rural Wisconsin.

Notes

1. Research for this study was supported by an Amy Louise Hunter Fellowship from the State Historical Society of Wisconsin and an Old Gold Fellowship from the University of Iowa.

2. Anne Farrington to Gretchen Knief Schenk, July 26, 1950. Archives, State Historical Society of Wisconsin Series 1967/110. Schenk, a native of Milwaukee, had worked in libraries in several states, including California, Illinois, and Washington. She retired from full-time librarianship in 1945 to become a library consultant. In 1948, she was editor of the "County Libraries" section of the *Wilson Library Bulletin.* Her correspondence with commission officials suggests that she enjoyed a close working relationship them, and that on occasion she played the role of friend and confidante.

3. There is an extensive literature on this subject. See in particular, Elaine Tyler May, *Homeward Bound: American Families in the Cold War Era* (New York: Basic Books, 1988) and Eugenia Kaledin, *Mothers and More: American Women in the 1950s.* (Boston: Twayne Publishers, 1984).

4. *Wisconsin Library Bulletin* 47, no. 2 (1951), 39.

5. For a comparison of contemporary studies that described library users' demographic characteristics, see Bernard Berelson, *The Library's Public* (New York: Columbia University Press, 1949): 19–50.

6. For the political background to this vote, see Christine Pawley, "Reading *versus* the Red Bull: Cultural Constructions of Democracy and the Public Library in Cold War Wisconsin" (*American Studies* 42, no. 3, 2001), 87–103.

7. William F. Thompson. *The History of Wisconsin. Vol. VI, Continuity and Change, 1940–1965* (Madison, WI: State Historical Society of Wisconsin 1988), 96.

8. Writers' Program. *Wisconsin: A Guide to the Badger State* (New York: Duell, Sloan and Pearce, 1941), 317.

9. For a discussion of women's strategy of justifying librarianship as an innovative activity by linking it to traditional activity, see Susanne Hildenbrand, "Women in Library History: From the Politics of Library History to the History of Library Politics" in *Reclaiming the American Library Past: Writing the Women In,* ed. Suzanne Hildenbrand (Norwood, NJ: Ablex:1996), 7.

10. Interview with Jane Livingston Greene, 23 October, 2000.

11. Interview with Lee Traven, 25 May, 2001.

12. Walter S. Botsford to the Anne Farrington Memorial Committee, February 1954. Archives, State Historical Society of Wisconsin Series 1967/110.

13. Interview with former librarian, Sturgeon Bay, 14 March, 2001.

14. Farrington's talk was transcribed and later published as "The Last Lap," in *The Idea in Action: A Report on the Door Kewaunee Regional Library Demonstration, 1950–1952* (Madison, WI: Wisconsin Free Library Commission, 1953) 10–12.

15. *Census of Population: 1950*, vol. 2 "Characteristics of the Population, part 49: Wisconsin" (Washington, D.C.: U.S. G.P.O, 1952), 49–122. For the farm population, the census data do not distinguish between men and women.

16. Franklin Eugene Rector. "Social Correlates of Eighth Grade Attainment in Two Wisconsin Counties." (PhD diss., University of Wisconsin–Madison, 1954), 21–22.

17. For a history of the mid-western rural school see Wayne E. Fuller, *The Old Country School: The Story of Rural Education in the Middle West* (Chicago: University of Chicago Press, 1982).

18. Interview with former student, Door County, 14 March 2001.

19. Interview with former teacher, Door County, 12 March 2001.

20. Ibid.

21. *Luxemburg News*, 18 September 1952.

22. *Algoma Record-Herald*, 11 June 1953.

23. Interview with former bookmobile librarian, Sturgeon Bay, 14 March, 2001.

24. The Wisconsin Historical Society archives contain records of the Wisconsin Free Library Commission, including some 6,000 library circulation slips drawn from both Door and Kewaunee counties—representing only a small fraction of those originally filled out, but providing the raw material for a database containing 5,819 usable records. The total number of individual named library users was 1,816.

25. Interview with former rural teacher, Door County, 24 May, 2001.

26. Sonya Salamon. *Prairie Patrimony: Family, Farming and Community in the Midwest* (Chapel Hill: University of North Carolina Press, 1992), 41; 194.

27. Katherine Jellison. *Entitled to Power: Farm Women and Technology, 1913–1963* (Chapel Hill: University of North Carolina Press, 1993), especially chapter 6, "The Postwar Era," 149–80.

28. Ronald E. Kline. "Agents of Modernity: Home Economists and Rural Electrification, 1925–1950." In *Rethinking Home Economics: Women and the History of a Profession*, edited by Sarah Stage and Virginia B. Vincenti (Ithaca, NY: Cornell University Press, 1997), 237–52.

29. Jellison, *Entitled to Power*, 150–51.

30. In 1936, Jeannette Howard Foster summarized the findings of five studies of urban reading conducted at the Graduate Library School of the University of Chicago between 1933 and 1934. According to these studies of about 20,000 readers in the Chicago area in and outside of libraries, 60 to 75 percent of all reading consisted of fiction. Foster's own study found that "Housewives'

interest in novels of family life is among the outstanding preferences . . . more than twice the percentage of married women read these stories" and that "all but two of the writers in the class ["Family"] are women." See Jeannette Howard Foster, "An Approach to Fiction Through the Characteristics of its Readers," *The Library Quarterly* 6, no.2 (April, 1936): 124; 160.

31. *Algoma Record-Herald,* 4 September 1952.

32. Tyler May, *Homeward Bound,* 26.

33. Farrington, "The Last Lap," 12.

Part 3

A Centrifugal Force

Gendered Agency through Print

Power through Print

Lois Waisbrooker and Grassroots Feminism

JOANNE E. PASSET

> We are rebels in the fullest sense of that word. We are determined to overthrow the ruling power, to dethrone it.
>
> Lois Waisbrooker, 1873

"A Queer Old Woman Thinks She Has a Mission to Perform," announced a headline in the *State Journal* of Topeka, Kansas, in August 1894. Indeed it must have seemed so to the editors of the newspaper. Defying the Comstock Act, passed in 1873 to prohibit the mailing of "obscene" material, an aged Lois Waisbrooker had since the mid-1860s devoted herself to publishing books and periodicals containing information about female sexuality and women's rights. Active throughout five decades characterized by periodic economic depression, political corruption, industrialization, immigration, and spiritual turmoil, Waisbrooker joined ranks with anarchists, freethinkers, and Spiritualists to critique an economic, legal, and social system that gave some men unfair advantages over other males—and over virtually all females. Only a thorough understanding of themselves and of institutionalized sources of inequality, she believed, would prepare women to claim their rights. Her frank prose did not result in an arrest until 1894, when a federal postal inspector charged her with publishing allegedly obscene content in *Foundation Principles*, the biweekly she published from her Topeka residence. Undaunted, Waisbrooker declared: "If prison will advance the work I am ready."[1]

Beginning in 1868 with the publication of *Suffrage for Woman: The Reasons Why*, this itinerant author wrote twelve novels, printed countless tracts and pamphlets; edited three periodicals *(Our Age, Foundation Principles*, and *Clothed with the Sun)*; and served as acting editor of an anarchist free-thought weekly titled *Lucifer, the Light-Bearer*.[2] A regular contributor to such Spiritualist publications as *Banner of Light*, *Religio-Philosophical Journal*, *Hull's Crucible*, and *Woodhull & Claflin's Weekly*, and to such anarchist weeklies as *Free Society* and *Discontent*, Lois Waisbrooker represents one of a small number of nineteenth-century women willing to link their names to the cause of sexual freedom. Yet though she represented a tiny minority, and a much-maligned viewpoint, many others read and responded to her words. Like historian of print culture Elizabeth Long, who challenges the hegemonic image of reading as a solitary act, I would argue that Waisbrooker's printed words facilitated the construction of an interpretive community of marginalized readers, many of them women alienated from white-gloved, middle-class suffragists, and separated from one another by geography. Empowered through print, Lois Waisbrooker and her readers stood on the periphery of power, where they contested male-prescribed definitions of freedom and claimed their rights as women.[3]

Waisbrooker's early life—punctuated by poverty, poor health, and marital failure—provided a foundation for her feminism. Born Adeline Eliza Nichols in Catharine, New York, on 21 February 1826, she was the daughter of Grandison Nichols, an impoverished day laborer, and Caroline Reed Nichols, a consumptive mother of seven who died at age thirty-six. From an early age, the girl recognized inequality and injustice, and sided with the oppressed. "I remember," she later wrote in a remembrance of her father, "the continuous toil, the coarse fare, and poor attire that was thine, in order that thy children might have bread, and that . . . others grew richer for thy toil." Because the Nicholses lacked adequate resources to provide their children with formal education, they allowed daughter Adeline to roam her grandparents' orchard and fields. This early sense of independence and her observations of the natural world would inform her evolving vision of women's rights.[4]

During her youth in the "Burned-over" district of New York and in the Western Reserve of Ohio (where the family moved in the early 1830s), Adeline Nichols also learned to question the logic of religious-sanctioned, male-dominated institutions. As she grew in knowledge—of the world if not of books—she became increasingly resentful when having to "sit Sabbath after Sabbath under the ministrations of an ignorant man" in order to avoid being branded an infidel. At times the family remained home from church "for want of proper clothing." Like other Christians who later left the church, the young girl believed in Jesus and his teachings but rejected "what is called the religion of Jesus." She cited two reasons: those calling themselves Christians who treated her in a condescending manner, and the hypocrisy of those who committed immoral acts even after they claimed to have achieved sanctification.[5]

Autobiographical references in Waisbrooker's speeches and novels suggest that she struggled to reconcile sexual desire with society's moral code. Pregnant at seventeen and forced to marry George Fuller on 12 April 1843 in Cuyahoga County, Ohio, she "rued her haste" and "the blighting desolation which bowed me to the very earth" after being legally bound to "a comparative stranger." The stigma she felt as a "fallen woman" (because she gave birth to a daughter only five months after marrying) fueled her nascent interest in women's rights and awakened her to the need for sexual reform. It also provided her with the narrative strand for such later works *Helen Harlow's Vow* (1870), a novel she dedicated "TO WRONGED AND OUTCAST WOMAN ESPECIALLY."[6]

In 1846, when she was widowed shortly before her twentieth birthday, Adeline Fuller quickly discovered the consequences of women's economic dependence on men. Lacking the financial means to support her son and daughter, she placed them with other families. Given the few employment options available to an uneducated widow at mid-century, Fuller chose to become a live-in maid. The sympathetic woman for whom she worked, she later reflected, "seemed to understand me better even than I understood myself," and she encouraged the young widow to seek education in order to become a teacher. Although it took two years to acquire six months' worth of schooling, Fuller recognized that this mistress had given her a far more valuable gift than money: "the encouragement which enabled me to use my own resources." Thus equipped, she set out to help another oppressed group when she accepted a position teaching African American children in a rural Muskingum County, Ohio, school.[7]

At age thirty, familial and social pressure led Fuller to relinquish her independence on 9 August 1856 when she entered into a brief and unhappy second marriage to Isaac Snell. Her father, she later recalled, pressured her to wed a man "for whom she had no attraction" because the marriage offered social and economic advantages. Such reasoning, and subsequent unhappiness, further informed her critique of this patriarchal institution. By 1860, Adeline Snell had left her marriage, moving to Miami County, Ohio. Her children, census data confirm, remained in the families with whom she had placed them; however, she appears to have maintained cordial relations with them, visiting both periodically for the remainder of her life, and at times making her home with them.[8]

In the late 1840s, Spiritualism, a belief in the possibility of communication with the dead, began spreading throughout the nation. This religious and reform movement, argues historian Ann Braude, "helped a crucial generation of American women find their voice" because it freed their minds from artificial constraints and provided a venue in which they could speak freely without fear of censorship. An alternative to paternalistic Christian denominations, it empowered women to reject externally imposed laws and social codes of behavior. Saying goodbye to her unhappy past, Adeline Nichols Fuller Snell joined many other Americans in discovering the liberating power of Spiritualism. By 1863 she also had chosen a new name—Lois Waisbrooker—to go with her new identity. Over the course of the next five decades, this movement challenged Waisbrooker's worldview, provided a marketplace for ideas, and offered a national network through which she could generate an income and cultivate relationships with reform-minded women and men.[9]

As a Spiritualist trance speaker—a vehicle through which spirits spoke—Waisbrooker drew upon her experiences as an impoverished child, widow, and unhappily married woman to critique the men who controlled the nation's purse strings, pulpit, press, politics, and women. By addressing such topics, she soon became branded by the press a "free lover." As Waisbrooker learned through her journey as a woman alone, men often expected independent women to have loose morals. In the early 1860s, while riding on a train, a soldier boarded the car and sat beside her. After a few minutes he proposed that they should spend the night together. "He had," Waisbrooker recalled, "but one idea of a woman who traveled." The seriousness of such subjects notwithstanding, Waisbrooker tried to retain her sense of humor. On one occasion, after hearing an enthusiastic woman in the audience exclaim "The Lord sent you here," she quickly rejoined: "Most of the people think the devil sent me."[10]

Tempered by her youthful struggles and subsequent experiences as a wife, widow, and divorcee, Waisbrooker fearlessly lectured on such controversial topics as illegitimacy, free love, motherhood, and women's rights. Like members of the National Woman Suffrage Association (organized in 1869 by Elizabeth Cady Stanton and Susan B. Anthony), she repudiated male spokesmen and women who thought like men, maintaining that only free women like herself could speak on woman's behalf. The survival of the human race, she asserted, depended upon women's liberation from social and economic constraints; only then could they conceive "a god-like race" and claim their birthright: freedom. One of the first steps toward perfect motherhood, she wrote late in the century, "is to secure to woman freedom from intrusion upon her person, even by a husband."[11]

Spiritualism provided a supportive network that sustained Waisbrooker and other self-supporting women financially. Such Spiritualist periodicals as Boston's *Banner of Light* and Chicago's *Religio-Philosophical Journal* contain numerous announcements of women's availability for speaking engagements and advertisements for their services as clairvoyants, psychometric readers, and healing mediums.[12] The Spiritualist network also served as a safety net for aging or infirm colleagues. During one of her periodic bouts with illness, Waisbrooker in the late 1860s took refuge with a Spiritualist and friend in Buffalo, Missouri. During that time, she devoted herself to writing, producing her first novel, *Alice Vale: A Story for the Times*, and a series entitled *Spiritual Tracts*. Her host, eager to aid Waisbrooker's work, announced the availability of the modestly priced tracts (bearing such titles as "What is Spiritualism," "Hell," and "The Laws of Mediumship") and urged readers to support the author by purchasing them. "These are documents which should be scattered broadcast over the land," wrote E. Hovey, a Spiritualist from Buffalo, Missouri. "They do lasting credit to the head as well to the heart of woman." In addition to praising the tracts' merit, Hovey encouraged readers also to "Remember the widows and fatherless in their inflictions, especially, such as do not wish to be numbered on the lists of "'The Indolent' or the 'Superannuated.'" While Waisbrooker disliked being categorized as "superannuated," she did not object too strenuously when her works began to sell.[13]

Many of the didactic novels and polemic tracts Waisbrooker wrote after 1868 portray young women victimized by the sexual double standard, and employ frank language to describe woman's sexual enslavement in marriage. Informed by her unsatisfying marital experiences, and those of women she had met while lecturing, she proclaimed: "If there is one act in heaven more criminal than another it is the crushing of a young and innocent girl into a loveless marriage." It was, she elaborated, "prostitution of the worst kind. . . ." Her readers concurred. While they found Waisbrooker's *Alice Vale: A Story for the Times* (printed by the Banner of Light publishing office in 1869) "interesting," their enthusiasm for *Helen Harlow's Vow* (1870) ensured that the latter would remain in print for most of the century. Recounting the story of a young woman's seduction and desertion, and her subsequent efforts to raise a son while coping with societal prejudices, *Helen Harlow's Vow* tackled the issue of the sexual double standard. Waisbrooker's message—that woman must free herself because no one else would—struck a responsive note with mothers who, like Mrs. Lavinia Woodard of Fruitland, Illinois, encouraged other readers to "place it in the hands of your daughters." They would, she explained, learn from the title character's example "that if woman respects herself, she will always command the respect of others." "There are few families in the land," observed a reader in Laona, New York, "that cannot apply some part of Helen Harlow's experience."[14]

On the lecture circuit and in her writings, Waisbrooker urged female listeners to claim the power inherent in their reproductive role. "How shall this power," she asked in a pamphlet based on a speech she had given before the Michigan State Association of Spiritualists in 1872, "be made to serve instead of ruling us?" Blaming women's economic dependence on men for their sexual bondage, she advocated that at eighteen every woman should receive a monthly stipend from the public treasury in recognition of her contribution to the reproduction of the race—and to free her from dependency on men. Society's problems, she believed, "must be finally solved through an application of the laws of maternity, woman having the power . . . to make proper conditions for her highest work." However, the use of contraceptives did not fit into

Waisbrooker's scheme. Regarding them as "unnatural," she observed that such devices rendered women subject to men's desires, not their own. Until such time as women could experience sexual satisfaction without fear of the consequences, they would have to exercise the self-control that men could not. As she declared: The "quickest way to raise the human [race] . . . is to thoroughly respect sex and sex relations . . . leaving woman to decide when, where, and with whom these relations shall be held, holding her responsible for the results."[15]

In the 1870s, with the nation caught in the grip of a devastating economic depression, questions of economics and power resonated with many working-class women and men. As they began to debate such issues, Spiritualists splintered into two factions: the many middle-class adherents who preferred to define Spiritualism as a religion, and those who, like Victoria Woodhull and Moses Hull, envisioned it as a broad social reform movement. That Waisbrooker sided with the latter camp is evident in the increasingly political focus of her publications. She explored causes of the nation's economic depression in a pamphlet titled "The Sexual Question and the Money Power" (1873) and in an introduction to Joel Densmore's *Economic Science; or, The Law of Balance in the Sphere of Wealth* (1875). Moving to Battle Creek, Michigan, a haven for health reformers and Spiritualists, she in 1873 began publishing *Our Age*, a short-lived Spiritualist reform periodical devoted "to the interests of Spiritualism in the broad sense of that term." No issues are extant today, yet editors of other radical reform periodicals of the era preserved some passages when they excerpted from its content. From the fragments of excerpts that survive, it is possible to discern Waisbrooker's sympathy for farmers and workers who contended with railroad monopolies and the aftermath of the Panic of 1873, prompting her to call for a national economic restructuring based upon a new, cooperative social order: "This present unjust, unbalanced condition of things must break in pieces of its own weight, and then we shall want something lasting upon which to reconstruct."[16]

Abandoning *Our Age* in 1874 because of her recurrent poor health and inadequate funding, the forty-eight-year-old editor attempted to express her views on such subjects as monetary reform and monopolies in the Spiritualist press. Rejecting her contributions, editors of Boston's *Banner of Light* and Chicago's *Religio-Philosophical Journal* sided with those who envisioned Spiritualism as a religious impulse, not a reform movement. They not only silenced her ideas but also sealed off a crucial outlet by which she supported herself by refusing to advertise her works. As Waisbrooker confided to free lover, Spiritualist, and Greenback Party supporter Moses Hull, the editors did not want to discuss the "bread and butter question."[17]

Physically and economically depleted, Waisbrooker traveled to California in 1874 and sought temporary refuge with her son Abner Fuller, who in the mid-1870s had moved from the Midwest to Contra Costa County. Using the small community of Antioch as a home base, she established herself in that region by connecting with reform-minded Spiritualists up and down the coast. During the next two years she sustained herself by visiting friends and lecturing in their communities. In San Francisco by 1876, Waisbrooker attempted to unite her geographically dispersed colleagues in reform who, like her, saw the questions of property and legal marriage as inextricably linked. Through the pages of *Woodhull & Claflin's Weekly* and *Hull's Crucible*, two reform-minded Spiritualist publications, she invited men and women who were "free" and "ready and willing to assert their freedom" to join her in a ring of personal correspondence.[18] (She also may have seen this venture as an outlet for the sale of her books and pamphlets.)

After the cessation of both *Woodhull & Claflin's Weekly* and *Hull's Crucible* in 1877, radical social reformers like Waisbrooker still could turn to Ezra Heywood's *The Word*, published with his wife Angela from their home in Princeton, Massachusetts, since 1872. In the eyes of some midwestern and western readers, however, Heywood's East Coast publication did not devote enough attention to the plight of rural laborers in the western half of the nation. Still, Heywood and Waisbrooker shared an avid interest in the relationship between the sex question and economic matters, and a belief that any meaningful discussion required the use of plain language. After Heywood was convicted and jailed in 1878 for publishing and distributing a free love treatise titled *Cupid's Yokes*, Waisbrooker was prompted to write *The Plain Guide to Naturalism* (1879), a tract in which she articulated her belief that sexuality would provide the human race with the key to immortality.[19]

In 1883 Waisbrooker returned to the Midwest and settled among longtime Spiritualist friends in the farming community of Clinton, Iowa. Home to a water-cure resort and the Mount Pleasant Park Spiritualist camp meeting (which is still in existence), Clinton served as headquarters for her new endeavor, an 11 x 17-inch bimonthly journal first issued in 1885. *Foundation Principles*, "the rock upon which

Motherhood Must Rest," circulated to several hundred subscribers who paid fifty cents a year for the four-page publication. To make ends meet, Waisbrooker often set the type and operated the hand press herself. A typical issue contained her opinions on current affairs, especially as they related to women and economics; her own works in serialized form; printed excerpts from reader correspondence; and advertisements for radical books, pamphlets, and periodicals, many of them her own. Thus, *Foundation Principles* became an important avenue through which Waisbrooker disseminated her feminist message while earning just enough to sustain her body. In 1886 yet another bout of poor health interrupted her editorial career. Turning over management of her publication to anarchist, freethinker, and Spiritualist Jay Chaapell, she returned to her son's California home.[20] Although she later resumed publication of *Foundation Principles* from Antioch, Waisbrooker lacked the resources to print more than an issue or two.

Until 1886, Waisbrooker found the thought of anarchy "hateful" or discomforting, but Chicago's Haymarket Riot (4 May 1886) and the subsequent execution of four anarchists caused her to reconsider and then embrace this cause. With other reform-minded Spiritualists, she looked to the anarchist press as an outlet for exploring the social and economic problems that plagued rural and urban working-class women and men during the economically tumultuous late-nineteenth century. Her readership did likewise. Many subscribers to *Foundation Principles* also read *Lucifer, the Light-Bearer*, an anarchistic free-thought weekly published in the rural community of Valley Falls, Kansas. Begun by Moses Harman in 1883, it advocated woman's emancipation from sex slavery and encouraged readers to engage in vigorous print-based discussions of sexual and economic topics. Like his counterpart, *Word* editor Ezra Heywood, Harman challenged Anthony Comstock and his army of postal inspectors by publishing frank words and "obscene" subject matter. Lending her support to Harman's endeavor, "Sister Lois" contributed frequent letters for publication and relied on *Lucifer* to advertise her publications.[21]

The Panic of 1893 and the ensuing years of economic depression created a receptive audience for socioeconomic critiques of society, especially in the nation's heartland, and provided a reinvigorated Waisbrooker with reasons to resume her role as an editor. Moving to Topeka, she resurrected *Foundation Principles* and continued lecturing to fund her endeavor. Supportive of her efforts, Harman gave Waisbrooker the use of his subscription list and arranged a "club" (reduced) rate for subscribers who wished to receive both publications. Additionally, Harman invited her to serve as acting editor of *Lucifer* in 1892–93 while he served a prison sentence after one of his four convictions for sending "obscene matter" through the mail. After his conviction, Waisbrooker decided that it was time for a female editor to challenge the Comstock Act of 1873, which made it a federal crime to send obscene material through the mail. As she anticipated, postal inspectors banned from the mail the issue of *Lucifer* in which she reprinted part of a government document discussing the horse's penis. However, the postal authorities decided not to press charges against her, perhaps because they may have regarded her as Harman's puppet, or did not wish to prosecute a woman.[22]

Stepping down from her acting editorship in 1893, Waisbrooker remained in Topeka, where she continued editing *Foundation Principles*. She also established the Independent Publishing Company because she knew that few publishers elsewhere would associate their names with "sex books." She whetted people's appetites for such of her works as *The Wherefore Investigating Company*, *The Occult Forces of Sex*, *A Sex Revolution*, and *The Fountain of Life, or, The Threefold Power of Sex* by publishing them serially in *Foundation Principles*. Typical advertisements contained endorsements from such well-known Populist speakers as lecturer Mary E. Lease, who praised *A Sex Revolution* (a small book about women who, as a sex, went on strike) for giving "expression to my thoughts so clearly that it almost startled me," and from the *Nonconformist* of Tabor, Iowa, which proclaimed: "Helen Harlow's Vow: Buy It. Read It. Then Lend it to your Neighbor. It will do more to kindle hope, revive the heart, and stimulate ambition . . . than the bible has ever done."[23]

No subscription list for *Foundation Principles* survives, yet it is possible to reconstruct some information about its readership by analyzing reader correspondence. Waisbrooker's publication circulated widely, with correspondents living in at least twenty-four states ranging from Maine to California. The largest numbers, however, resided in rural Kansas, Illinois, and Iowa, where the population had for years suffered the consequences of prolonged drought, unfair working conditions, and economic depression. A female reader from Lily Dale, New York, wished that the fifty cents she sent could be fifty dollars "to help fight woman's battle which she doesn't know enough to know needs fighting." Many struggled to accumulate enough money to renew subscriptions and purchase the radical books and pamphlets for which they yearned. "Of course I desire to help on all reforms," wrote Harriet from Chicago in 1894, "but what good does it do when you have no money in your pocket." Signing herself "Not a Nickel," another reader confided that after selling cattle, paying debts, and taxes, her family only had five dollars left. "We need so many things I don't know what to get first, but it seems as if I could hardly live without some good paper. My papers are about the only real company I have." Although Waisbrooker carried subscribers after their subscriptions lapsed, she had a low tolerance for readers who claimed they could not pay for subscriptions or publications, accusing them of refusing to make sacrifices. "Do you not believe that if your soul went out to the cause of woman's emancipation as earnestly as your words seem to imply," she admonished, "you could save that much a week toward sustaining a paper devoted to woman's cause?"[24]

Women comprised slightly more than half (52 percent) of the ninety-four individuals whose letters appeared in *Foundation Principles* from mid-1893 through November 1894, making it one of the few, if not the only, sex radical periodical in which women's voices outnumbered men's. (Indeed, the percentage may be even higher if one considers that some correspondents disguised their gender by using initials when they wrote.) Correspondents ranged from young girls of ten to octogenarians, and included anarchists, dress reformers, free lovers, freethinkers, Spiritualists, and advocates of women's rights. Little-known women like Mattie E. Hursen, a Michigan dressmaker who earned her living by sewing for prostitutes, Kansas farmwife Ada Starke, and Chicago anarchist Lizzie M. Holmes joined such well-known figures as California social reformer Caroline Severance and dress reformer Mary E. Tillotson in airing their views. Mothers and daughters like Mrs. Annette and Loretta Nye of Northwood, Iowa, eagerly ordered and discussed books and pamphlets.[25]

Readers who corresponded to *Foundation Principles* and its sister periodical, *Lucifer, the Light-Bearer*, developed and sustained a sense of community that spanned both distance and time. Some knew each other from their earlier involvement in antebellum reform causes. Regular contributors included lapsed Quaker author Elmina Drake Slenker, who conducted a correspondence bureau for radical men and women in search of their spiritual affinities. Siblings Lillie D. White, Lizzie M. Holmes, and C. F. Hunt had lived as children among the Berlin Heights Free Lovers in north-central Ohio. Holmes, who served as assistant editor of *The Alarm* (published by Haymarket anarchist Albert Parson), remained dedicated to radical social reform for over forty years. Spiritualism served as the connecting link for several editors who read and commented upon Waisbrooker's works. One of them, English-born James Vincent, a farmer of Tabor, Iowa, evolved from Spiritualism to free thought and edited a periodical titled *The American Nonconformist*. Another, Chicago-based dress reformer and member of the National Woman Suffrage Association (NWSA) Lucinda B. Chandler, found supportive colleagues among readers of *Foundation Principles* and *Lucifer, the Light-Bearer* after NWSA members shunned her for printing works about sexual topics at her deceased husband's publishing firm. Many others found similar comfort in the sense of community Lois Waisbrooker's publications afforded them. "I cannot do without your paper," wrote Ellen H. Taylor in August 1894. "Its arrival is welcomed as I would receive an old friend whose thoughts are congenial with my own."[26]

In addition to connecting with one another, many of Waisbrooker's subscribers came to regard her as a trusted friend and confidante. "There are near me very few lady friends," wrote one woman, "who are not astounded and mortified when I approach such a subject as sex slavery." "You seem nearer and dearer to me than many of my blood relations," confessed a correspondent from Junction City, Washington. "I never write what I feel to any of them."[27] Readers credited Waisbrooker with awakening them to their constraints as well as their potential. "I am not the only one that your books have saved from the insane asylum," wrote a devotee in 1898. Others concurred. "I don't know what would have become of me but for reading [Waisbrooker's books]," confided a young teacher. "I have realized the hell of a broken home, but with the knowledge I have gained by reading *The Occult Forces of Sex*, *The Fountain of Life*, and *My Century Plant*, I have learned how to live and am happy in my second marriage."[28]

Those who shared Waisbrooker's reformist zeal supported her work by sharing copies of *Foundation Principles* with their friends and relatives. A woman wrote from Council Bluffs, Iowa, "I wish every mother in the land could have it to read." Some, in their eagerness to proselytize, sent Waisbrooker money and asked her to mail *Foundation Principles* to distant friends.[29] Others attempted to recruit subscribers in their communities but discovered that not everyone was receptive to its content. "The trouble is," complained E. H. Underhill of Elmira, New York, that "so few people are intelligent or progressive enough to appreciate thoughts on such an advanced plane." Undeterred, George McNinch of New Basil, Kansas, promised to "keep right on distributing the papers" even though people thought they dealt "with spiritualism and immoral topics."[30]

During her seventeen-month-long editorship of the revived *Foundation Principles*, the "small woman with a pleasant and intellectual face" insisted on maintaining an uncompromising stand on free speech. Consequently, in June 1894, one of Anthony Comstock's agents named McAfee entrapped her by posing as a sexually dissatisfied husband in search of marital advice. Waisbrooker published his letter verbatim in *Foundation Principles*, someone forwarded the issue to Washington, D.C., and on 1 August 1894 a postal inspector arrived in Topeka to arrest her. She did not flinch; indeed she relished the prospect of martyrdom, declaring that "if Prison will advance the work I am ready."[31]

Readers of the 1 September 1894 issue of *Foundation Principles* learned of the arrest in an article titled "Arrested! Noticed at last!" Rallying to her defense, they sent words of encouragement and enclosed small donations—ranging from fifty cents to one dollar—in support of the legal battle that ensued. Eliza H. Fales of Tonawanda, New York, could not send money but declared that in the past fifteen or twenty years that she had read Waisbrooker's publications, she "never saw a word or sentence that ever reminded me of anything that was obscene." Writing from Madrid, Iowa, Abbie C. Culver declared that "every fiber" of her soul vibrated "in sympathy with your efforts to inform woman and elevate the standard of social purity." Some viewed Waisbrooker's case as part of the class struggle. "We never hear of any great and wealthy papers," observed W. A. Wotherspoon from Abilene, Kansas, "being prosecuted under this infamous statute. It is only poor and struggling advocates of social reform . . . that are selected as victims."[32]

Federal officials were determined to stop Waisbrooker's defiant actions once and for all. "Mrs. W.," wrote U.S. attorney W. C. Perry in 1896, "has been a cause of serious complaint for a number of years. The Post Office Department has no desire to be severe with her, but desires that the case be so disposed of that she be made to cease her filthy publications for all time to come." Because of her age, Perry offered Waisbrooker's attorney, Populist Ben S. Henderson, a deal: if she would plead guilty, the sentence would be suspended "on account of ill health and extreme age during good behavior." Upon learning of this offer, Waisbrooker declared that she would never confess herself guilty to save herself from the consequences. "No! not to escape the gallows. If I have so long been a cause of serious complaint why have I not been informed?"[33]

Waisbrooker printed her last issue of *Foundation Principles* in mid-November 1894, but she remained in Topeka until 1896 because of her legal battles. The numerous delays in the prosecution of her case, which finally ended in a dismissal in the spring of 1896, heightened her hostility toward government.[34] Returning to San Francisco, home to the anarchist publishers of the periodical *Free Society*, she rented a room on Market Street from a German-born family whose other boarders included factory workers and mining experts. Waisbrooker thrived in the midst of this supportive group of working-class radicals who read voraciously and met frequently to engage in vigorous debate. Increasingly politicized, her articles addressed such socioeconomic issues as Chicago Mayor Carter Henry Harrison's plan for poor relief in Chicago, polygamy in Utah, conditions for working women everywhere, and prostitution. The solution to these and other problems plaguing the nation, she asserted, was "to set woman wholly free and secure her in her right to her own person. . . . Give us anarchy here, secure woman self-government, and all else will follow as a matter of course."[35]

Despite financial struggles and ill health, Waisbrooker remained determined to continue her agitation on behalf of women's social and economic independence. The Panic of 1893 and its lengthy aftermath, however, had had a disastrous impact on the rural and urban working-class women (and men) who consumed her works. "I am receiving no orders for books," she lamented in 1897. "Have the friends forgotten that I need bread, shelter and street car fare—yes and postage and paper? I could speak every Sunday to good audiences were I able, but there is no pay in it. . . . The landlord gets what is collected." Determined to advance the cause, she freely gave pamphlets to her radical colleagues, much to the chagrin of *Lucifer* editor Moses Harman. "Cost," he observed, "is a ploughshare which opens the soil of people's mind." People will read "contraband truth," he elaborated, "when they would not use it free."[36]

In January 1900, on the eve of her seventy-fourth birthday, Waisbrooker announced plans from her rented San Francisco quarters to begin yet another small monthly, this one to be titled *Clothed with the Sun*. Although she was a freethinker, Waisbrooker took the title from Revelations 12:1 because it celebrated woman as the giver of life and underscored the importance of embracing light, or truth, if women wished to achieve their destiny. Contributors sharing this sentiment included the poet and author Charlotte Perkins Gilman. Calling for the scientific study of woman's sexual desire, Waisbrooker remained determined to awaken women to their sexual and economic enslavement: "Oh, woman, WOMAN! Wake up and demand your Liberty!"[37] From the onset, however, *Clothed with the Sun* was plagued by such obstacles as a small base of subscribers and postal rulings that denied her affordable postage rates. The subscription list of a publication mailed as second-class matter, she explained to readers, must be approximately 50 percent of the copies issued. Evidently Waisbrooker either gave away or sold in person more copies than she sent through the mail. Issuing an urgent call to her supporters, she informed them that the publication would be delayed until "those who are willing to aid me in paying this extra postage" stepped forward with cash donations or subscriptions.[38]

In 1900 the publishers of *Free Society* decided to move their editorial offices to the supportive environment of Chicago, but Waisbrooker remained behind. She recalled the effect prior winters spent in the Midwest had had on her health. After issuing a few numbers of *Clothed with the Sun* from San Francisco, she moved instead to Puget Sound in Washington State where she joined comrades living at the small settlement of individualist anarchists known as the Home colony. According to historian Charles LeWarne, Home "tended to attract individuals united by their very differences and their receptiveness to new ideas."[39]

Little known before 1901, Home became the target of attacks after the assassination of President William McKinley by the self-proclaimed anarchist Leon Czolgosz on 6 September 1901. Short of vigilante action, one way to inhibit an anarchist community's functioning was to prosecute publishers of its periodical, *Discontent: Mother of Progress* (begun in 1898) for violating the Comstock Act. Like *Free Society*, it provided anarchists and freethinkers with an open forum for views on a wide range of topics, including sex and economics. The judge in the case found in favor of *Discontent*, but the grand jury next indicted Waisbrooker for publishing an allegedly obscene article entitled "The Awful Fate of Fallen Women" in *Clothed with the Sun*, and Home postmistress Mattie D. Penhallow for mailing it. Supporters across the country rallied to the septuagenarian Waisbrooker's aid by sending money and words of encouragement to Home for her legal defense. Penhallow was acquitted, but the jury found the editor guilty. A sympathetic judge assessed Waisbrooker the minimum penalty: a fine of one hundred dollars.[40]

Waisbrooker returned to Home, where she continued to subsist by publishing intermittent issues of *Clothed with the Sun*, selling her works, and providing consultations through the mail. She promised to respond privately, for a fee of one dollar, to readers who did not wish to have their inquiries about sex and marriage appear in print. Additionally, she offered a service known as "name reading." For fifty cents she would "read the character" of a correspondent's name. Charging less than the usual price of one dollar, Waisbrooker explained that she was "not proficient." At age seventy-seven, she also continued to lecture on her reform ideas, both at Home and in other states. Longtime supporters like Spiritualist Olivia Shepherd expressed admiration for her determination: "Ever earnest in the cause of woman's full emancipation, she continues to pour solid shot into the reactionaries." Readers recalled hearing her as children, and commended her for the new ideas she had awakened in them.[41]

In 1903 Waisbrooker informed readers of *Lucifer* that she had "put up another number of the magazine on the little press." She actively involved readers in the production of *Clothed with the Sun*, informing them "Only two more numbers and then another volume. Think how much the paper depends upon PROMPT RENEWALS." Additionally, she promised to give as many copies as readers wished, "for distribution," to all who contributed to the paper's cost. And if this was not enough, she reminded them of her sacrifices: "I am glad to give MYSELF to the work. Please help to furnish needed tools." Such pleas prompted concern and a measure of pity on the part of her friends, who expressed sadness to know that the fiercely independent woman "should feel the sting of making a personal appeal for the sale of her books."[42]

Discontinuing *Clothed with the Sun* in the spring of 1904, Waisbrooker moved to Denver, Colorado, where she boarded with friends and continued to lecture and issue books and pamphlets. By then, however, her readership had begun to shrink. Some of her ideas about women's economic self-sufficiency now appeared in mainstream publications, but many "New Women" of the 1890s and early 1900s did not share her uncompromising view of men as destructive and [utterly?] lacking in self-control. Nor did they share her belief that contraceptive devices enslaved rather than liberated women. Some supporters had grown uncomfortable with her embrace of anarchism; others, aged like herself, struggled to remain financially solvent. Dependent upon subscriptions and sale of her books and pamphlets for a livelihood, Waisbrooker's plaintive pleas for support gradually diminished her power as an editor. It pained friends and colleagues in reform to see the woman they had called "the mother of coming generations" making personal appeals for the sale of her books so she might have bread and shelter.[43] Penniless and dependent upon others for sustenance, she returned to her son's home in Antioch, California, where she died on 3 October 1909. Active to the end, her last article, "The Curse of Christian Morality," appeared posthumously.[44]

Reflecting on her editorial career, Lois Waisbrooker in 1903 concluded that *Foundation Principles* had accomplished "a work for the Freedom of Mothers and for the right to be Born Well that is quite impossible to estimate in words or figures."[45] Through her periodicals *Our Age* and *Foundation Principles*, and in the publications to which she contributed—the spiritualistic *Banner of Light* and *Religio-Philosophical Journal* and the anarchistic *Free Society*, *Lucifer, the Light-Bearer*, and *Discontent*—she joined with like-minded readers to construct an interpretive community devoted to the discussion of woman's freedom. Because of her role as an author and editor, Waisbrooker played a central role in this network, which collectively preserved an alternative strand of feminist thought as it evolved from antebellum Spiritualistic roots to a more anarchistic phase by the close of the century.

By the time of her death in 1909, Lois Waisbrooker had spent over forty years promoting assertive womanhood and the positive power of female sexuality. Her rural roots, her poverty, marital experiences, and exposure to Spiritualism all informed her critique of woman's status in society, and her writings resonated with rural and urban working-class women and men. A believer in progress—the idea that imperfect beings had the potential to advance to a higher plane of development—she regarded the demystification of sexuality as a necessary first step. As she achieved higher levels of understanding—of sexual politics and economics—she grew disillusioned with Spiritualism's increasingly cautious tendencies. Aligning herself with oppressed groups against the monopolies of business, church, and state, she also agitated on behalf of currency reform, free thought, and freedom of expression.

A competent, if not charismatic, speaker, Waisbrooker reached out to women through the printed word. Poor for much of her life, and largely self-taught, she wrote both to inform others and to support herself. Personal circumstances led her to focus on the economic roots of sexual inequality and to align herself with impoverished individualist anarchists and experimental cooperatives. With them she tested the limits of government tolerance by publishing material deemed obscene by Anthony Comstock and his army of postal inspectors. The venue of print enabled this editor to reach geographically, economically, and intellectually marginalized readers. After digesting her works in the privacy of their homes, those women and men interacted with one another by means of the letters that Waisbrooker reprinted in *Our Age*, *Foundation Principles*, *Lucifer, the Light-Bearer*, and *Clothed With the Sun*. The interpretive community they formed not only sustained Waisbrooker ideologically and economically but also helped to make sure that her radical vision of what women's rights must entail would endure after her death.

Notes

1. "A Queer Old Woman Who Thinks She has a Mission to Perform," *Topeka State Journal* (15 August 1894): 5; Lois Waisbrooker to E. B. Foote, 1 August 1894, Ralph Ginzburg Papers, Mss. 8652, Box 6 folder 2, Wisconsin Historical Society, Madison, Wisconsin.

2. Waisbrooker's books included *Suffrage for Woman: The Reasons Why* (St. Louis: Clayton and Babington, 1868), *Alice Vale: A Story for the Times* (Boston: William White and Co., 1869), *Helen Harlow's Vow* (Boston: William White and Co., 1870), *Mayweed Blossoms* (Boston: W. White, 1871), *Nothing Like It, O, Steps to the Kingdom* (Boston: Colby & Rich, 1875), *From Generation to Regeneration* (Los Angeles, 1879), *Facts and Figures for Working Men* (Antioch, CA, 1886), *Perfect Motherhood, Or, Mabel Raymond's Resolve* (New York, 1889), *The Wherefore Investigating Company* (n.d.), *The Fountain of Life, or the Three Fold Power of Sex* (Topeka, KS: Independent Publishing Company, 1893), *A Sex Revolution* (Topeka, KS: Independent Publishing Company, 1894), *My Century Plant* (Topeka, KS: Independent Publishing Company, 1896), *The Temperance Folly; or, Who's The Worst* (1900), and *Eugenics; Or, Race Culture Lessons* (Chicago, 1907). She edited *Foundation Principles* (Clinton, IA, and Antioch, CA, 1885–86; Topeka, KS, 1893–94), served as acting editor of *Lucifer, the Light-Bearer* (Topeka, 1892–93), and edited *Clothed With the Sun* (San Francisco, CA, and Home, WA, 1900–1904).

3. Elizabeth Long, "Textual Interpretation as Collective Action," in *The Ethnography of Reading*, edited by Jonathan Boyarin (Berkeley: University of California Press, 1993): 180–211.

4. Lois Waisbrooker, "My Father," *Mayweed Blossoms,* 137; for the reference to her lack of education as a child, see Waisbrooker, *Suffrage for Woman,* 12, and for a discussion of her observations of nature, see *Mayweed Blossoms,* 12–13.

5. For the "ignorant man," see Waisbrooker, *Suffrage for Woman,* 13; for the "religion of Jesus," see *Alice Vale,* 243; for "proper clothing" and sanctification, see *Mayweed Blossoms,* 55–56.

6. For the quote about her marriage, see Waisbrooker, *Mayweed Blossoms,* 84. Daughter Pauline M. Fuller was born on 10 September 1843, and son Abner Burton Fuller was born before 1846. Waisbrooker descendent James B. Hardin provided Fuller's death date, e-mail message to the author, 25 January 2000. For a discussion of Adeline Nichols' adolescence, see "Social Reform Convention, February 28-March 1, 1875, *Hull's Crucible* [March 1875], Ralph Ginzburg Papers, Box 3, Folder 19, Wisconsin Historical Society Archives, Madison, Wisconsin. For additional biographical data about Waisbrooker, see James C. Malin, *A Concern About Humanity: Notes on Reform, 1872–1912 at the National and Kansas Levels of Thought* (Lawrence, Kansas: James C. Malin, 1964); and Ann D. Braude, "Lois Waisbrooker," in *American National Biography,* ed. John A. Garraty and Mark C. Carnes (New York: Oxford University Press, 1999), 22:453–55.

7. Waisbrooker, *Mayweed Blossoms,* 87. For information about her teaching career, see *To-Morrow Magazine* (October 1906): 6.

8. According to James B. Hardin, e-mail message to the author, 25 January 2000, Adeline Nichols Fuller married Isaac Snell in Morrow County, Ohio. The 1860 federal manuscript population census locates him there in 1860, and Adeline Snell in Troy Township, Miami County, Ohio.

9. According to family legend, Adeline Snell changed her name to Waisbrooker because relatives disapproved of the controversial ideas she espoused, one of which was Spiritualism. "It was more than a 'pen name,'" James B. Hardin states. "Her granddaughter never mentioned her in her 'diary' as other than 'grandmother Waisbrooker.'" Historian of Spiritualism Ann Braude attributes Waisbrooker's lack of national notice to the fact that "she shunned urban centers, choosing agrarian populists as the audience for her radical message," yet my research indicates that she also gave speeches in such urban settings as Boston, Chicago, Denver, and San Francisco. See Braude, "Lois Waisbrooker," *American National Biography,* 454.

10. Waisbrooker is described as a trance speaker in "Minnesota Quarterly Convention of Spiritualists," *Religio-Philosophical Journal* (10 April 1869): 6. For another description of her speaking style, see *Banner of Light* (6 February 1869): 4. For the anecdote about the soldier, see Waisbrooker, "I Wonder How Many," *Free Society* (11 February 1900): 3. For the reference to the devil, see Waisbrooker, *Suffrage for Woman,* 31.

11. Waisbrooker, "The First Step," *Foundation Principles* 4 (August 1893): 4.

12. Ann Braude, *Radical Spirits: Spiritualism and Women's Rights in Nineteenth-Century America* (Boston: Beacon Press, 1989), 201.

13. E. Hovey, Buffalo, Missouri, "Illness of Lois Waisbrooker," *Banner of Light* (30 January 1869): 8. Waisbrooker left nearly 2,000 of the tracts with C. C. Colby, of Carthage, Missouri. See "Mrs. Waisbrooker's Tracts in Southwestern Missouri," *Banner of* Light (20 March 1869): 8.

14. Braude discusses Waisbrooker's writings in *Radical Spirits,* 137. Waisbrooker descendants claim that *Mayweed Blossoms* is an autobiographical novel. *Helen's Harlow's Vow, or Self-Justice* (1870) tells the story of a young woman seduced and deserted, scorned by society, and left alone to raise a son. Reprinted as late as 1890 by the Murray Hill Publishing Company, the novel remained in print at the close of the century. For the Woodard quote, see *Banner of Light* 30 (27 January 1872): 2; for the quote from a Laona, New York, reader, see *Banner of Light* 30 (6 January 1872).

15. Waisbrooker aired these ideas at a meeting of the Michigan State Association of Spiritualists in 1872, and refined them in a pamphlet, "The Sexual Question and the Money Power," published in 1873 (n.p.). For her ideas about the monthly stipend, see "Wisconsin, Southern Spiritual Association," *Religio-Philosophical Journal* 10 (13 May 1871): 6. For a discussion of Waisbrooker's ideas about contraception, see Waisbrooker, *Lucifer, the Light-Bearer* (23 March 1894): 3. The quote about sexual relations is from "Mrs. Waisbrooker on Diana," undated clipping from *Foundation Principles,* located in the Ralph Ginzburg Papers, Box 13, Folder 3, Wisconsin Historical Society Archives, Madison, Wisconsin.

16. Waisbrooker, [untitled letter], *Woodhull & Claflin's Weekly* (16 October 1875).

17. Waisbrooker, [untitled letter], *Hull's Crucible* (week ending September 29, 1877): 2.

18. D. Edson Smith, Santa Ana, California, recalled that Waisbrooker had "sowed Liberal seed" in his community. See Smith, *Lucifer* (22 October 1903): 325. For one version of her advertisement, see Waisbrooker, "Wanted—Correspondents," *Hull's Crucible* 5 (17 June 1876): 3.

19. Heywood, after having met Waisbrooker at an 1875 social freedom meeting in Boston, described her as a Roman Sibyl, Margaret Fuller, and Sojourner Truth, "all rolled into one." See Hal D. Sears, *The Sex Radicals: Free Love in High Victorian America* (Lawrence: The Regents Press of Kansas, 1977), 232.

20. Chaapel, born in 1829 in Pennsylvania, married at least five times. His fourth wife, Velma, was from Clinton, Iowa, where they kept a sanitarium for a few years. See Chaapel Papers, Labadie Collection, University of Michigan Libraries, Ann Arbor.

21. During this time she published *Facts and Figures for Working Men: Usury and Land Monopoly Must Go or All Freedom Must Go* (1886), as well as new editions of her novels.

22. Sears, *Sex Radicals,* 229–31.

23. Mary A. Lease, *Foundation Principles* (July 1893): 1; Ad for Helen Harlow's Vow, *Foundation Principles* 3 (26 October 1886): 3.

24. Myra F. Paine, Lily Dale, New York, *Foundation Principles* 5 (15 September 1894): 3; Harriet, from Chicago, and "Not a Nickel," *Foundation Principles* 5 (15 July 1894): 6; Waisbrooker, "A Prostitute," *Foundation Principles* 4 (15 December 1893): 5.

25. For information about the Abel and Annette Nye household, see the manuscript federal population census for Worth County, Iowa, 1880.

26. Ellen Taylor, *Foundation Principles* (14 August 1894).

27. For the quote about "few lady friends," see Anonymous, *Foundation Principles* 4 (October 1893): 6. For the Junction City quote, see N. M. M., *Foundation Principles* 5 (15 July 1894): 1.

28. For the quote about the insane asylum, see *Lucifer, the Light-Bearer* (23 July 1898); and for the teacher's quote, see *Lucifer,* (10 September 1898).

29. E. H. Underhill, *Foundation Principles* 5 (1 July 1894): 6; S. L. Woodard, *Foundation Principles* 5 (15 July 1894): 6.

30. B. Childs, Council Bluffs, *Foundation Principles* (August 1893): 3; for an example of readers requesting copies be mailed to friends or for distribution in their counties, see Sylvina L. Woodard, Golden Eagle, Illinois, *Foundation Principles* (August 1893): 3, and Mrs. Rose C. Dunham, Mammoth Springs, Arkansas, *Foundation Principles* 4 (April 1894): 5; E. H. Underhill, *Foundation Principles* 5 (1 July 1894): 6; George McNinch, New Basil, Kansas, *Foundation Principles* 5 (July 15, 1894): 6

31. "And Still Another Arrest," *Foundation Principles* (15 August 1894): 4. Waisbrooker's response to her arrest is contained in Waisbrooker to Dr. E. B. Foote, 1 August 1894, Ralph Ginzburg Papers, Mss 82, Box 6, folder 2, Wisconsin Historical Society Archives, Madison, Wisconsin. The case was dismissed June 30, 1896. While waiting for its resolution, Waisbrooker published *Anything More My Lord* (Topeka, KS: Independent Publishing Company, 1895).

32. Eliza H. Fales, *Foundation Principles* 5 (15 September 1894): 3; Abbie C. Culver, and W. A. Wotherspoon, *Foundation Principles* 5 (1 September 1894): 1, 4.

33. W. C. Perry to Ben S. Henderson, 1 January 1896, Ralph Ginzburg Papers, Box 6, Folder 1, Wisconsin Historical Society Archives. The Waisbrooker response is appended to the Perry/Henderson letter.

34. Anarchists claimed credit for her release, reporting that their systematic letter-writing campaign had influenced the judge in the case. See Stephen T. Byington, "Anarchist Letter-Writing Corps," *Liberty* (August 1897).

35. For the occupants of the household in which Waisbrooker lived, see federal manuscript population census, 1900, B. Greenwood household, Market Street, San Francisco, California. For her discussions of socioeconomic problems, see Waisbrooker, "Dividing Up," *Free Society* (21 November 1897): 7; Waisbrooker, "Signs of Progress," *Free Society* (December 17, 1897): 5. The quote is from Waisbrooker, "Some Facts," *Free Society* (10 December 1899): 3.

36. Waisbrooker, "Things as I See Them," *Lucifer* (22 December 1897): 407; Moses Harman, untitled editorial comment, *Lucifer* (16 February 1898): 53.

37. *Clothed With the Sun* (January 1902), unpaged.

38. Lois Waisbrooker, "The New Ruling," *Free Society* (25 March 1900): 4.

39. Charles P. LeWarne, *Utopias on Puget Sound, 1885–1915* (Seattle: University of Washington Press, 1975), 174.

40. "The Home Case," *Free Society* (30 March 1902): 4.

41. Quote is from *Discontent* 27 May 1903, 2. For more on her determination, see *Discontent* 25 March 1903, 4. An account of her lecturing is given in Discontent 25 1 April 1903, 4 and 13 May 1903. J. E. C., Port Angeles, Washington, *Clothed with the Sun* 3 (15 August 1902), 4, recalls Waisbrooker speaking before the Progressive Lyceum in Chicago.

42. For the references to "another volume," "PROMPT RENEWALS," and distribution copies, see *Clothed With the Sun*, 1 (November 1900), 1. The plea for "needed tools," is in "Among Lucifer's Exchanges," *Lucifer* (7 May 1903). The reference to "personal appeal" is from *Lucifer* 10 September 1898).

43. X. X., Des Moines, Iowa, *Lucifer* (September 10, 1898).

44. Waisbrooker is interred in an Antioch, California, cemetery with her son Abner Fuller.

45. *Lucifer* (7 May 1903): 134. No known collection of Waisbrooker manuscripts exists. Issues of *Foundation Principles* are available at the Kansas State Historical Society in Topeka, and at the Labadie Collection, University of Michigan, Ann Arbor. Scattered issues of *Clothed with the Sun* are available at the Wisconsin Historical Society Archives and at the University of Michigan.

Woman's Work for Woman

Gendered Print Culture in American Mission Movement Narratives

SARAH ROBBINS

In their writing, reading, and circulation of texts for the American foreign mission movement, late nineteenth-century women used print to address religious objectives while also supporting self-fashioning processes based upon shared social beliefs and activities. Their publications reached eager (if highly specialized) audiences all over the world and, directly or indirectly, influenced Christian women's religious beliefs and social practices for generations. Yet this rich ground of analysis for studying print culture at work in a gendered context has, until now, been underexplored. With that in mind, this essay offers a preliminary survey of a terrain that merits even more attention.

Beginning in the 1870s, and well into the early twentieth century, women stationed at overseas posts and home-based supporters of the American Christian foreign mission movement used print to maintain intense, productive connections that clearly bolstered the goals of their international evangelical endeavors. In terms of medium and reach, women's writing for the foreign mission movement began with an informal antebellum stage when early pioneers (who were mainly unpaid adjuncts providing moral support for their husbands' preaching) wrote personal letters keeping family and friends informed. In a second stage, as married women took a more active, formally recognized role in mission activities, and as some single women gained official sponsorship for service overseas, an expanded network of textual exchange evolved. Some women missionaries began drafting multiple copies of their letters and/or organizing round-robin "pass-alongs" so that their stories could reach more readers, thus subtly inviting more support for particular stations or projects.[1] Some of these texts also found their way into print publications, therefore reaching an even broader audience beyond the personal circle of friends who would have received the original handwritten missives. In a third stage, as typewriters made writing ever faster and more efficient, and as mission magazines developed from relatively modest publications with somewhat limited circulation patterns to far more ambitious business enterprises with some paid professional staffs, much of the writing produced by missionaries stationed abroad (and by their loyal supporters back home) was prepared, from its very first drafting, with the idea that it would quickly be seen in print by many readers in and outside of the United States.[2]

When women's stories about their foreign mission movement activities moved into print, they gained ideological force. As Anne Ruggles Gere and I observed in a study of print texts created for the women's club movement in the early twentieth century, "an ideological model" for studying print assumes that, "like other aspects of culture, [it] interacts with, shapes, and is shaped by the various contexts in which it appears and that even the practices of its technology are structured as a meaningful dimension of print culture."[3] Like the clubwomen who used print to redesign their literacy and social identities for their own needs, women reading and writing for the publications of the foreign mission movement acquired a gendered agency through their use of print—one that clearly influenced the larger enterprise in which they were participating.

One window that offers a meaningful glimpse of how print publication operated in the social context of the American women's foreign mission movement is *Woman's Work for Woman*, one of the many specialty magazines produced between the 1870s and 1920s to support the American women's foreign mission movement. As a particularly popular example of the periodicals flourishing during that era, *Woman's Work* is an apt choice for a case study that not only suggests outlines for further scholarship on the larger phenomenon of women's multifaceted mission movement writing but also, and more specifically, links it to print culture in general.

Woman's Work celebrated and guided the mission-oriented activities of white, middle-class Presbyterian women, primarily in the United States, but also at overseas stations funded by loyal movement members at home. Analyzing the range of material that appeared in the magazine while tracking its highly gendered history, we can gain a sense of how print served needs of the movement's middle-class female participants as well as the mission endeavor itself. My analysis begins with a representative account by one regular reader (who was also a writer) reflecting upon her own and her whole discourse community's use of print stories about women's foreign mission work. I will then describe and apply an interpretive framework for examining such narratives' contributions to print culture. Finally, I will trace connections between the missionary enterprise's evolving use of print and the increasing professionalization (and publication business orientation) of the movement itself.

In a letter appearing in the October 1882 issue of *Woman's Work for Woman*, a regular subscriber enthusiastically portrayed her love for the publication while describing a print-made communications circuit linking dedicated missionary authors, well-organized lady publishers, and devoted readers. Writing to the editors just after "reading the March number," the East India missionary Mrs. Tracy proclaimed: "I always immediately tear off the wrapper and give a glance through it to see that all my friends are well, just as I do my own home letters; and then when I have a leisure hour I sit down and enjoy it."[1] The "friends" Mrs. Tracy possessively claimed were indeed far-flung, scattered across the United States and abroad in such remote outposts as China and Japan, Syria and Siam. Different and physically removed as the daily lives of these other women were from her own experiences, however, Mrs. Tracy felt an intense kinship with them, largely due to the shared literacy practices sponsored by and embodied in the print texts of their beloved magazine. Whether working in some mission station overseas or supporting the movement through donations and study sessions in their American homes, these women formed an interactive network united in large part by reading, writing, and discussion of the literature in their own publication. Accordingly, Mrs. Tracy declared to the editors: "The Woman's Work is to me like receiving letters from . . . all over the world, for where there is any work being done in telling the gospel story, there I have a friend, and what a pleasure it is to hear from her in this way!"

The "way" Mrs. Tracy heard from her *Woman's Work* cohorts was actually somewhat similar to the handwritten "home letters" she received from close friends and relatives. After all, the stories published in the periodical were written in an intimate tone and often took the form of first-person epistles about daily "woman's work" at mission stations. They vividly described, in personal terms, duties such as teaching at a school for native children, organizing local "Bible women," studying the host country's language, or writing accounts of just such activities to inspire supporters at home. Yet, despite its echoing the personal letters written by missionary women to family and friends, Mrs. Tracy's descriptions of the impact of the publication itself emphasized how its identity as a printed text heightened its power for her and, presumably, for others linked to its vast network. Marveling at how *Woman's Work* made the experiences of others in faraway places accessible to her at a remote station in India, she reported appreciatively: "Now I do not suppose I have more than one or two personal acquaintances in either Syria or Persia, yet I watch eagerly for letters from those fields."

To explain her enthusiasm for reading their stories, Mrs. Tracy explicitly noted parallels between her own endeavors and those of other lady missionaries:

> Several years ago Miss Bassett interested me very much in an account of her daily life in the school to which she chiefly devotes her time. It just filled my dreams of missionary life. God marked out another sphere for me, but I look for news from that school almost as though it were my own. Another work I have been watching with interest is the school Mrs. Graham opened in Panalla. I commenced one about the same time, on the same plan, and it has been very pleasant to compare them (333–34).

When she characterized her reading of these colleagues' mission narratives, Mrs. Tracy was also signaling how the creation and consumption of print bound her together with others, reinforcing their shared commitment to social action. In other words, she was identifying the role of her group's print publication as similar to that community-building endeavor Yumei Sun and Rudolph J. Vecoli have assigned to immigrants' print publications in the United States between about 1850 and 1920. As Vecoli has observed, "Rather than simply serving as transmitters of information, communication media" like the immigrant press and the missionary magazines were "forces actively constructing social reality and identity in the minds of their audiences."[5]

An important aspect of the "social reality" and identity-shaping experiences publications like *Woman's Work* helped construct was the aims and strategies of the mission movement to which its readers were so firmly committed. For members of this widely scattered community, print helped make achievable many goals that would have seemed difficult to face alone. Along those lines, to characterize the "new courage" she often derived "from reading these letters" in *Woman's Work for Woman*, Mrs. Tracy lauded the degree to which the missionary narratives helped her step outside of her own situation, enabling her to see both similarities and differences between her experiences and the ones she read about in the magazine. Thus, Mrs. Tracy described an identification process that would be echoed in others' accounts of reading mission literature in venues like *Woman's Work*—namely, using interaction with print to create an imaginatively shared space of gendered cultural work. Equally significant, she pointed to a powerful benefit of writing for the periodical's congenial audience, as she extolled the thought-provoking effect of seeing her own stories return to her in printed form, where she could more easily recognize "the good to be found in it" than when she was caught up in the "surrounding rubbish" of everyday life.

Meanwhile, though especially valuing the publication's portrayals of life at the foreign missions, Mrs. Tracy also praised another of its key components—the so-called "Home Department," where the goals and methods of U.S.-based women supporting the foreign missions were also portrayed through exemplary narratives about their meetings, fund-raising, and study sessions. After stating that reading that section always provided "a very great source of encouragement" for all the movement's workers, Mrs. Tracy declared that the at-home supporters often "had far more to contend with than we on the field," making her feel ashamed for every being disheartened (334). Thus, while terming the movement's U.S. workers as saintly as their foreign counterparts, Mrs. Tracy framed the whole (foreign and home) group's shared literacy, centered in the magazine's printed missionary stories, as broadly humane, educational, and nurturing for all those who partook of it.

Mrs. Tracy was certainly not alone in her appreciation of how managing the technology of print played a crucial role in sustaining the gendered community of readers and writers to which she belonged. Reviewing copies of *Woman's Work for Woman* from the height of its publication history—which coincided with the heyday of the American women's foreign mission movement—I have found numerous self-conscious reflections by readers, writers, and editors on the crucial importance of being able to circulate their stories in print. Of course, *Woman's Work* was but one of an array of publications dedicated to promoting the American woman's foreign mission movement from the 1870s to the First World War. Like *Our Mission Fields* and *Royal Service* for southern Baptist women, *Woman's Work for Woman* concentrated initially on reporting about the mission activities of women affiliated with a particular region (the Northeast and the Midwest) and religious denomination (Presbyterian), but increasingly broadened its focus and goals to present the movement as a gendered national enterprise, spreading distinctively American Protestant ideals all around the world.[6] In casting the mission enterprise as inextricably linked to American values, while also suggesting that these values and their transmission were being influenced by women leaders, *Woman's Work for Woman* and its sister publications claimed an important social role for their readers and writers. To understand that role and the ways print contributed to its enactment, we would do well to heed the advice of David Hall for studying the cultures of print: besides examining "reading and writing as practices that reveal the presence of domination, subversion, and resistance," we need to construct a social history including "patterns of actual consumption"—in this case, the practices women in this discourse community developed for producing, circulating, and interpreting their texts.

Accordingly, my characterization of these gendered texts builds upon the framework suggested by Wayne Wiegand in *Print Culture in a Diverse America*. He characterizes print culture studies as answering Robert Darnton's call to interpret "'the social and cultural history of communication by print'" so as "'to understand how ideas [have been] transmitted through print and how exposure to the printed word [has] affected the thought and behavior'" of its users. Furthermore, Wiegand observes, print culture studies should view literature, as Michael Winship argues, as "'a human institution, part of a matrix of social and cultural forces from which it emerges, rather than a pure or abstract idea, independent of history.'"[7] With this conceptual framework in mind, I will analyze how the printed narratives appearing in publications like *Woman's Work for Woman* enacted many of the complex, constructive social processes described by Wiegand. Much the same as the digital text that is transmitted on the worldwide web today for specialized yet widely dispersed audiences, *Woman's Work* drew upon a specific institutional context (the women's foreign mission movement), shaped the ideas and actions of a far-flung yet coherent discourse community, and depended upon interactive networks of textual exchange to bolster social power for a group whose very identity was closely tied to its shared involvement with particular print texts.

I want to focus initially on one element in Wiegand's suggested interpretive framework; namely, to study print culture by viewing a particular body of literature as part of a "matrix of social and cultural forces" in a particular historical context. For foreign mission literature like that in *Woman's Work for Woman*, such a perspective is essential. First of all, this literature needs to be situated within the larger body of texts produced by the American women's foreign mission movement, which also generated many other kinds of print text, including formal financial reports, curriculum for home study, organizational agendas, travelogues, and testaments of personal salvation. As one element in this multigenre didactic array, women's missionary literature both benefited from and contributed to the institutionalization of the women's foreign mission movement itself. By the turn of the twentieth century, this process of institutionalization evolved from the loose and informal clusters of individuals and groups of the nineteenth century into a large and multifaceted collection of overlapping organizations with impressive budgets, sophisticated governance structures, and regulated communication procedures.[8]

On the one hand, then, we might view printed mission narratives as participating in what Anne Firor Scott has described as women's nineteenth-century enthusiasm for organized social activity.[9] Seen in that light, the stories in specialty magazines like *Woman's Work for Woman* were participating in an ongoing cultural enterprise dedicated to institutionalizing feminine benevolence in missionary service and reflecting that institutionalization in material products. By setting up their magazines' issues with a recurring organizational structure (e.g., separating "Foreign" and "Home" reports), by establishing rhetorical techniques for their writing (e.g., presenting financial data within a spiritual narrative; placing biblical allusions in new contexts), and by adapting an increasingly businesslike tone, print publications like *Woman's Work* contributed to readers' sense that they were part of an efficient, productive enterprise.

On the other hand, however, literature written and read for the American women's foreign mission enterprise was, like the movement itself, closely bound up with a distinctively Protestant commitment to evangelism. Along those lines, when we read an 1880s or 1890s *Woman's Work* narrative questioning the practice of arranged marriages in Asian countries, and bemoaning how some of the best students at mission schools for girls were "lost" to Christianity when their parents decreed weddings with unconverted spouses, we should observe how such a narrative operates at the intersection of several conflicting cultural forces.[10] Specifically, to take this particular example, we would need to critique how these women writers' print texts tended to depict the divergent social practices of non-Christian Asians as inherently flawed in spiritual terms. By contrast, when we read celebratory descriptions of students on American Indian reservations rejecting the "heathen" practices of their ancestors for Christian Bible study, we need to temper our discomfort with missionary women writers' unwillingness to exalt tribal culture by recognizing the sincerity of these women writers' efforts to present their students in a better light than in prevalent critiques of "savage" Indians dangerous to American values.[11] In other words, as they reported their impressions of the people they tried to serve, the missionary women who wrote these narratives tended to embody, in print, characterizations that were consistent with the limited views typical of the white, middle-class Americans of their own day. For us, reading these works in another time offers a window into gendered, racialized (and sometimes racist), and class-based beliefs about The Other in an earlier era—beliefs that, in both their caring and their prejudiced dimensions, were also influenced by Protestant religious ideology.

In addition to helping us historicize the attitudes of mission movement women toward the would-be converts they served, Wiegand's recommended emphasis on "social and cultural forces" at work in print culture also underscores ways in which readers' religious beliefs and needs influenced the mission magazine's presentations. For instance, a concept called "reflex influence," closely associated with the movement's emphasis on spiritual improvement among its participants, often appeared at the heart of these publications. Thus, mission stories frequently included explanations of how home-based women could nurture their own purity and piety by helping support the mission movement. According to this theory, such activities, even though they extended women's sphere into a politicized, international arena, did not at all undermine their essential feminine natures. Instead, their own souls accrued virtues that had been associated with American middle-class motherhood from the earliest days of the Republic. Therefore, texts seeking to galvanize the home support strand of the movement often stressed its ennobling influence, as in an article published in *Woman's Work for Woman* in 1879. One subscriber from Nebraska reported: "I have been thinking on the 'reflex influence of missions' in my own case. My Christian life and love grow and strengthen, and are less fluctuating since I entered more heartily into service. Isn't it sweet to feel that we are co-workers?"[12] Another from Iowa noted: "It is wonderful to see the change that comes over a woman's heart after she becomes interested in the salvation of the world at large" (392).

Along with their links to the mission movement's organizational context, testimonials like these affirmations of a "reflex influence" also exemplified another element in Wiegand's interpretive framework: the tendency of print to influence thought and behavior. Moving to that second component in the framework—including Wiegand's related call to explore interactions between print and its users—we find countless examples in the *Woman's Work* printed text of the magazine's readers and writers crediting their periodical as a guide for their spiritual thinking, their daily use of literacy as a social practice, and their long-range life choices. Consistent with Pierre Bourdieu's analyses of how self-defining groups can employ cultural activities and products for social action, women reading and writing within the community of *Woman's Work* used print to define a meaningful identity for themselves.[13] Along those lines, for example, stories for *Woman's Work* explicitly called upon what might be termed an "equivalency" principle, using the authority of print to accentuate (and thereby to strengthen) bonds between missionaries stationed overseas and their supporters laboring back in the United States. The equivalency strategy was intended, at least in part, to assure home supporters that their less dramatic involvement in the movement was as important as the more romantic, adventurous enterprise of serving overseas. It was also used to cast the work of the most faraway mission stations, which otherwise might have seemed remote and unfamiliar, into accessible (and therefore appealing) terms. Accordingly, the principle operated in two directions, using two related equivalencies.

First of all, having women at foreign mission stations portray their work as mirroring well-bred women's activities back in the United States enhanced would-be mission supporters' ability to identify with their counterparts overseas. In that vein, Miss Fannie Cundall's 1883 story for *Woman's Work for Woman* reported on her life in Tripoli by picturing herself as engaged in traditional American women's home literacy management. Like so many other mission movement texts, Miss Cundall's repeatedly employed the second person, addressing her audience directly to assert a comfortable bond, while depicting herself as doing tasks just like her readers' work in their homes. "You know that thirteen little girls compose our family of boarders, and I think you are familiar with some of their names," she declared early on.[14] Describing a lesson using religious songs, Miss Cundall noted: "I wish you could have seen them when they were finally gathered around the piano." She then used her own narrative to help her audience imagine themselves not only seeing but also participating with the eager group, singing familiar tunes such as "Come, Thou Almighty King" and "What a Friend We Have in Jesus." Next, she crafted a scene reminiscent of traditional, middle-class maternal domestic teaching models in the United States, which were so often portrayed in nineteenth-century women's literature as fireside literacy management. She described herself gathering her young charges by the fire in her own room, as they "sat down on the rug" while everyone "told some of the good old Bible stories."[15] To emphasize that she was replicating a familiar American middle-class social pattern of preparing older sisters to assist with home-based management of spiritual life, Miss Cundall recounted how one of the older girls had been trained to tell Bible stories. To suggest that her surrogate family was, indeed, learning just the kind of lessons readers' children might be studying in Protestant homes within the United States, she outlined how she quizzed the group on their reading from the book of Revelation. Finally, with modest pride, she confided how, before bedtime, one "dear little face was lifted to [hers] before the good-night kiss," asking if heaven itself might be like this idealized scene of domesticated learning: "'Will we see each other there, and can we come and sit around you as we do here?'" (158.) By invoking a scene reminiscent of those taking place in readers' own houses in America, Miss Cundall equated her work overseas with women's work at home.

By sharing such stories of motherly instruction as an inspiring yet familiar enterprise, women involved with the foreign mission network at home or abroad could maintain a strong sense of connection. Even in the most remote and unusual places, these narratives demonstrated, foreign mission workers drew on gendered teaching practices like those used back in the United States to impart the social practices and belief systems central to Protestantism. Reporting from "A School in Rawal Pindi" in 1883, Margaret M. Given described the progress of her mission work in just such terms, using an internationalized version of the antebellum American narratives that had first begun the cultural work of constructing neighborhood schoolteaching as maternal labor and evangelical benevolence as appropriate women's work.[16] Describing herself as going alongside Miss Downs and a local "Bible woman," Miss Given limned multiple visits to "a Mohammedan house on the edge of the city," where the lady evangelists first met with "decided hostility for the gospel."[17] However, after initially teaching the three "young girls" there while enduring "cold politeness" from the mother, Miss Given and her colleagues soon celebrated one daughter's "rapid progress in her reading," followed by a successful move to give her "the Gospel of Matthew for a reading book." As their first dedicated student progressed from the gospel itself to *Barth's Scripture History* under their guidance, she also began "helping the other two girls" and eventually "gathering in some of the neighbor children and teaching them as well" (378). All in all, Miss Given carefully repeated the plot line of U.S.-situated stories that had, for several decades, been depicting the extension of enlightened motherhood into the community by way of religious teaching. Thus, her print account of this gendered teaching process reinscribed links between her endeavors and parallel Christian education led by women at home.

Another equivalency-oriented technique associated with these texts' blurring of home/foreign boundaries involved writers' imaginatively situating themselves with readers in a gendered discursive space emphasizing how shared print use itself could bind distant locations and social agents together. An exchange of material objects, especially ones including print text, could facilitate this imaginative process and was duly celebrated in many narratives. So, for example, Miss Lillian Green invited her *Woman's Work* readers to experience an 1882 "Christmas in Tullahassee" by visualizing the many "gifts that had been kindly sent by societies in Bloomfield, Ill., and Allegheny, Pa." and were now hanging on a "nice cedar tree" in the Creek mission school where she taught.[18] In particular, she "wish[ed] the children who sent the nice cards with verses could see how pleased and eager the boys are to get them," and she encouraged that border-crossing identification process by showing how her students were using the cards "to learn their verse for the evening prayer-time." Such a story indicated that, like the continually essential infusion of money into the movement's coffers, the exchange of gifts incorporating print text bound American women teaching and studying in their own parlors to related pedagogical enterprises going on in faraway locations—public sites of action that, through the equivalency principle, were no longer viewed as extra-domestic.

In that same vein, Miss S. L. McBeth wrote from Idaho about her work at an Indian mission, inviting her readers to contribute and participate via a literacy exchange: "Do some of the friends who cannot go to the heathen wish to do like missionary work among the Spokanes and Umatillas? They can do it by sending there . . . Bible pictures and picture cards. They cannot well send too many."[19] Characterizing the striking successes she had already had teaching with "picture cards illustrating Bible scenes and truths," Miss McBeth described her approach, made possible through readers' donations: "Some of these pictures and picture cards I made into little books, and our boys in leisure hours would go with them from lodge to lodge, and tell the listening, wondering groups around the fire or door the story of the picture, which they in turn would tell to others. Often a picture given to a visitor would carry its story to distant neighborhoods" (8–9). To prompt her own readers to see how they could literally send Christianity "to distant neighborhoods" far from their parlors simply by extending their own print-based literacy practices, McBeth asked for "Sunday-school papers" and more pictures, which she assured her readers would be "a great attraction in the children's homes," thereby directly helping with the "the enlightening" aims of mission work (8).

As Benedict Anderson has observed, the nineteenth century was an era when individual nations actively worked to define their particular identities by creating "imagined communities," grounded in such shared social markers as a common language, but also in various social products. In highlighting the "coalition between Protestantism and print-capitalism," Anderson has focused on such products as mass-produced popular texts aimed at "large new reading publics" within the United States.[20] Significantly, rhetorical strategies such as the equivalency strategy in literature of the woman's foreign mission movement show how Anderson's concept of such an alliance between print culture and Protestant Americans' ongoing self-construction could be adapted to reinforce a national sense of identity within an internationalized religious context. At the same time, many aspects of the cultural work being celebrated and guided in publications like *Woman's Work* were also framed in highly gendered, racialized, and class-oriented terms. Consequently, we need to note how print culture in this particular context imagined (and supported) a multidimensional version of national identity that continually reinforced itself through writing and reading networks.[21]

Readers of *Woman's Work for Woman* often argued that responses like the reflex influence and the equivalency principle were made even more likely by constructive, self-conscious use of the magazine. We can recognize that shared understanding of, and intense appreciation for, print's distinctive social power in the ways the periodical's authors often wrote about the print exchange process itself. For one thing, in line with Wiegand's call for emphasis on "how ideas circulated through print," we should take note of such essential elements in the network of *Woman's Work*-type publications as the international shipping routes dependent upon European and American colonialism.[22] However, besides such material factors as the transportation systems supporting textual exchange, there were also crucial affective connections—shared, highly gendered feelings about the enterprise that were continually being strengthened by cultivating the specialized reading and writing processes associated with these print texts. For instance, in the words of women like Mrs. Tracy, whose gushing praise of *Woman's Work* we encountered earlier, we see how such feeling-based literacy practices were themselves being explicitly celebrated in print, even as they were also bound up with intellectually significant educational strategies for producing and consuming text.

Telling the story behind the making of print texts that readers would encounter was one recurring rhetorical approach for tapping into what we might call an "affect/intellect" circuit. For example, the missionaries who contributed to *Woman's Work* often described themselves as writing letters they knew would later be printed for the movement's broad audience. Similarly, home support groups wrote narrative essays explaining the study practices they used, so that those techniques could be printed for dissemination to others in the movement. In addition, the periodical's editors depicted various tasks involved in preparing and circulating the printed material their audience was reading.

By the 1870s and 1880s, *Woman's Work for Woman* had actually developed a two-pronged strategy for writing about the movement's print network in action: features explaining "how to" carry out mission-based literacy as envisioned by the magazine's discourse community, and stories focused on the powerful impact of these same textual exchanges.[23] While the former type of piece tended to present textual production and consumption as a rational enterprise managed through intellectually rigorous preparation and study, the latter stressed the role of feeling as an avenue to meaning. In practice, these two strands might be woven together within the same printed text.

"How-to" pieces were sometimes presented as celebratory reports on conferences, auxiliaries, and home-based study groups as intimately linked with communal literacy practices—activities which readers of the magazines would certainly be better prepared than others to carry out.[24] Along those lines, *Woman's Work* gradually printed more and more stories explicitly guiding readers as to how they should be adapting their own literacy practices to respond to changing times.[25] In the 1880s, these directive stories were increasingly being supplemented with printed bibliographies of recommended reading and calendars with topics for study and discussion at mission meetings.[26]

Stories demonstrating the positive social effects of mission literacy complemented the wide-ranging "how-to" features. Among the most striking of the "impact" narratives were those picturing the salutary effect of print-related exchanges on foreign mission stations. These stories often took the form of letters thanking readers for support—especially books and letters—which were aiding the literacy management efforts of the missionary teacher. So, for example, Mrs. Fitch wrote from China in 1877 that the "packages of beautiful cards" sent by loyal readers were spurring attendance and outstanding schoolwork in her Sunday-school class, where a number of "the scholars" now "recited to [her] *without the least mistake*" because they were so eager to have the beautiful religious pictures.[27] In a similar move, Miss McBeth wrote from the Nez Perces mission to thank readers who had responded to a short article about her work by sending her affirming letters: "That little extract in Woman's Work perhaps has been the means in God's hand of prompting kind Christian hearts in the East, South, and North to send me words of cheer and Christian sympathy which have done me good." Apologizing for not having time to answer each letter individually, Miss McBeth nonetheless asserted the continued power of the magazine's literacy network by asking not only for more prayers directed to "the Nez Perces and their teacher" but also for "*more letters.*"[28] Although Miss McBeth herself longed for personal writing from her readers, she suggested that the intimate underpinnings of the mission magazine could make the print versions of her own greetings a comparable alternative for her multiple correspondents.[29]

Woman's Work contributors writing from foreign stations also told stories of how the magazine's printed accounts of home-based activities enhanced their work far away. For instance, Miss S. Dougherty wrote from a station serving Indians in Wisconsin about how much she and her colleagues appreciated being able to read the periodical: "The reports of the meetings at '48' do truly make us feel blessed and stronger with such earnest workers helping us; and often the thought of the 'prayer hour' is restful when I feel very weary, as though the answer was before the petition."[30] Along similar lines, Mrs. W. W. Eddy wrote two years earlier that she had used *Woman's Work* home study pieces from the companion publication *Children's Work* as valuable instructional tools, having her students in Sidon, in Lebanon, try to translate articles, then discussing the texts in "a delightful hour" just like a "missionary meeting" back home.[31] Occasionally correspondents working at foreign stations sent submissions imagining how their own writing might have a similar impact for readers at home. For example, Mrs. Eddy wrote on another occasion that she knew her counterparts in the United States could picture her "examination of the day-school" from reading about it. In fact, she said, just reflecting on the potential influence of her printed record of the event had made it far more special for her too: "My heart was full of joy that day, and every day since, as I recall what I was permitted to see and hear," she explained, in large part "because these facts [would] give joy to others as well as myself" when they read in *Woman's Work* about her school's success.[32]

Stories touting the impact of *Woman's Work* among foreign mission stations, as well as narratives about its influence on home-based supporters, emphasized connections among shared literacy practices, knowledge-building, and moral development. All of these were cast as dependent upon the movement's ongoing print text exchange. To bolster both mission study and the journal itself, for instance, a December 1877 issue focused on the home audience, setting a goal that subscribers could attain by reading the periodical. "To have an intelligent sympathy in the work of missions we need knowledge, and our sympathy grows with knowledge. . . . Let us inform ourselves and teach the children of the Church, so that the geography and history of missions shall be as familiar as any other that they are taught to consider indispensable."[33] Using this anecdote as lead-in to a series of stories about foreign mission locations, the periodical presented itself as meeting a community-building need. Another classic example of this strategy had appeared under the title "Home Work" earlier that year. Describing "Mrs. J. G. Johnston" as writing "from her sick bed," this parable-like story urged the *Woman's Work* audience to read and write about missions, even if they were not healthy enough to serve at foreign stations themselves. Recording the personal experience of a reader from Peoria, Illinois, this text began with a sketch of her invalid status, which had her feeling cut off from God's religious work until she asked herself: "'Is there nothing, however small, that you can do with your pen and your knowledge? Is there nothing you could write which might reach some hearts, and find an entrance into some home?'"[34] Sure enough, the story continued, Mrs. Johnston began to write articles like this one, which, she came to realize, could help the mission movement by raising awareness—and money—to support its overseas initiatives. Illustrating the impact of her own reading and writing, Mrs. Johnston's story presented an adaptable role model of printed writing's social power.

Of course, behind the printing of accounts like Mrs. Johnston's, editorial decisions were being made. A seemingly simple editorial feature such as "Extracts From Letters" was of course a product of editorial selection and sequencing, not a haphazard printing of all that had arrived in the mail. The socially constructed nature of the movement's literacy practices underlay much of the magazine's content. For example, one letter the editors chose to print in 1877 lauded the influence that studying the periodical had exerted on the correspondent and simultaneously offered advice about how to read publications like *Woman's Work* to greatest effect. "Although my sphere of action to-day lies within four square walls," wrote the correspondent, "yet I have had such a feast in reading your Annual Report that I seized my pencil to express my sympathy and joy in your arduous work of the closing year. . . . I have carefully read and pondered the whole contents, and I have read some of the addresses twice over."[35] Portraying a sense of "sympathy and joy" her fellow readers would surely want to emulate, this same correspondent also suggested how they might all achieve a religious state of mind—by reading attentively ("twice over," if necessary); writing in response to reading ("seiz[ing one's] pencil to express" a reaction); and thereby becoming one of the "sharers" in the movement's energy (250).

In printing the enthusiastic missive of that anonymous 1877 letter-writer, the editors of *Woman's Work for Woman* underscored a close relationship between readers' personal responses to their publication and the contents of the magazine. They also hinted at ways their magazine was blurring boundaries between formally (and widely) published print text and other products of collaborative interpretation and composition that had always been central to the American women's foreign mission movement. Such text-sharing activities included readers discussing the magazines together; movement members writing response papers to be read aloud to each other; and local organizations publishing their own informal, limited-circulation print documents whose contents drew upon the national-level material.[36] Overall, in fact, print periodical texts like those in *Woman's Work for Woman* interacted continually with writing that, in other situations, might have been decidedly "ephemeral." This ongoing interplay, in effect, blurred the distinctions between print and nonprint, as well as between occasional, limited-circulation publishing (e.g., tracts and newsletters) and large-scale print publications like the national missionary books and magazines. A "Home" article in the July 1879 issue of *Woman's Work* illustrates just how easily so-called ephemera could pass into a more permanent form under the auspices of a mission periodical, as the "Our Young People" article for that month was printed in the journal after being "Read at the Ninth Annual Meeting of the Woman's Foreign Missionary Society."[37] The same issue included an announcement that two other speeches originally delivered at the annual meeting had "been published in leaflet form," and could "be had on application to the Editor" (233).

Keeping such venue-crossing in mind, the term "ephemera" is problematically applied to the enormous body of missionary narratives that first took the "disposable" form of tracts, church bulletins, club programs, speeches for study groups and conferences, and other print or handwritten documents that, in another context, might have had a more tenuous or short-lived circulation.[38] A great many pieces first disseminated in "ephemeral" form were later reprinted in more "permanent" sites such as issues of periodicals and hardbound study books, just as personal letters sent back and forth across the ocean between mission stations and U.S.-based movement supporters often became printed pieces in book-length epistolary biographies or in issues of the mission magazines.[39] The energy and dedication of women involved in the mission movement ensured that various pieces which might otherwise have been viewed as "intended for short-term use and disposal" were disseminated, then saved and catalogued.[40] In fact, strategies for preparing and circulating print texts through a range of venues represented a favorite topic for magazines like *Woman's Work*, suggesting how the periodical medium itself could be used to encourage the translation of nonprint texts (e.g., letters, a study group's notes, a member's oral presentation) into the more permanent and authoritative form of print. Movement leaders, acutely aware of the need to support women's sustained involvement in the community, recognized that "ephemeral" forms were broadly accessible avenues for the membership's writing, reading, discussing, and disseminating needs. Then, when such ephemera did gain added force in formal print publication, they could be reextended in still more oral texts and new informal study papers, guaranteeing a self-sustaining and interactive textual production cycle.

So-called "ephemeral" forms were particularly suited to combining records of particular events with directions for future literacy practices. Along those lines, a paper presented at a missionary auxiliary meeting might include all of the following: a vivid anecdote commemorating a successful missionary teaching experience (usually involving circulation of print text, presumably supplied by mission supporters), a description of how to teach this success story to others (e.g., at a Sunday school class or a ladies' study club), and a call for donations to enable others to carry out similar work. A prime example of this pattern was "The Home Side of Foreign Work," which began as a "paper read at a meeting of the Marion Presbyterial Society," but which later was printed in *Woman's Work for Woman*. To create multiple layers of reflection on the process of fund-raising for foreign fields, the story introduced a narrator who "eavesdropped" on the conversation between an experienced movement supporter and a novice who had encountered both discouragement and success in her first canvassing. After reviewing the "excuses" and "objections" she met from the less generous, this text used its story-within-a-story dialogue between "Aunt Margaret" and her protégée to outline how readers could use effective arguments to counter such resistance. Closing with a rallying call consistent with the piece's having first been an oral presentation, the narrator affirmed Margaret's advice, then reminded her listeners/readers to "give—heart, hand and voice to woman's work for woman."[41]

These overtly reflective depictions of texts being socially constructed and disseminated by the *Woman's Work* discourse community heightened the awareness participants in this mission publication network had of print's role in their lives. Such stories of literacy in use—of a vast communication circuit reaching otherwise isolated (and hence less effective) individuals and groups—helped unify missionary groups around their shared publications. With such community-building goals in mind, periodical reports on the movement's progress often combined with descriptions of the magazine's links to its readers, as in the "Seventh Annual Report of the Woman's Foreign Missionary Society of the Presbyterian Church," published in *Woman's Work* in June 1877. Here, as so often in *Woman's Work*, writers emphasized how subscribers and publishers shared a strong sense of ownership in the publication. As evidence, the editors cited the frequent visits paid to the magazine's offices at 1334 Chestnut Street in Philadelphia. Asserting that "delightful" subscribers came "from every quarter of the land," the editors described their own great pleasure in "find[ing] that to so many" their "pilgrimage" to Chestnut Street "was one of the main points of interest in their visit" to the city.[12] In acting upon a wish to "see face to face and take by the hand those who were so well known to them by name and through letters," the editors concluded, these readers were reiterating a feeling of connection all subscribers had already achieved imaginatively through reading the periodical. Equating that print-based exchange of ideas and feelings with a telegraphic energy, the editors urged their readers to maintain and strengthen the connection. "Take hold with your own hand," they advised, "this more than magic wire that encircles the world with its magnetic power of prayerful sympathy" (112–13). By continuing to be regular readers of and writers for *Woman's Work for Woman*, in other words, women could achieve a collaborative "power" centered in the creation, dissemination, and use of printed text.

Descriptions like the one above (echoing the language presented earlier from Mrs. Tracy's personal account) particularly emphasized the affective bond connecting members of the *Woman's Work* discourse community. Imbedded within the editors' celebration of the powerful feelings shared in this community, however, is an acknowledgement of the business behind the network. Over the course of its history, *Woman's Work for Woman* became increasingly professionalized, in a trajectory that parallels the women's foreign mission movement itself. Overseas, spousal helpers gave way to single women working as paid mission schoolteachers. Eventually, teaching itself became secondary to administration for some professional lady missionaries, such as Laura Haygood, who, as their careers developed, concentrated more on such duties as fund-raising, monitoring other mission workers' teaching, and educational management. In the United States, even the volunteers leading the home support movement acquired many highly professional skills, partly through attending regional and national conferences—on program management, curriculum development, and fund-raising—but also through reading magazines like *Woman's Work*. Over time, then, the content of such publications expanded beyond accounts of home study and foreign-based religious instruction (both of which had always been cast as maternal activities) to include advice on directing the activities that would help build up the institutional structure of the movement itself. Even the magazine's annual index, which became increasingly elaborate year by year, became a marker of enhanced professionalization.

Nonetheless, despite this professionalization process, the rhetoric of *Woman's Work* and its sister publications continued to stress the personal dimensions of the foreign mission movement enterprise. In fact, to help keep the business end of the publication's activities successful, the editors depended upon readers' personal affiliation with the magazine through a highly gendered bond. Tracing the history of *Woman's Work* in a financial context, therefore, includes taking note of editors' determination to maintain a tradition of woman-to-woman Christian benevolence, alongside changes reflective of the professionalization of publishing that was going on nationwide in the secular realm as well. A look at the magazine's frequent printing of short narrative articles about its own financial history and status reveals how determined the managers of *Woman's Work* were to maintain the health of the magazine without sacrificing its gendered Christian identity—but also how challenging a task that goal could be. Though overseen by the Woman's Foreign Missionary Society of the Presbyterian Church, the magazine was expected to be self-supporting and also to help generate revenue for the overseas stations, whose workers received their stipends from the Presbyterian ladies' organizations.[13] Maintaining a healthy number of subscriptions for the monthly issues was crucial for the magazine, which began by charging a modest sixty cents per year in the early 1870s.

Both the success of the subscription system and its ever-tenuous status are clear in articles from across the life history of the magazine in its original form, April 1871–November 1885.[14] For example, in June of 1877, the editors touted the growth of the overall institutional structure for the Presbyterian women's mission movement (with "one hundred new [local] auxiliaries," bringing "the whole number . . . up to seven hundred and forty-eight"). They congratulated their readers on the magazine's seventh anniversary, and the second anniversary of *Children's Work* (intended to serve young readers); yet they worried over the difficulty of managing subscription revenue for the two publications at once:

> What of our two little messengers to the women and children of our land—Woman's Work and Children's Work? . . . Well, their life is vigorous and their progress healthful, although, concerning the latter, there were grave anxieties towards the close of its first year. It tottered on its feet, and there were not wanting fears lest it might fall not to rise again. The year 1876 was not a very good one for young periodicals; but there was a stretching forth of hands from those nearest to this one, and it was borne up for a little time so successfully that it was able to recover itself and stand, even more firmly, than it had done before. The managers of this Society could not see Children's Work go down after it had so good a beginning, nor could they consent to carry a debt on its account[;] therefore, by a united effort, they cleared off nearly the whole of the indebtedness that was crushing it, and January of 1877 saw it almost free, while the incoming subscriptions since then has given good reason to believe that in future it will sustain itself.[15]

Blending a language of maternal nurturance (e.g., "stretching forth of hands") with rhetoric invoking financial management skills, this segment from the "Seventh Annual Report" embodies the editors' continuing efforts to professionalize (maintaining a balanced ledger) *Woman's Work* without undermining its traditional foundation in gendered, motherly benevolence (like that guiding a toddler's first steps).

Both the stress and the possible benefits of such a balancing act continued to be in evidence in the magazine's comments on finances throughout the late 1870s and into the 1880s. For instance, in September 1877, an article titled "Shall It Be Done?" raised the possibility of changing *Woman's Work* from a monthly to a bimonthly format. The magazine's editors then invoked both financial and gendered religious language to try convincing the readership that such a change would be an unfortunate "backward step." Declaring that "the more frequent issue of this magazine was begun two years and a half ago . . . in response to an urgent demand from many readers and friends," the editors bemoaned the fact that "the belief that full support would be given" to the expanded publication calendar had not held up. So, they warned, "unless very speedy relief be found in a large increase of subscriptions, we must return to the old basis of . . . six numbers a year instead of twelve." Reminding readers that "This magazine is not ours any more than yours," the editors described themselves as "servants" happy to work for the good of the movement, but dependent upon choices that only the readers could make. By speaking to their audience directly ("What shall we do, readers?") and asking for a resolution to the problem of balancing the books, the editors distanced themselves rhetorically from the business management issue their article was actually guiding.[46]

Continuing the same strategy in a follow-up article the next month ("What Will You Do?") the *Woman's Work* staff again emphasized that the personal actions of readers would determine whether or not the magazine could sustain its publication schedule and still be "entirely self-supporting" rather than beholden to the Mission Board for financial assistance. At the same time, however, this second article gave evidence of sophisticated editorial decision-making at work, aiming to make the publication more appealing (and hence more profitable) through decisions about publishing content. Specifically, the editors announced a new plan for having a unifying theme for each issue—one tied to the topic of study that the Board had designated for each auxiliary to follow that month. Although the editors described this move as intended to make the magazine "more useful in the monthly meetings," they also hoped this change would "give to their readers just as much as it is possible to give them in return for the small subscription price, and to make the magazine as useful and attractive as it can be made."[47] The closely linked language of anxiety over finances and efforts to manage them through a combination of appropriate content and gendered appeals to readers recurred throughout the magazine's history. For example, a call to readers in February 1883 echoed those of the 1870s in observing that "If every one now subscribing would get one new subscriber, the end would be accomplished." Although the goal by then was more ambitious (to "bring the [subscription] list right up to twenty thousand"), the tactics remained consistent with earlier years.[48]

And clearly many readers did respond, some at a notable personal cost. In 1879 one reader, for instance, wrote "Cheering Words" about how she stretched her "little income" to maintain her subscription, even though her choice meant forgoing other comforts at Christmas.[49] Another raised money to donate to the magazine when she "accosted" several "gentlemen who were not in the Sabbath-school" and preyed upon their guilt to collect "a little money" for *Woman's Work*.[50] Still another tried to help pump up subscriptions by writing a letter to the editors that told of how a widowed acquaintance had struggled to keep up a subscription in the face of virtual poverty, determined that she could not do without her magazine or without *Children's Work* for her "four little boys."[51] How indeed, such personal accounts seemed to ask, could an upright, middle-class Presbyterian woman possibly do without *Woman's Work*, given the sacrifices that some were taking on to maintain their connection to the magazine?

Blending as they did these apparently sincere accounts of the periodical's power with strategic selection and presentation of information about finances, such recurring entries underscore for us today the significant place of *Woman's Work for Woman* in a complex social context. Like the mission movement itself, the printed texts of *Woman's Work* played a productive role in the lives of many middle-class American women; but it did so in ways more complicated than a mere surface reading of their beliefs and actions would suggest. *Woman's Work* and many other mission-based periodicals of the late nineteenth and early twentieth centuries are worthy of deep and prolonged research for the multitude of insights they reveal into a diverse and far-flung community. Through analysis of the print culture that was so central to this gendered community, we can gain a clearer understanding of the mixed motives and complicated value systems that helped to shape the identities of both magazine and readers—as well as the cultural and social work of an earlier generation.

Notes

1. Nellie Arnott, a California woman who traveled all the way to West Africa as member of a multiperson missionary team that included several women, was especially prolific in her letters to potential supporters in various cities within the United States, and she sometimes gave very explicit directions as to how her letters should be circulated through a set sequence of readers

for maximum impact. I thank colleagues at the University of California's Bancroft library for alerting me to the Nellie Arnott Darling collection of letters, journals, and scrapbooks. Before returning to America, marrying Paul Darling, and settling down to a quieter life, Nellie produced numerous examples of mission writing representing all of the stages described here. At first she wrote individual letters. Soon, though, she used carbon paper to make multiple copies, increasing her person-to-person network substantially. (Some of these pieces were later published in printed mission periodicals.) Later, she began to use a typewriter and to send more of her writing directly to mission publications.

2. The three stages I have described above were not, of course, neatly sequential. On the one hand, for instance, Progressive Era women involved in the mission movement continued to handwrite private, personal letters after they could count on having print publication venues. On the other hand, in the antebellum period when most of their writing might have been envisioned initially as private letters, some women's correspondence was eventually published by "compilers" who collected and edited writing mission women had sent to personal correspondents. See, for instance, J. B. Jeter, *A Memoir of Mrs. Henrietta Shuck, The First American Female Missionary to China* (Boston: Gould, Kendall and Lincoln, 1846).

3. Anne Ruggles Gere and Sarah R. Robbins, "Gendered Literacy in Black and White: Turn-of-the-Century African-American and European-American Club Women's Printed Texts," *Signs* 21.3 (Spring 1996): 653–54.

4. Mrs. Tracy, "Woman's Work." *Woman's Work for Woman* 12.10 (October 1882): 333–34. In succeeding citations, I will abbreviate the journal's title as *WWW*.

5. "The Italian Immigrant Press and the Construction of Social Reality, 1850–1920," in *Print Culture in a Diverse America*, ed. James P. Danky and Wayne A. Wiegand (Urbana: University of Illinois Press, 1998), 19. Vecoli draws on Antonio Gramsci's "concept of ideological hegemony" to argue that "communication" can be "viewed as the means whereby the ruling element manufactures and secures consensus to its view of the world among subaltern groups. Since such hegemonic conceptions are subject to challenges by oppositional views, the media become the site of ideological contestation, of a struggle over meaning." In the case of mission movement publications like *Woman's Work*, the publishers, readers, and writers being middle-class Protestant women meant that they were often asserting traditional values based on the power they wielded in terms of their social class, even as they were sometimes resisting (if tactfully and carefully) constraints associated with their gender. See also Yumei Sun, "San Francisco's Chung Sai Yat Po and the Transformation of Chinese Consciousness, 1900–1920," also in *Print Culture in a Diverse America*, 85–100. Yumei Sun points out that "print culture was not only an integral part of the lives of the Chinese in America, it also played a leading role in shaping

the thinking of the Chinese community," not only those who could not speak English and therefore were linguistically dependent upon Chinese-language publications, but also for those who could read English but sought information not available in the American press (88). For women involved in the foreign mission movement, as will be discussed in more detail below, print texts played a parallel role, since theirs was also a subculture with unique needs and interests both served and shaped by their publishing.

6. While the women writing in this venue consistently depicted their work as contributing to "American" goals, their version of a national vision for interacting with people from other cultures was different from the more overtly aggressive ideals of colonialism developing in much male discourse about international incursions during this same time period. Nonetheless, as Amy Kaplan has shown, even as they continued to invoke an ideology of domesticity, many American women involved in international culture between the Civil War and World War I were implicated (at the least) in the colonizing impulses of the period. See Amy Kaplan, "Manifest Domesticity," *American Literature* 70.3 (September 1998): 581–606. See too Laura Wexler, *Tender Violence: Domestic Visions in an Age of U. S. Imperialism* (Chapel Hill: University of North Carolina Press, 2000).

7. Wayne A. Wiegand, "Introduction: Theoretical Foundations for Analyzing Print Culture as Agency and Practice in a Diverse Modern America," in *Print Culture in a Diverse America*, 4. This anthology brought together work from the 1995 conference sponsored by the University of Wisconsin and the State Historical Society of Wisconsin—clearly a watershed moment in print culture studies.

8. For excellent histories of the women's foreign mission movement, see Patricia R. Hill, *The World Their Household: The American Woman's Foreign Mission Movement and Cultural Transformation, 1870–1920* (Ann Arbor: University of Michigan Press, 1985); Jane Hunter, *The Gospel of Gentility: American Women Missionaries in Turn-of-the-Century China* (New Haven: Yale University Press, 1984); and Dana L. Robert, *American Women in Mission: A Social History of Their Thought and Practice* (Macon: Mercer University Press, 1996).

9. Especially helpful to my own research has been Scott's analysis of how "women learned," through organizational participation, "to conduct business, carry on meetings, speak in public, manage money" (2), since these skills were all important to the shared literacy practices of the foreign mission movement's use of print. Additionally, Scott's interpretation of how "values and attitudes were developed" through "collective experience" parallels my own more specific sense of how reading and writing printed mission literature shaped the social selves of women in this specific literacy community. See *Natural Allies: Women's Associations in American History* (Urbana: University of Illinois Press, 1991).

10. An apt example of American women missionary writers struggling (and beginning) to develop a sense of cultural relativism, even as they continued to assume that Protestant middle-class norms were naturally superior, is seen in the article called "At Home: Child-Marriage," *WWW* 7.2 (February 1877): 412–15.

11. Because the authors of *Woman's Work* articles used "Indian" to refer to the mission stations serving Native American reservations, I will follow their terminology. Significantly, both the work of missions serving such tribal groups located inside the continental United States. and those serving Chinese immigrants in California were designated "foreign" assignments by the magazine's editors, who placed those reports alongside writing from women stationed in places like Japan, China, Africa, and East India.

12. "Gleanings," *WWW* 9.11 (November 1879): 393.

13. For helpful interpretations of Bourdieu's sociology of culture, see Craig Calhoun, Edward Li Puma, and Moishe Postone, eds. *Bourdieu: Critical Perspectives* (Chicago: University of Chicago Press, 1993). See especially Edward Li Puma's essay, "Culture and the Concept of Culture in a Theory of Practice," 14–34, and Bourdieu's own "Concluding Remarks," 263–75.

14. Miss Fannie Cundall, "The Twilight Hour in Tripoli," *WWW* 13.5 (May 1883): 157–58.

15. Cundall, 158. Authors of antebellum domestic literacy narratives whose works helped establish these social patterns in literature included Lydia Sigourney, Lydia Maria Child, and Catharine Maria Sedgwick. See my "The Future Good and Great of Our Land," *New England Quarterly* 75 (December 2002): 562–91. For a discussion of Frances Harper's writing of narratives in this tradition around the time when the foreign mission movement was just beginning to adapt the genre, see my "Gendering the Debate over African Americans' Education in the 1880s: Frances Harper's Reconfiguration of Atticus Haygood's Philanthropic Model," *Legacy: A Journal of American Women Writers* 19.1 (Spring 2002): 81–89.

16. For analysis of schoolteaching's gradual construction as appropriate women's work grounded in models of maternal nurturing, see Jo Anne Preston, "Domestic Ideology, School Reformers, and Female Teachers: Schoolteaching Becomes Women's Work in Nineteenth-Century New England." *New England Quarterly* 66.4 (December 1993): 531–51. Susan Ryan describes antebellum links between benevolence and women's pedagogy in *The Grammar of Good Intentions: Race and the Antebellum Culture of Benevolence* (Ithaca, N.Y.: Cornell University Press, 2003).

17. Margaret M. Given, "A School in Rawal Pindi," *WWW* 13.11 (November 1883): 377.

18. Lillian Green, "Christmas in Tullahassee," *WWW* 12.3 (March 1882): 81. Although Miss Green's mission was situated in what we tend to think

of as the United States, *Woman's Work* classified her work as in a "foreign" location since she was teaching on a Creek reservation.

19. "N. A. Indians." *WWW* 13.1 (January 1883): 8–9.

20. Benedict Anderson, *Imagined Communities: Reflections on the Origin and Spread of Nationalism.* Revised Edition (London, Verso, 1991).

21. Michael Fultz has described a similar process happening in ethnic terms in the print culture of African Americans in the early twentieth century. Noting that "black America as a sociological and psychological entity" was developing into a "'Nation within a Nation,'" Fultz attributes an important role in this process to the "black periodicals [that] served as mediums of internal communication," so that, "between 1900 and 1930 the black middle class created a 'universe of discourse' through its monthly periodical literature"—a discourse supporting group identification in both national and racial terms. See "'The Morning Cometh': African-American Periodicals, Education, and the Black Middle Class, 1900–1930," *Print Culture in a Diverse America,* 143.

22. Women missionaries often wrote about waiting impatiently for a ship to arrive, so that they could receive letters from home and send their own letters back to loved ones there.

23. Certainly, as in the case of other rhetorical patterns discussed here, *Woman's Work* was only one of many magazines including "how-to" stories and paeans honoring the effect of these social practices; nor were such strategies limited to the 1870s and '80s. A look at *Missionary Talk,* a newsletter primarily serving southern Baptist women, suggests how pervasive these strategies could be, even in less formal publications with more limited circulations. The lead article for an 1893 issue of this newsletter for the Woman's Missionary Union offers an apt example of the frequent blending of "how-to" and impact stories in mission publications. The front-page "how-to" piece called upon mission-supporting women to organize a program for the Sunday schools at their own churches and pointed out that "the Executive Committee of the Union [had] spared no pains in preparing for Sunday-School Missionary Day" by crafting a transportable study agenda "composed of scripture selections, songs and music, recitations and fact, combined in just the right proportion" to be "instructive, interesting, and striking." [*Missionary Talk* 6.9 (September 1893): 1–4.] The "Children's Column" prescribes hymn number 97, scripture from the book of Revelation, recitation of a poem, a lecture on a foreign mission, and the reading of letters from missionaries. Later in the same issue, a proposed program was listed, along with a copy of the poem recommended for recitation and material that could be used for a lecture (4). Printed alongside this agenda, meanwhile, was a "Directory for Use of Woman's Missionary Societies," including such items as appropriate nearby "Fields" for local boards to support (e.g., "Indians," "Destitute Sections of Southern States" and "The Colored People"), other distant missions also needing financial aid (e.g., China, Africa,

Brazil), and a listing of the "duties" of the "Woman's Missionary Societies" (e.g., to "awaken and maintain the interest of the women and children of the churches in missions, and to increase their contributions to Foreign, Home, and State Missions"). In this case, while the individual front-page story provided a general set of directions for literacy activities, the associated articles offered more detailed directions for drawing upon the printed resources of the publication for social action. Taken together, this cluster of stories demonstrated ways that print, even in informal publications like a newsletter, could help ensure the movement's success by organizing the work of its affiliates, thereby insuring the maintenance of their affective bond.

24. For examples of stories depicting the importance of literacy practices associated with conferences and general meetings of the association, see "At Home: Semi-Annual Meeting," *WWW* 7.9 (November 1877): 285–90; "Our Anniversary Meetings," *WWW* 7.4 (June 1877): 109–10; and "Abroad," *WWW* 9.11 (November 1879): 385–87. For stories depicting the efficacy of home societies' study, see "For the Young People: Many Days After," *WWW* 13.7 (July 1883): 233–37; "For the Young People: Many Days After II," *WWW* 13.8 (August 1883): 278–85; "For the Young People: Making the Best of It," *WWW* 13.1 (January 1883): 15–21; and "Monday Evenings at Mrs. Gray's," *WWW* 15.11 (November 1885): 390–94.

25. See, for instance, "The Week of Prayer," *WWW* 12.3 (March 1882): 31–32; and "At Home: How to Study the Mission Fields—China," *WWW* 13.2 (February 1883): 62–63.

26. "Current Literature and Missions," *WWW* 12.7 (July 1882): 246–47, and "W.F.M.S. of the Presbyterian Church: Topics for the Week of Prayer; Subject for Prayer Meeting," *WWW* 13.1 (January 1883): 28.

27. Mrs. Fitch, "China." *WWW* 7.7 (September 1877): 224, emphasis in original.

28. "Letter from Miss McBeth." *WWW* 9.7 (July 1879): 225, emphasis in original.

29. As the circulation of the magazines grew, one way they assisted women posted overseas was by reducing the quantity of correspondence expected to be sent home. In the early days, before periodicals like *WWW* were readily available, sponsoring organizations at home pressured women stationed overseas to write numerous potential supporters on a regular basis so as to keep contributions flowing. While that need was never fully met by the magazines, they did lead to fewer demands for detailed letters.

30. "North American Indians," *WWW* 9.7 (July 1879): 242. This article was published when the journal was still printing material gathered by the eastern regional office separate from submissions sent to the midwestern headquarters in Chicago, where room 48 at the McCormick street offices was occupied by the Woman's Presbyterian Board of Missions of the Northwest,

which also paid Miss Dougherty's salary.

31. "From Sidon," *WWW* 7.10 (December 1877): 307.

32. "Mrs. W. W. Eddy, Beirut, Syria." *WWW* 9.10 (October 1879): 335.

33. "Abroad: Syria." *WWW* 7.10 (December 1877): 301.

34. "Home Work." *WWW* 7.2 (February 1877): 428.

35. "Extracts from Letters." *WWW* 7.7 (September 1877): 250.

36. *Woman's Work* editors also reprinted and adapted material originally printed in other publications, especially compatible pieces from journals of other denominations and from the interdenominational branch of the movement.

37. Miss H. M. Johnson, "At Home: Our Young People." *WWW* 9.7 (July 1879): 231. Similarly, "The Home Side of Mission Work," which appeared in *WWW* in March of 1883, had originally been "A paper read at a meeting of the Marion Presbyterial Society" (13.3, 94).

38. The editor of a publication dedicated to the study of such texts recently offered this definition of ephemera: "printed or handwritten materials intended for short-term use and disposal." "Letter to the Editor," *Ephemera Canada* 6.2 (Fall 1996): 5.

39. For an example of this epistolary genre, see Oswald Eugene Brown and Anna Muse Brown, *Life and Letters of Laura Askew Haygood* (Nashville: Smith and Lamar, Publishing House of the M. E. Church, South, 1904).

40. See, for instance, "Extracts from Letters," where a contributor described the plan her local mission group had developed for distributing "some of the best leaflets of the various woman's societies . . . into the hands of ladies in different parts of the town to circulate." Declaring that this process had allowed their auxiliary to reach "many who never attend our mission circle," this letter writer clearly exemplified the high level of planning and energy women often gave to managing others' interactions with print via the mission movement's "ephemeral" publication circuits. *WWW* 13.3 (March 1883): 99.

41. *WWW* 13.3 (March 1883): 94–97.

42. Letter from the editors, *WWW* (June 1877): 111–13.

43. In the early years, *Woman's Work* was jointly published by the Woman's Foreign Missionary Society of the Presbyterian Church (headquartered in Philadelphia) and the Women's Presbyterian Board of Missions of the Northwest (headquartered in Chicago). Over time, the Philadelphia office at 1334 Chestnut Street took on more and more responsibility and leadership. This shift is mirrored in the organizational structure of the magazine itself, which went from printing two sections of articles—one set of submissions from each of the two regions—to a single collection presented within a more national than a regional framework.

44. For an inside view of the history of the magazine in its initial form,

see "Woman's Work for Woman: April 1871-November 1885," *WWW* 15.11 (November 1885): 367. Explaining that the joint venture of the Northeast and Midwest regional societies needed to be replaced by a publication which would represent all regions served by the national Board of Foreign Missions, the editors announced that this November 1885 issue would mark the "end" of *Woman's Work for Woman* "in its familiar form and as the organ of only two societies." Beseeching readers "to carry over to this new form of your old friend your heartiest sympathy and support," this historical review, like so many previous *WWW* articles, placed the health of the discourse community in the hands of its reader-subscribers.

45. "Seventh Annual Report," *WWW* 7.4 (June 1877): 114.

46. "Shall It Be Done?" *WWW* 7.7 (September 1877): 234.

47. "What Will You Do?" *WWW* 7.8 (October 1877): 263.

48. "What Remains?" *WWW* 13.2 (February 1883): 64.

49. "Cheering Words," *WWW* 9.2 (February 1879): 56.

50. "Children's Work for the Sabbath-School," *WWW* 7.2 (February 1877): 430.

51. "Encouraging Words," *WWW* 7.8 (October 1877): 265–66.

"When Women Condemn the Whole Race"

Belle Case La Follette's Women's Column Attacks the Color Line

NANCY C. UNGER

In 1931 Belle Case La Follette was hailed by the *New York Times* as "perhaps the least known, yet the most influential of all the American women who have had to do with public affairs in this country."[1] More than seventy years later, her legacy remains under-appreciated. Once a powerful force in progressive politics, both in Wisconsin and on the national scene, she merits much closer scrutiny—and greater recognition than she has heretofore received.

Belle Case La Follette was first of all a major political influence on her husband, who was a congressman from 1885 to 1891, Wisconsin governor from 1901 to 1906, and U.S. senator from 1906 until his death in 1925. "Fighting Bob" La Follette sought to bring the "Wisconsin Idea" of a truer democracy to the entire nation. He embraced a broad spectrum of reforms, including state regulatory commissions, the direct election of senators, the conservation of natural resources, and the concept of a university working in tandem with the legislature to create a modern service state. He was a major player on the national scene for decades. Unlike many other men of his time, Bob La Follette depended enormously on his wife's advice and counsel, seeking it eagerly and often, openly acknowledging to fellow politicians that he would not make key decisions without consulting his wife. The La Follettes could and did differ publicly over political issues, but even at such times Bob would listen to Belle's clear and measured thinking. She had a first-rate mind and a keen instinct for public policy. Among other achievements, she was the first woman to graduate from the University of Wisconsin Law School.[2] Despite their occasional differences over political strategy and tactics, Bob La Follette called his wife "my wisest and best counselor."

While Belle La Follette's influence on her spouse is undeniable, this was not the only sphere in which she made her mark. She also had a talent for reaching the public and influencing public opinion—frequently through speeches, but most often through the hundreds of articles she wrote over a period of more than fifty years, primarily for *La Follette's Magazine*, which premiered in 1909 and continues to this day as *The Progressive*. Of exceptional importance is her skillful use of the written word, especially in the years prior to the attainment of woman suffrage. In particular, her columns attacking the racist practices of President Woodrow Wilson's administration during the period when women were still denied the vote demonstrated her ability to galvanize one disenfranchised and oppressed group (women) to take up the cause of another (African Americans), with empowering results.

Bob La Follette intended the weekly (later monthly), sixteen-page magazine to be "the vigilant champion of True Representative Government" and of course a vehicle for his own political views. Its pages provided "an uncensored forum in which to justify and rationalize, defend and attack, criticize and promote" any and all issues the La Follettes found worthy of discussion.[3] Just as Eleanor Roosevelt later utilized the forum of her regular column "My Day" to promote various causes, Belle La Follette made use of her own featured department within the magazine. While La Follette's readership never matched Roosevelt's in numbers, the reactions evoked by her department are evidence that through her printed words she created a powerful relationship with her readers nationwide. Her words in response to the racist policies of the Wilson administration inspired her readers not merely to critical thought but to protest and to action.

Belle Case La Follette passionately, tenaciously, and publicly promoted not just women's suffrage but feminism, world peace, public service, and other movements contributing to sweeping, liberal, even radical change. She shrewdly used her husband's political influence to publicize and promote her own reform agenda, forging powerful relationships and contributing materially to social change. Her life story, though less well known than those of various First Ladies, has hardly been ignored. It is the subject of a full length biography, a dissertation, scholarly articles, websites and a documentary film.[4] Each details to varying degrees the depth of her commitment to political reform; yet the woman who emerges too often appears to be "merely" the staunch supporter and helpmeet to her husband, a woman who championed idealistic causes, but from a safe distance. In fact she was as actively involved in reform efforts as any progressive of her day—a woman who managed to be both complex and reserved emotionally, while at the same time politically passionate. Her commitment to various reforms earned her much scorn and derision, involving her in ugly public and private debates and disputes that she endured at great personal cost. Her opposition to America's entry into World War I, and the vilification which she and her husband endured as a result, caused her, in 1919, to suffer a nervous breakdown whose symptoms included amnesia.[5]

Belle Case La Follette often campaigned in support of world disarmament and civil rights, especially for African Americans but always most avidly for women's rights.[6] She is probably best known for her dedication to attaining the woman's vote (for which she spoke, wrote, and marched), but all three of the causes she held most dear were, she believed, inextricably bound together: "This business of being a woman is in many ways, like being a member of a despised race."[7] As a woman—that is, a member of a group that had suffered from generations of discrimination—La Follette was well aware of the toll that bigotry had taken on the pride, dignity, and incentive of its various targets. Yet she remained unshaken in her faith in the unsung, often even untapped, courage, integrity, and ability of victims of discrimination. It was her fervent belief, for example, that despite the limitations imposed on women by the prescribed gender roles of the day, "if women had a larger voice in the counseling of nations, there would be no war slogans, no dreams of empire which could lead to the great sacrifice of life, which woman alone knows the real value."[8]

Following World War I, La Follette became a prominent member of the national board of the U.S. section of the Women's International League for Peace and Freedom. She had long believed that women could, and should, change the world. In her "Home and

Education" department in *La Follette's Magazine*, she offered her readers advice and encouragement to do just that. In describing the goal of her department (whose column frequently spilled onto two, even three pages) she stated that, contrary to the advice of others, "I have written upon the supposition that no subject is too broad, too dignified, too advanced for women readers."[9] Clearly, she and others viewed her column as an agency for social change. Consequently she was hailed by the *Cincinnati Inquirer* as "a pioneer in the establishment of a new sort of women's page."[10] As the editor of "one of the cleverest and most readable women's pages in the country," she garnered praise for providing women with "stronger intellectual food" than the usual fare of "vaseline and cold cream."[11] Rejecting the notion that women's inability to vote rendered them politically powerless, La Follette believed fervently in the importance of even traditional perceptions of women's proper role in the political well-being of the nation.[12] Women's contributions could not be made in the form of a completed ballot, but through the printed word their political wisdom could be made known. For the first several years of *La Follette's Magazine*'s publication, the motto under her "Home and Education" title read: "The Home is the real seat of government and the Wise men of all nations bring their gifts to the cradle." She explored a vast variety of topics, from advice on nutrition, housekeeping, and child raising to such decidedly undomestic subjects as race relations, party politics, and foreign affairs. Although the desire for women's rights remained the closest to her heart, La Follette's columns on race published during the second decade of the twentieth century are deserving of special attention. It was there that Belle La Follette truly demonstrated her ability to use the printed word to inspire women to action while showcasing the depth and breadth of her commitment to civil rights during a particularly trying time in the nation's history.

In the 5 August 1911 issue of *La Follette's*, a story titled "Colored Folk of Washington" takes up nearly two pages of the "Home and Education" section. It is illustrated by six photographs, mostly of smiling African American faces. Ostensibly, the story offers a simple comparison between La Follette's impressions of Washington's African American population during her husband's tenure in Congress during the 1880s and her observations of their status some thirty years later. La Follette details the changes she has observed in both the white and black populations. Washington's African Americans in the 1880s, she recalls, were but one generation removed from slavery. She praises the "old types" for their wholesome manners, habits, and traditions, but presents the new generation of that postwar era as inexperienced, ill-educated, and undisciplined, "foolishly imitative" of white folks because "they did not realize that abolishing slavery had not removed the barriers of race and color; nor had they awakened to the possibilities of separate racial development." Whites in Washington in the 1880s were much involved with the "race question," their positions clearly distinguished by their choice of the term "nigger" or "negro." But whatever their viewpoint, notes La Follette, whites assumed it was up to them, as the nominally superior race, to solve the "Negro Problem": "[N]ot even their strongest champions considered the possibility of black folks settling it for themselves." To be sure, La Follette's language reflects the casual racism of that earlier day. She describes the children of the cook at the boardinghouse where she and Congressman La Follette resided as "happy little coons," and the describes the mother of a faithful nurse as "a typical mammy."[13]

But there was more to Belle La Follette's column than mere reminiscence. The remaining, and much longer, portion of her story is in fact a spirited defense of Washington's African Americans. She emphasizes the popular movement away from assuming whites to be the sole providers of any potential solution to the "race problem," noting instead the self-reliance of Washington's African Americans. "Colored," La Follette notes, is the nearly universal adjective indicating Washington's African American population, and said "quite unconsciously," reflecting much less division among whites as to black status. "Very little thought seems to be given to the race question, either public or personally," La Follette asserts, because "Colored folk are presumed to settle their own problems and carry their own burden," and were doing so with a good deal of success. No longer a burden on the white population, African Americans were, according to La Follette, an important asset. They constituted about one-third of the population of Washington and performed nearly all the city's manual labor. (With a population of 94,446 in 1910, Washington, D.C., had the largest African American population of any city in the United States, a population that enjoyed an elevated social status when compared to those of their race in other southern cities). La Follette wonders "what Washington would do without the colored help." African Americans are wage earners and, she notes quite pointedly, wage spenders, with great purchasing power. There is, she reminds her readers, "a class of very wealthy and prosperous negroes," and observes that even many of those in domestic service are saving toward buying a home.[14]

After reminding her readers that African Americans were vital players in the Washington economy, La Follette then refutes, in some detail, the negative stereotypes middle-class white women in Washington perpetuate about African American domestic servants. "When women decry the whole race,—as women are wont to do,—because of their hard experience with servants," La Follette urges white women in Washington to consider their good fortune to live in area where domestic servants are plentiful. In fact, much of the readily available help was "very good," in La Follette's opinion. She urges her readers not to be "thoughtlessly uncharitable," but instead to make allowances for the "disadvantages in opportunity and environment" of the "colored help." In this portion of her column, young African Americans are no longer "happy little coons," but rather "children who are interesting, and often beautiful," neatly and tastefully dressed, with "bright attractive faces," and "good manners," qualities La Follette credits to their mothers' care and attention. African American women living in their "little homes," she observes, take in washing and sewing when they are not serving in the homes of white women. They also raise flowers, vegetables, and eggs for sale. Indeed they "reflect the spirit of the pioneer home-makers of this country—the sacrifices, the varied occupations, the industry, and the love of the land," and she wonders if, "considering all the circumstances, there is a class of people more deserving of a word of appreciation than the colored folk of Washington."[15]

La Follette's Magazine had a circulation between 30,000 and 40,000, with about half its subscribers in Wisconsin. Presumably most subscribers were sympathetic to the family's progressive views on most issues, creating what print culture scholar Elizabeth Long calls a "social infrastructure," making the reading of *La Follette's* a communal activity grounded on shared interpretative frameworks and practiced in shared institutions.[16] But many of the magazine's readers vehemently disagreed with Belle La Follette's "casual observations" on the "Colored Folk of Washington." Rather than eliciting only appreciation for Washington's African American community, as she had intended, her words brought angry reactions from readers who brought their racist orientation to her text.[17] The article cost the magazine subscribers and "called forth letters of bitter denunciation." So chastened and upset was she that she waited two full years before mentioning in print the storm of criticism and protest that erupted after publication of her column. In her follow-up article (23 August 1913), La Follette states that it was not her purpose to offend her readers and acknowledges that she is no expert investigator. However, she also expresses that she finds it "the very essence of editorial obligation to stand firmly for well grounded convictions on important matters, especially where human rights are involved." She then makes plain her real agenda in revisiting the 1911 column: since the inauguration of the Wilson administration, southerners were determined to have the citizens of the nation's capital be officially segregated by race. The existing policy of no official discrimination on the streets of Washington was under attack in the form of bills mandating segregated street cars introduced by members of Congress from Florida, Mississippi, and Oklahoma. Belle Case La Follette printed in full the advertisement for a public meeting held two weeks earlier at which Senator James K. Vardaman of Mississippi and other "prominent speakers" addressed the question "Shall the Negro Rule?" and discussed "fully and freely" "the policy of appointing Negroes to government positions." The senator and his fellow speakers appeared under the auspices of the National Democratic Fair Play Association, a nongovernmental group advocating "the segregation of the races in government employment, and the 'reorganization of the civil service' as declared in the National Democratic Platform of 1912." La Follette describes this unprovoked announcement as "a proclamation of hate [that] strikes terror to the hearts of the colored race," causing "fear and suffering."

Although Belle La Follette had been more indirect in defending African Americans from white women in Washington who did not sufficiently appreciate their value, once politicians—and demagogues—became involved, she took off the gloves. While La Follette's class and race granted her a certain level of privilege in society, her disenfranchisement and other political and social constraints based on her gender placed her on the periphery of power. Undaunted, she skillfully and aggressively used one of the few powerful means of expression available to her. Within the "women's section" of her family's magazine, La Follette, clearly seeking her readers' support, used the printed word in an effort to shape race relations in America. With her column of 23 August 1913, she officially launched her very public attack on the Wilson administration's efforts to racially segregate all government agencies and eliminate African Americans from federal service.[18]

The column, frankly titled "The Color Line," makes a two-pronged attack on the racism suddenly pervading Washington. The first, a more pointed effort than she had attempted in her column previously, emphasizes the contributions of African Americans to the nation's capital. La Follette invites her readers to imagine the scenario resulting from the fulfillment of Nevada Senator Francis Newland's desire for all blacks to be resettled outside the United States, possibly even shipped back to Africa. Whites would be the first to feel what she terms the "economic tragedy." Far more dramatic is her second attack: a detailed account of her personal efforts to discover and combat the impact of the government's as yet unofficial but pending efforts to segregate the federal civil service. The new requirement that all applicants submit a photograph was evidence of the effort to make race a criterion in what had been a color-blind hiring process. La Follette's involvement was motivated by a desire to bring attention to actions that the government clearly intended to be kept quiet. She was inspired by a letter she had received from Nannie Burroughs, president of the National Training School for Women and Girls, protesting the racial segregation being instituted in the Bureau of Engraving and Printing. La Follette wrote directly to J. E. Ralph, director of the bureau, and published the parts of his reply pertaining to women employees. Ralph noted that about 10 percent of the employees in his bureau were African American and declared that no general order to segregate had been issued. He did acknowledge, however, that when three "colored girls" persisted in disregarding the "kindly suggestion" that "it would be best for them to occupy [lunch] tables with girls of their own race," he found it "necessary" to give them "positive directions" to restrict themselves to those tables assigned to "the colored assistants." At La Follette's request, the bureau provided her the names of the three African Americans, each of whom agreed to be interviewed by Belle La Follette.

These interviews, conducted on 9 August 1913, revealed that two of the women had been employed at the bureau for eleven years, and the third, Rosebud Murraye, for nine years. During those years the quality of their work had earned them several promotions. They had eaten where they liked within the lunch room, with no white opposition. When a white woman suddenly objected to their presence in the lunch room, they replied that they heeded orders only from the director. During the subsequent meeting with the director, strong suggestions rather than direct orders were issued, prompting La Follette to ask if they were still eating in the lunch room. "No," came the reply, "it was no use trying. Our food choked us." Two days after these interviews, Rosebud Murraye brought La Follette a copy of a memorandum from her immediate supervisor calling for her dismissal for "insubordination and disrespectful behavior, " which La Follette duly appended to her column. La Follette's own concluding remarks rather dramatically informed her readers that the fate of Murraye had yet to be resolved.[19]

La Follette's column of 13 September 1913 includes a letter she deemed typical of the many she received criticizing "The Color Line." Dr. Leon Peek of West Palm Beach, Florida, justifies forwarding to her his critical reaction by noting that because La Follette had presented her views in a public forum, she invited responses. Peek chided La Follette for her ignorance about racial differences, noting that "Negroes, at least many of them, like to push themselves into company where they are not wanted," and he urged her to respect the opinions of "normal" white people who opposed racial equality, especially northerners who express racist sentiments after visiting the South. In response, La Follette freely acknowledged the limitations of her experiences but pointedly rejoined, "I believe my views in this field are entitled to consideration at least equal to that according the views of Northerners who go South, and speak with authority of the whole colored race." She wrote that "the policy of drawing the color line in the United States Civil Service was the occasion of my writing the article" and concluded that "the South should not try to set up its Standards for the North or for the District of Columbia," because "merit, not sympathy, demands that [Negroes] should not be discriminated against and should be accorded the justice due them as citizens of a democracy."[20]

A month later La Follette summarized in *La Follette's Magazine* a report on segregation in the civil service in the District of Columbia instigated by the New York chapter of the NAACP. The report noted that, despite a lack of official orders, systematic enforcement of segregation was being carried out under the Wilson administration. Federal administrators denied any racial motivation for the creation of segregated facilities, instead attributing the "changes" to a desire to "increase efficiency."[21]

The impact of La Follette's "Color Line" columns, especially upon the higher levels of government is impossible to gauge with any real accuracy. Robert La Follette had copies of each issue delivered free of charge to each of his colleagues in the House and the Senate, but distribution does not guarantee readership. However, in January 1914, Belle La Follette received a letter from a writer she termed as "a refined, intelligent colored woman" in Paris, where the news had reached of the "splendid articles appearing in *La Follette's* regarding segregation."[22] The woman decried the persecution of her race within the United States and warned of the legacy of bitter hatred and even bloodshed that would be the inevitable result. La Follette printed her letter in "Home and Education" alongside to an article by Margaret Woodrow Wilson on an unrelated matter.[23] Since President Wilson's attention was likely to be drawn to this issue of *La Follette's Magazine* featuring his daughter's words—which were introduced in extremely flattering terms by Belle La Follette—it is probable that the juxtaposition of her article with the letter from the African American woman in France was not entirely coincidental.

Whether the impact was lost on Woodrow Wilson remains unknown, but Belle La Follette did not hesitate to confront the president directly. Two weeks later, in "The Color Line to Date," she noted the criticism resulting from her speeches (one before an African American audience at the Washington YMCA, the other at the annual banquet of the New York NAACP), before providing an update on the status of Rosebud Murraye. Murraye's employment at the Bureau of Engraving and Printing was terminated 21 August 1913, nine years after she began work and just twelve days after she openly discussed the new racial restrictions with La Follette. La Follette printed in full Murraye's letter of protest to President Wilson, together with portions of her own letter that she attached to Murraye's appeal. She also printed in full the response from Wilson's secretary, who directed La Follette to an attachment by the president's son-in-law, William McAdoo, Secretary of the Treasury. McAdoo's terse note that "the Department . . . sees no ground for reopening the case" is likewise reprinted in *La Follette's Magazine*.[24]

Having used the Murraye debacle to personalize the injustice wreaked by the government's efforts to segregate the civil service, La Follette repeated in her column what she had said in her public speeches; namely, that African Americans had for too long been forced to submit to discrimination in travel, in hotels, at public entertainments, in schools, and in churches. Her outrage that public service was being added to the list is plain: "But to have the United States Government take a backward step, to have the color line drawn in places they have won their merit, to be humiliated, repressed and degraded at the capital of the nation by their own government, which has no right to discriminate among its citizens, is a body blow to hope and pride and incentive."[25]

As Belle La Follette noted, it was not only the immediately oppressed who would suffer if such practices were perpetuated: "Continued violations of fundamental principles of human rights touching a race that constitutes one-tenth of our citizenship must ultimately degrade our standards, corrupt our ideals, and destroy our sense of democracy."[26] And time proved her prophecy correct. The systematic effort to oust African Americans from positions of any power continued. As the more influential African Americans were purged from government positions, those blacks on rungs much farther down the civil service ladder who managed to retain their positions were racially segregated. These and a variety of other oppressive actions moved Booker T. Washington to observe in 1913, "I have recently spent several days in Washington and have never seen the colored people so discouraged and so bitter as they are at the present time."[27] Calling whites to consider what such unjust discrimination against civil service employees meant to national life, Belle Case La Follette wrote that the issue is "in no way a matter of social privilege. It is a matter of civil right."[28] Nonetheless, by 1916 only one African American maintained a federal appointment—municipal judge Robert Terrell, husband of the noted educator and social activist Mary Church Terrell of the District of Columbia.

La Follette concluded "The Color Line to Date" by reprinting excerpts from a few of the multitude of letters generated by her writings and speeches on race. Many of the critical letters came attached to accounts of La Follette's speeches and articles clipped from southern newspapers such as the *Roanoke Times*; supportive letters were accompanied by clippings from the *New York Evening Post*, the *Washington Evening Post*, and similar papers in the North. One anonymous writer warned her that "for a white lady to address a Negro Audience is out of place," noting that while such behavior might garner Senator La Follette some black votes, "it does not raise you very much in the estimation of decent white people." (Wisconsin then had fewer than 5,000 African American voters, constituting less than 0.2 percent of the state's total.) Other critics were far less restrained. One reader, so determined to have the prevailing racial values confirmed, termed Belle La Follette a disgrace to the white race and suggested that the only true reason she might have written such a column was that she was herself black—but only "a little light in color." It was signed, "[A] real white person with no black stripes down the back like you."[29]

Two months later, La Follette offered readers of *La Follette's Magazine* another sampling of reader response in "The Color Line: Various Points of View." One correspondent from Tennessee denounced the "idiotic demands" for social equality of the races being popularized by La Follette. But the printed and spoken words of Belle La Follette also generated support, demonstrating the power of her words as agents of meaningful change. A white southern woman expressed her admiration for La Follette and her sympathy for the racially oppressed. An unidentified brigadier general of the U.S. Army who had served as an officer in a "colored regiment" was inspired by La Follette's coverage to publicly declare racial segregation of America's armed forces a clear violation of the Constitution. And an African American woman tried to describe the "tremendous effect upon all who heard" La Follette's stirring speech concerning race relations delivered to an audience of color at the Washington YMCA. It was, she reported, "the topic which overshadows all others" in the African American community. A white employee of the Government Printing Office (and a Civil War veteran) concluded his lengthy tribute to his black colleagues by addressing La Follette directly: "Again I thank you. The black race needs such as you to aid them. The white race needs you to bring it to its senses."[30]

During the first four months of 1914 Belle La Follette continued to print letters expressing a variety of viewpoints concerning her views on the color line. Her correspondents ranged from an "absolute segregationist" in Topeka, Kansas, to a grateful Wisconsinite thanking La Follette for the "never-forgotten steps you have taken to protect a downtrodden race."[31] She also reprinted in her column the speeches and columns of others who shared her views on civil rights. In "Fair Chance for the Negro," retired Brigadier General Richard H. Pratt demonstrated the illogic of a variety of prevailing racist stereotypes and practices, concluding, "The Negro is entitled to a full, fair, and equal chance to develop all his best powers to the highest extent. Until he has that full chance and proves by that alone what is he capable of, all assertion of lower order or incompetence is baseless."[32]

In the end, the Wilson administration failed in its attempt to impose racial segregation throughout the federal civil service. Black and white advocates of civil rights refused to acquiesce in the giant step backward, swelling the ranks of the Washington NAACP from the original 143 (of which Belle Case La Follette was one) to 700 dues-paying members.[33] The president personally received letters of protest from every state, written by both blacks and whites, some doubtlessly inspired by La Follette's outspoken columns.[34] La Follette urged her Washington female readers in particular to consider how an "absence of purpose that characterizes the social life of the national Capital reacts unfavorably on the country," reminding them that they are "not supposed to belong to the butterfly and parasitic class," but "should represent the earnest, intelligent womanhood of the nation."[35] Mass meetings were held and petitions circulated. By early 1914 the "rain of complaints" that activists had brought down on segregationists forced an official end to the federal segregation efforts, prompting many victory celebrations within the offices of the NAACP, their joy shared by all proponents of civil rights, black and white.[36]

But Belle La Follette did not relax in her vigilance. Her final direct assault on Wilson's racial policies appeared in *La Follette's* in December 1914, decrying the President's ongoing defense of "unofficial" segregation in certain federal departments, which he continued to declare necessary to prevent friction resulting from the racial prejudice that already existed.[37] Even as Wilson's segregation plan foundered, La Follette remained alert to violations of African American rights. Until her death in 1931, her "Home and Education" department of *La Follette's Magazine* carried articles decrying segregation and lynching while promoting racial harmony and cooperation.

Leaders of the African American community nationwide never forgot Belle La Follette's public stance on their behalf during what was called at the time "the most serious blow to Negro rights since the days of slavery."[38] Even in the midst of a disagreement with La Follette over troop removal from Russia following World War I, Mary Church Terrell noted La Follette's total lack of race prejudice and praised her for always having the courage of her convictions. "[B]y word and by deed," she wrote, Belle La Follette strove to "place herself on record as being in favor of any legislation or any effort designed to give colored people all the rights and privileges which other people enjoy."[39]

The "new kind of women's page" she created within her family's magazine allowed Belle Case La Follette to establish a unique relationship with her readers. Through her skillful use of the printed word, she challenged thousands of Americans, most of them women, to think deeply on the political, social, and economic ramifications of racism.

She encouraged and enabled them to see an attack on one race as an attack on all. By publicly exposing the segregationist activities of the Wilson administration, she also showed by example how women, without the benefit of the vote or economic power, could use their own printed words to battle injustice—and win. As they strove to empower African Americans, American women of all races who heeded La Follette's call empowered themselves. Belle La Follette was undeniably a politically influential spouse of the highest caliber—and a remarkable American in her own right who used to fullest advantage one of the most important tools available to her and to oppressed others: the printed word.

Notes

1. "Wisconsin's Matriarch," *New York Times*, 20 August 1931, p. 18.

2. Bob refused to share his wife's pacifism, however, which led to a number of public disagreements, including Belle's refusal to support Bob's efforts in 1923 to maintain the Wisconsin National Guard. See Dee Ann Montgomery, "An Intellectual Profile of Belle Case La Follette: Progressive Editor, Political Strategist, and Feminist" (PhD diss., Indiana University, 1975), 159.

3. Nancy Unger, *Fighting Bob La Follette: The Righteous Reformer* (Chapel Hill: University of North Carolina Press, 2000), 184–85.

4. See Montgomery, "An Intellectual Profile," as well as Lucy Freeman, Sherry La Follette, and George Zabriskie, *Belle: A Biography of Belle Case La Follette* (New York: Beaufort, 1986); Nancy C. Unger, "The Two Worlds of Belle Case La Follette," *Wisconsin Magazine of History* 83, no. 2 (Winter 1999–2000): 82–110; Bernard Weisberger, "Changes and Choices: Two and a Half Generations of La Follette Women," *Wisconsin Magazine of History* 76, no. 4 (1993): 248–70, and Jocelyn Riley, *Belle Case La Follette, 1859–1931* ([videotape and brochure] Madison: Her Own Words, 1987). Extensive web-based projects include Nancy C. Unger, "How Did Belle La Follette Resist Racial Segregation in Washington, D.C.,1913–1914?" *Women and Social Movements in the United States*, ed. Kathryn Sklar and Thomas Dublin, http://www.alexanderstreetpress.com/products/wasm.htm (New York: Alexander Street Press, June 2004); and Sarah Lochen, "Belle Case La Follette," *Women's Legal History Biography Project*, http://www.law.stanford.edu/library/wlhbp/profiles/LaFolletteBelle.html (Stanford University, 2004).

5. Montgomery, "An Intellectual Profile," 152.

6. Ibid. See also Genevieve McBride, *On Wisconsin Women* (Madison: University of Wisconsin Press, 1993).

7. Belle Case La Follette (BCL), speech, "On Segregation," 5 Jan. 1914, in the Belle La Follette Papers, box 40, La Follette Family Collection, Library of Congress, Washington, D.C.

8. Ibid.

9. BCL, quoted in Selene Armstrong Harmon, "A New Sort of Women's Page," *Cincinnati Enquirer* quoted in *La Follette's Magazine* (*LM*), 13 June 1914, vol. 6, no. 24, 6.

10. Harmon, "A New Sort of Women's Page," 6.

11. Ibid.

12. See Unger, "Two Worlds," and Unger, *Fighting Bob*, 47–68.

13. BCL, "The Colored Folk of Washington," *LM*, 5 August 1911, vol. 3, no. 31, 10–11.

14. Ibid., 11.

15. Ibid.

16. Elizabeth Long, "Textual Interpretation as Collective Action," in Jonathan Boyarin, ed., *The Ethnography of Reading* (Berkeley: University of California Press, 1993), 180–211. Cited in James P. Danky and Wayne A. Wiegand, eds., *Print Culture in a Diverse America* (Urbana and Chicago: University of Illinois Press, 1998), 3–4.

17. Stanley Fish refers to this kind of raiding of a text for readers' own purposes as "poaching," a powerful indicator that readers do not read like literary critics, but are active agents who exercise creativity in making sense of a text. Stanley Fish, *Is There a Text in This Class? The Authority of Interpretive Communities* (Cambridge, MA: Harvard University Press, 1980). Cited in Danky and Wiegand, *Print Culture*, 3.

18. BCL, "The Color Line," *LM*, 23 August 1913, vol. 5, No. 34, 6.

19. Ibid., 6–7.

20. BCL, "The Adverse Point of View on 'The Color Line,'" *LM*, 13 September 1913, vol. 5, no. 37, 6.

21. BCL, "Segregation in the Civil Service," *LM* 13 Dec. 1913, vol. 50, 6.

22. BCL, "A Mother's Question," *LM* 10 Jan. 1914, vol. 6, no. 2, 6.

23. Margaret Woodrow Wilson, "The Social Center and Home Economics," *LM*, 10 Jan. 1914, vol. 6, no. 2, 6.

24. BCL, "Color Line to Date," *LM*, 24 Jan. 1914, vol. 6, no. 4, 6. La Follette ultimately arranged another position for Murraye. Montgomery, 17.

25. Ibid., 7.

26. Ibid.

27. Booker T. Washington, quoted in Kathleen Wolgemuth, "Woodrow Wilson and Federal Segregation, *Journal of Negro History* vol. 44, no. 2 (April 1959): 163.

28. BCL, "Color Line to Date," 7.

29. Ibid.

30. BCL, "The Color Line: Various Points of View," *LM*, 28 March 1914, vol. 6, no. 13, 6–7.

31. BCL, "The Color Line: Various Points."

32. BCL, "Fair Chance for the Negro," *LM*, 11 April 1914, vol. 6, no. 15, 6.

33. Montgomery, "An Intellectual Profile," 115.

34. Wolgemuth, "Woodrow Wilson and Federal Segregation," 165.

35. BCL, *LM*, 20 Dec. 1913, vol. 5, no. 51, 6.

36. Wolgemuth, "Woodrow Wilson and Federal Segregation," 171.

37. BCL, "Segregation in the Civil Service," *LM*, Dec. 1914, vo1.6, no. 46, 10.

38. Wolgemuth, "Woodrow Wilson and Federal Segregation," 165.

39. Montgomery, "An Intellectual Profile," 155.

Contributors

Index

Contributors

Jane Aikin is senior academic advisor at the National Endowment for the Humanities and a historian of late-nineteenth- and twentieth-century America. Her publications include *The Nation's Great Library: Herbert Putnam and the Library of Congress* (University of Illinois Press, 1993), "Valley of the Shadow," *Humanities* 18 (March/April 1997): 18–22, and "High Culture, Low Culture: The Singular Duality of the Library of Congress," *American Studies* 42 (Fall 2001): 43–61.

Terri Castaneda is assistant professor and director of the Anthropology Museum at California State University, Sacramento. Castaneda earned her PhD in cultural anthropology at Rice University in 1993, where she specialized in museum studies and the anthropology of tourism. From late 1999 through the summer of 2001, she worked as an archivist for D-QU Tribal College, in Davis, California. Castaneda is currently working on a cultural and political account of the early to mid-twentieth-century relations between California Indians, museum anthropologists, and Indian agents in north-central California.

Michele Valerie Cloonan is dean and professor, Graduate School of Library and Information Science, Simmons College. Prior to coming to Simmons she was associate professor and chair, Department of Information Studies, UCLA. She has published widely, mostly in the areas of book trade history and the preservation of cultural heritage materials.

James P. Danky became director of the Center for the History of Print Culture in Modern America when Wayne Wiegand relocated to Florida in 2002. In addition to *Print Culture in a Diverse America* (University of

Illinois Press, 1998), Danky has written and edited reference works, bibliographies, and monographs on the radical press, women, and minorities. With Wiegand, he edits the series Print Culture History in Modern America for the University of Wisconsin Press.

June Howard is professor of English, American culture, and women's studies at the University of Michigan, Ann Arbor. She is the author of *Publishing the Family* (Duke University Press, 2001), which examines early twentieth-century literature and culture through a microhistory of the collaborative novel *The Whole Family* and other contributions to American literary history.

Elizabeth Long is associate professor of sociology at Rice University. She majored in history at Stanford University and worked for several years in publishing for Simon & Schuster and Alfred A. Knopf, Inc., in New York City before earning her doctorate at Brandeis University in 1979. Professor Long has published in the fields of cultural sociology, sociology of gender, the sociology of knowledge, qualitative sociology, and contemporary sociological theory, as well as in the interdisciplinary fields of American studies, cultural studies, and women's studies. Her most recent book is *Book Clubs: Women and the Uses of Reading in Everyday Life* (University of Chicago Press, 2003).

Kristin Mapel Bloomberg is director of the Hamline University Women's Studies Program, where she is associate professor of women's studies and English and holds the Hamline University Endowed Chair in the Humanities. She is author of *Tracing Arachne's Web: Myth and Feminist Fictions* (University Press of Florida, 2001).

Joanne E. Passet is assistant professor of history at Indiana University East. She is the author of *Cultural Crusaders: Women Librarians in the American West, 1900–17* (University of New Mexico Press, 1994), *Sex Radicals and the Quest for Women's Equality* (University of Illinois Press, 2003), and coauthor with Mary Niles Maack of *Aspirations and Mentoring in an Academic Environment* (Greenwood Press, 1994).

Christine Pawley is an assistant professor at the School of Library and Information Science at the University of Iowa. Her research focuses on the reading experiences of "common" readers in the American

Midwest. Her book *Reading on the Middle Border: The Culture of Print in Late Nineteenth Century Osage, Iowa* was published by the University of Massachusetts Press in 2001 and won the Benjamin F. Shambaugh Award for 2002 from the Iowa State Historical Society. Other publications have appeared in *Libraries and Culture, Library Quarterly, Book History,* and *American Studies.*

Sarah Robbins is professor of English and English education at Kennesaw State University. Director of the NEH-funded Keeping and Creating American Communities program (http://kcac.kennesaw.edu), Sarah is also director of the Kennesaw Mountain Writing Project and winner of the University System of Georgia's award for excellence in the scholarship of teaching. Sarah's interdisciplinary essays on American women's literature and culture have appeared in journals such as *Signs, New England Quarterly,* and *American Quarterly.* With historian Ann Pullen, she has created a growing website on women's work in nineteenth-century America (http://www.kennesaw.edu/hss/wwork). Her most recent book is *Managing Literacy, Mothering America: Women's Narratives on Reading and Writing in the Nineteenth Century* (University of Pittsburgh Press, 2004).

Toni Samek is associate professor of library and information studies at the University of Alberta, where she teaches in the area of intellectual freedom. She is the author of *Intellectual Freedom and Social Responsibility in American Librarianship, 1967–1974* (McFarland & Company, Inc., 2001). She is currently researching contemporary progressive library discourse. Toni serves as convenor of the Canadian Library Association's Advisory Committee on Intellectual Freedom. She lives in Edmonton, Alberta.

Barbara Sicherman is the William R. Kenan Jr. Professor of American Institutions and Values, Emerita, at Trinity College. She is the author of *Alice Hamilton: A Life in Letters* (Harvard University Press, 1984), which was reissued in 2003 by the University of Illinois Press, and coeditor of *Notable American Women: The Modern Period* (Harvard University Press, 1980).

Nancy C. Unger is associate professor of history, women's, and gender studies, and environmental studies at Santa Clara University. Her publications on the La Follette family include the prize-winning biography *Fighting Bob La Follette: The Righteous Reformer* (University of North Carolina Press, 2000) and "The Two Worlds of Belle La Follette" in the *Wisconsin Magazine of History*. Her current book project is *Beyond "Nature's Housekeepers": American Women and Gender in Environmental History*.

Wayne A. Wiegand is the F. William Summers Professor of Library and Information Studies and professor of American studies at Florida State University. He is author of several award-winning books (including *Irrepressible Reformer: A Biography of Melvil Dewey*), and from 1992 through 2002 served as codirector of the Center for the History of Print Culture in Modern America while a faculty member at the University of Wisconsin–Madison School of Library and Information Studies.

Index

Compiled by Amanda Grell

Print Culture History in Modern America
James P. Danky and Wayne A. Wiegand, General Editors

Libraries as Agencies of Culture
Edited by Thomas Augst and Wayne Wiegand

Purity in Print: Book Censorship in America from the Gilded Age to the Computer Age, Second Edition
Paul S. Boyer

Women in Print: Essays on the Print Culture of American Women from the Nineteenth and Twentieth Centuries
Edited by James P. Danky and Wayne A. Wiegand

Bookwomen: Creating an Empire in Children's Book Publishing, 1919–1939
Jacalyn Eddy

Apostles of Culture: The Public Librarian and American Society, 1876–1920
Lora Dee Garrison